D1274921

BEACONS IN THE NIGHT

*With the OSS and Tito's Partisans
in Wartime Yugoslavia*

STANFORD UNIVERSITY PRESS
STANFORD, CALIFORNIA

BEACONS IN THE NIGHT

*With the OSS
and Tito's Partisans in
Wartime Yugoslavia*

FRANKLIN LINDSAY

Stanford University Press, Stanford, California
© 1993 by the Board of Trustees of the
Leland Stanford Junior University
Printed in the United States of America
CIP data appear at the end of the book

Title photo

A weary Fourth Zone Partisan unit approaching a village in Stajerska (Styria), winter 1944
(*Lindsay*)

To Margot
with love

The past is never dead.
It is not even past.

—William Faulkner

FOREWORD
by John Kenneth Galbraith

I have known Franklin Lindsay ever since the end of World War II, just short of half a century. For quite a bit of that time I have been encouraging him to write this book or waiting for it to appear. Now that it is here, I take modest pride in my effort; it is, as the reader will discover, a remarkable piece of work. And it is remarkable not only in one dimension but in several. I'm not sure that there has been any memoir from the war years greater in diversity, breadth, and, I must add, compelling interest.

There is, first of all, the adventure. That for the reader begins on the very first pages. One rides with the author hour by hour and sometimes moment by moment on those flights over the Yugoslav landscape, shares the tension and even more the relief when a safe landing by parachute is finally accomplished. (Alas for that bottle of whiskey with the radio that didn't make it.) The excitement, the sense of involvement, the ever-present danger, continue throughout the book. Were this all, a truly accomplished adventure story, it would be enough for many readers.

But there is much more. There is what until now has been a sadly missing chapter of history. In the accounts of the war in the Balkans there has been no slight mention of Churchill's mission to Tito. This is hardly surprising; the British who went—Fitzroy Maclean, Randolph Churchill, Evelyn Waugh—are not known for anonymity. Much less has been made of the intervention of the Americans, which, as this book tells, had its own influence on the larger events of the time and after. The Americans, as did their British counterparts, helped to hold in the Balkans German divisions desperately needed elsewhere for combat, and thus made their own contribution to victory. Even greater, needless to say, was their contribution to Marshal Tito's turn to the West and away from Moscow just a few years on.

Further, and for the historian as well as for the serious student of this part of the world today, there is here a compelling view of the ethnic and religious divisions of the region as the author experienced them, which live on so powerfully in our own time. Some of what we now read daily in the papers begins here.

Franklin Lindsay had a more than remarkable public career. A high-ranking member of the Office of Strategic Services in the years of which he tells in these pages, he went on to work on the Marshall Plan and for the Ford Foundation, to serve on numerous public and private commissions and then to pursue a highly successful and admirably rewarded business career. Not necessarily combined with such achievement is one quality much in evidence here. That is a gift for clear, concise, and highly readable English expression and a wonderful ability to remember and recapture past, even distant, personal history. We live in a world of accomplished people who, alas, cannot make their experiences known; even, on occasion, with the assistance of one or more toilers from our now vast reserve army of ghostwriters. With all of his other qualifications, including that superior power of memory and retrieval, Franklin Lindsay is a very good writer. Thinking again of all the virtues of this book, I might well have put this one first.

PREFACE

Largely hidden by the German military occupation of Yugoslavia during the Second World War, a violent civil war raged for postwar control of the country. Tito and his Partisans won that war and installed a full-fledged Leninist government. It was the first successful Communist revolution since the 1917 Bolshevik revolution a quarter century earlier. In 1948, Tito broke with Stalin. Again it was a first—the first Communist government to declare its independence from Moscow and the Comintern.

The Partisan wartime revolution, and that in neighboring Albania, were the only successful Communist revolutions in which a few officers of both the United States and Britain served on the ground with the Partisan forces. I was fortunate to be one of those few—the conflict provided us with a ringside view of Communist strategy and tactics as they fought both the Germans and their internal enemies.

At war's end, at 29, I returned to civilian life and in 1946 became executive assistant to Bernard Baruch, the American representative for the first United Nations negotiations for the control of nuclear energy. Former president Herbert Hoover was then living in New York. Through a friend, he learned of my assignment with the Yugoslav Partisans and asked me to come to see him. During two long evenings he questioned me deeply on what I had seen and heard. He then asked me to dictate as detailed a record as possible, the transcript to be deposited in the Hoover Library at Stanford University. Although my memory was then fresh, because of wartime security I had been able to keep only a few reports and notes. The files of my messages and reports were still classified and remained so for many years. I did not complete Mr. Hoover's assignment, although the pages I did complete have been a starting point for this book.

Until I could have access to these files there was no possibility that I could reconstruct a record of the events in which I was directly involved; I could not rely on memory alone. It was not until the 1970's that the declassification of these wartime British and American archives was begun. By 1988, when nearly all had been declassified, I was able to lay out almost day-by-day events. In the process I have found that my memory has been both stimulated and disciplined by the archival records.

The most important single source has been nearly a thousand pages of radio messages sent by me and to me while I was with the Partisans in Slovenia, Styria, and Carinthia in 1944. Because my radio communications were primarily with a British Special Operations (SOE) station in Italy these records, along with those of Brigadier Fitzroy Maclean, the head of the Allied mission with Tito's Partisans, and Lieutenant Colonel William Deakin and the other Allied officers under Maclean's command, are held by the British government in the Public Record Office in London.

The declassification of these British records of wartime Yugoslavia was unusual. Nearly all of SOE's wartime records are still held by the Secret Intelligence Service. The Yugoslav records, however, were considered to be British War Office rather than secret intelligence records because Maclean had reported directly to the Supreme Allied Commander, Mediterranean, and to the prime minister. They have therefore been declassified in accordance with War Office policies.

During this period I also had a radio link with Office of Strategic Services (OSS), and after December 1944 my radio and courier communications from Croatia and Serbia were solely with the American

OSS headquarters in Italy. Most of these records were declassified in the 1980's and turned over by the Central Intelligence Agency to the National Archives in Washington. Unlike the well-organized British archives, my OSS messages were widely dispersed in many different places and I was unable to locate all of them. Several are still classified and held by the CIA, according to "withdrawal notices" in the declassified folders.

A third major source has been the Ljubljana historical archives of the Slovene Partisans. Dr. Dusan Biber of the Institute of Modern History and Professor Tone Ferenc of Ljubljana University have been extraordinarily helpful in providing copies of original Partisan internal messages and reports, as well as Slovene historical studies covering operations in which I was involved. The bulk of the documentation for this book has thus come from these three sources. Where I have drawn on other sources I have so indicated with specific notes. I have also drawn on the recollections and records of a few of my associates during this period.

In respect to a few episodes, I have not found either confirming or conflicting documentary records. Because my memory on these is strong, however, I have included them—noting the lack of confirming documentation.

I have purposely chosen not to write a history of the whole resistance movement in Yugoslavia, but to describe the events in which I took part or of which I had firsthand knowledge.

Slovene and Serbo-Croat place and person names are loaded with diacritical marks as an aid to pronunciation. These marks have been omitted from this text for the sake of simplicity for the English reader.

The pronunciation of some letters in Slovene and Serbo-Croat is different from their English pronunciation, and trying to pronounce them as they are normally used in English becomes quite awkward. There are a few simple rules that can help with the most difficult words without resorting to a full study of pronunciation:

> c is never pronounced as k; it is either as tz or ch
> s is pronounced either as English s or sh

j is pronounced as *y* in *yet*

z is pronounced as *z* in *zero*, or as *s* in *measure*

In the book I have used the term "Russian" rather than "Soviet" because this was the way both we and the Partisans referred to the Soviet government and to the Soviet officers with the Partisans at the time. I have also used the term "Partisan" throughout to refer both to the armed units and to the wartime political organization of the Communist-led national liberation movement. Again, this was the shorthand term we normally used in our messages and reports. In 1943 the term "Army of National Liberation" replaced the earlier term "Partisan Detachments" and in 1945 this in turn was replaced by "Army of Yugoslavia."

The British organization to which I was assigned during most of 1944 had a quick succession of names: Force 133, Force 266, Force 399, 37 Military Mission, and MacMis (Maclean Mission). I have used Force 399 throughout for simplicity. The British Secret Intelligence Service, which operated separately in Yugoslavia, was also called MI-6. I have used the latter term. The Allied military headquarters in Caserta, Italy, to which Force 399 and OSS were responsible was known as Allied Force Headquarters Mediterranean, or simply AFHQ.

British and American officers serving behind the German lines and Partisan officers as well often used assumed names. I have referred to those whose real names I knew by their real names. In those cases where I knew only one name I have necessarily used that name, though I do not know whether it was assumed or real. I myself did not use an assumed name with the Partisans, but I later discovered that OSS in processing my messages referred to me by the impersonal label X–84 or by the rather inelegant term "Dogfish." The latter prompted more than one querulous query, "Who the hell is Dogfish?"

CONTENTS

Contents

MAPS

FRANCE

Munich

Berchtesgaden

Zürich

Innsbruck

SWITZERLAND
(neutral)

BRENNER PASS

GERMANY

Geneva

Simplon

SIMPLON TUNNEL

Line

Line

Brenner Pass

Ljubljana

Milan

Verona

Trieste

Venice

ITALY

ADRIATIC

AXIS FORCES

Gustav Line
(1-15-44 through 5-11-44)

⊛ Rome

Anzio Beachhead
1-23-44 through 5-23-44

ALLIED

Caserta

CAPRI

Naples

	Double-track rail lines across Alps
	Axis-controlled area

MEDITERRANEAN SEA

Map 1: Southeastern Europe, 1944; for wartime partition of Yugoslavia, see Map 2.

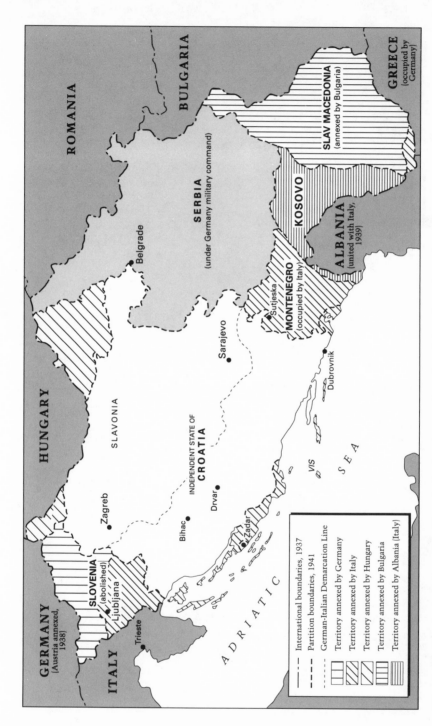

Map 2: Wartime boundaries within Yugoslavia, showing greatly enlarged Croatia, truncated Serbia, and partitioned Slovenia.

GERMANY
(Austria annexed, 1938)

ITALY

HUNGARY

ROMANIA

BULGARIA

GREECE
(occupied by Germany)

SLAV MACEDONIA
(annexed by Bulgaria)

KOSOVO

ALBANIA
(united with Italy, 1939)

SERBIA
(under Germany military command)

Belgrade

MONTENEGRO
(occupied by Italy)

Sutjeska

Dubrovnik

SLAVONIA

Sarajevo

Zagreb

INDEPENDENT STATE OF
CROATIA

Drvar

Bihac

Zadar

VIS

SEA

SLOVENIA
(abolished)

Ljubljana

Trieste

ADRIATIC

International boundaries, 1937
Partition boundaries, 1941
German-Italian Demarcation Line
Territory annexed by Germany
Territory annexed by Italy
Territory annexed by Hungary
Territory annexed by Bulgaria
Territory annexed by Albania (Italy)

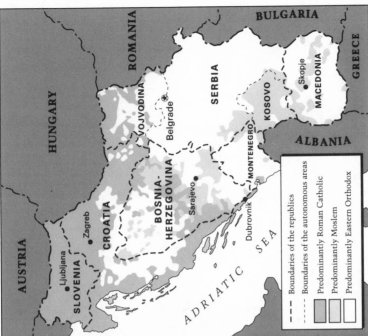

Map 4: Religious-ethnic concentrations and postwar political divisions in Yugoslavia; see also Appendix. From Stephan Clissold, "Croat Separatism, Nationalism, Dissonance, and Terrorism," *Conflict Studies* 103, 1979 (Institute for the Study of Conflict).

Boundaries of the republics
Boundaries of the autonomous areas
Predominantly Roman Catholic
Predominantly Moslem
Predominantly Eastern Orthodox

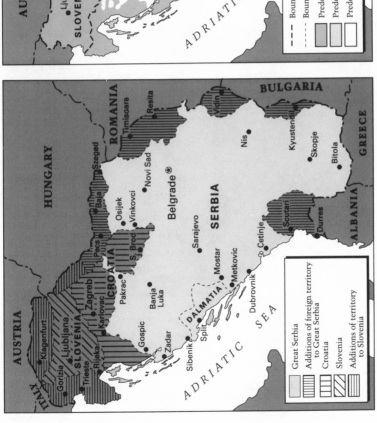

Map 3: Wartime Chetnik plan for a greatly enlarged Serbia. From Jozo Tomasevich, *The Chetniks: War and Revolution in Yugoslavia, 1941–1945* (Stanford University Press, 1975), p. 168.

Great Serbia
Additions of foreign territory to Great Serbia
Croatia
Slovenia
Additions of territory to Slovenia

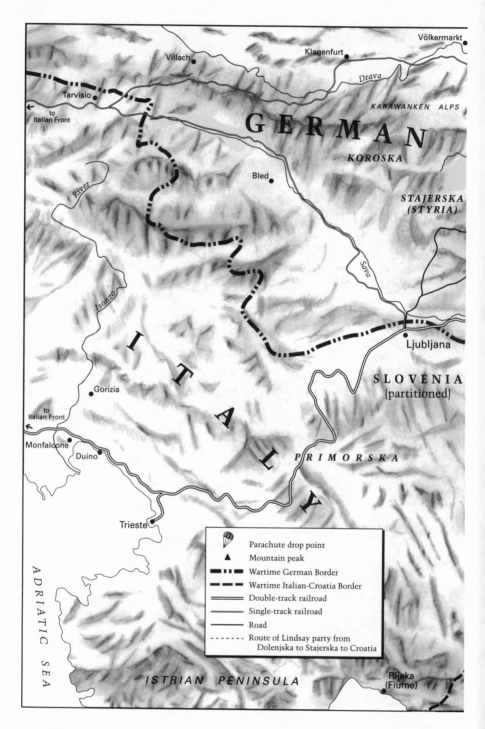

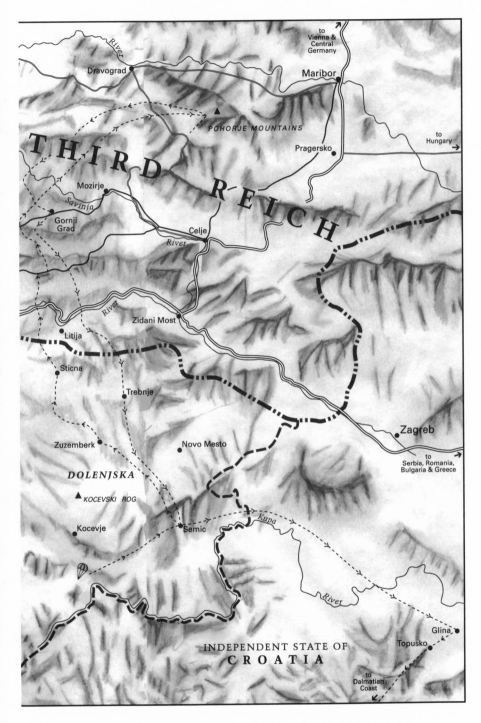

Map 5: Operational map of wartime Slovenia.

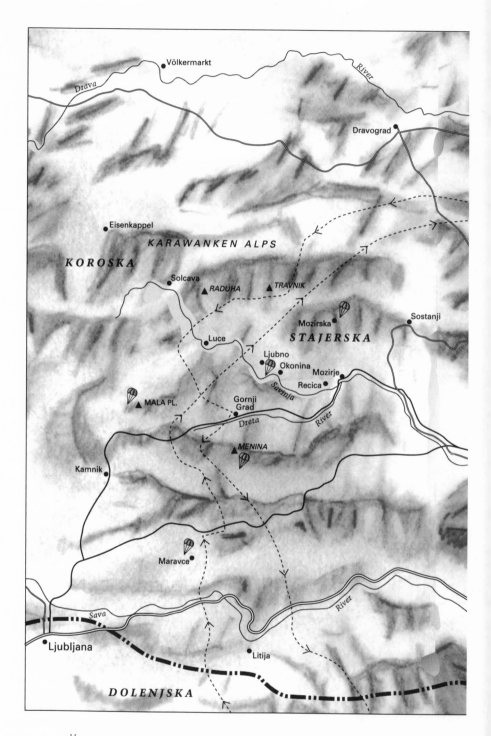

Drava

River

Völkermarkt

Dravograd

Eisenkappel

KARAWANKEN ALPS

KOROSKA

Solcava

▲ *RADUHA*

▲ *TRAVNIK*

Mozirska

Sostanji

Luce

STAJERSKA

Ljubno

Okonina

Mozirje

Savinja

Recica

▲ MALA PL.

Gornji
Grad

Dreta

River

▲ *MENINA*

Kamnik

Maravce

Sava

River

Ljubljana

Litija

DOLENJSKA

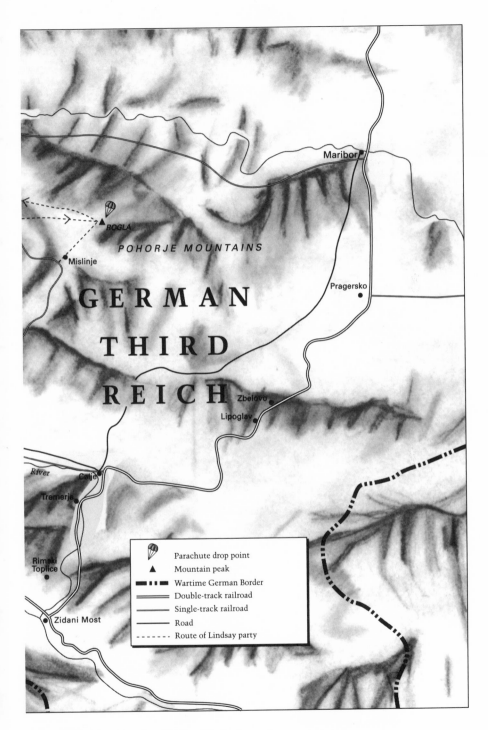

Map 6: Operational map of Stajerska region.

BEACONS IN THE NIGHT

With the OSS and Tito's Partisans
in Wartime Yugoslavia

CHAPTER 1

To Slovenia by Parachute

O ur first two attempts to find the reception party on the ground had failed. This was our third try.

We had been four hours in the air. In our flight plan the TOT, time over target, was 23:45. It was now midnight, May 14, 1944. The dispatcher, a Royal Air Force sergeant, came aft from the cockpit. He removed a wooden cover from a hole, about four feet in diameter, in the floor of the bomb bay. The sides of the hole were about three feet deep, enough to allow a man to sit on the edge and still keep his feet from the plane's rushing slipstream below. Through the hole there was only the black of a moonless night.

Alongside the hole Lieutenant Gordon Bush, Lieutenant Schraeder, and I, sweating out our parachute drop, watched the flight dispatcher as he went about his business; Corporal James Fisher, my radio operator, slept as soundly as he had during most of the flight. The navigator had brought the Halifax long-range bomber to the area in which, if his navigation was accurate, the aircraft commander should be able to see the reception signals on the ground. After several wide, searching turns, he spotted a fire. As he flew closer a flashlight winked the prearranged Morse code recognition signal. It was the letter "D," the right one for that night. We were set to jump.

The plane circled, dropped to 3,000 or 4,000 feet above ground.

The bomber commander had explained before we left Brindisi that he would drop the cargo chutes first to lighten the aircraft as much as possible before we jumped. He could then drop us at as low an altitude as he dared to minimize the drift of our own parachutes before we hit the ground. He made the first run across the drop area to cut loose the parachuted containers of guns and explosives attached to the underside of the wings. Since there was no moon, he was evading the surrounding mountains by starlight alone. We in the bomb bay, where there were no windows, could see nothing, and were totally dependent on the crew sergeant to relay bits of what was going on in the cockpit.

We could feel the slowing of the aircraft as the flaps were lowered and engine power cut. The bomber lost altitude rapidly. After a minute or two the engines again came on full power and we could feel the plane lunge forward, climb steeply, then bank in a sharp turn. The wing containers had been dropped to the ground party. We were now circling for the next pass.

As the plane turned, the dispatcher moved the cargo containers with our two radios, the batteries for the radios, our packs, and the medical supplies for the Partisans to the edge of the hole. He then attached the ends of strong webbed lines—static lines—about 25 feet long to rings on the parachutes of each container. The opposite ends were already attached to rings on the inside of the aircraft. When the lines were pulled tight as the containers fell from the plane the chutes would be pulled open automatically. As a precaution the dispatcher wore a body harness that tied him to the plane so that he could not fall through the hole as he wrestled the containers to the edge. As the aircraft moved over the drop area the pilot would try to judge the probable wind drift of the parachutes after they opened, and to compensate for the drift by timing the drop signal to the dispatcher. In our case, as we were flying into a slight head wind, he would delay the signal a few seconds after passing directly over the target area, so that the parachutes would drift in the wind back toward the waiting ground party.

A red warning light in the top of the bomb bay over the hole came on as the pilot started his second pass. Again the engines were throttled back and the flaps lowered. I had the sensation of abruptly dropping several hundred feet. When the green light went on, the sergeant quickly pushed out each of the containers. The static lines, having pulled open their chutes as they fell away from the plane, rattled dryly against the underside of the aircraft. I was acutely aware that we ourselves would go out in the same way.

The sergeant pulled the lines in quickly as the plane circled again. It was our turn. I shouted above the roar of the engines to wake Jim Fisher as we got ready for the jump. I was not as calm as he about what lay ahead. The "etiquette" of British military drops dictated that the senior officer always went first. As a major I would be first. Schraeder would follow as soon as I cleared the hole. Bush and Fisher would be dropped on the next pass. Schraeder and I now hooked our own static lines to the rings on the sides of the fuselage while the dispatcher hooked the other ends to the parachutes strapped to our backs. We then took our positions sitting on the edge of the hole across from each other.

My training jumps had all been from a standing position in the door of a plane. For reasons I don't understand even today the thought of passively dropping through a hole into the night was infinitely more disagreeable than jumping from an open door. Now I sat on the edge of the hole looking down at absolute black nothing.

I knew that a replacement radio operator had been killed in a drop to the same area a month earlier. Both he and the dispatcher had been in such a funk immediately before the drop that neither had remembered to hook up his line to open the chute. In British operations, unlike American, a reserve chute was not provided, and there was no way the main chute could be opened once one had dropped through that hole.

Being sure I was hooked up at both ends totally consumed those last few minutes. What I would do after I got on the ground seemed so far in the future as to have no reality. The static line was coiled at my side. I pulled first on the end attached to the plane until I was sure it, and not some other line, had been firmly attached. Then I reached over my shoulder to feel if the other end was attached to the parachute on my back, and then with my hand I ran the length of line at my side to be sure it was the same one that was attached to the chute. I must have repeated this instinctive bit of reassurance four or five times.

By now the red light, indicating we were again approaching the drop area, was on. I put my hands on the edge of the hole ready to shove off. The dispatcher was standing across from me. As the green light went on, he gave the thumbs-up sign and shouted to me over the roar of the engines, "It's a piece of cake!"

Out I went.

■ This was our third try to get into the mountainous northwestern corner of Yugoslavia. In planning our operation we had two alternatives. One was to drop to a Slovene Partisan group in Dolenjska, a province of prewar Slovenia south of the Sava River. This offered the security of a drop area known to be safe, in which a reception party on the ground could be arranged in advance by radio. The other was to fly further north to the lower Alps in Stajerska (Styria in English, Steiermark in German) between the rivers Sava and Drava (or Drau) and make a blind drop into the Third Reich itself, where lay the rail lines we were to cut. The first alternative put some 70 miles, to be covered on foot, between our landing and the area in which we intended to operate. The second, while saving us the time such a trip through German-occupied territory involved, meant even greater risks.

The American Office of Strategic Services (OSS), in which I was serving, and its British counterpart, the Special Operations Executive (SOE), believed that there was a small resistance group in Stajerska, but their allegiance was uncertain. There was no way to contact them to arrange a safe drop area and a recognition signal. The aircraft navigator would have had to find the spot he was aiming for after flying nearly 500 miles over enemy-held territory on dead reckoning—relying only on compass, air speed indicator, star-fixes, and estimated winds along the course. There was also no certainty we would find

4

the resistance group before we were picked up by the Germans. And had we found the group but turned up unannounced, they would certainly have suspected that we were Germans masquerading as an Allied team—leading to considerable difficulties, and possibly to the same fate we would meet at German hands.

In the end, Force 399, the British Special Operations command that controlled these Balkan operations, decided against a blind drop, so we proceeded with the plan to drop to the Slovene Partisans south of the Sava. This required approval by Josip Broz Tito, the Yugoslav Communist leader, commanding some 200,000 of his countrymen as Partisans in their war against the occupiers of Yugoslavia. After Tito's approval had been obtained from his mountain headquarters, a radio message went from there to Partisan headquarters in Slovenia authorizing our parachute drop. It also directed the Slovene Partisans to provide an escort for us to the north, to the region the Slovenes call Stajerska, and authorized our operations there in collaboration with the local Partisans.

Our first attempt to drop failed when we encountered heavy ground fog over the entire area surrounding the drop zone in southern Slovenia. Having taken off as the sun was setting, we returned to the RAF base in Brindisi, in the heel of Italy, as the sun was rising the next morning. We stumbled out of the aircraft, turned over our chutes to the waiting ground crew, and went into the mess for breakfast. I felt as though I had a heavy hangover.

Cots were set up at a nearby house requisitioned by OSS, and I slept on and off during that day. Thereafter, we were told each day about noon whether we would be "on" that night for another try. RAF operations each morning assigned aircraft for the coming night based on the weather forecast, on radio messages from "inside" confirming that a reception party was still in place and able to receive a drop safely that night, and on the priority assigned to the mission. For three days the decision was negative because of bad weather over Slovenia. On the fourth night we took off again.

This time the ground was clear of fog. The navigator advised the aircraft captain when he should be able to pick up the signal from the ground reception party. After a few searching turns of the aircraft, a flashlight blinking a Morse code recognition signal—a letter that had been transmitted by radio to the ground party at midday—was picked up. But it was the wrong letter.

I was so anxious not to make another four-hour return flight to Brindisi that I convinced myself we were at the right place and that someone had simply made a mistake in transmitting the recognition signal. The commander, however, was quite firm. His orders were that no one would jump unless the recognition signal on the ground was correct.

Again we tried to sleep on the long flight back and again landed as the sun was rising over the Adriatic. Another wait of four days in Brindisi stretched out interminably. Finally we were "on" again for another try. But this time there would be no moon to aid the pilot as he maneuvered to get us to as low an altitude as possible over the drop area. Because of the urgency of our mission to support the coming Allied offensive in Italy—the breakout of the Allied armies from the Anzio beachhead and the liberation of Rome—it was decided by Force 399 to risk a drop without moonlight.

At sundown we arrived in a jeep at the assigned aircraft. Thinking to make a little light conversation with the tail gunner as he helped us climb aboard—more to boost my own morale than anything else—I said we had made two dry runs already, and I certainly hoped we could get in tonight. I couldn't help taking his reply ambiguously. "Oh, don't you worry, sir," he said in good Cockney, "this captain never brings anyone back."

■ A few seconds pass after leaving the plane before the static line pulls tight and the chute opens. These few seconds of free-fall were, for me, the most exhilarating moments of a jump. Perhaps it was because I was more concerned that I would freeze than I was that my chute wouldn't open. The elation I felt must have been the relief that I had got myself out of the plane.

Jumping into what was in effect a 120-mile wind tossed and buffeted me much like being tumbled in a heavy surf. The chute opened and I found myself swinging violently at the end of the risers connecting my harness to the chute above. I was facing in the direction of the departing Halifax. I could see four small blue points of flame from the four engine exhausts rapidly growing smaller as the plane climbed out of the long valley. My reaction was simply, "You damned fool, now look what you've gone and done." I might have felt even more strongly if I had known then what the next nine months would bring.

After the sound of the aircraft engines died away and the swinging stopped, it became completely quiet except for the rustle of air against the silk parachute. I had the sensation of being suspended completely motionless in the black night around me.

In the distance I could see the fires marking the drop area and I now began to think about the landing. We had been taught never to try to anticipate landing, especially at night. Because one's reflexes are conditioned to the acceleration of a jump off a wall or rock, the natural reaction is to expect to hit the ground a fraction of a second before it actually happens. Legs are broken by misjudging the instant of hitting the ground, and we had been trained never to try to judge when we would hit. We were instructed to keep our feet and knees together with knees slightly bent, to avoid breaking a leg by landing on one foot, while using our arms to hold onto the risers and thus protect our heads in the event of a hard landing.

All this sound instruction I forgot completely. Instead, I tried to see where the ground was and where I would land. I dimly spotted a winding white line that I took to be a narrow road still some distance below me. Just as I was trying to see the terrain more clearly I quite unexpectedly hit the ground. Fortunately I landed in a plowed field on the side of a slope. I wasn't hurt at all, but my mental processes were not at their best. After I picked myself up, the wheels inside seemed to be going very slowly as I considered what to do next.

The first thing, I finally decided, was to take off the parachute, which now lay collapsed on the ground. I then heard shouting in the valley below and saw flashlights blinking as the reception party searched for us and for the cargo chutes. I was far from sure they were Partisans and not Germans. But I now had no choice. I signaled with my flashlight in their direction. Soon two or three Partisans with rifles slung over their shoulders arrived with whoops and yells, and there was much slapping on the back. I responded with enthusiasm—enthusiasm that I had made it at least this far without mishap.

One of them gathered up my parachute and we headed down the slope. Another who spoke a few words of English arrived and communications became somewhat more intelligible. The other three Americans from the plane soon turned up, having been found by other Partisans. We were taken to a nearby peasant house where we were given shots of slivovitz, the local plum brandy, to noisy toasts. After a few I was able to get across that I wanted to recover the cargo chutes, especially the radios, as quickly as possible.

The group that had set up the reception area numbered about twenty men and had come from Slovene Partisan headquarters, a day's march away. We all fanned out on the hillside and began our search. As each container was found it was brought to the house for unpacking.

I had felt strongly that we should have a reserve radio at all times and therefore we had brought two on the initial drop. The reason for my insistence had to do with the radios of those days, which functioned by means of fragile glass vacuum tubes. Had we only a single radio, its failure, loss, or capture would cut us off from our base in Italy. Without communications we would not be able to call in supplies and explosives by air, or to send out intelligence on German military movements.

The radios were powered by heavy wet-cell batteries, similar to automobile batteries. A small gasoline-powered generator called "Tiny Tim" had been designed for recharging them. But since it weighed sixty pounds it was not practical to man-pack one from southern Slovenia to Stajerska. The generator would be dropped to us when we reached our destination.

While I was at the packing station in Brindisi, supervising the assembly and packing of our kit, a British major, in a truly noble act, had presented me with a bottle of Scotch, undoubtedly out of his personal ration. We decided the safest place to put it was with one of the radios, since their containers were the most heavily padded to protect them against the shock of landing and had, I was told, the best parachutes. On the ground in Slovenia we soon found one radio container intact. It was still black night as we searched for the other. Suddenly I smelled calamity in the air. I had bet an invaluable bottle of Scotch on the wrong parachute. We found the container, parachute unopened, radio smashed, and the whiskey aromatically soaking into the Slovene hillside. No other chute had failed.

■ We now divided up the equipment we had brought. The ammunition and weapons in the wing containers would remain with the Partisans. Schraeder, a weather officer, had brought several container-loads of weather station equipment. He would remain near Slovene Partisan headquarters to set up a weather station for the Allied Air Forces. Bush, Fisher, and I would take our radio, batteries, and personal equipment north across the German border into Stajerska. The Partisans took all the parachutes to make clothing and bandages for the wounded. (I cut one panel from my chute, which was made of natural silk; it survives today as a scarf.)

As daylight came I could begin to see a lovely little valley. There were fruit trees around the peasant house the Partisan detachment was using—all in the full bloom of spring. In the daylight I saw with what skill the RAF pilot had flown his Halifax into the valley between two mountain ridges. He had maneuvered between and then below them to drop us and the cargo containers as low as possible, and he then had put the aircraft into a steep climb to clear the ridge and circle back for the next pass—all by starlight alone.

In this beautiful mountain setting, and in the warm early sunlight, I couldn't believe that a war was going on, particularly a violent civil war for the ultimate control of the country, overlaid by a Nazi occupation that ruthlessly exacerbated the age-old hatreds among the different South Slav nationalities.

As the sun rose several Partisans, for the moment oblivious to the war, sat in the warm grass, their shirts off, patiently picking lice from their clothing. I was startled: this had not been included in my brief-ings. But after a few days I too learned to hunt lice. They hide in the seams of clothing and are so small that one has to learn how to spot them. Lice don't bother you when you are on the move, but when you are still and trying to sleep they begin to crawl across your body. The sensation is most unpleasant. Later, when we called for supply drops to Stajerska, louse powder was always high priority. This is not simply a matter of comfort. Typhus is transmitted by lice. Among the Partisans—and that came to include all the Allied personnel serving with them—every week or two everyone's clothing was put into a boiling kettle and handed back supposedly louse-free. Fortunately ty-phus was not a problem in our area, though further south typhus epidemics struck both the Partisans and the German forces.

As the Partisans occupied themselves picking lice in the pleasant sunlight, the final four-day delay in our arrival still troubled me. I asked the leader of the reception party if they had heard our aircraft overhead four nights before we finally made our jump. No, he said. They had waited all that night, but had heard no aircraft. After a thoughtful pause, he added that a Partisan underground worker had subsequently reported that an aircraft had circled that night about ten miles east of the agreed drop zone, in an area controlled by the Germans. A German officer had gone into a nearby field with a flash-light and had done a little night fishing to see what he might be able to bring in. So much for my impatient insistence that the wrong sig-nal that night was only a "clerical error."

■ We were safe and, for the moment, in an idyllic mountain val-ley. But that fell far short of describing the reality into which we had been dropped. Our objectives, as set out in my orders, were strictly military: we were to avoid any implication of Allied support for Par-tisan postwar political aims. Our immediate mission was to cut the rail lines that ran through the Southeastern Alps, in order to block the transfer of German reinforcements from Austria, Hungary, and the Balkans to the Italian front, as the Allied armies approached

Rome and pushed further north. With their advance, the blocking of those same lines would later become a key to helping bottle up German divisions in the Balkans.

Our mission was an integral part of the decision of the American and British governments to support the Communist-led Partisans because they were judged to be an effective fighting force. Their postwar political objectives were not considered in that decision. We were, after all, allied with the Soviet Union in a common effort to defeat Hitler. It would have been inconsistent to have withheld support from the Partisans simply because they were led by Communists. The Allies believed that, with our help, the Partisans could increase their contribution to the common effort by tying down German divisions that would otherwise be sent to the Eastern front or to fight the Allied armies in Italy, and later in France. The Partisans could also inhibit German troop movements through the area of Partisan operations. But these were, in effect, short-term, pragmatic decisions that brushed aside the realities in Yugoslavia.

It was naive, for example, to assume that our mission with the Partisans had nothing to do with politics in the broader meaning of the word. The British and American officers with Partisan groups were fighting with a Communist-led organization and were arranging deliveries of arms and explosives to them. Our presence with them was in itself taken by the Partisans and the local populations as evidence that the Western Allies, Britain and the United States, were on the Partisan side, not only in the fight against the Germans, but also in the civil war that increasingly had become the Partisans' first priority.

Between the briefings I had received in Cairo, and in Bari in Italy, and our experiences once on the ground, it was soon borne in upon me that I was involved in more than the war against the Germans. Instead, several separate conflicts were all taking place simultaneously in what had been the territory of Yugoslavia. Which side individuals and groups were on depended on which level of conflict one was involved in at the moment. Allies in one conflict were at the same time foes in another. Actual armed conflict, or the threat of it, was almost universally present.

For Britain and the United States, as my orders made clear, the war against Hitler was the only conflict that mattered. They would support the Partisans despite their Communist leadership. But, as I had been told during my briefings, the Western Allies had also made contact in Yugoslavia with the Chetniks, a resistance group led by Draza Mihailovic, a Royal Yugoslav Army colonel, with a similar objective of tying down German and Italian forces but with a different postwar goal in mind. Mihailovic and his Chetniks were fighting to restore the monarchy, to continue the prewar dominance of Serbia over the remainder of the country, and to prevent a Communist takeover. The Partisans were fighting to create a totally new federated republic that would be under the control of the Communist Party, and fashioned on Leninist principles. Conflict between the two was inevitable, and in fact fighting between them had broken out within months after the German occupation and continued with increasing violence throughout the war. By 1942 the Partisans and the Chetniks had each openly declared the other, rather than the German and Italian occupiers, to be the principal enemy.

Another conflict was an ethnic one, illustrated by George Wuchinich, an OSS lieutenant recruited for his command of Serbo-Croat language, whom I was to meet in Slovenia. In his final report after leaving Yugoslavia he wrote, "My background was that of a second-generation American of Serbian parents. I was taught to believe in the superiority of the Serb in war, and also that nothing was impossible for a Serb to do, whether in war or peace. Fundamentally, I was taught to hate Croats, and brand them as the greatest traitors the world had known." The mirror image of this was often expressed by the Croats about the Serbs.

These ethnic conflicts—which led to renewed armed combat four decades later—had as one central element the age-old religious differences among the Catholics of Croatia and Slovenia; the Eastern Orthodox of Serbia, Montenegro, Macedonia, and parts of Croatia; and the Moslems, centered primarily in Bosnia-Herzegovina.

Hitler dismembered Yugoslavia in a manner calculated to exacerbate these ethnic conflicts. The lid was not only off the Serb-Croat hatreds and other ethnic rivalries, but they were all fanned by the Nazis as a means to divide and rule. The venom was released. Unspeakable atrocities were committed by elements of each against the others, and stories of the ensuing horrors are as alive today as they were then.

The growing antagonism of the Partisans toward the West became, as time wore on, a major source of friction in the daily lives of those of us working directly with them. At the time we regarded it as a symptom of expansionist Communist orthodoxy under Moscow's direction, but whatever its origins, by the fall of 1944 relations between ourselves and the Partisans soured drastically, and at war's end it brought Tito's Yugoslavia and the Western Allies to the brink of armed conflict.

We could not see clearly a further conflict that came into the open only after the war. This was the insistence by Tito and his Partisans on the independence of Yugoslavia from what they perceived to be the outside domination of Moscow. Because of the Partisans' adoration of the Soviet Union and because they were Communist-led, we believed that they were becoming a totally loyal satellite of Moscow. This last conflict, which began as early as 1941 in secret communications between Stalin and the Yugoslav Communist leadership, surfaced in 1948 when the Yugoslavs refused to knuckle under to Stalin.

CHAPTER *2*

Preparing for the Mission

T he OSS had taken me on because I was an engineer who was expected to know something about bridges and railroads, because I had inflated my claims to fluency in German and Russian, and because I had volunteered.

I had graduated from Stanford in 1938 and in June of 1940, the month France fell to Hitler, I left graduate school for the army. After two years in the War Department in Washington, in 1942 I was ordered to Iran, to work on the supply line from the Persian Gulf to the Caucasus in support of the Russian armies, which were being driven back all the way to the northern slopes of this mountain wall by the advancing Germans. Before the war German engineers had built a railroad from the ports at the head of the Persian Gulf almost to the Soviet border. The Iranian supply line to the Red Army, begun by the British, then taken over by the U.S. Army Engineers in 1942, used both the uncompleted railroad and a highway across a thousand miles of mountains and deserts from the Persian Gulf to the Soviet border. But by 1943 it was clear that the Russian armies had held at the Caucasus. The danger of a German breakthrough to the Persian Gulf had passed. Iran had become a backwater of the war, and I wanted out.

Through contacts I had made in the U.S. command in Cairo I wangled a transfer to the Egyptian capital, where I soon learned of

OSS operations based there for the penetration of the German-occupied Balkans. This led to a series of conversations with OSS officers that slowly became more precise. The question eventually surfaced: Was I prepared to go into German-occupied Europe?

This took some thought. It would mean a major, and welcome, change from the headquarters staffs to the cutting edge of behind-the-lines operations. It would also mean more than ordinary wartime personal risk. But the chance it offered to break out of the mass anonymity of a military headquarters was tempting. I sensed that in ways that could not be charted it would change my life after the war—as it did. The question became still more precise. Would I parachute at night into enemy-held territory? Having invited the question, I could only say yes. So after the inevitable paperwork was done, I was sent off to the British parachute school in Palestine.

■ The school was at Ramat David, about 15 miles east of Haifa at an RAF Coastal Command base. The curriculum was four days of ground school followed by two days of jumps. Our instructors, RAF sergeants, were part of a permanent corps of physical training instructors. They had honed their jobs to a fine art, not unlike the drill instructors at American boot camps. Each day began with the usual push-ups until arms and backs ached or refused to function, the instructors haranguing and berating us all the while as the worst they had ever seen. The rest of the ground-school days were spent in tumbling on mats and practicing landings by jumping off towers into sawdust pits while hooked to cables to simulate parachutes.

When the day arrived for an actual jump from an airplane we assembled at the parachute packing sheds, and drew and strapped on our chutes. As we were each handed our chute while hoping it was not, as rumored, just a bundle of rags, one British rule eased our anxiety somewhat. The rule was that once every three months each enlisted chute packer was given a chute randomly selected from those he had packed and required to jump with it. It kept the packers' attention focused on what must have otherwise been a boringly repetitive job.

While waiting to board the aircraft there was a certain amount of black humor traded, and in our anxiety the urge to urinate hit us all. The entire group of a hundred or more were watering the ground or lined up facing the hangar walls when we were called.

After jumping above a plowed field, we were expected to practice several maneuvers to control our oscillation and to turn the chute so we faced in the right direction for landing. We were harangued from the ground by our instructors with bullhorns. But once on the ground we instantly became seasoned veterans. There was not a little swagger as we rolled up our chutes and headed off the field.

A military ambulance, known as the meat wagon, was drawn up at the edge of the field. On the ground in front the medical corpsmen had placed pipe and wire net stretchers. Like U.S. Navy stretchers they were shaped to fit the average human body. One had been foreshortened so that while it still had the outline of the human body it was only two feet long. We laughed, but rather hollowly.

After I had finished the course I wondered if practice jumps were all that necessary for the type of clandestine drops we would be making—either the chute opened or it didn't. Practice jumps might help minimize a bad landing or a broken leg, but there was no reason it couldn't be done right the first time. Scots Guards Major John Clarke, who was to be a colleague in Yugoslavia, was smarter than I. He refused to go to parachute school himself, and instead sent his batman (orderly). From him he learned what he needed to know, practicing by jumping off the bureau in his Cairo billet.

The week following parachute school I spent at a British school for special operations located south of Haifa, on Mount Carmel. Although the full course ran three months, I was given a special cram course of one week. I was sorry to miss the final field problem of the full course, which involved being put ashore for seven days, without identification documents, on the island of Cyprus, a British garrison in a ticklish part of the world. Each student was given specific intelligence he was to get on the defenses of the island.

My mornings at Mount Carmel consisted of training with German and Italian weapons, and demolition exercises using plastic explosives and various types of timers and detonators. Afternoons were spent on codes and ciphers, on arranging clandestine meetings, and on resisting interrogation.

Evening mess at the school was a formal occasion with full uniform required. The commandant of the school, a lieutenant colonel, was addicted to liar's dice. He would assemble eight or ten of us after dinner each evening to play. Each time someone lost he was required to buy a round of drinks. I was the only American student and the commandant, on starting the game, always called out: "Where's my American major?" The game lasted until after midnight, through quite a few rounds of drinks. The commandant was rumored to base our grades entirely on how we played his game. It was probably true since we never saw him at any other time.

Thanks to the commandant's addiction, the mornings were sheer hell. I was roused out of too short a sleep at six with a cup of "sergeant-major's tea"—very strong, very sweet, and lots of canned milk. The mornings were spent setting off explosive charges, or running through an obstacle course with sudden pop-out targets that I was expected to hit accurately with a submachine gun—all with a raging headache.

But one afternoon made up for it all. It was the fulfillment of a lifelong fantasy. I was taken down to the Haifa railroad yards and taught to run a steam locomotive. My instructor and I spent three glorious hours running the engine up and down the tracks blowing the whistle as we went—boyhood's ultimate dream become reality. The school's theory was that if one were being chased by the enemy and suddenly came upon a locomotive sitting on a track with steam up, a well-prepared person should be able to jump aboard and drive the locomotive off. While it was great fun and, I thought, would make a great movie escape scene, I figured the odds were heavily against ever being able to use that particular skill. I was wrong. A group of Yugoslav Partisans, including Tito himself, had escaped German capture by driving off on just such a fortuitously parked steam engine.

■ Returned to Cairo in late 1943 from my quick education in destruction and self-preservation, I was summoned before Lieutenant Colonel Paul West, head of OSS Special Operations for the Balkans, to receive my orders. In suitably brisk words he told me I was to be dropped to Partisans in Slovenia. My mission would be to cut German rail lines connecting Austria, Italy, and the Balkans.

Not being sure where Slovenia was, I walked over to the map of the Balkans and Central Europe that covered the entire wall behind him. On scanning the floor-to-ceiling map I found Slovenia, Slavonia, and Slovakia. Which one had he said? He was decent enough to admit he wasn't sure. He riffled through his papers and finally raised his head. "Slovenia," he said.

I was now introduced to the organizational intricacies of OSS and Allied organizations. The U.S. Office of Strategic Services, wartime predecessor of the CIA, had been set up at the beginning of the war to be our first national intelligence service. Its principal sections reflected their several missions:

> Secret Intelligence, SI, was the arm for the clandestine collection of intelligence.
>
> Special Operations, SO, was the activist arm to work with the indigenous resistance organizations in occupied countries.
>
> Research and Analysis, R&A, staffed largely by leading academics, converted to summary estimates and evaluations the raw intelligence collected by SI, the military intelligence services, the State and Treasury departments, as well as from public sources such as foreign newspapers.
>
> Morale Operations, MO, was expected to use propaganda, both white and black, to encourage and support our friends and allies, and to subvert and undermine the morale of the enemy.
>
> X-2, the counter-intelligence arm, protected the organization from enemy attempts to penetrate and subvert our operations.

These operating organizations were supported by sections for technical research and development, secret funds, communications, personnel, training, and registry. Registry was the important repository of all the information flowing into OSS, and the orders, directives, reports, and other communications flowing internally and to users outside OSS.

The British counterpart of the Special Operations branch of OSS was the Special Operations Executive, SOE, a wartime creation. After France fell, the British chiefs of staff had concluded that the wartime mission of aiding resistance forces in occupied Europe was so important that it should be given to a new organization, rather than left to MI-6, which had had several sabotage failures in the early days of the war. Churchill agreed and SOE was set up, with Churchill's order to "set Europe ablaze."

My OSS assignment was to SO, and I was to be a member of the Allied group operating in Yugoslavia under Brigadier Fitzroy Maclean, who had been personally chosen by Churchill a few months earlier to head a military mission to the Yugoslav Partisans.

Before the war Maclean had served in Moscow in the British diplomatic service. When war broke out he had tried to become a soldier, but had been told he would not be released by the Foreign Office. However, he discovered in the fine print of regulations a way to leave the Foreign Office by becoming a candidate for Parliament. He successfully stood for Parliament and joined the Cameron Highlanders. Churchill later referred to him as "the young man who has used the Mother of Parliaments as a public convenience."

The British had taken the lead in establishing contact with both the Partisans led by Tito and Mihailovic's Chetniks. In 1943 General William J. Donovan, the head of OSS, had worked out an agreement with the British to include American OSS officers in the missions to both the Partisans and the Chetniks. Donovan had won the Medal of Honor in the First World War, had practiced law in New York between the wars, and had unsuccessfully run for governor of New York.

These missions would, however, remain under British operational control. American officers and radio operators were therefore being sent into Yugoslavia both to Partisan and Chetnik headquarters and to subordinate Partisan and Chetnik units in other parts of the country. British parachute supply operations were based at Brindisi. British Halifax and American Liberator bombers and C-47 transport planes (military version of the famous DC-3), were fitted out to deliver guns, ammunition, and explosives to both groups; and, where needed, food, blankets, clothing, boots, and medical supplies as well. From now on most of my briefings, as well as detailed operations plans, would be done by and with the British.

■ It would have been impossible for me to deal with all the currents and countercurrents of the Yugoslav conflict without understanding some of what had gone before. It is one thing to be part of a massive invasion force, but it is quite another to work in hostile territory alone, or as part of a small team working closely with local resistance forces. One needs some understanding of the country and the people to whom one is going to be dropped in the latter case. So first I read all of the OSS and British intelligence reports and analyses that I could find. These gave me the beginnings of an appreciation for the military and political complexities and uncertainties I would encounter on the ground.

At the end of the First World War the Southern Slav peoples were united in an independent country, Yugoslavia, or "land of the South Slavs," under a Serbian king. But old religious and ethnic differences soon surfaced in the new body politic. Though known initially as the Kingdom of the Serbs, Croats, and Slovenes, the country was dominated by the Serbs.

In the spring of 1941, as Hitler was making final preparations to invade Russia, the Germans put heavy pressure on the Yugoslav prince regent and government to join the Axis—the German, Italian, and Japanese alliance. But the Yugoslav generals balked, and forced a new government and the abdication of the regent in favor of the young King Peter. Hitler, apparently enraged by the Yugoslav action, ordered an immediate attack on Yugoslavia, to be carried out, he ordered, with "unmerciful harshness." It took only ten days to prepare.

The attack began on Palm Sunday, 1941, with wave after wave of Stuka dive-bombers hitting Belgrade. German and satellite armies crossed the frontiers from Hungary, Romania, and Bulgaria. Immediately after the German attack began, the young King Peter and the government abandoned Belgrade and fled to the safety of Athens and then Cairo. By April 17 it was all over. The Yugoslav army had disintegrated. The king, safely in Cairo, and later in London, and supported by the British and Americans, played out the charade of a government-in-exile, while Hitler dismembered the nation. In London the now-exiled Serb and Croat ministers immediately began feuding, to the disgust of both the British and the Americans.

Slovenia, the northernmost province, was divided between Germany and Italy. The northern half was annexed to the German Third Reich; the southern half became a province of Italy, and a small piece in the east was picked up by Hungary. Croatia, enlarged at the expense of the other Yugoslavs, became a separate kingdom under Italian control. A truncated Serbia was put directly under German military authority. The Italian surrender to the Allies in 1943 simply resulted in one master's being exchanged for another. Germany had quickly moved in forces to control the areas that had been given to the Italians (see Maps 1 and 2).

Only a million strong, the Slovenes had maintained their separate language and culture for centuries in spite of continuous foreign domination. Now their nation had been literally wiped off the map. The Communist leadership astutely saw this as an opportunity; as the ground for a nationalist rallying cry that could enlist the support of the Slovene people.

The Italians had installed at the head of the government of their newly proclaimed Kingdom of Croatia a murderous terrorist, Ante Pavelic, the leader of a fascist Croat band, the Ustashe. It was the Ustashe who in 1934 had murdered King Alexander, a Serb, while he was on a state visit to France. The organizers of the assassination had escaped capture and been given protective internment in Italy by Mussolini.

Pavelic, who was possibly even more racist than Hitler, set out to eliminate the Serbian minority in Croatia, then about a third of the total population, as well as the Jews and Gypsies. Hundreds of thousands of Serbs were murdered. Those who could fled to Serbia. Others were forced to convert to Catholicism as the price for their lives. Still others went to the forests to join resistance bands. One Partisan later told me that he had seen the Ustashe break open the locked doors of freight cars in order to murder Serbs inside who were being sent by rail through Croatia to German labor camps. Even the Germans in Yugoslavia, in their reports to Berlin, were appalled by the violence. But this did not deter them from arming the Ustashe and employing them with German units in their several offensives against the Partisans during the next years.

Because of the mountainous, sparsely populated terrain of most of Yugoslavia, the Germans, Italians, and their Yugoslav collaborators did not attempt at first to control the countryside, but instead limited themselves to the cities and main lines of communication. The conquerors' ability to police the country was also markedly diminished when nearly all of the German combat divisions were withdrawn after the swift, bloody takeover to take part in the attack against Russia seven weeks later. Isolated areas throughout the country thus first became areas of refuge for those escaping the German and Italian occupations in 1941. They included remnants of the Yugoslav army, members of the Communist Party, and others who were at risk of internment or imprisonment.

Some of those escaping the German net joined Draza Mihailovic, while others formed into independent bands, initially for self-preservation. Mihailovic concentrated his operations in Serbia where, as a Serb, he was most likely to find sympathizers who would provide support, and where he was safest from the danger of betrayal. Tito and the Communist Party leadership assembled in a secret villa in Belgrade, but soon moved into the Serbian hinterland to the southwest. They too began recruiting among the refugees but did not begin attacks against the Germans until after the German attack on Russia in June. By September their attacks intensified. The German reaction was immediate and violent. German forces brought back into Yugoslavia launched an offensive against both the Communist Partisans and the Chetniks and took most of the territory held by both resistance groups. The Partisans were soon forced to move the bulk of their forces into neighboring Bosnia, Montenegro, and Croatia.

■ I now began my operational briefings. My first meeting at the British SOE headquarters in Cairo was with Lieutenant Colonel F. W. D. Deakin, at that time deputy head of the Yugoslav Section. Bill Deakin was by profession an Oxford historian. Small, thin, blond, with smiling eyes over a prominent nose, he was friendly and warm in his approach, and given to the usual British understatement. He was also exceedingly modest about his own role as the first British liaison officer assigned to Tito's headquarters. He had been dropped on the night of May 27–28, 1943, into the midst of a savage German attack aimed at destroying Tito and the main Partisan forces. After six months of bloody fighting he had been picked up from a clandestine airstrip, and flown out to Cairo in December, just a few weeks before I met him.

Because he had been with the Partisans in a trying and dangerous time, Deakin had had an unusual opportunity to know Tito and his senior staff. He had arrived at a time when the Partisan leaders were anxious to develop firm relations with the Western Allies, and had used the periods of quiet between the intense fighting to learn all he could of the Partisan capabilities and objectives. As I later learned myself, the intense experience of breaking out from successive enemy encirclements made for personal bonds that at times surmounted the Partisan compulsion for secrecy and their intense suspicion of the West.

Deakin emphasized how important it was that I understand as much as possible of the complex evolution of the Yugoslav resistance, which had now crystallized into the two violently opposed guerrilla forces of Tito and Mihailovic, each demanding exclusive Allied recognition and support.

With the German invasion on April 6, 1941, a dense curtain dropped over the entire country. The first information to seep out came from couriers who crossed Bulgaria and reached British intelligence officers in Istanbul. They brought reports of resistance groups in Serbia and Montenegro under the leadership of Mihailovic. Then in August a weak radio transmission from Mihailovic was picked up by a British naval intercept station near Portsmouth in southern England. Messages could now be exchanged, but only in clear text since Mihailovic and the British had no common ciphers. As a consequence, the Germans and the Italians could easily listen in.

For the first months of German occupation SOE remained almost completely ignorant of even the existence of the Partisans. Then on the night of September 20, 1941, British Captain D. T. Hudson, two Royal Yugoslav officers, and a radio operator were put ashore from a submarine on the Montenegrin coast. Before the war, Hudson had served as a mining engineer in Serbia and spoke the language fluently. His mission was to find and assess any resistance groups in those areas he could reach. Soon after being put ashore Hudson and his party were picked up by a small resistance band which, Deakin said, were remnants of a Communist-led uprising in Montenegro that had been suppressed by the Italians that summer. Hudson's evaluation of the group, which he radioed to an SOE station in Malta, was favorable. They were actively fighting the occupiers and he recommended that Allied supplies be sent to them.

After this first Partisan contact Hudson had been taken to Partisan headquarters to meet with Tito and several of the other leaders of the Partisan movement. Hudson had had to abandon his radio because it was too heavy to carry to Tito's headquarters, so SOE remained completely ignorant of these meetings with Tito and of Hudson's more thorough assessment of what became the Partisan movement.

Because Mihailovic still had no ciphers with which to communicate securely, Hudson was directed to find him and deliver a cipher system he had brought with him for this purpose. He left the Partisan group and arrived at Mihailovic's headquarters on October 25, where he delivered the ciphers. He now had access to Mihailovic's transmitter using his own ciphers.

Deakin said that on November 9, 1941, only seven months after Yugoslavia had been invaded, Hudson had signaled to London that fighting had broken out between Partisans and Chetniks. The conflict that would make unified resistance to the Germans an impossibility had already begun.

■ Our drop to Slovenia was tentatively scheduled for April 12, three days before the end of the April moon period, so we flew to Italy a few days in advance. But on reaching Bari, where both OSS and SOE had advance bases, it became apparent we would miss the April moon period. In spite of the clearance from Tito's headquarters, the one from Slovene Partisan headquarters, which was also required, had not yet been received. The wait until the May moon period gave us additional time to learn more about conditions inside Yugoslavia from British and American officers with firsthand knowledge.

Major Linn Farish had just returned to Italy after his second trip into Partisan territory. Farish was, as was I, an engineering graduate of Stanford, so we had much in common. Farish was tall, craggy, and built like an oak. Fourteen years older than I, he was a man of strong passions, not of cool judgments. We spent many hours together as we waited for the moon, the weather, and the Partisan clearances to come together for our projected drops, he on his way to Serbia, I to Slovenia.

Farish had first parachuted to Tito's headquarters in Bosnia with Fitzroy Maclean on September 19 the previous year. Only six weeks later Farish had returned to Italy filled with the urgency of convincing the American government of the importance of the Partisan movement. He had not been outside Partisan headquarters, so he had been exposed only to the enthusiastic rhetoric of the Partisan leadership and to the propaganda of the skillful Agitprop section. His report, which OSS sent to President Roosevelt, was an eloquent plea for greatly expanded supplies for the Partisans, both by sea to the Dalmatian coast and by airdrops inland.

Farish was convinced that a new order would emerge at the end of the German occupation, and that it somehow would be a blend of Western democracy and Soviet communism. He was aware of the leading role of the Communists but believed that the broader political spectrum of the Liberation Front would provide the freedom for the political system he foresaw. In this he proved to be quite wrong.

OSS brought Farish to Washington where he saw the president and the senior military and State Department people. He was the first American to have seen Tito and the Partisans at first hand; everyone was eager to hear his story.

In January 1944 Farish returned to Tito's headquarters by parachute. He remained there for two months and again came out to Italy. When I saw him there a month later he was disillusioned and greatly depressed. In his first report he had been certain the Partisans were fighting and would continue to fight the Germans. Now he believed that both the Chetniks and the Partisans were committed to fight each other to the bitter end.

In one of his reports he wrote that "both sides believe that their first enemy is each other, with the Germans and Bulgarians second." He became obsessed by the realization that American weapons, dropped from American planes flown by American crews, were used by both sides to kill each other: "We saw both Chetnik and Partisan casualties. To us they were only poorly clothed, barefoot, and hungry peasant farmers, some of them badly wounded, who had borne their pain with a forbearance one would hardly believe possible. . . . I couldn't tell who was left or who was right, who was Communist or reactionary. . . . Rifles stamped 'U.S. property' firing Remington Arms ammunition, flown by American airmen in American aircraft, [were] being fired at people who had rescued other American airmen and who are doing everything to make them comfortable and to return them to safety.

"The senseless killing of these people by each other must be stopped," Farish wrote. "It is useless now to try to decide which side first did wrong. Too much blood has been spilled, the feeling is too bitter." He was profoundly discouraged, yet hopeful that something could be done to stop the fratricidal killing and get both sides back to fighting the Germans. It was inconceivable to him that the combined strength and influence of the Soviet Union, Great Britain, and the

United States could not put an abrupt end to the civil wars in Yugoslavia and guarantee the people a free election.

■ While waiting for the next moon period I also spent time with Major William Jones, a Canadian who had parachuted to the Croatian Partisans in May 1943, about the same time Deakin had dropped to Tito's headquarters. He had just been relieved of his assignment and ordered to leave Yugoslavia by Brigadier Maclean. Jones was a small and wiry man in his forties who had had a gallant record in the First World War, having won the British Military Cross for bravery. One eye was glass, and when he fixed you with that unblinking glass eye he was quite ferocious. How he came to find his way to SOE and Yugoslavia I never learned. He, like Farish, had been captivated by the Partisans, but unlike Farish he never lost his total and quite uncritical enthusiasm for them.

After his drop to the Croatian Partisans Jones and his radio operator soon moved to Slovene Partisan headquarters where he continued to make promises of Allied aid far beyond his instructions and the capabilities of the British and Americans to deliver. Four days after his arrival he asked that arms to equip four (British strength) divisions be dropped immediately. His messages were filled with exaggerated claims of Partisan capabilities, including an underground intelligence net throughout Italy as far as Rome itself.

Before being dropped to the Partisans he had been given an operational fund the equivalent of several thousand dollars. At a Partisan political rally in Slovenia in a burst of exuberance he had stood up and presented his entire fund to the Anti-Fascist Women of Slovenia in the name of the nonexistent Anti-Fascist Women of Canada.

■ Although I was officially a part of Brigadier Maclean's mission, OSS officers also wanted me to take on jobs for them. The most ambitious briefing of this sort came from OSS officers of the Morale Operations section. It was obvious that they had a mission in life and were desperately trying to find a way to carry it out. They had wanted to send an officer to Tito's headquarters but so far their request had been turned down. They also wanted to send an officer to me to conduct propaganda and psychological warfare operations against the Germans. This also was turned down.

They had to be content with trying to brief me on what I should do when I arrived. As one task they gave me pictures of Adolph Hitler framed with a black border and announcing his death in heavy German script. These, they said, were to be dropped on mountain trails and in villages where they would be found by German soldiers who presumably would be "demoralized" by the revelation.

More serious, and quite at odds with my basic orders, were their instructions on political issues, which they gave me in writing:

> Convince them [the Slovene Partisans] that the Julian March and Istrian peninsula taken by Italy and the Klagenfurt area taken by Austria [after World War I] will be returned to them.
>
> Convince them that our apparent appeasement policy with respect to Italy does not mean we will take sides with Italy in territorial disputes between Italy and Slovenia, rather the contrary.
>
> The more the Slovenes take an active part against the Germans the greater the support they will receive from us both in postwar relief and in honoring their territorial claims against Austria and Italy.

This was in direct contravention of the American policy to defer all decisions on postwar territorial changes until peace treaties were negotiated. Another of their instructions was directly contrary to the strongly held views of the president and the joint chiefs against any commitment of American combat forces in the Balkans. Either the Morale Operations staff were unaware of that policy, or they were prepared to make promises they knew would not be honored. Their instructions to me were:

> Don't imply that we envision Russian occupation of Slovenia, rather that we expect to arrive in Slovenia before the Russians.

At the time the immediacy of cutting German rail communications was foremost in my mind and I ignored this misguided guidance.

Of my many briefers, only Bill Deakin combined the direct experience of having been with the Partisans with a mature and dispassionate assessment of their capabilities and limitations, together with timely warning of problems I would face with them.

■ My orders from Maclean's headquarters, Force 399, were prepared. They read:

Major Lindsay is appointed Commanding Officer of the Allied Military Mission to the Partisan forces in the Stajerska area.

As such, he is fully empowered to represent the Allied Military Authorities in this area. He or his delegate is the sole representative of Brigadier Maclean and through him of the Allied Commanders-in-Chief, on all matters which involve liaison with Partisan Military Authorities in the Stajerska, including military plans and supplies.

CHAPTER 3

First Days with
the Partisans

After our spring morning in the lovely Alpine valley, we set off for Slovene Partisan headquarters more than twenty miles away. Our remaining radio and batteries, together with several hundred pounds of Schraeder's weather observation equipment, were loaded onto farm wagons. The entire trip would be through liberated territory. The Partisan patrol of twenty men armed with German rifles and machine pistols accompanied us. In two villages through which we passed stone walls of houses and churches, blackened by fire, stood starkly open to the sky, the wooden floors and roofs completely consumed by flames—reprisals inflicted by the Germans and Italians in earlier sweeps. It was a sight that was to become all too familiar.

On this march we met several Slovene men who had worked in the mines and steel mills of America before the war and, having built up a small stake, had returned home to their families and villages. One old man who had worked in the steel mills of Gary, Indiana, hobbled out to greet us. With great difficulty he tried to recall a few words of English. All he could get out was "Jesus Christ, God damn." Jim Fisher, my radio operator, still had a pack or two of American cigarettes and offered the old man one. He took it carefully, looked at it lovingly, and finally managed to ask if he could have a second one. The first was to smoke, the other was to show to his friends.

At one point we passed a section of a branch rail line being repaired by Germans taken prisoner by the Partisans. They were a bedraggled-looking lot. The Partisans explained that they were already getting ready for the end of the war when railroads would be vitally needed for relief and reconstruction. The final linking of this line to the main Slovene rail network would not be made until the war ended so that it could not be used in the interim by the Germans during their periodic sweeps in force through liberated territory.

We also passed tank traps built by the Partisans to impede any German movement to retake the liberated area. These were built at points where the road was cut into a steep slope along a stream. The shelf of earth on which the road itself rested was dug away for 10 to 20 yards and replaced by a very light wooden bridge, strong enough to support men on foot or a farm wagon but sure to collapse with the weight of a light tank or armored car. In addition, these roads were mined with plastic explosives received by airdrop and planted in wooden boxes immune to mine detectors. The mines were set to explode only if triggered by the weight of a heavy vehicle. Road mines were used sparingly, however, because of the danger they posed to the peasants on whose support the Partisans very much depended.

The purpose of these defenses was not to stop the Germans, but to oblige them to commit large forces in their attacks on Partisan territory. The need to use large forces limited the number of offensives the Germans could mount—and gave the Partisans, with their extensive intelligence network in the towns and valleys, ample warning of such attacks as well.

After nearly forty-eight hours awake and a twelve-hour march through liberated territory in Dolenjska, we arrived at Slovene Partisan headquarters at one o'clock in the morning. The headquarters was near Semic, a tiny village of some twenty peasant houses located on the lower slopes of a mountain. Here we met Captain James Goodwin, an American who was head of the Allied Liaison Mission, and Lieutenant George Wuchinich, the Serbian-American OSS intelligence officer whose family views of the Croats I have quoted earlier. Goodwin had a tiny room behind the one-room schoolhouse, and during my stay I slept there on the floor.

Goodwin, assigned to Brigadier Maclean's Anglo-American military mission to the Partisans, had parachuted in January to Tito's headquarters at Drvar in Bosnia in central Yugoslavia along with Brigadier Maclean, American Major Linn Farish, Major Randolph Churchill (the prime minister's son) and Lieutenant Eli Popovich of OSS. Goodwin's first two months in Drvar were spent receiving parachute drops and organizing an airstrip. In early March Maclean asked Goodwin to go to Slovenia to work under the Canadian Major Jones with whom Maclean was increasingly dissatisfied. Goodwin had made the trip of more than 200 miles on foot through German-controlled territory, over the mountains in two to three feet of snow, finally arriving at Slovene headquarters in late March. Only a week after his arrival, the removal to Italy of the irrepressible Major Jones was decided upon, and Goodwin took over the duties of senior liaison officer. Given this chance by Maclean to prove himself, Goodwin had done well.

Goodwin was a big man in his middle twenties. He had grown a large moustache and wore his military visored cap jauntily cocked on the side of his head. An engineer officer, he was a practical, down-to-earth doer and busied himself arranging airdrops, evacuating downed airmen and working with the Partisan command on attacks against the German lines of communication.

Wuchinich, also a big man, seemed quite the opposite. He was filled with an emotional empathy for the Partisans. He radioed reams of propaganda material to OSS that had been given to him by the Slovene Partisan Agitprop section—and very little hard intelligence. He recognized that the Partisan movement was directed and controlled by the Communist Party, but in one of his reports he concluded, "Communism as we see it can be dismissed without any fear. The Communist Party is working within the Freedom Front, which is trying to give each Slovene the equivalent of our American Bill of Rights."

Later, in reading both his reports and those of British Lieutenant Colonel Peter Wilkinson, head of the Austrian section of SOE, who was in Slovenia at about the same time, I have been struck by their great differences in quality. Wilkinson's reports were analytical and balanced politically and militarily. He had, for example, quickly identified Slovene nationalism and the desire for freedom from prewar Serb domination as a strong motivating force.

Wuchinich's reports were emotional and ill-informed. He simply accepted uncritically the handouts of the agitation and propaganda section. After attending a Slovene Partisan congress held in liberated territory he radioed: "The scope of this parliament and its fundamental laws in Hitler's Europe were all that I as an American could wish or expect. The enthusiasm of the people at the parliament knew no bounds." He reported almost nothing on the hard intelligence targets of German order of battle, their tactics in securing the railroads, the strengths and weaknesses of the Partisan forces, and their effectiveness against the German lines of communication.

In part this reflected the differences between the British intelligence organizations and OSS. OSS had impressive strengths in political and economic analysts recruited from the top universities, but General Donovan, the head of OSS, had concentrated most of them in Washington and at major overseas headquarters, such as those in Britain and Italy. People to work behind the lines were often chosen for their potential for sabotage operations and for their languages, learned from their immigrant parents. By contrast the quality of work of people like Deakin, Maclean, and Wilkinson, who served directly with resistance organizations, was impressive.

■ We now parted with Schraeder who, with his weather instruments, went off to set up his observation station near a German airfield. It was vitally important to the Allied air forces to have as complete a picture as possible of the weather over German-occupied Eu-

33

rope in order to assign targets to their bombers during the next 24-hour period. Improved weather forecasts were also vital to military land and sea operations, such as the timing of the planned Allied landings on the coast of France. OSS dropped weather observers like Schraeder at several locations in occupied Europe to help piece out the Allied weather maps.

These weather observers served an additional purpose. Since all German weather observations were radioed in code to their weather central, there was no way that these much more numerous observations could be used by the Allied meteorologists unless the German code could be broken. As it was known that each German airfield was equipped to make weather observations and radioed reports every four hours, a second and potentially even more important purpose of OSS weather observers was to get as close to German airfields as possible and make their observations at the same time. By comparing the radio intercepts of coded German reports with the observations of our own weather observers it should be possible to break the German weather code. This would make it possible to read all of the German weather reports from occupied Europe as soon as they were sent, a feat I later heard was ultimately accomplished.

Establishing another weather station in the Karawanken Alps was a possibility I was to investigate when we arrived there.

■ The morning after our arrival at Slovene Partisan Headquarters I was introduced to a young lawyer from Ljubljana who was the Partisan liaison officer between Goodwin and Slovene Partisan headquarters. We spent several hours together, during which I got my first view of their operations. Couriers who had recently arrived from Stajerska across the German border reported that a German offensive against the Partisans there was now in progress. I was told it would be impossible for us to get through until that offensive was over, which might be a week or two. I was acutely aware of the urgency of getting to Stajerska to cut the railroads there in support of the Allied spring offensive in Italy—but for the time being I could only wait and use the time to learn more about the Partisans and their operations.

Politically, the Partisan movement in Slovenia had grown out of the prewar Popular Front in which the illegal Communist Party was the guiding force. After the capitulation of the Yugoslav government in Belgrade to the Germans in 1941, it had been renamed the Liberation Front of Slovenia. The Liberation Front was the political device used by the Communist Party throughout Yugoslavia during the war to broaden the internal political support for resistance without diluting Communist direction and control.

I soon had my first experience with their electoral processes. While at Semic I was invited to witness the election of a district council at a nearby village. On arrival we were taken to the local schoolhouse, which was packed with peasants. I was given a front seat, and the proceedings began. The election started with very long nominating speeches for each of the seven candidates for the seven seats on the council, followed by seconding speeches for each, fortunately of somewhat shorter length. Still unused to Communist politics, I waited for competing candidates to be nominated, but none were forthcoming. The election was then held, its form a unanimous vote of acclamation, accompanied by much cheering and stamping of feet. The seven members then took their places at a table at the head of the room, and the newly elected chairman pulled from his pocket his speech of acceptance covering several closely written pages. I am told by Dusan Biber that other local elections were by secret ballot, but with only one nominee per office, a secret ballot didn't make much difference.

I asked one of the political commissars if it was usual that there were no opposition candidates. But he did not find it at all inconsistent with the slogan of democracy that they had so wholeheartedly embraced. Their "democracy," I learned, made no room for pluralism or opposition candidates. At that, I may have been too critical of the proceedings. This was probably the nearest thing to political participation the ordinary citizens of the village had ever seen.

The two founders of the Slovene Partisan movement begun in 1941, Edvard Kardelj and Boris Kidric, had been prewar leaders of the Slovene Communist Party. Before the war Tito had personally brought both men into his inner party group, and they proved to be among his most loyal and trusted lieutenants both during and after the war. Kardelj had joined the illegal party at 16 and at 19 had been caught by the police, tortured, and imprisoned. After release he had gone to Moscow for extended training at the Comintern. Back in Axis-occupied Slovenia, now aged 30, he took the lead in organizing the Slovene resistance to the German occupation. By the time I arrived in Slovenia, he was spending most of his time in Bosnia as a member of the Partisan high command and was becoming Tito's alter ego.

Boris Kidric, also a member of Tito's prewar party leadership, had, at 29, been an organizer of the resistance in 1941. Now, in 1944, he was secretary of the Slovene Communist Party, a member of the Slovene liberation government, and the most powerful man in the Slovene resistance leadership.

The Partisan government of Slovenia was not at the Partisan military headquarters at Semic, but in a camp hidden in the forested mountains of Kocevski Rog, a four-hour march away. Consequently we saw almost nothing of the political leadership during our wait to go north. But we were made well aware of their existence. All important political or military questions, the military command impressed on us, had to be referred to the government.

Semic was much better off than other Slovene villages I visited during our stay. Several that I saw had been completely burned out by Italian troops during their occupation. Practically all the inhabitants of these villages had disappeared, but there were still a few people in each who had formed primitive shelters by laying a few planks across the tops of the stone walls remaining from their burned-out homes.

Partisan officers described in detail the Italian occupation of southern Slovenia, which had been every bit as cruel and violent as the subsequent German occupation. The taking and shooting of hostages, the burning of villages and farms, the looting—all were pervasive under the Italians. In 1942 the Italian High Command issued a harsh proclamation in what had been the region of the

Slovene capital of Ljubljana. OSS had secretly obtained a copy, although I did not see it until after the war.

IN THE ENTIRE TERRITORY OF PROVINCIA LUBIANA FROM
THIS DAY ON:

ALL local passenger trains are discontinued;

ALL persons are prohibited to travel via transit trains; with the exception of individuals in possession of passports for foreign countries or to other provinces of Italy;

ALL bus transportation is discontinued;

ALL traffic between inhabited places, either on foot or any type of vehicle is prohibited;

ALL loitering or trespassing on either side of the railroad tracks—except in towns—within the distance of 1 kilometer is prohibited; the transgressor to these regulations shall be shot without warning;

ALL telephone, telegraph, and postal service in the city and outside is discontinued.

FROM THIS DAY ON, IN THE ENTIRE TERRITORY OF THE
PROVINCIA LUBIANA THE FOLLOWING SHALL BE SHOT
WITHOUT FURTHER WARNING:

ALL those who shall have in any way acted inimically toward the Italian authorities or the Italian Army;

ALL those in whose possession arms, ammunition, or explosives shall be found;

ALL those who in any way shall aid the rebels;

ALL those who shall be detected in possession of forged passports, transit permits, or identification cards;

ALL qualified male persons who, without an approved reason, shall be found within the military zone, behaving suspiciously.

IN THE ENTIRE PROVINCIA LUBIANA FROM THIS DAY ON
THE FOLLOWING SHALL BE COMPLETELY DEMOLISHED:

ALL buildings in which Italian troops shall be insulted;

ALL buildings in which arms, ammunition, or explosives, as well as any material of military character shall be found;

ALL dwellings whose inhabitants, of their free will, give shelter or render hospitality to the rebels.

Certainly during actual hostilities, no occupying army is a boon to those being occupied. But the Italian decrees in Slovenia had two characteristics which made them exceptional—and put them on the same level with their Nazi allies in their effort to control all of Europe. One was the fact that these decrees were put into effect in annexed territories; that is to say, in what the Italian authorities themselves claimed was Italy proper. The other was that the Italian command regularly issued notices of execution of hostages. OSS had also obtained copies of these:

THE HIGH COMMISSIONER FOR PROVINCIA LUBIANA AND THE
COMMANDER OF THE XI ARMY ANNOUNCE:

In the morning of May 14 certain Communists kidnapped two men and two women. In the morning of May 14 certain terrorists fired on the train Novo Mesto–Lubiana. The given period of time having passed without the perpetrators being found and in accordance with the decree of April 24, 1942, in retaliation for these terroristic acts, 6 persons were shot, all of them reliably guilty of Communistic activities. They were shot this morning at 6:30 A.M.

May 16, 1942

Similar announcements of other hostage executions continued to be issued almost weekly. An OSS report from inside Slovenia in those days, after describing the Italian destruction of the village of Ravnik, and the eviction and torture of its inhabitants, concluded, "The sight of Ravnik today is pitiful. You find no other living creatures among the debris but half-starved dogs and cats who have not deserted the place as their masters were forced to do." Of such places I saw many.

Except during the occasional enemy sweeps, the liberated areas of Slovenia were spared such horrors. Civil government in those areas, dominated by the Communists, was already well organized. Liberated areas provided the opportunity to set up Communist or Communist-controlled local governments that became the building blocks for regional political organizations, and then for a Yugoslav-wide organization for all liberated areas. Step by step, and already visible to us in the late spring of 1944, this provisional Communist shadow government was being transformed into a national Communist government, ready to move to the cities and assume control whenever the war ended.

A thin facade of a multiparty system was maintained, yet only candidates nominated by the Front were permitted. In the words of Milovan Djilas, a wartime Partisan leader and later a prominent Yugoslav dissident, "The participation of individuals or groups from [other] parties was for show and symbolic. . . . It never went further than that." The Front quickly developed grass-roots political organizations, from people's committees at the village level to the Slovene National Liberation Council at the top. In October of 1943, two and a half years after war had come to Slovenia, the Liberation Council, still functioning secretly in its mountain hideout, had declared itself to be the sole legal government of Slovenia. Indeed, with the country parceled out among Germany, Italy, and Hungary, and under a brutal military occupation, there was no other.

A few days after our arrival, the commander and commissar of the Slovene Partisans returned from the Partisan Ninth Corps in Primorska, the Slovene littoral. That evening Goodwin, Bush, and I had dinner with them and their staff in the peasant house they were using as their headquarters. The hut was a primitive, one-room affair, the entrance to which was through the pigsty. It turned out to be a tremendous spread—sausage, ham, bully beef, and potatoes, followed by cake with wine sauce, all washed down with lots of local wine. Much of the food was prepared from supplies that the Allies in Italy had dropped by parachute.

Franc Rozman, the commander, had been the commander in Stajerska in the first half of 1943. Rozman was, like many senior Partisans, a veteran of the Spanish Civil War. The deputy commander was one of the few Royal Yugoslav Army officers who had joined the Partisan movement in its early days. He later was transferred to Tito's headquarters as chief of supply.

Dusan Kveder, the chief of staff, was direct and vigorous in his speech. In his late twenties, he was a "no-nonsense" officer. He was thoroughly committed to the Partisan revolution and appeared to consider the larger conflict between the Western Allies and Germany as of lesser importance. Of the Partisans, he was one of the most rigid in what appeared to us to be a pro-Russian and anti-West attitude.

He too had been in Stajerska in 1943, as political commissar of the Partisan group there.

Boris Kraigher, the political commissar, was quietly friendly and thoughtful. Rather surprisingly, Boris Kidric himself assumed the position of Slovene commissar a few months later while retaining his positions in the shadow government of Slovenia and as secretary of the Slovene Communist Party. At the time we believed he did this to strengthen his political control of the Partisan army during the critical last months of the war.

The deputy commissar, Viktor Avbelj, whose war name was Rudi, later came to Stajerska where we became good friends. During the dinner in the peasant house, a courier arrived from the north with a message for the commander saying that the German offensive in Stajerska was continuing unabated, and that approximately 20,000 German troops were being used against the Partisan brigades there. The brigades had been dispersed into the higher mountains to escape the larger and better-armed German forces. Kveder told us he had just returned from there a few days earlier. The trip had taken him fourteen days. He had been ambushed three times by German patrols, and in one ambush his courier had been killed. We would have to continue our wait.

As Rozman and Kveder had been in Stajerska as commander and commissar during the previous year, they were able to give us a full rundown on what to expect. They both emphasized that I would find it quite different from life here in the liberated territory. We would find no liberated territory there. The German control was rigorous and we would live in the forests and move only at night.

■ We found that relations between the Partisans and the British and ourselves were normally conducted by the commissar, rather than by the military commander. Kraigher, the senior Slovene commissar, his deputy Rudi, and I therefore sat down after the dinner to spell out the working relationships I would have with the Partisan Fourth Operating Zone (as the command in Stajerska was termed), the Slovene headquarters, and Brigadier Maclean's headquarters with

Tito. We agreed that because of the extremely slow and difficult communications between the Fourth Zone and Slovene headquarters, I should arrange by radio directly with Allied headquarters in Italy the specific requirements for supplies to be dropped to the Fourth Zone.

Availability of Allied aircraft set the limits on the supplies we could deliver from Italy to Partisan units. Each month Allied headquarters would advise Tito through Maclean of the number of sorties that could be flown during the following month. Tito's headquarters then allocated these sorties to each Partisan resistance group. The volume of supplies for each was thus determined by Tito's headquarters, although the composition of the loads would be worked out by each Allied liaison officer together with the Partisan command with which he was working. Tito's purpose was to ensure that the British did not allocate supplies to specific areas for their own political reasons, or limit supplies to other regions to minimize the strength and influence of the Partisans there. Tito was thus able to control the allocation of Allied supplies to meet his own political and military objectives.

■ The enforced stay at Semic, while frustrating, was an opportunity to get to know my hosts. A good thing, since the Partisans were, after all, the forces on whom I had to depend for accomplishment of my mission, and for the survival of my companions in this operation.

Thus, a few days later, while still waiting for the situation in the north to quiet down, we visited one of the brigades of the Seventh Corps near one of the German "hedgehog" garrisons—well-fortified towns from which they launched periodic offensives into Partisan-controlled territory. The Partisans had just completed a successful offensive against Zuzemberk, a town that had been held by several hundred Slovene collaborationist troops. The last two days of the battle, more than a hundred of the defenders had barricaded themselves in the town church. The Partisans had shelled the church with an Italian 75-mm gun and had almost completely destroyed it. Not a single defender had gotten out alive.

The brigade was well armed and appeared to be well disciplined. The majority of men appeared to be in their teens and early twenties, with a few in their thirties. Officers were all in their twenties, most in their early twenties. They looked healthy and fit.

For the most part the Partisan rank and file wore German uniforms and boots. Officers were in brown British battle dress with Partisan insignia of rank, or in Partisan-designed high-collared tunics cut from British blankets that had been dropped with the loads of guns and explosives. Uniforms and boots, especially in winter, were among the highest priority needs for supplies to be parachuted by the Allies. The brigade commander told us that since they had no uniform factories they had to capture German and collaborationist soldiers for their clothing. Captured, they would be stripped to their underwear and sent back to their units, where they would be reoutfitted. The Partisans then would capture them again and the cycle would be repeated. This, he quipped, was the way the Partisans manufactured their uniforms. It must have been a popular joke. I later heard Tito had told Maclean the same story.

The troops were armed with German rifles, some of which they had captured, and some of which had come from German stocks captured by the Allies in North Africa and Italy and subsequently dropped to the Partisans. In order to minimize differences in ammunition some units were equipped with Italian weapons and others, as was this brigade, with German guns. Although the British Bren light machine gun used a still different ammunition it was one of the best weapons for Partisan warfare. It was light enough to be carried easily by one man, highly accurate and capable of automatic fire. Large numbers had been air-dropped and the brigade had several. The German Schmeisser machine pistols were prized by Partisan officers and many in this unit had them. Many units carried German MG38 and MG42 machine guns. A few light mortars rounded out their armament.

■ The several talks with the Partisan officers gave me an appreciation of the fighting that had taken place since the German and Italian occupation of Slovenia. The Partisans' armed organization had grown from a few isolated units of 50 to 100 men each in 1941 to a few thousand men in 1942, organized into brigades of 200 to 500 men each. By launching attacks against isolated Italian garrisons in Dolenjska southeast of Ljubljana they had forced the withdrawal of the Italians from an area around the town of Kocevje, which became the first liberated territory under Partisan control. That same year the first Partisan units were sent across the Reich frontier to Stajerska to pick up recruits who were evading German mobilization.

The big event in 1943 was the capitulation of Italy. The Partisan brigades in Slovenia and all along the Adriatic coast moved in forced marches to capture the weapons of the Italians before the Germans were able to secure the area and intern Italian troops. There were six Italian divisions in Slovenia alone. Glad to get out of the war, the Italians willingly turned over their arms and supplies to the Partisans.

Before the arrival of the Germans, the Partisans worked frantically to move food, weapons, clothing, and other supplies out into the forests, where most of it was hidden for future use. The Slovene Partisans, who previously had had to kill a German or local collaborator for every gun they acquired, now were on a more solid footing, with considerable quantities of ammunition, guns, clothing, and food buried or stored in the mountainous hinterland. This had allowed them to more than double the number of men under arms.

By the time we arrived the Partisans in Slovenia controlled two areas that had been liberated from the Germans. One was in Dolenjska, extending from the Kupa River in the south to just outside two towns on the north from which strong enemy garrisons from time to time launched heavily armed attacks. The liberated area—farming valleys separated by ridges of hills and low mountains—was roughly 12 by 25 miles. The second area, in the hills and mountains of the littoral between Rijeka (Fiume) and Ljubljana and astride the main railway connecting the two cities, was roughly 12 by 18 miles. The two areas were sufficiently large and stable to support more than 20,000 armed Partisans.

The Partisans' Seventh Corps, with a strength of about 15,000 men, operated in the first liberated area; their Ninth Corps of about 5,000 men operated in the liberated area of the littoral; and the Fourth Operational Zone in Stajerska, the mountainous area between the Sava and Drava rivers, had about 2,000 men. As there was no liberated territory in Stajerska, now inside the German Reich, Partisan units there were organized in smaller guerrilla groups, each of one to two hundred men, operating in the forest and largely independent of one another except when brought together for a major offensive operation. The Fourteenth Division, with less than 1,000 men, had been sent from Dolenjska across the Sava to Stajerska two months before we had arrived. A third of the men in its three brigades had no weapons at all.

Each commander in the Partisan military hierarchy was paralleled by a political commissar, down to the lowest level of a platoon of 15 to 40 men. Officially, the military commander was responsible for all combat functions. The commissar was responsible for education, political indoctrination, supply, and political organization of the several areas under Partisan control as well as for secret organization in adjoining areas under German control. In early 1942 Tito's Supreme Headquarters had defined the role of the commissars, saying: "The political commissars are the soul of the units. They are the representatives of the people and the guardians of the people's interests in the units. They are the initiators and the leaders in the elevation of the political, military, and ideological level of the units." In more down-to-earth terms, the commissars organized political indoctrination and propaganda, saw to it that the civilians were organized to support the Partisans unswervingly and that any "subversives" within the civilian or Partisan ranks were quickly removed.

When I arrived Tito had just issued an order substituting the western open-palm military salute for the clenched-fist Communist salute, though most of the Partisans still used the clenched fist through force of habit. This change was probably one of several made at the direction of Moscow in order to play down the visible Communist appearance of the Partisan leadership. The Comintern in Moscow in 1941 and 1942 had complained to Tito about the open use of Communist symbols by the Partisans. One message asked why it was necessary to call the Partisan brigades "Proletarian Brigades." Another objected to the red stars sewn on the Partisan caps.

As for the opposition we faced, German occupation troops in the area consisted in part of third-rate border and line-of-communication guards. They were backed up, however, by tough SS troops and by Wehrmacht units that had been pulled out of active combat elsewhere for major offensives against the Partisans.

In addition to their own troops, the Germans had taken over from the Italians a very sizable Slovene collaborationist force, the White Guard. They had been renamed the Slovene Domobrans, or home defense force, but the name White Guard persisted. The Germans, playing upon the strongly conservative Catholicism of the Slovene population, had expanded the White Guard for the proclaimed purpose of defending the church and conservative institutions against Communism. In this respect they were quite successful: they had probably recruited a greater number of Slovenes than had the Partisans. The garrison at Zuzemberk, which had been wiped out in the Partisan attack there, were all White Guardists. The White Guard were in some ways more dangerous in encounters than the Germans because they spoke the same language and often dressed in a nondescript fashion similar to the Partisans. Being natives of the area they were equally familiar with the local terrain.

While at Slovene headquarters I also spent a few hours talking with the head of the Russian mission there, a colonel who had spent many months commanding Soviet Partisan units behind the German lines in Russia. I found him friendly though not very informative, possibly because we were using a Partisan interpreter and we both felt inhibited.

Goodwin told me that the Russians were far more warmly received than either the British or Americans, and appeared to have greater access to information on Partisan operations and on German intelligence picked up by Partisans. The Russian officers with the Partisans were, on the whole, military men rather than political officers in uniform, though there was no indication that they exercised any command function over Partisan troops. It was possible that they gave advice from time to time which, if given, was likely to be readily accepted by the Partisan military leaders—at least in the early days.

■ While we waited, Jim Fisher, our radio operator, ran trial radio contacts with both the OSS and SOE bases to check our own equipment before we would have to leave Goodwin's functioning communication link with the SOE base station. Jim set up his radio in the attic of a peasant hut, stretched an antenna to a nearby tree, and began to call Italy. I never ceased getting a thrill from watching Fisher tapping his brass key to call the base station, and then hearing the answering call come back from several hundred miles away across the German lines and the Adriatic. He was able to establish two-way contact with SOE but not with OSS. Later an OSS message came in over Goodwin's link saying they heard Jim's calls loud and clear, but apparently he could not hear the base station. It took two months to work out dependable radio communications with the OSS station.

While we were still waiting at Semic Lieutenant Colonel Peter Moore, Brigadier MacLean's field deputy, arrived by parachute. He brought word that the Allied drive on Rome was imminent, and that it was urgent that we go north as soon as possible. The Ljubljana-Zagreb railroad line could only be attacked effectively from Stajerska because the southern approaches were blocked by a string of German strong points. The north-south rail line to Vienna could only be reached from Stajerska. He and Tito's staff had allocated ten tons of explosives to be dropped to us as soon as we arrived.

Peter also brought news of a German parachute attack on Tito's headquarters. Suspense was high. As the attack had taken place only a few days before Peter left Italy, no one knew whether Tito and the Allied and Russian missions there had been able to avoid capture. In fact, as we learned in due course, Tito had escaped by climbing up through a hole in the top of the cave in which he had been living. Most of the Partisan staff and the British, American, and Russian missions had also escaped. The village of Drvar, however, had been burned and most of the civilians who had not escaped had been lined up and shot by the attacking Germans.

CHAPTER 4

Crossing the Border

At last, on May 25, a courier arrived at Semic with a report that the German offensive in the north was over. We prepared to depart. It would be impossible to use either wagons or packhorses after we left liberated territory. We therefore would take only two batteries for our radio, which we had charged to the limit. We hoped that by restricting the number and length of our radio contacts to an absolute minimum, we would be able to arrive at our destination and have a generator dropped by parachute before the charge in our two batteries was completely exhausted.

We had anticipated that most of our equipment would have to be dropped to us in Stajerska and I had decided that Corporal Edward Welles, the fourth member of our group, should stay in Italy and drop to us in Stajerska along with radios and other equipment too heavy to carry from Dolenjska. He was keenly disappointed, but he was invaluable in assembling the equipment we asked for from Stajerska. Neither he nor I anticipated the incredible sequence of foulups that delayed his arrival for weeks after we called for him.

We prepared three packs of the radio equipment, putting a battery in each of two packs and the radio itself in the third. Partisans would carry these as we went north. Our own equipment was reduced to what we could carry in our knapsacks. Needless to say, the extra shirts, trousers, and underwear that in Italy had seemed essential were discarded.

One of the unexpected lessons of our months with the Partisans was how little we needed in personal possessions to make out very well. My own equipment was reduced to code books, a pistol, submachine gun and ammunition, maps, a flashlight, raincoat, mountain sleeping bag, an extra pair of socks, first-aid kit, toothbrush, soap, and razor. Subsequently we found that even the first-aid kit was not worth carrying, and discarded all but a small bottle of aspirin and a bottle of iodine. We each carried a bar of chocolate in the bottoms of our packs as an emergency ration.

I did make one improvement on the standard-issue mountain pack. Before our parachute drop, the British had issued to each of us a foam rubber headband sewn into a cloth cover to cushion a bump on the head should we have a hard landing. After landing I had cut the band in two pieces and slipped each half under the shoulder straps of my pack. My "invention" was a great success as a cushion between the straps and my shoulder bones.

A young Partisan lieutenant, Vlado Valencak, was assigned to us as our interpreter, watchdog, and general link with whatever Partisan unit we happened to be with. Although a Slovene, Vlado had been at the University of Belgrade when the Germans invaded Yugoslavia. At the university he had joined the illegal Communist Party and after the German invasion had joined the Partisans. He was selected because he combined some facility in English with party reliability. His dogmatic Communism became increasingly irritating. His English was not as good as he thought it was, particularly in the first few months, and there were often difficulties in communicating through him.

He had one particularly infuriating phrase that he worked to death over the months he was with us. Whenever we would find ourselves in a difficult spot, he would observe, as though it was great wisdom, "It is bad but it is so." He would proclaim this in a sort of singsong lilt.

Notwithstanding my earlier claims to OSS, my Russian was poor, although it was of some help in learning Slovene, which is also a Slavic language. My other linguistic claim, to proficiency in German, was unfortunately also exaggerated. I say unfortunately because German was the second tongue in Slovenia, and in the area north of the new German frontier it was of course the official language. Since Slovenia had been an Austrian possession for centuries there was nothing new in German being the official language. There was thus no sign of resentment when I resorted to German, and I often used it—as best I could—as a way of getting over stumbling blocks with Vlado's English, and in talking with the Stajerska peasants. But perhaps their lack of resentment was because I spoke such horrible German that they knew I couldn't be anything but American.

We were to be accompanied north by Lieutenant Dan Gatoni, a Jewish Palestinian serving in the British Army. A Major McNeff of British MI-6 had gone to Stajerska just before the German offensive and had not been heard from since. Gatoni was being sent to find him and establish radio communications.

After we reached Stajerska he confided to me his true identity and mission. Dan Gatoni was an agent of the Jewish Agency in Cairo, the organization fighting to create a Jewish state. He had joined MI-6 as a radio operator in order to carry out his real mission, which was to get as close as possible to the German concentration camps in Austria so that when the war ended he could quickly help any Jewish survivors who could be found.

This rang a bell. Corporal Rose, Bill Deakin's radio operator, had revealed to him the year before, when they were with Tito, that he had been placed in SOE by the Jewish Agency. His real name was Peretz Rosenberg, and he was a Sabra born in Palestine of German parents. His real objective was to find out whatever he could about the situation of the Jews in Yugoslavia. Rose was an excellent radio operator and after the Second World War he became head of the clandestine radio service of Haganah, the Jewish insurgent organization dedicated to forcing the British out of Palestine.

■ The journey from Slovene headquarters to the northern edge of liberated territory took two days, most of it on foot, and the remainder in a farm wagon drawn by two horses and driven at a fast trot by a peasant wife. With no springs whatsoever, every bump and rut in the dirt track felt like a pile driver going up my spine. Before we had gone a mile I was ready to bail out and walk.

We spent the first night in a small village that had received horrible treatment at the hands of the Germans a few months before. The village church was a burned-out shell, and most of the houses were burned out as well, victims of a German sweep in force to retaliate for Partisan attacks on German garrisons and installations. The village was currently the headquarters of the Partisan Seventh Corps, commanded by a Montenegrin who had been sent to Slovenia by Tito to help in the organization of the larger Partisan units. The corps commissar impressed me as a very well-educated and sensible man, quite unlike some of the more fanatical, crusading commissar types.

We were told there would be a Partisan dance that evening, and that we were expected to attend. It was held in one of the few buildings with a roof still intact. There were about fifty Partisans and civilian political workers, and the wine flowed freely. The dances were traditional Slovene dances, somewhat like American square dances, the music provided by an accordion and robust singing of Partisan songs. At one point I found myself spinning around with a buxom Partisanka who had hooked a hand grenade by its safety pin ring to her German military belt. At a particularly wild swing the hand grenade flew out and hit me below the belt. I dropped to the floor in pain. Everyone thought this wonderfully funny and loud cheers went up as I attempted to hide the pain and struggle back to the dance. As the evening continued Jim Fisher became the life of the party by teaching the Partisans the latest American songs, such as "My Blue Heaven" and "Ma, He's Making Eyes at Me."

At the end of the second day we arrived at the village of Sticna, a small group of houses clustered at the foot of forested hills that marked the end of the liberated territory. This was the point beyond which we no longer could move safely in daylight. The coming night we were to cross the frontier of German-occupied Yugoslavia and enter the Third Reich itself, then cross the Sava River and the road and railroad paralleling it in order to reach the mountains on the north side by daylight the next morning.

This village was the temporary headquarters of a Partisan unit known as an *odred*—the original Partisan organizational unit. Odreds were local commands with authority over small units operating in areas where the Partisans controlled no territory, but simply lived in the forests or at isolated farms and carried out occasional raids against small German garrisons or supply lines. They were also the centers for clandestine political organization work in nearby villages under German control. The odred at Sticna manned the courier line across the frontier and to the Sava River, and provided armed escorts for parties such as ours. The odred commander told us his men had returned from the border area a few hours earlier and had reported that it was now quiet. We would make the crossing that night.

As the sun was setting the leader of the patrol that would take us across the frontier and to the Sava explained that the patrol would consist of thirty men and two British Bren light machine guns to get us to the river—an unusually heavy escort. This, we learned, was the standard way in which a Partisan patrol was described: so many men (armed with rifles), and so many light machine guns. A more usual patrol would be ten men and one machine gun or, in safer areas, four or five men and no machine gun.

The patrol leader said that the border itself was a cleared area two to three hundred meters wide along which the Germans had erected watchtowers and a double barbed-wire fence. Antipersonnel mines were planted on both sides of the barbed wire. On the north side German and White Guard patrols of a hundred or so men with dogs moved constantly. The fences would be cut and a path cleared through the minefield by an advance party as soon as it was dark. Local Partisans would scout the area for enemy patrols so that we could hide till they passed or be guided around them. If we ran into a German ambush or a roving patrol, part of our escort would engage them while the rest would guide us around them. Our job was to get to the Fourth Zone safely and not to get involved in fights along the way if we could avoid them.

One Partisan was assigned to carry our radio and two others would each carry a battery. I carried a 9-mm Marlin submachine gun and a German Luger pistol. The latter was useless for partisan warfare, and I should have got rid of it long before. If I had ever found myself close enough to an enemy to use it, I would have been in serious trouble. I also carried two phosphorus smoke grenades to use to screen our withdrawal should we be caught in an ambush.

As darkness closed in we set out in single file along a path leading up the forested hillside toward the border about twelve miles away. A half-moon lighted our way. Well before midnight the column halted at the spot where we were to meet the next courier, who would take us across the frontier. The new courier was not there and after nearly an hour's wait it was increasingly clear that the contact had somehow failed. Since the meeting points between couriers—or guides—were constantly changed for security, the leader of the patrol thought that there might have been a mix-up on the meeting point. He was right. The new courier was found waiting nearby for us and we moved out toward the frontier.

As we approached the frontier area two men were sent forward to check the crossing point and to be sure there was no waiting ambush. When they returned with a report of all clear we shouldered packs and guns and headed for the frontier itself. Outlined in the light of the setting moon we could see the barbed wire along a ridge before us. Again we stopped in the protection of the forest just before the cleared area. The leader of the patrol told us in a whispered voice that a path across the minefield had been cleared by cautiously removing the mines by hand. We were to follow precisely the man ahead, with ten-meter intervals between us, so as to avoid being bunched closely together if caught by surprise.

The head of the column moved out and each man followed at the prescribed interval. When I reached the mined area I not only was watching the man ahead in order to follow his steps, but I also tried to see and remember exactly where he had made each step. Whether I stepped precisely in his footprints or not I don't know, but we all crossed the frontier successfully.

The lights of Ljubljana, the prewar capital of Slovenia, ten miles to the west, were clearly visible. We felt a thrill on being within the German Reich, possibly the first Americans to infiltrate the Reich since America entered the war—though three British officers had crossed into this area a few weeks before.

■ From the frontier onward traveling became more difficult. We crossed several steep and wooded ridges; on each one we had to scramble over loose rocks and roots and through small streams. By now the moon had set. The forest was dark and it was almost impossible to see the next man in the column. The only way to keep in the column was to listen for the steps of the man ahead and walk blindly in that direction, hoping not to fall into an unseen hole or slip off the path down the mountainside. About 2:30 in the morning we arrived at a small mountain cabin that was being used as a courier station. A courier had just arrived from the river and reported that a contact had been arranged with the boatmen between 3:30 and 4:00 for the crossing.

It was already 3:30 when we reached the last ridge south of the Sava. As we dropped down toward the river we could from time to time hear trains climbing up the steep river valley. As we were about to cross the tracks a train came in sight around a bend and moved onto the line immediately before us. We lay in the long grass a hundred yards away and watched a heavy freight pass, the light from the open firebox flickering in the early morning ground fog as the fireman shoveled in more coal. Armed guards were visible on the rear car. This was the section of the railroad that connected Vienna and central Europe with northeastern Italy; it would be one of our targets when we received our supply drops of explosives.

After the train passed we crossed the two tracks and went into the wooded area along the river. Most of the Partisan patrol left us on the south bank to return to their base. Because we were about one hour late the boatmen who were to get us across the river had assumed we were not coming and had hidden their boats and disappeared. Again we waited while they were found and came back to launch their boats. The boats turned out to be made of rough planking, and nailed together into flat-bottomed craft big enough only for a boatman and two passengers. They had to be light enough to be carried by two men and small enough to be hidden among the little trees and bushes along the river.

The crossing took well over an hour. It was daylight by the time all of the party reached the far side of the Sava. Fortunately a morning mist had formed over the water and both shores so that we continued to be hidden from sight from both the railroad on the south side and the road on the north. We expected to be met by a new patrol from the odred in the mountains to the north and a new courier as guide. But as none had appeared a part of the patrol that had come with us from Dolenjska would go with us into the mountains on the north side. As soon as the river crossing was completed we moved across the road, fortunately deserted, and headed up through the forest on the mountain north of the river.

Although we had been on the move for twenty-four hours, it was not safe to stop until we were well into the higher levels and away from the river and road. When we did finally stop at the odred's farmhouse headquarters most of us slept while guards were posted on the approaches to the house. Exhausted, we had been asleep for two hours when we were awakened and told a German column was a half hour away and headed in our direction. After another three-hour march we arrived at a mountain farmhouse which the Partisans told us confidently was quite safe.

I now learned for the first time that during the night one man in the patrol that had taken us across the frontier had quietly dropped out of the column. It was so dark his disappearance had not been noticed until dawn. It was almost certain that through him word had reached the Germans that a group including Allied officers was moving into Styria (Stajerska). They had to assume that we intended to expand the Partisan organization and to attack the rail lines within the Third Reich itself. They were bound to take this more seriously than Partisan operations in occupied areas to the south.

The next morning, while I was shaving in a water trough outside, we were surprised by a German patrol that opened up on our "safe" farmhouse with machine-gun and mortar fire. The Partisans panicked and ran into the forest, leaving our radio behind. I ran into the house, grabbed my pack and gun and followed the Partisans up a steep grassy slope to the protection of the forest above. I shall never forget the peasant wife, tears of fright running down her cheeks, holding out to me a glass of schnapps as I ran through the door. It was the first time I had come under small-arms fire, and as I struggled up the slope I was puzzled by short "tssk" sounds in the dry grass until I realized they came from bullets hitting the slope around me. The only casualty was the first-aid Partisanka, who got some mortar fragments in her back. Fortunately they were small and not deep.

Our radio, forgotten in the emergency, was lost to us. But because Lieutenant Gatoni was bringing a radio for MI-6 that had been saved, we could share it until one was dropped to us. It was likely that our own radio had been found by the Germans and we decided not to try to retrieve it.

We spent the day in the forest and that evening a courier brought a report that a large column of German troops was concentrating in the valley below and fanning out along the foot of the mountain. The mountain where we were hiding might be encircled by morning. Lookouts reported that the road we had just crossed along the river had not yet been sealed by German troops but it was our assumption that the troop movements below were intended to encircle us. We decided that as soon as it was dark we would go back across the highway and river to the hills on the south side before the encirclement was complete.

As soon as it became dark we moved south to the road, found it still free of troops, and went on to the river. The boatmen had been alerted and were ready for us this time. We were on the south bank by midnight. We decided that we would not retrace our steps all the way to Slovene liberated territory but would hide out in a remote area in the hills between the river and the frontier. We spent three days waiting for a courier from the north. Finally one arrived and reported that the German encirclement had been discontinued and the troops withdrawn. Apparently we had been able to recross the river without being detected, since there was no unusual German troop activity on the south side. As we had not been found in the trap set for us, the Germans must have assumed that we had somehow slipped out of the net and had continued to the north.

That night we crossed the river for the third time. We then found that the main road in the next mountain valley to the north, which we had to cross, was blockaded and we had to wait three more days before pushing on. This time we decided to stay at a peasant farm on the north side of the river. Nearby there was a small chapel on a promontory overlooking the river. Lieutenant Gordon Bush and I passed several hours each day lying on the grass surrounding the chapel and watching German freight and troop trains moving across the rail line along the river below.

While we thus passed the time, three American airmen were brought in by the Partisans. Their plane had been shot down several days earlier while bombing the Maribor railroad yards. They had been picked up by Partisans who had spotted their chutes coming down, and who now were sending them south to Slovene headquarters for eventual evacuation to Italy. They had had two or three brushes with German patrols and couldn't wait to get out. They thought we were absolutely mad to deliberately go into the area from which they had come. I gave them some German reichsmarks to buy food along the way.

While waiting we discovered near the village of Maravce a small area between two ridges in which there was a large open field. The field looked to be wide enough to be used for a parachute drop of explosives. The combination of the delays in our own drop and the delays in moving north meant we would be very late in launching our attacks against the railroads. The railroad we had crossed on the south side of the Sava, across which troop reinforcements could be moved into Italy, was one of our priority targets. I proposed to the odred officers that we arrange a drop here without waiting to reach the Zone headquarters. With explosives we could attack the line immediately. The Partisans, however, had only 150 men and doubted that they could collect and hide the drop before the Germans arrived. Ljubljana was only ten miles away and German troops in trucks could be there within a half hour after an unidentified low-flying plane was heard. Reluctantly we abandoned the idea.

The evening of the third day we watched from a nearby hill as a German patrol moved in and burned down a village as punishment for aiding the Partisans. A courier now arrived to report that the roads to the north were no longer blocked, and so at dusk we moved down the north side of the mountain into the narrow valley. We were to be preceded by a patrol that was to go well ahead of us and flush out German ambushes along the path. This was the main road connecting Maribor with Ljubljana, and was used by the Germans in switching troops and supplies by truck between Austria and Hungary to the north and east and Italy to the southwest.

About ten o'clock we stopped a few hundred yards short of the road. A scout was sent ahead, and a few minutes later he reported back that a German patrol had moved in between the time our advance patrol had crossed the road and our arrival. After a conference, which I was sure neighboring Germans must certainly hear, we decided to move eastward along the ridge south of the road and make another attempt to cross a few miles away. The Germans, as we learned the next day, had a hidden machine-gun ambush at the point of the road at which we had expected to cross. For two hours that night we stumbled along rocky mountain paths in the dark to our new crossing point. We stopped short of it while a patrol was sent to scout the road ahead. This time we waited for nearly three hours in a cold rain that soaked us all through. Finally the scouts reported back that the road at this point was free. At dawn we crossed the road and climbed another two hours to a farmhouse on the north side, where we rejoined the advance patrol. We were across the German frontier, we were across the Sava, we were into Stajerska, and we were now well inside the Third Reich itself.

CHAPTER 5

Inside the Third Reich

fter its 1941 incorporation into the German Reich, the part of Stajerska in which we found ourselves became the scene of intensive German efforts to completely Germanize the land and the people. All place names and all family names were Germanized. Viewed by the Germans as an integral part of Germany, their defense of the region was more determined than in the territories that, though under German occupation, were nominally under the sovereignty of the various local collaborationist governments. And even more drastic measures against the local population were taken in Stajerska than in the occupied areas.

Shortly after the new Reich frontier was established, the Germans decided to remove all Slovenes from the areas near the border. Some were sent to that part of Silesia between the former Czechoslovak and Polish borders, and others sent to Croatia and Serbia. A proclamation issued in October 1941 stated that for political reasons the population would be removed from a belt that included the entire area south of the Sava River to the new border, and those areas we had now crossed north of the river. Insofar as transportation facilities permitted, the order said, the emigrants would be allowed to take along only their underwear, clothing, bedding, and articles of everyday use.

In 1942 and 1943 approximately 30 percent of the Slovenes, including 90 percent of the intellectuals and professional classes, were deported or sent to concentration camps and to industrial centers as forced labor. Germans were brought in to staff the local government offices. German teachers were used exclusively in the schools. Hitler had ordered that Lower Styria was to be made German; every trace of Slovene culture was being eliminated. As a result of the deportations, many farms were left uncultivated. The German government announced that these would be given to veterans of the Wehrmacht when the war was over. Meanwhile, the application of Nazi law in Stajerska, and the Gestapo's ministrations to the Slovene populace, meant torture and terror for innocents and resisters alike.

Through this land of great beauty, of ostensibly conquered and seeming conquerors, of cruelty and heroism, we continued on our way. The three nights following our final crossing of the Maribor-Ljubljana road we were able to make long marches and spend the days resting in the forest. The countryside became much more mountainous and typically alpine. Both the terrain and the architecture of the farmhouses reminded me of Bavaria, which I had known in the summer of 1938 after graduation from Stanford.

On June 6 we reached a farm near the top of one of the mountains. We had expected to find the Fourth Zone headquarters here but were disappointed. The courier line had apparently completely broken down during the German offensive. We had no way to find Zone headquarters without the couriers who alone knew its location. There was nothing to do but wait here until the broken links of the line were reconnected.

We could now see the higher peaks of the Karawanken Alps to the north. The upper levels were sheathed in large snowfields. The peaks were bare rock that pushed up through the forest-covered lower slopes. The remnants of a winter snowdrift lay in the shadow of the farmhouse. Crocuses had pushed through and were in bloom. It was magnificent country, and when I had a peaceful moment to absorb it, I often felt more on a summer holiday than on an assignment of carefully targeted destruction.

A mile or so below us in the valley was the small town of Gornji Grad (Oberburg). The peasants told us that there was a German garrison of three to four hundred men in the town. (The relations between town and countryside were so intimate that when I ran out of paper the Partisans provided me with the official stationery of the Burgermeister of Oberburg, Nazi swastika and all.)

As there was some danger the German garrison there might have learned of our location, a little girl of about fourteen, daughter of one of the peasants near whose house we had stopped, was sent to town to see what the Germans were up to. A few hours later she came back and reported that there appeared to be no special activity there. So we decided to stay on. This was a measure of the support of the population. Any one of the twenty or so peasants in this group of highland farms could have slipped away to inform the Germans of our presence; but none did.

During our stay above Gornji Grad we decided to use Lieutenant Gatoni's radio and some of our battery power to try to establish a contact with the British station in Italy to report our progress. Fisher was able for a few minutes to pick up the base station calling us, but he soon lost their signal. Before switching off the set he tuned in on a BBC shortwave broadcast. It was obvious from the sounds of battle, heavy gunfire, the roar of low-flying aircraft, and the excited voice of a radio correspondent that something big was going on somewhere.

It was, we decided, some sort of Allied landing. But where? As we listened, I with one earphone, Jim with the other, the voice continued to describe the battle but made no mention of where it was. Our guess was that it must be the long-expected Allied landing in France: we were right; it was June 9, 1944, and we had tuned in on the third day of the Normandy landings.

In spite of their strong ideological and emotional identification with the Soviet Union, the Partisans invariably preferred the BBC news broadcasts to those of Radio Moscow. The BBC provided more, and more reliable, news of the war than what they could get from Radio Moscow. They would often stop on the march at the time of the

BBC news broadcast to Yugoslavia, unpack a beat-up Telefunken radio, and gather around to listen.

The second day on the mountain above Gornji Grad the deputy commissar for Slovenia, Viktor Avbelj (Rudi), arrived with an escort. He was a small man, quiet in speech and always to the point. He too was on his way to the Fourth Zone headquarters. I told him of our attempt to establish a dropping point just north of the Sava. He agreed on its importance and felt that a drop could be made successfully if all the loads were dropped in a single night. We decided that Gordon Bush, my second officer, would return to that area—about three days' march—with a patrol of three or four men. As he would have no radio with him, we would have to decide in advance the recognition signals to be used, the amount of stores to be dropped, and the exact time that he would be waiting.

We calculated that the best compromise between the urgency of receiving the drop and the possibility of his being delayed in reaching the drop point would be to allow him five days' time for traveling and organizing the reception. The odred where we had previously stopped near the village of Maravce would be used to secure the area and to dispose of the supplies dropped.

Bush was a small, wiry man in his early twenties. He had left his new wife in Washington, where she worked in a government department. He was tough and aggressive, and a good man with the Partisans. While he was with me he cultivated a long and scraggly mustache which he carefully trained to cantilever out into space from his upper lip.

We sent off a radio message to Bari, our headquarters in Italy, outlining our plan and requesting a drop the first night weather would permit after the fifth day. The stores we wanted totaled four planeloads: half explosives and half light machine guns, rifles, and ammunition. Bush and his patrol then left almost immediately with Rudi's written orders to the odred.

The next day the courier link was reestablished. The arriving courier brought messages that the previous week the Fourth Zone headquarters had been surrounded twice by German units and had been forced to fight its way out. The commander had been seriously wounded and the Zone headquarters apparently was moving slowly eastward to another range near Maribor called the Pohorje.

I made these notes on the ensuing trip to the Pohorje:

> About two last night, while moving along a mountain trail, we heard gunfire and saw flashes in the distance. In true Partisan fashion, a conference was held in a nearby farmhouse. The entire party crowded into the kitchen, and all tried to look at the commissar's map at once. The meeting started with the commissar and the cook having an argument as to the position from which the gunfire was coming. Then the farmer's wife joined in, and finally the farmer himself. It ended with the farmer and his wife having a first-class battle on the subject while everyone else listened. We finally went off again without anything having been decided.

I was beginning to learn the different sounds of each weapon, from the slow thump, thump of the Italian Breda machine gun to the rapid fire of the German automatic weapons.

By now I had become convinced that if there was an option of going around the side of a mountain or going straight over the top the Partisans would go for the up-and-down route every time. Every three or four hours we would change to a new courier who was a native of the land that lay ahead. He was, of course, fresh and would set a fast pace. By the time dawn came we were well ready to call it quits.

Early one morning as the sky began to lighten I noticed clumps of ripe wild strawberries along the trail—the delicious *fraises des bois* for which one pays so dearly in Paris. I eagerly bent down to pick one. It was luscious beyond anything I remembered. But here the price was straightening up with a forty-pound load and regaining the few steps I had lost. For the next hour or two every time I spotted one I went through an all-consuming argument with myself: Should I stoop to pick it up or let it go by? Either way I paid a price. Sometimes picking won out, sometimes my aching back and legs won out.

Food was not plentiful. The staple diet was called "zganci." It was rough ground meal moistened with hot water and patted into a rubbery ball. If we were lucky it would be sprinkled with a few crumbles of pork rind that looked and tasted like bacon. One day I caught myself intently eyeing the patrol leader cutting each man one slice of a loaf of rough bread he had obtained from a peasant house. It was the only food thus far that day. Was my slice as thick as the others? And if it looked just a little smaller, I felt cheated. It gave me a sudden insight into what concentration-camp prisoners must have endured every day in a much more extreme way as starvation rations were handed out.

The evening before arrival at Fourth Zone headquarters in the Pohorje a courier met us with a message from the Zone commissar to please wait until morning before arriving so that an honor guard could be assembled to properly greet us. The next morning we found the headquarters in a forest encampment. The honor guard was suitably drawn up, bearing a Partisan flag—a red star superimposed on the prewar blue, white, and red Yugoslav national flag.

The honor guard consisted of ten men, some in worn German uniforms and some in civilian clothes with Partisan cloth caps, red stars sewn on. The only honor guards I had ever seen were in movie newsreels of foreign heads of state arriving in Washington. Nevertheless I tried to play my role by walking down the line with the commander, returning the salute and then addressing "the troops," saying, as I often did later to other Partisan gatherings, that they were not alone but had the strong support of powerful allies in the West and in the East, and together we would finish the war against Hitler and the Nazis.

The Zone headquarters consisted of the staff and a headquarters guard of about a hundred. We found Major McNeff from MI-6, who had reached the headquarters a few days before. Lieutenant Gatoni soon had a working contact with the base radio station in Italy. McNeff left via the courier line to return to Italy a few days later. Gatoni and the radio remained with us. That radio was our only link with the outside world.

We also found a Canadian Yugoslav, Vuchko Vuchkovic, who had been sent into Slovene headquarters by Force 399, Brigadier Maclean's Allied command. During the previous winter he had been sent north to establish a drop point. As he had no radio and as his fire signal plans and recognition codes were all out-of-date, he had been more or less written off. Apparently, however, Force 399 had become extremely anxious to deliver explosives to us for the forthcoming operations. As they had not had radio contact with us for several days, they had sent six Halifaxes loaded with explosives to this area three nights before in hope of finding us. Vuchkovic had been camped on the top of the Pohorje mountain since midwinter waiting every night for planes to show up. Fortunately, when he heard the Halifaxes in the area looking for us, he had lighted signal fires and flashed a recognition signal. Although neither the fires nor the recognition signal were correct, the Halifax crews had decided to take a chance and dropped their loads anyway. The weapons and explosives had been gathered by two Partisan brigades that were then on the Pohorje and had been hidden in underground bunkers by the time we arrived.

A radio message from the base asked if we had received a radio, generator, and batteries that had been sent to us in the drop. We had not. Fifteen of the containers had dropped six kilometers away to the Germans.

Two days later a courier came in with a message from Bush saying his group had successfully received a drop of supplies as scheduled. Within a half hour after the drop a German mobile column of several hundred men had arrived on the scene. Machine guns and rifles had been pulled from the parachute containers, and during the fight that followed, nearly a hundred Germans had been killed. The Partisan group had suffered considerably lighter losses. Practically all the explosives had been successfully picked up and hidden in spite of the German attack. Bush reported that they would move against the Zagreb-Ljubljana railroad immediately.

■ By now I had had the chance to observe and to use the courier lines under difficult circumstances. They were among the best of the Partisans' major organizational achievements. Without secure and reliable communications a resistance organization is no more than a collection of isolated bands operating quite independently of each other, with little chance of success. Courier lines, along with radio links, provide secure communications through enemy-occupied territory to other resistance units, to liberated territories, to underground organizations in the cities, and across national frontiers to areas in friendly countries where safe haven and training can be provided.

In Slovenia regular courier lines consisted of many segments, each manned by natives of that area and linked together in a continuous chain as much as 50 miles long. The courier line to Fourth Zone headquarters from Slovene Partisan headquarters in Dolenjska not only provided for our safe transit from Slovene liberated territory across the German frontier into Stajerska, but also carried political directives, printed propaganda, and operational orders from Slovene Partisan headquarters, and intelligence and operational reports from Fourth Zone to Slovene headquarters.

The courier lines also took walking wounded south across the German border to hidden hospitals in Dolenjska. Escaped Allied POW's and downed Allied airmen were moved to safer territory whence they would be sent to the Dalmatian coast to be picked up by boat or aircraft, or to Slovene liberated territory, where they would be flown out when possible by an Allied C-47 or light aircraft from dirt strips.

Throughout Yugoslavia courier lines provided the means by which national Partisan leaders could safely visit the regional political and military headquarters, coordinate their political and military activities, evaluate on site the competence and loyalty of regional leaders, replace those who didn't measure up, and ensure that directives from Tito and the Central Committee were faithfully followed.

Before taking off from their bases, British and American aircrews of Allied fighter and bomber forces studied maps showing the general area of Fourth Zone operations—copies of which they were forbidden to take along. If their aircraft were shot up on bombing missions to Germany so that they could not get back to their bases in Italy or England they were to try, before bailing out, to get their damaged aircraft to our area, the nearest "safe haven" to Allied bombing targets in Austria and much of Germany. There was a good chance that here friendly peasants or Partisan underground workers could pick them up before the Germans did. Their chances were enhanced by Partisan activity that discouraged the Germans from venturing very far off the roads and into the forested areas except in large units. Altogether well over 300 prison-camp escapees and downed airmen were picked up and evacuated over the courier line in the seven months I was in Stajerska. Every week we radioed updates on the safe area map so that the Allied air forces would know precisely what areas were safe for aircrews to drop to.

One downed American airman picked up by the Partisans told me a disturbing story. On an earlier mission he had found his target covered with low clouds and had headed back to Italy. Standing orders were that bombs were to be jettisoned harmlessly over the Adriatic. Bombers could not land with bombs still aboard because of the weight and the danger of detonation on the runway. Instead, the pilot had picked out an isolated farmhouse and barn in Austria and had dumped his entire load of bombs, obliterating the buildings and presumably all the family. Another airman who had jumped over our forests told of being so enthralled by his free fall from 20,000 feet that he forgot to open his chute until he was about to hit the ground. The chute blossomed and braked his fall when he was only a few hundred feet in the air.

Another escapee was Sergeant Winterburn of the British Sixth Commando. He had been captured in the 1942 Dieppe raid against occupied France, had escaped from a German prison camp in Breslau and made his way by rail on prison-forged documents to our area. There he simply got off the train and came into the forest to join us. Unlike many we helped, he remained full of fight and we would have liked to keep him with us.

Winterburn regaled us with wonderful stories of his private psychological warfare against his captors. He and a buddy had been assigned to work in a brewery near the prison camp; when the guards were not looking they regularly relieved themselves in the beer vats. From time to time the prisoners received Red Cross packages from Britain containing chocolate, among other delicacies. At the end of one day, as his work detail was being rather loosely marched down a crowded street from the brewery back to camp he took a Red Cross chocolate bar from his pocket and ostentatiously unwrapped it in front of German passersby. Not having seen chocolate since the war began, the Germans were overcome by the sight and smell. Winterburn waited until they had crowded around him. Then, with a flourish, he turned to a dray horse standing at the curb and fed him the chocolate. When the crowd groaned in protest, he explained that he felt sorry for the horse, who clearly was not getting enough to eat. Not many had his fighting spirit. Unfortunately our request to keep him with us was turned down and we reluctantly sent him south along the courier line.

The courier lines were manned by young farm boys and sometimes girls who were seldom over 14, and who had grown up in peasant farms in the more isolated upper levels of the mountains. The segments of the lines were roughly a four-hour march each. As each segment was manned by couriers from the immediate area, they knew every inch of the land in daylight or darkness.

The contact points, or courier stations, linking each adjoining segment were the most sensitive elements of the line. These contact points were known only to the couriers themselves and to the chief courier, who had overall responsibility for the security and functioning of the line. Contact points, which could be a hut on a mountain trail or a point in the forest near a farmhouse or on a mountain ridge, were changed every few days to prevent a person being taken across the courier line from divulging a location.

In the more dangerous areas the couriers did not make personal contact. Instead, "mailboxes" such as a hole in a tree trunk or a crevice in a rock were used. These are now known in the intelligence trade as dead drops. One courier could deposit his mail and leave, unseen by the next courier. The second courier could, if he was uncertain, watch the mailbox area for strangers before venturing to pick up his mail. Mobile Partisan units, as they moved about the mountains, could tap into the courier line by sending their own man to the nearest courier station to deposit and pick up their mail without revealing their own location or having messages to them include their physical location.

But if a link was broken it could be days before the line could be reconnected. In our move into Stajerska we did not know where the Zone headquarters was located. We simply traveled the courier line, link by link, until we were taken to it by the final courier.

The reason for this heavy attention to security was the special vulnerability of the courier line to penetration by the German or local collaborationist security forces. If a courier were captured he could at most give the identity of two adjoining couriers, and by that time the courier contact points could already have been changed and the line rerouted. If an enemy agent posing as a Partisan traveled over the courier line, the information he would have that might expose others subsequently using the line to ambush or capture would be limited. Such an informer was in the escort unit that took us across the German border on our way to Fourth Zone headquarters.

But there was no guarantee of perfect safety in spite of the most rigorous precautions. While I was in Yugoslavia, in occupied Norway the courier line into neutral Sweden from the Norwegian underground was secretly controlled by the Germans for several months before the war ended. A Norwegian resistance group that operated the courier line across the Swedish border had been penetrated by the Nazi intelligence service, the Sicherheitsdienst.

This courier line was regularly used to bring out to the safety of Sweden those Norwegian underground workers who had been identified by the Gestapo and were in danger of being picked up. The Germans controlling the last leg of flight to the safety of Sweden wanted above all to protect their covert control of the resistance group and to do nothing that would arouse Swedish or Norwegian suspicions. When small fry were taken across the line they were allowed to go to Sweden without hindrance. But when important leaders of the Norwegian resistance used the line, either to seek refuge or to meet outside Norway with Allied officers, there would be an elaborately staged German interception, made to appear an accidental capture so as to throw no suspicion on the controlled resistance group itself.

The more I saw of the operations of the courier lines the more I appreciated the importance of the support of the mountain people for the Partisan movement. Their sons and daughters served as couriers, their barns were used for sleeping and hiding by people traveling along the courier lines, and they fed and warmed us in their tiny houses. They ran terrible risks of being exposed to the police. Indeed, many subsequently were shot or sent to labor camps in Germany and their houses burned in reprisal for having sheltered Partisans, or for simply failing to report our presence. They often ran greater risks than the Partisans because they stayed unarmed with their farms and animals while we were free to hide ourselves in the forests.

Late one night in Stajerska we stopped at a peasant house for a few hours' rest. Nailed to the wall of the house next to the door was a large red placard printed in heavy German script. It was addressed to the inhabitants of the area, and stated that there were armed bandits in the area who were assaulting the civilians, stealing their food and burning their buildings. The German authorities were taking all steps to apprehend these bandits in order to protect the peasants. But in order to do so all persons were ordered to report immediately the presence of the bandits or any other information about them. It ended with the warning that anyone failing to so report would be subjected to the severest penalties. It was a thinly disguised threat of deportation, burning of buildings, or summary execution. It was signed: "Steindl, SS, Gauleiter, Untersteiermark."

The civilians were caught in the middle, because neither Germans nor Partisans would hesitate to take reprisals against them, the one if they helped us, the other if they informed against us. For this reason the more disciplined and experienced Partisan leaders were careful to take action only when they had good evidence of betrayal. In contrast, wholesale reprisals by the occupiers and their collaborators against entire villages tended to unite the population against the Germans.

CHAPTER 6

Blowing Up
Germany's Railroads

The morning of our arrival at Fourth Zone headquarters the Partisan leaders and I went to work on our plan of attack. Our conference room was two logs in the fir forest. The group included the Zone commissar, the deputy commander, and the chief of staff. Mile Kilibarda, the commander, had been wounded a few days earlier and his deputy was now acting commander. Kilibarda, an experienced Serb Partisan officer, had been sent by Tito to Slovenia a few months earlier to provide aggressive leadership for the expanding Zone operations.

Commissar Rudi from Slovene headquarters was also there. Vlado interpreted. Maps were spread out on the ground and we all pored over them, looking at likely places to cut the railroads. Our maps were of Yugoslav origin, printed in 1932, with longitude measured from Paris. The British army had obtained the plates and reproduced them with Greenwich longitude overprinted. In order to save on scarce map-quality paper they were printed on the back of highly detailed maps of Spain, which in turn were overprinted "Void." This gave us an unusual insight on Allied wartime strategy in respect to neutral Spain. The maps had originally been printed against the possibility that Allied sabotage operations in Spain might be necessary if Hitler had moved to take over Spain and attack Gibraltar.

I was tremendously impressed by the eagerness of these Partisans to attack this main rail net across the Alps—so important to the Germans as they tried to stem the advances of the Allied armies. At this stage no operation seemed too hard for them to take on.

For centuries the Alps have been a natural barrier to the movement of armies and supplies between Central Europe and Italy. In the Second World War the Germans were dependent upon a very few railroads to move troops and supplies to and from the Italian front. Only two were double track. One crossed the Brenner Pass into the Tyrol and Germany. The other went through the only natural break between the Alps and the solid mountain chain running from Slovenia south almost to the tip of Greece. This is the famous Ljubljana Gap, and has been used for centuries by both armies and traders. A third main line went through the Simplon tunnel, and because it ran through Switzerland its availability to the Germans was limited.

Three legs of the railroad that passed through the Gap came together at a junction called Zidani Most on the Sava River in prewar Slovenia (see Map 5, showing the railroads). The southeastern leg followed the eastward-flowing Sava into the Danube plain and was the principal supply route for the German armies in the Balkans. The western leg provided access through Ljubljana to Trieste and the Italian front. The third leg ran north, along river valleys on the eastern edge of the Alps, to Vienna, Germany, and Central Europe. The northern and western legs, called the Südbahn, were built by the Hapsburgs to connect Vienna with the Adriatic port of Trieste. The principal segments of interest to us were the main double-track lines, although single-track lines provided bypasses and should be attacked also.

The three lines that came together at Zidani Most provided the German high command with the ability to shift its divisions quickly between Germany, the Balkans, and the Eastern and Italian fronts; to supply weapons and fuel to the Italian front; and to bring raw materials from the Balkans, chiefly oil, bauxite, copper, zinc, lead, and chrome, to German war industry—and to transport the slave labor to work in German factories. After our first strikes we would also operate against the Balkan and Italian segments of the line. If we could cut these lines and keep them closed for a good part of the time we could deal a strategic blow to Hitler's ability to fight.

In those days aerial bombardment was the only way to reach almost all German targets. It was also the least efficient because of its inaccuracy—a large number of bombs had to be delivered to ensure that one or two hit the target. If one could get close enough to a target to hit it with long-range artillery, it would be destroyed with far less explosive power. But if one could get next to the target and plant the explosives by hand right on the most vulnerable parts of, for example, a bridge, the probability of its destruction could be increased greatly and the explosives used would be a tiny fraction of that used in aerial bombardment.

The Pohorje was an ideal base from which to attack the northern segment. To the south was the key junction of Zidani Most. A few miles to the east was the main line of the Südbahn serving Vienna and Germany. An alternate line paralleled it to the west. Both had to be cut if German north-south traffic was to be halted. We examined these lines on the east and west sides of the Pohorje in detail. The pros and cons of each likely target were intensely debated. I had been promised 10 tons of plastic explosives immediately. The high priority of our rail targets led me to believe we would also get the guns and ammunition to expand the Partisan forces rapidly.

Our planned attacks also had to be based on a realistic picture of Partisan and enemy strength and dispositions in the Fourth Zone. The information we had obtained during our stay in Semic turned out to be generally accurate—in outline. But the Fourteenth Partisan Division, sent to Stajerska in March from liberated territory south of the Sava (Dolenjska) had since lost about 300 men in fighting and was now about 600 strong. The Partisans told us that its strength was 1,500, but we knew that two of its three brigades were under 200 men each, so 600 seemed the upper limit. Even at this reduced strength fully a third of the men had no weapons.

In 1943, two small battalions within Stajerska had been expanded to separate brigades: the Eleventh "Zidansek" brigade and the Sixth

"Slander" shock brigade. (Brigades were named for poets, writers, and early Partisans who had died heroically in battle.) In all there were now five brigades in Stajerska. In addition there were several hundred men without weapons whom we would arm by parachute drops. There were also the odred on the north side of the Sava and two odreds on the north slopes of the Karawanken Alps. A small odred was being organized to guard the prospective drop area in the Pohorje and to receive the drops. The total strength of the Fourth Zone was probably under 2,000 men spread out in a forested mountain area roughly 70 miles by 25 miles. Partisan designations of battalions, brigades, and divisions were misleading at first because they were so much smaller than in the conventional armies we knew. A brigade in Stajerska at that time was anywhere from 150 to 300 men. (A Second World War U.S. Army infantry brigade was about 5,000 men).

We were told by the Fourth Zone officers the Germans had at that time a total of 36,000 men in the area of the Zone. This was probably overstated, and some of these were older Slovenes who were not aggressive fighters but who knew the territory almost as well as the Partisans. They were used for garrison duty to supplement the German army forces in Stajerska.

Rudi and I told the Zone officers of the Slovene headquarters' decision that the Zone command and I should work out directly with Force 399 the mix of weapons, ammunition, explosives, food, medical supplies, blankets, boots, and battle dress to be sent in the sorties allocated to us. The great need for weapons was all too evident. Hundreds of recruits who had been brought into the Stajerska brigades were without weapons. The Partisans rightly considered that having unarmed men in the fighting units was terribly destructive to the morale of the entire brigade. I radioed Force 399 that "the Partisan command practically guarantees 20,000 recruits if we can supply them arms." It was a brave but overconfident statement. During the next five months we were able to provide arms for an additional 4,000 men. Additional arms were captured from the enemy. Several hundred recruits were also sent to Dolenjska where they were armed and trained with Allied weapons delivered there.

One recruit was Janez. Shortly after joining the Fourth Zone headquarters we were assigned a 15-year-old red-headed Caliban with a wild laugh and blazing eyes as our courier, bodyguard, and general "gofer." Janez would fetch batteries, get us food on occasion, and keep an eye on us. A few weeks before he joined us, Janez had been living in a nearby village, where he had received notice of his induction into the German army. He was ordered to report to a nearby railway station where he would be given a ticket for a train to the induction center. He climbed on the train, left his small bag and induction orders on the seat, got off the train on the other side and went into the forest to join the Partisans. The train proceeded to Graz, a major city, just in time to be hit in an Allied bombing raid on the marshaling yards. The train was destroyed. His bag and orders were later found in a wrecked coach. The German authorities assumed that he had been killed in the raid, informed his mother, and thereafter dutifully sent her a monthly check. The tale delighted him each time he told it.

Explosives continued to be high priority since the possibility of capturing explosives from the Germans was low. Rifles, submachine guns and light machine guns made up the bulk of the weapons we requested and that were dropped to us. Because of the ammunition problem German and Italian rifles, of which thousands had been captured in North Africa and in Italy, were sent to Yugoslavia in preference to British and American rifles. The Partisans were already armed with captured German and Italian weapons. By standardizing, using a few types of weapons, our ammunition supply problem within Stajerska was greatly simplified. This led to some problems later on when, for political purposes, the rumor was circulated that we were deliberately sending them cast-off weapons that malfunctioned instead of new British and American models. Small numbers of British shoulder-fired short-range rocket launchers that had hollow-charge projectiles for piercing steel armor, called PIATs, were sent to us as antitank weapons.

Every Partisan officer had a side arm, usually a small Italian Beretta pistol. It added a bit of dash and swagger. Nevertheless, during my time in Stajerska I saw three Partisans kill themselves cleaning or just fiddling with their pistols. None that I knew of were ever fired in combat. As in Dolenjska, the German Schmeisser machine pistol was highly prized by officers.

One of the weapons dropped by the thousands into occupied Europe was the famous Sten, a small submachine gun. It was not much more than a piece of pipe, a clip magazine, a simple firing mechanism, and a folding metal stock. It was a close combat weapon with an accurate range of a couple of hundred feet. In Slovenia it became legendary.

One day a German Storch light reconnaissance plane flew very low over a Slovenian peasant Partisan driving his team of horses down a country road. The driver pulled his Sten from its hiding place under his wagon seat and fired a burst at the plane. Miraculously, one of the bullets carried far enough to hit the plane in a vital spot and caused it to crash. The driver achieved instant fame among the Partisans. Now everyone wanted to shoot down his own plane. As a result, thousands of rounds were shot off as people opened up on anything flying, no matter how high.

■ As we conferred on the Pohorje mountain, we concluded that our strategy should be to take the fullest advantage of surprise. Up to now the Partisans, for lack of explosives, had made no major attacks on the German railroads. Bridges and tunnels were reported to be lightly guarded. After our attacks began the Germans would quickly reinforce their guards on all the major targets and it would become much harder and more costly in lives to destroy them. Now was the time to go after those targets that would take the longest time to repair and would later be the most heavily guarded. In these first discussions, the Partisans were enthusiastic and eager to get on with the rail attacks, even though they clearly would bring down reprisals on themselves and the civilians who sheltered us. No target was too remote, too well guarded, too difficult for them to propose.

We quickly settled on our initial targets: a 350-foot stone viaduct on the western line just south of Mislinje, a 700-foot tunnel at Li-

poglav and nearby bridge at Zbelovo, and a second bridge at Tremerje south of Celje on the eastern line. Destruction of both lines could
stop all rail traffic in the region for several weeks. The only other line
connecting Central Europe and northeastern Italy ran from Maribor
westward along the Drava River and thence into Italy through Tarvi-
sio. It was single track and already loaded to capacity.

The Partisan position in the Pohorje, besides its access to our targets, was ideal for supply. Rogla, the summit of the Pohorje, was perfect for receiving parachute drops. The very top was a flat grassy
meadow of several acres completely surrounded by forest. It was the
highest point for several miles around. Even on a dark night supply
aircraft could fly a few hundred feet above the meadow without danger of hitting a higher mountain nearby. If the pilots came in low the
parachutes would not be carried laterally by wind before touching
ground, thus simplifying the collection of the containers, and preventing them from drifting into German hands. Finally, the ring of
forest around the drop area shielded us and our fire signals from any
German observation except from the air.

Since one of our chosen targets was a multiple-arch stone viaduct
and the other a tunnel and masonry bridge, the explosives required
would amount to several thousand pounds. Plastic explosives had
twice the power of TNT per pound, and were used exclusively behind
the lines because an aircraft, or a man on the ground, could thus carry double the explosive power. Every bomber diverted from bombing
missions had to be fought for, and there were always fewer than we
needed: when available, they had to carry the maximum payload for
our purposes. We argued that we could do more lasting damage with
air-dropped explosives than could the same commitment to bombs
dropped directly on a target.

Later that first morning I enciphered and sent out a message by
radio giving our location in latitude and longitude, the fire pattern
and the recognition signal, and asked for a drop of guns, ammunition, and explosives—and I also asked, as a priority, that we be sent
Ed Welles and a replacement radio and generator. We were still shar-

ing the one radio belonging to MI-6's Lieutenant Gatoni, and it was tempting fate to have no backup.

In the afternoon contact an incoming message read:

"Four Halifaxes tonite. TOT Beer."

"Beer" specified the anticipated TOT (time over target), and I have long since forgotten the hour it stood for, but it was probably midnight or thereabouts. Whatever the hour, excitement began with our deciphering the message, and immediately alerting the Partisan command. They promptly moved the two brigades in the Pohorje to defend the drop area, and made preparations to disperse the materials received to safe hiding in the event we were attacked before we could carry out our plans.

Amid mounting anticipation shared by all, we were at the drop area at least two hours before the planes were expected. At the scheduled time of the drop all of us listened in silence for the sound of approaching aircraft. From time to time one of us was sure he heard an aircraft in the distance but it was the tricks our minds played on us. Nothing came that night. We were a dejected lot, wondering what had happened—which of course the Base Air Operations could not or would not tell us.

The next morning we received a message saying the drop was on again for the following night. There was no mention of the failure to show up the night before. Again we assembled at the drop area. This time, a half hour or so after the designated time, we did hear aircraft faintly. Certain this time that we had heard correctly, the Partisans lit the fires that had been laid out in the pattern of the letter E in the open meadow where we wanted the containers to drop. The sound we heard grew louder and we were sure the first aircraft was headed directly toward us. Then the sound grew fainter and we lost it completely. Were they looking for us? Had they been off in their navigation, searching in the wrong place? Had they given up and gone back? The questions tumbled through our minds.

Then the sound returned faintly. And then faded again. The tension was almost unbearable. The Partisans were beside themselves with excitement. Jim Fisher could no longer contain his anxiety and started shouting: "We're here! We're here! Come this way!" And finally the lead aircraft did—flying directly overhead. I flashed our identification signal and the pilot responded with his confirming signal. It was the right one.

The big plane flew beyond us, turned so that it was headed into the wind as it crossed above us again, and began dropping its load. First the large containers slung under the wings were dropped, and on subsequent passes padded bundles carried in the waist of the aircraft were tossed out by a crew member. The large containers were of light metal at least six feet long—long enough to hold rifles, mortars and machine guns. The lower ends were crushable to cushion the shock of landing.

We could hear the quiet rustle of silk as the opened parachutes descended, but could not see them. Then suddenly we could see the dim outline of parachutes and containers a few feet away as they silently drifted to the ground. Finally, bags of white flour were dropped without parachutes. The flour had apparently been added to the loads to completely fill up the carrying capacity of the planes. It was a very welcome supplement to our food supply. Some ingenious person had devised a system of placing the flour sack in an empty outer sack much bigger than the inner one which of course broke on impact. But the loose outer sack was there to catch the precious flour. (How precious was shown in a later drop when one of the outer bags broke and spilled the flour. Next morning I saw a peasant wife with a bowl carefully spooning up the flour from the ground and separating out the bits of earth and leaves.)

As soon as the first aircraft completed its drop the second arrived, then the third, then the fourth. There was pandemonium on the ground. Partisans began picking up containers and parachutes while others were dropping. No one paid any attention to the free-falling flour sacks as they hit the ground around us. They would have killed anyone who received a direct hit. By dawn all the supplies had been carried off the drop area and were sorted and dispersed to temporarily secure hiding. In addition to explosives and flour the drops had included medical supplies, rifles, Bren guns, and ammunition. We were inside Germany and surrounded by German troops. Yet we had been able to call forth planes from hundreds of miles away by means of a radio transmitter no larger than a shoebox.

But neither Welles nor the replacement radio had arrived. I sent off a querulous message to the base, and the answer came back that Welles had not been dropped because we had not formally confirmed the drop ground as safe for bodies. It seemed to me obvious that I would not have asked that he be dropped if the ground had not been safe. It was an early example of the irreducible communications gap between "headquarters" and "the field."

■ The night after the successful airdrop to us, we attacked the granite masonry viaduct on the rail line at the foot of the Pohorje to the west. It was important to strike quickly before the Germans reacted to the parachute drop—which they would be alerted to by their informers in nearby areas. The attack was to be carried out by the Eleventh "Milan Zidansek" Brigade. The weather changed during the day and by nightfall we were in a heavy mountain rainstorm.

I had expected to supervise the placing of the explosives and detonators, fusing them and tying them together so that they could be set off simultaneously. My intensive training in the British school at Mount Carmel had prepared me to do just that. However, the brigade commander made it quite clear to me that he had men who were very competent to do this and it would all be handled by them. I found myself in an awkward situation. To have insisted on participating in the detailed planning and execution of the operation probably would have been regarded as an affront to the Partisan demolitions unit. I was told that they had been miners in civil life and were thoroughly experienced in the use of explosives, so I accepted their assurances. This turned out to have been a mistake.

At about dusk the brigade commander took me on a tour of the camp where the preparations were being made. There were several groups of men around campfires preparing supplies and equipment. At one campfire I was horrified to find a grinning Partisan, a coil of fuse around his neck, unwrapping packets of plastic explosive and carefully placing them in a circle around the fire, almost at the edge of the glowing coals. When he saw my look of horror, he reassured me that all was well; the explosive worked better, he said, "if it was warmed up first." Fortunately the plastic required a detonator to make it explode; had a glowing coal landed on the plastic it would only have burned intensely—but we could lose a lot of our limited supply that way.

The Partisans estimated that a total of 1,700 German troops— three major and several smaller garrisons—were within 6 miles of our target. The closest, a garrison of 350 men at Mislinje, could reach the viaduct within 10 minutes; the furthest within a half hour.

One battalion of the brigade was ordered to set up blockades and ambushes on the road and railroad north and south of the viaduct. The second battalion would provide immediate protection for the demolition unit who would place the charges. The Zone headquarters guard company was to set up ambushes on a third road leading into the mountain to the east.

About 10 P.M. the second battalion and the demolition group were formed up. Each man had more than 20 kilos of plastic explosive in his knapsack, and nearly a hundred men were needed to carry the explosives, shovels, picks, and equipment we needed. But we had only a few miles to go, and it was all downhill. Jim was left behind with the Partisan camp guards and the MI-6 radio.

Our column halted just before reaching the viaduct. Three Partisans went ahead to scout the track for German guards and to remove them quietly before we arrived. There was the German garrison of 350 men less than a mile from the viaduct and we fully expected that it would be well guarded. While the scouts were gone, Commissar Rudi, the Partisan commander and his staff, and I waited in a small wayside inn, there for summer hikers in more peaceful times. The inn was opened for business and a round or two of local schnapps was ordered up. It helped to relieve the tension—perhaps a little too much—for at one moment I found myself demonstrating with my submachine gun the "killer crouch," as I had been taught it by the

British, to the laughs of everyone, especially when I put my foot in a bucket of fresh milk.

To our great surprise, the patrol on returning reported that there were no guards at all on the viaduct. Our column immediately formed and we moved to the viaduct to place the explosives. It quickly became apparent to all of us that the 1,000 kilos of plastic the Partisans had brought were inadequate to blow up all six of the columns. I later learned that neither the demolition unit nor the brigade intelligence officer had made a reconnaissance in advance. The individual columns were much larger than we had expected.

Three of the seven massive columns which supported the four center spans were selected to be blown, as shown in the sketch reproduced on this page, done by one of the Partisans. The next step was to dig holes for the explosives in the rocky soil next to the columns on the uphill side. The more confined the explosive when it is detonated the more efficient it is in its destructive effect. Explosives placed in these holes would thus have some degree of "tamping" in comparison to placing them on the top of the ground next to the column.

More than an hour was spent digging these holes. The almost continuous thunder of the mountain storm fortunately masked the sounds of digging. The center columns were massive—12 feet by 20 feet—and it would take a lot of plastic to knock them down. In each

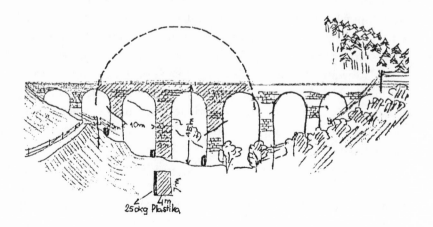

of two of the holes were put 250 kilos, and 150 kilos went in the third, for a side column. Detonators were attached to wires leading to the hand plunger that sent an electric current to the detonators. Two charges of 100 kilos were pushed up against the arched top of the immediately adjoining tunnel and held in place by poles. These charges were also connected to the detonating wires.

We moved back along the tracks a safe distance and Rudi, the commander, and I, along with a few others, crouched behind a small stone track maintenance shed while the Partisan explosives experts brought electric wires to the plunger that set off the charges. When all was ready the explosives chief pushed down the plunger with great verve. The noise of the explosion seemed of an order of magnitude greater than any thunderclap I had ever heard. It reverberated up and down the mountain valley for several seconds.

To cover our withdrawal, the brigade commander had placed Partisans with Bren guns on a ridge overlooking the nearby German garrison. Immediately after the blast the Brens opened up on the garrison. The Germans were completely surprised—and at least as scared as we were. The sound of the explosion, immediately followed by machine-gun fire directed at them, must have totally confused them about what was happening. Fortunately, they did not leave the garrison to investigate, but instead defended themselves against what they thought was an attack on the garrison itself.

Meanwhile, as soon as the rocks thrown into the air by the explosion stopped falling, we went forward to see what damage we had done. The charges had not been enough to completely topple the three columns and the four arches they supported, but had only blown away a large part of the base of each of the columns. In this condition, the columns could be shored up with concrete or masonry in a relatively short time and the bridge made usable again. Fortunately, we still had about 250 kilos of plastic and the Partisans now proceeded to load it into the cavities.

The night air was now crisscrossed with tracer bullets. The Germans continued to defend themselves in their bunkers rather than coming out after us. The reloading of explosives took another hour.

Then the new charges were detonated. When the echo of the explosion died away I was sure I heard another quite distinct crash. The columns of the bridge had shuddered for a few seconds, then disintegrated.

Again, we went back to the site. This time the columns and the arches they supported were completely destroyed. Broken stone masonry was scattered on the ground below. I suspected that the plastic we had kept back was the precise amount necessary to finish the job. In any case, there was a gap of more than 150 feet in the viaduct, and the reconstruction would take weeks if not months. The tunnel blast unfortunately accomplished nothing other than blowing rubble onto the tracks. We had wasted 200 kilos of plastic. By my own calculation, unfortunately made after the fact, we should have used at least double the amount of explosives in the first shot against the three viaduct columns. We were lucky to have had enough left over to complete the job.

When I left Stajerska six months later the line was still closed to through traffic. It is probable that the viaduct was not rebuilt until well after the war ended. My radio message the next morning reported that the operation had been carried out without a single casualty.

Three days after the attack the chief of operations of the Fourth Zone sent a report of the operation by courier to the Slovene Partisan headquarters. The report concluded:

> After this first operation there was suddenly a greater interest in sabotage operations. There was an increase in optimism among the Partisans who took great pleasure in seeing the ruins—aware that it would take the enemy a long time to rebuild the demolished target.

Yet the Partisans' failure to get in advance the measurements of the columns and to calculate the amount of explosives to be brought nearly caused the operation to fail.

Two nights after the first attack, the main double-track line north to Vienna, which was on the eastern side of the Pohorje, was attacked by three brigades using more of the explosives we had received in the airdrop. This was a more ambitious and complex operation—and it was only partly successful. The report of the Fourth Zone command to the Slovene command in Dolenjska (which I was not shown) was severe in its critique. It began:

> The Zidani Most–Maribor railway line represents for the enemy the most important communication line, especially now that the front line in Italy has been set in motion.

The report then detailed the targets and the various assignments in the plan of operation.

> At every designated target the enemy garrison defending the above objectives shall be wiped out. After their liquidation a thorough demolition shall be carried out.

The attacks against the two bridges failed. The operation against the tunnel was only partially successful. The operational report of the Zone tells the story in clear and unvarnished words:

> The bridge at Zbelovo is a very important objective on the Celje-Maribor railway line, especially if the road bridge is included. With the demolition of the road bridge the traffic would be cut on two important arteries, especially one leading to Hungary and being used by the enemy for the transfer of its troops from Danubian regions to Italy.
>
> All the chances were in favor of a completely successful operation. . . . The first battalion under the brigade commander reached the bridge and drove away the sentries who fled without firing a shot. After the target area had been secured, the miners began their work.
>
> They laid a 150 kilo charge and rammed the earth into the hole. This charge did not detonate. It was evident that the miners had been nervous and careless. For the fact that the fuse burned out and that there was no explosion there can only be one explanation, viz., that the miner before lighting the fuse pulled it from its detonator. After the fuse had been lit, the flame merely ignited the explosive, which burned out without exploding. The responsibility for this failure lies with the careless miners and the commanding personnel overseeing the operation. Thus a great opportunity to demolish the bridge was lost. Any renewed attempt at the demolition of the bridge will cost us many more lives since the enemy reinforced immediately all the garrisons guarding communications objectives. . . .
>
> The Thirteenth Brigade, ordered to attack the bridge at Tremerje, aborted the attack after finding the bridge guarded by a 100-man garrison, including 4 antiaircraft guns and 2 mountain guns. The comman-

der decided that an attack would fail because the brigade was too weak and poorly armed to overcome the garrison.

At the Lipoglav tunnel, where the Eleventh Brigade attacked with 143 men, there was plenty of action. The Zone operational report continued:

> The tunnel at Lipoglav is one of the most important objectives along the Celje-Maribor railway line. With the complete demolition of the tunnel all traffic would be stopped for a long time.
>
> The approaches to the tunnel are easy, the terrain is hilly, but it represents no obstacle. . . . Near the tunnel no enemy sentries were observed. Consequently, the column entered the tunnel. Soon a "Halt" challenge was heard. Because the column did not stop, two more challenges "Halt" followed. The column stopped and Comrade Viktor fired two bursts from his Sten gun in the direction of the voice. After several demands for surrender no answer was forthcoming. Comrade Viktor threw a hand grenade and moaning sounds came from the interior, but they soon subsided. The patrol continued on its way and after close inspection found in a recess two sentries who surrendered. One was wounded. The rest of the battalion surrounded the outpost above the tunnel.

After exchange of fire between the Partisans and the Germans who were holed up in the outpost, one of the Partisans got close enough to lob a 15-kilo explosive package into the building. After the explosion what was left of the garrison surrendered.

> In the meantime the demolition inside the tunnel was under way under the command of the mining Second Lieutenant, Comrade Marjan Kurolt. The charges were laid in one compartment at either end of the tunnel. After the detonation a large hole appeared in the arch of that part of the tunnel nearer to Ponikva. At the other end the damage was not so heavy, though the effect was still satisfactory.
>
> If the problem had been correctly understood and the situation thoroughly evaluated, the demolition of the tunnel could have interrupted the traffic over a much longer period of time. Luckily, the surrounding material was loose, otherwise all our exertions would have been in vain.

In concluding its report to Slovene headquarters the Fourth Zone command was extremely critical:

The entire operation was well conceived, yet badly executed. The preparations themselves were poor. The demolition job was completely overlooked. No calculations were made as to the amount of explosives needed for the demolition of specific objectives. Insufficient explosive was taken along by the units so that all these tasks were only partly executed. The odds were in favor of all these actions being completely successful as planned. The targets were not guarded and were easily accessible.

It also became clear that the miners are still incapable of executing such works, that they are not trained sufficiently for it, and that demolition of such targets is still beyond their powers. . . . Responsibility for failure should also be laid at the door of the intelligence service which failed to provide plans for the units who had to undertake sabotage operations without information.

Tunnels are normally not good targets for sabotage because the explosives are likely to simply enlarge the tunnel diameter, which becomes usable again as soon as the rock debris is removed. However, this tunnel targeted by the Partisans had a lining over which there was sandy earth rather than solid rock. When the tunnel was originally built, in the Hapsburg days, holes for explosives were placed at intervals on both side walls along the length of the tunnel, in order to be able to block the rail line in event of war.

During the Second World War the Germans had overlooked the potential danger and failed to block up the holes. They were thus ready-made for the Partisans, who used them to emplace the explosives. Earth above the tunnel continued to fall through the destroyed shell as soon as the Germans began to dig it out. The Partisans later reported that they could see slumps in the hill over the tunnel where the hillside was falling into the tunnel. A few days later a repair train that had been brought to the tunnel was destroyed by the Partisans. This tunnel, and thus the main line through Austria to the heart of Germany, was completely blocked.

In the immediate aftermath of the operation, the Partisans did not tell me the full story. In spite of their own harsh assessment of the operation, the Fourth Zone officers were very cagey with me at the time about the results of the attacks. I was told of the damage to the tunnel. That was no mean achievement. The other failures were glossed over. They were too proud to admit them to me, and probably they feared we might cut back our supply drops if failures were known. Had Welles been dropped to us when I called for him he would have accompanied the brigades and we would have promptly had a more complete appraisal of the operation. With that in hand we might then have been able to organize a timely joint training program on demolition.

Partisan intelligence reported that the German military railroad headquarters was using 500 men to reopen the main line. They were threatened with death if the work was not completed by August 2. It was reopened July 23, after having been completely blocked for five weeks. It was not a bad result for a bungled attack.

Bush rejoined us on the Pohorje a day or so after these attacks. He reported that his group had indeed cut the Zagreb-Ljubljana main line by filling deep cuts with rock blown down by explosive charges from either side of the cuts. The line had been completely blocked for a week. We had begun our work.

The next issue of the *Marburger Zeitung*, a German-language paper, carried a lead article blaming the actions on Allied saboteurs and offering a considerable reward for our capture. At the time we were never sure what would happen to us if we were captured. Intensive interrogation certainly, but would we be shot? The Geneva Conventions state that no prisoners of war shall be shot, but we doubted the Germans would abide by the rules in our case. Partisans captured were usually shot and we had no reason to expect better. An OSS party put ashore in Northern Italy to cut a rail line were, after capture, all shot. It became known after the war that Hitler had ordered that all Allied *Sabotagetruppen* caught in occupied Europe be "completely exterminated." Since we had been called "saboteurs" by the German press we presumably would have come under Hitler's order. Still, it was not something we thought about a great deal.

LEFT: Major Franklin Lindsay, OSS, in British parachute school at Ramat David, Palestine (*Lindsay*)

RIGHT: Joze Borstnar, Commissar and later Commandant of the Partisan Fourth Zone in Stajerska (Styria) (*Lindsay*)

BELOW: Franklin Lindsay with officers of the Partisan Fourth Zone (*Lindsay*)

A village set afire by German troops in retaliation for Partisan attacks (*Museum of the People's Revolution, Ljubljana*)

OPPOSITE: A group of women being executed for aiding the Partisans by a German firing squad in Celje, Stajerska (*Museum of the People's Revolution*)

ABOVE: Slain Partisans, members of the Savinja Battalion, and prisoners forced to stand on display wearing signs listing their "crimes," Celje, November 1942 (*Museum of the People's Revolution*)

CHAPTER 7

Night Marches and Hidden Hospitals

We had fully expected German retaliation for our strikes. But for the next week we were left quietly to ourselves atop the Pohorje mountain. The weather was frightful all that time. Having no shelter, we remained thoroughly soaked. The continuing bad weather prevented planes from reaching us with additional supplies. At the end of the week the weather broke and we were told on June 25 that five Dakotas were coming to us that night. We received the drop successfully—but there was still no Ed Welles or radios.

The next morning a message came in saying five more Dakotas were coming that night. About noon I was with Jim Fisher in a hut where we had the radio transmitter, a few hundred feet below the top of the Pohorje. Returning to the top of the mountain, I heard small-arms fire and an occasional grenade exploding. Angry that the Partisans were having a little fun with the weapons that had just been dropped, I intended to deliver a lecture about wasting ammunition that had been delivered by air at great cost and great risk from a distant base. Instead, on arriving at the top I found a battle under way. An SS force had been sent up the mountain after the "bandits." Fortunately, the two Partisan brigades were still close by and they quickly engaged the enemy.

By nightfall we were completely surrounded. The Partisan chief of staff passed word to me that as soon as it was dark we would start moving to break out of the encirclement. One of the brigades would cover our breakout.

The moon had not yet risen. It was a black night and the heavy forests shut out the starlight that normally provides enough light to see by on moonless nights. Those of us with watches tied them on string around our necks and hung the watches on our backs so that the man behind could follow the luminous dial on the man ahead. We attempted to make as little noise as possible but I thought we must have sounded like a herd of elephants as we slipped on rocky slopes and tangled with heavy branches. We moved all night long, only stopping from time to time to listen for possible German movements. In the midst of all this the Dakotas arrived overhead and circled, looking for our signal—which of course we could not give. Because of the attack we had been unable to radio to cancel the drop.

For the next several months the RAF continued to believe that if a drop was successful on one night, it should be followed up with another drop the next night. We could never convince them that a successful drop often stirred up a hornet's nest, and that they should stay away from us for at least a week. Instead they later made things even worse by sending in one aircraft alone the first night "to test the water"; if that drop was successful they would send several the next night. Most of the second-night sorties aborted because we were on the run and unable to receive a second drop. Our plea was "Send us all you can in a single night, then leave us alone for awhile." Although I twice sent this plea, a month later we received this message: "One Halifax trying tomorrow 25th. If succeeds will try six planes 26th so stand by."

As we worked our way out of the SS encirclement, we saw, toward morning, a large fire burning in the valley below. Partisans had slipped undetected to the German barracks and set it afire. In the early days of the war Tito, in his instructions to Partisan units, told them to meet an enemy offensive both by withdrawing from an unequal battle with a superior force, and by slipping behind them to destroy their bases. By dawn we were out of the encirclement and on a nearby mountain. We had been led all night by a peasant boy who had grown up on the Pohorje and who knew every ridge and ravine, every path. It was another lesson in the importance of winning the support of the local population to provide safety, protection, and support, without which no armed group could have survived. We stopped long enough to make a radio contact and received a message asking us to "give explanation why 5 planes failed Pohorje last night." We replied: "Yesterday afternoon and evening 2,000 SS attacked drop area. Impossible to receive planes."

The decision was now made to leave the Pohorje and to move westward into the lower slopes of the eastern Karawanken Alps. During the month of July we moved nearly every night in the highland forests and farms on the southern slopes of the 6,000-foot peaks of Raduha and Travnik. We would arrive about dawn without advance notice at a farmhouse where we would spend the day before moving on the next night. Guards were immediately posted a quarter of a mile from the house to cover each of the possible approaches. As added security the Partisans enforced the rule that no one, including the peasant family and any visitors, would be allowed to leave until we had departed.

One house where we spent the day was in sight of a small town in which there was a German garrison. One side of the house was screened by trees but the other side was in full view of anyone in the town who might happen to look our way. During the day a Partisan was posted next to the house to prevent anyone from inadvertently walking into view of the town.

■ All the males, except the old men and the boys under sixteen, were either in the German army or with the Partisans. The farm work fell on the women. We often saw women in the fields plowing, or scything the grain. An old man often would be seated under an apple tree sharpening the scythes for the women. Sometimes sturdy women were pulling plows themselves. Their oxen had been taken either by the Germans or by the Partisans.

A few Italians had joined the Partisans, probably to avoid internment by the Germans when the Italian government surrendered. For two or three weeks an Italian deserter barber traveled with us. Not only did I get a haircut but also regular shaves. He would sit me on a stump in the forest, tie a white cloth around my neck, lather my face, and go after the stubble with a straight razor. The first time I was apprehensive about that straight razor, but I concluded that if he had slit my throat he would not have lasted long himself.

The Partisans, and especially the officers, were rigorous in shaving every day they possibly could. The Chetniks, in contrast, had taken a vow at the beginning of the German occupation not to shave until the Germans had been ejected. This was in the tradition of the Balkan chetnik bands of earlier times.

During the summer I developed a tooth cavity. An Italian dentist, also a deserter, was sent for. Again in the forest he set up shop with a drill powered by a foot treadle, and drilled out the cavity. He then filled the hole with an amalgam of silver and mercury. I had no further problem with the tooth. After the war I had the filling checked. To my surprise the American dentist said it was sound and there was no need to touch it.

The area to the west to which we had moved lay on the mountain slopes above and to the north of the villages of Luce and Ljubno in the Gornja Savinjska Dolina—the upper Savinja valley. All the towns and villages in the area were garrisoned by German troops. Food was always a problem, and sometimes a serious one. The higher we were in the mountains the safer we were, but the further we were from the valleys where food could be obtained at night. A foraging party we sent one night into the valley for food ran into a German patrol; all of the Partisans were shot.

Our diet was varied, but not balanced. Occasionally on our marches the party would include an ox procured from a peasant farmer. It might be driven along with us for two or three days (at a very slow pace) until it was slaughtered. We would all live on meat for the next few days. Then it would be only fruit, then only potatoes, then only meat, and finally a return to the ubiquitous zganci, the rubbery ball of grain. On rare occasions a peasant wife would offer me a small bowl of *kislo mleko,* whole milk that had been allowed to sour to form a yogurt. It was pure heaven.

The food problem was the worst in areas that were under German control during the day and Partisan control at night. The Germans sought to deny us the food on which they knew we depended by confiscating the peasants' reserves for the winter. In the liberated areas in Dolenjska south of the Sava, which were under Partisan control nearly all the time, there was some degree of food distribution management, and stocks could be set aside for winter and rationing to peasants and Partisans. But even in Dolenjska, as the 1944–45 winter approached, stocks were dangerously low. Seed for the next planting and the animal population for breeding were below minimum requirements for the next season. To this was added the drive to add thousands of recruits to the Partisans. The latter, combined with (perhaps based on) the expectation that the war might end in the fall of 1944, led to imprudent short-term consumption and consequent misery.

One night while traveling from one Partisan group to another my escort and I stopped at the house of a well-to-do Slovene. I was urged to spend the night in the house and was shown to a bedroom. After being reassured that there were no German troops nearby I swallowed my caution and accepted. It was the first time since leaving Italy that I had slept in a bed. It was wonderfully soft. Before falling asleep I looked up at a shelf on the opposite wall. There I saw three German steel helmets neatly lined up side by side. But the bed was too comfortable to leave. The German soldiers could have been out manning an ambush on a forest path. As I thought about it I remembered the nursery tale of the three bears who returned home to find someone in their house. "Who's been sleeping in my bed?" growled one bear. I didn't propose to wait for that question. We left early in the morning before they returned.

■ Before leaving Italy OSS had asked me to investigate the possibility of setting up a weather observation station in Stajerska. Now, in an exchange of messages, I was told I must guarantee that the station could remain in one place for at least a month at a time. This I could not do, and so the drop of a weather officer and station was canceled.

We continued to report on weather conditions during the days before drops to us were scheduled. One of the required reports was our estimate of cloud cover, to be reported in tenths. As we were always eager to get supplies, we soon fell into the habit of reporting "one-tenth clouds" for a sky at least half cloudy. Any time we caught only a single glimpse of the sun during the day the weather was reported as "five-tenths clouds." But I doubt we ever fooled the base weather officers very much.

■ In the early days Partisans were forced to abandon wounded in their efforts to escape from German encirclements, and almost without exception those left behind were killed by advancing German, Italian, and collaborationist troops. In at least one instance the pursuing Germans laid the wounded out in fields and systematically ran their tanks back and forth over them.

As the war progressed, the Partisans constructed hidden hospitals high in the mountains where it was unlikely that German troops would come. This eased the terrible burden for the fighting brigades of carrying their wounded: on the march four able Partisans were required to carry one wounded man plus all their weapons. These hospitals were often underground, with hidden entrances that were carefully camouflaged. A wounded man would be brought within a mile or two of the hospital and left alone at a prearranged spot, the location of which was often changed. Hospital couriers would then arrive to pick him up and take him the rest of the way, thus ensuring that only the hospital's staff knew of its location. If German patrols did come into the area, the hospital personnel would often leave water and food for the patients, and then depart after covering the entrance completely with sod and leaves. Only disguised air vents remained open. The wounded would be left alone, hidden, for as long as a week if necessary.

Elaborate precautions were taken not to leave a trail from the pick-up locations to the hospitals themselves. In summer parts of the paths were routed across rocky ledges, in flowing streams or on logs placed on stones and removed as soon as an incoming or departing group had crossed. Moss-covered stones were turned upside down for people to step on, then returned to their undisturbed mossy sides. In winter, easily followed tracks in the snow were a major problem. False trails were often made. Junctions with the secret routes to the hospitals would be carefully hidden by evenly tramping down the snow into natural contours, then sifting new snow over the packed and smoothed surface.

The Germans and White Guards often used dogs to follow human scents. To throw them off an arm or leg that had been amputated in the hospital was dragged along false trails.

When the patients were well enough to leave they were blindfolded and led out of the hidden area so that they could never tell under German torture the location of the hospital they had been in. Most of the hospitals survived detection, although a few were discovered. I and other officers with other Partisan groups reported that in those cases the wounded were murdered in their bunks and the hospitals burned on top of them.

In Stajerska we were never able to arrange a landing strip, so the wounded who could walk made the long march south to the clandestine airstrip in Dolenjska. The others had to be carried to the hospitals hidden high in the mountains.

■ Our new base was the relatively isolated lower eastern slope of the Karawanken Alps. There were many peasant farms, some in small groups and some standing quite alone. Nearly every cluster, too small to be called a village, had its own tiny chapel. Some were in the midst of the houses and some at the top of nearby promontories with winding paths leading upward to them. Some were so small that they would hold no more than a dozen parishioners. Each had its ornate altar that filled the entire front wall. Like the larger churches in the villages in the narrow mountain valleys, some had baroque towers with the traditional onion-shaped domes culminating in a sharply pointed spire. Most domes were the gray of pewter and may have been made of sheet lead. Others had simpler spires formed by steeply sloped four-sided roofs. Like the houses they all were of stone, plastered white both inside and out. Roofs were usually the same flat red-brown tile that were used on the houses. There were many wayside shrines on mountain paths just before a house or a group of houses. Some were in the form of crucifixes and some held tiny figurines of the Virgin Mary. There were often tiny altar lights.

The peasants must have resented the way the Partisans would arrive and take over their homes, dump hay from their barns on the floor to sleep on, and requisition their meager food. But they seldom said so in my hearing. They must also have been terribly afraid of what the German patrols that regularly moved about the region would do to them for having helped the Partisans.

The Partisans tried to minimize antagonizing the peasants by not requisitioning food whenever that could be avoided. Payment was made either in cash or notes that the Partisans promised to repay at the end of the war. Cash was obtained by taxation, and by extracting it from wealthy individuals and from companies who either sided with the Partisans or who hoped to buy a little protection in the event of a Partisan victory at the end of the war. Often the responsibility for supplies would be placed with the local Liberation Committees. The peasants were made a part of the Partisan movement, and they had a say in the way food was collected and distributed. The Germans would often redeem these Partisan promissory notes held by the peasants to maintain the fiction that the Partisans were only marauding "bandits."

As the Partisan strength grew, we tended to stop at isolated peasant houses for food and sleep rather than stay in the open, although we continued to move every day. The mountain farmhouses were almost always on gentle slopes. Open grassland alternated with evergreen forests. Alpine summer rains kept the grass a brilliant green throughout the summer and fall. The grass was cut several times a year for winter feed for the cows and horses.

The cut grass was dried on large racks set near the farmhouses and in the fields. Each rack was constructed by sinking two posts into the ground 8 to 10 feet apart. Smaller horizontal poles were placed between the uprights about a foot apart. The cut grass was hung over each of the horizontal poles, and when the rack was filled, the hay looked like a shaggy green rug hung between the two end posts. The structures were capped by narrow roofs of shakes overhanging the racks on either side to protect the drying grass from rain.

Sometimes two drying racks were placed side by side and roofed over to shelter farm wagons. Lofts for storing the dried hay were built above the wagon shelters. In the winter after the hay had been stored in lofts, the bare weathered racks set out across the fields formed arresting geometric patterns against the snow.

The walls of the farmhouses were usually of stone plastered and whitewashed or painted white. The roofs were either of flat orange-red tiles or weathered shakes. Over the years the tiles accumulated gray lichen, which softened their color to dull reds and oranges. The interiors of the houses were so much alike I soon found I could enter one for the first time and know exactly the layout, even in the dark. The main room was always on the left of the entry. A tile or brick Dutch oven was in the back right corner and provided both room heat and an oven for baking. A narrow wooden bench was attached to the walls around the perimeter of the room and stove. In the far left corner a shrine, usually holding a plaster figure of the Virgin Mary, was attached to the wall and adorned with colored paper flowers.

Although the bench was so narrow that one shoulder stuck out resting on air, I learned to sleep on it without tipping onto the floor. The officers shared the benches while the Partisan soldiers slept in the barns. When we were crowded, hay was brought in and we slept on the floor with barely room to move.

I soon learned, after a couple of nasty surprises, to always place my gun in the same position next to me by my side, and my pack close on the other side so that I could automatically grab each in the dark should I need to move fast. I kept my boots on and never zipped up the sleeping bag. In bathing, usually in a mountain stream or an animal trough, I learned never to have more than one boot off at a time and to keep it always handy. Shirt and trousers were never off at the same time.

■ OSS had provided me with a small fund before leaving Italy which I used to supplement Partisan resources from time to time, and to pay peasants for having run the risk of sheltering and feeding us when we were not with an organized Partisan headquarters. Before leaving Italy I had stopped to see David Crockett, the OSS special funds officer. We tried to decide which currencies I might need, but it was a case of the blind leading the blind. He had no more idea than I of what currencies would be useful, or how much I should take. We finally settled on Swiss francs, gold seal dollars, reichsmarks, and the famous French gold Louis, accepted throughout all of Europe. Gold seal dollars were special paper bills with the seal of the United States printed by the Treasury in yellow rather than the normal green. The purpose was to provide a currency that could be used abroad but would be recognizable if large stocks were captured by the enemy and used to fund intelligence agents in the United States or other areas of the world. The reichsmarks had come from captured German army paymaster stocks in North Africa; they were in abundant supply. I think I took 10,000. Crockett also tried to push off a stack of Italian lire, which I refused. The dollars were in fives, tens, and twenties; the Swiss francs were in comparable denominations. We settled on 100 gold coins which I placed, one coin at a time, between two strips of adhesive tape, and which I strapped around my waist.

Once we were in the Reich itself I found reichsmarks still to be completely acceptable. I knew that they weren't going to be worth anything when the war ended and so it seemed logical to get rid of them while they still had some value. After two or three months most of my supply was gone. I sent a radio message to the British special funds officer asking for more reichsmarks to be sent in the next supply drop of explosives. Back came a message inquiring why I wanted reichsmarks, and offering Italian lire instead. I radioed back frostily, pointing out that we were forty miles inside the Third Reich and that reichsmarks were still legal tender. I thought this would end the matter.

Then came another message asking why I needed all that money. I needed it to say thank you to peasants who took care of us, who risked their lives for us, to pay crews at the drop grounds, and to assist escaped POWs and downed airmen, I rejoined. Back came still another message:

> Specify separately how much money required for mission expenses and how much for assisting POWs as funds for latter come from different source. Do you propose to use marks for direct purchase of commodities or exchange into lire as we can provide lire at more favorable rates.

This British special funds officer must have been a junior bookkeeper in civilian life! He was still pushing lire and must have had a truckload of the stuff—God knows what he thought I could use them for. At this point I said to hell with it and when the reichsmarks ran out I began to spend Swiss francs and dollars. I saved the gold in case I really got in a jam and had to buy my way out. After nine months tramping the mountains of Carinthia, Styria, Slovenia, and Croatia I returned to Italy with some dollars and all but twenty of the hundred gold coins (having lost, not spent, the twenty), and turned them in to the special funds office. Only then did I realize I had been living proof of Gresham's law in economics, which states that when two currencies are in circulation the weaker one will always drive out the stronger. More simply, the bad money always drives out the good.

■ While on the march one night, the head of our escort patrol heard the footsteps of men approaching us. At a whispered command everyone went flat on the ground, guns ready. The other group reacted in the same way and the two groups found themselves about a hundred feet apart, each unsure whether the others were Partisans or White Guard collaborators. After preliminary challenges a shouted dialogue began between the leaders of the two groups: "Who are you?" "What village are you from?" "Who is your father?" "Where is your house?" "Who lives in the next house?" "When did you join the Partisans?" Finally, each was satisfied that the other unit was also Partisan and we continued on our way.

There were no identification cards to be shown, and no passwords to be exchanged. Yet it was a very effective way of determining friend or foe, since the leaders of the patrols usually were natives of the area and knew intimately the details of village and farm life, especially whether or not another person was a collaborator or a Partisan. No false documents or cover story could be designed to stand up to this sort of questioning.

One day we stopped for several hours near a mountain farm. The night before several horses had been captured and were now tied to nearby trees. One, a stallion, was in a near frenzy because of the mares nearby. He had soon worn a deep circular track around the tree to which he was tied. One of the Partisan officers came by and asked if any of us would like a ride on one of the mares. Squadron Leader Mervyn Whitfield, an MI-6 officer who had replaced McNeff, said he didn't know much about riding but would like to try. A very quiet mare was produced and saddled. While we gave him not very helpful advice he mounted and rode off. A little while later he returned at a slow walk filled with his newfound equestrian skill. At the moment he was preparing to dismount, the stallion somehow slipped out of his halter and, unnoticed by Mervyn, circled behind the mare. The next moment the stallion's head, wide-eyed and nostrils dilated, appeared over Mervyn's shoulder. Mervyn was sandwiched between the two animals and had no idea of what had happened or what to do. We grabbed him and the mare and extricated him just in the nick of time from a "fate worse than death." We never let him hear the end of it.

■ On clear days during the summer we would often see the entire strength of the American Fifteenth Air Force passing overhead. It was an awesome sight that only those within occupied Europe were able to see. Minutes before seeing the first planes we would become conscious of a low-pitched penetrating sound that came from nowhere and from everywhere. It would steadily grow in intensity as we searched the sky in all directions. Then the bomber formations began to appear, coming from the south and headed north.

They had started from many airfields in and around Foggia on the Adriatic coast of Italy, and by the time they passed over our area the individual formations had formed up in a single column and had slowly lifted their heavy loads of bombs and fuel to their operating altitude. At this altitude each of their engines left behind its white vapor trail of ice crystals in a very blue mountain sky. Long-range fighters accompanying the bomber formations constantly wove back and forth above the bombers like sheepdogs working their flocks, their S-shaped vapor trails stitching patterns against the arrow-straight trails of the bombers.

We stopped whatever we were doing to watch the display of power, knowing that in less than an hour thousands of bombs would be released over the industrial sections and rail yards of Vienna, Wiener Neustadt, Bruck, Linz, or perhaps even Munich. As each wave passed another followed. The procession continued for two full hours and the roar that filled the sky never slackened until the last wave disappeared to the north.

As for German aircraft, the only ones that regularly bothered us were Fieseler Storches, light slow reconnaissance planes that carried machine guns strapped vertically along the fuselage. They were often out looking for Partisans. When they spotted us they would fly into the wind a few feet above the treetops so that they appeared to be almost stationary, their machine guns firing straight down. On such occasions I would find myself looking for the biggest nearby tree and would carefully slide around, trying to keep the tree trunk between me and the plane. The worst damage I recall was a direct hit on a cooking pot—our one and only, serving the whole unit.

■ The coordination of the airdrops became increasingly difficult, both on the ground and with Air Operations in Italy. On the first of July we asked for five sorties to Mozirska, a new drop point. "Send Welles and radio equipment without fail. Do not send more planes after first successful drop." On the night of July 3, one Halifax was sent to us. The next morning I signaled: "Surrounded and attacked last nite. Rec'd stores one plane after trying to signal it to Rogla [in the Pohorje]." Because we could never be sure that any single drop point would still be in our hands by the time the aircraft arrived, we set up several drop points. Pilots were given a primary drop point and two or three alternates in the expectation that at least one would be open. Air supply operations now increased in volume. Almost every night that the weather was good we received drops of anywhere from one to ten planes.

But this created a new set of problems. Unlike the large Partisan-held liberated areas in central Yugoslavia where drop points were typically ten to twenty miles from the nearest German units and were not moved for weeks or months, we held no liberated territory. The German strategy was to move units around constantly and to attack first one area and then another with the object of preventing the Partisans from taking the initiative, and also of destroying the Partisans if they could. They also blockaded key areas so that for several days running it was impossible to get couriers in or out. Strong German patrols would often occupy a drop point without warning between an afternoon radio contact and the arrival of planes.

Fire signals and recognition codes needed to be changed almost daily in order to be sure the stuff was dropped to us and not to the Germans, who increasingly were using false signals to lure unwary or careless pilots. Because some of the drop points required three or four days for couriers to reach them, we had set up the fire and recognition signal plans a month in advance. But this was frustrated by Air Operations in Italy, which frequently changed the signals on 24 hours' notice—or less. It was then too late to get the word to the drop points.

For example, we radioed:

Yr Four Eight rcd today tenth stop Mala will flash new signals tomorrow stop Other pts will probably use old signals for four more days until couriers can get there stop This [your abrupt changes in signals] raises hell here.

As a result of these last-minute changes several sorties were aborted.

The only way these failures could be reduced was to supply the Partisans with radios they could use to communicate with the drop points and with their brigades. A few radios would do more than anything else to get badly needed weapons to the Partisans, to make their brigades effective fighting forces, and to improve the effectiveness of rail sabotage. I now put first priority on radios, including twelve sets for the Partisans.

Peter Moore had told me that the base in Italy had had an ample stock since March. But even the radio, batteries, generator, and fuel for our own communications, which we had asked for several times, had not been delivered by the end of July, although we had received more than forty sorties that month. Admittedly, in part this was bad luck: the radio equipment on one sortie had been dropped to the Germans, and another sortie bringing Welles and a set of equipment had aborted with engine trouble before reaching us, and the entire load had been jettisoned so that the plane could limp back to Italy.

Still, there were avoidable errors, costly delays, and failures to inform. On several occasions brigades went to the drop areas to receive supplies we had requested several days in advance. At times either the supplies never came or the wrong supplies were dropped. Had we been told by the base that our requests could not be filled we could have told the Partisans, who would have altered their plans accordingly. Once a hundred men without arms waited eight days for a drop of arms, and when it finally came there were no guns—only ammunition.

Much to my frustration, and over my strong protest, Air Operations finally landed Welles in Dolenjska in a C-47 on July 26 instead of dropping him directly to us. From there he came across the courier line, which required three weeks. He had been equally frustrated by the weeks he had had to spend waiting in Italy.

Edward Welles was in his sophomore year at Yale when the Japanese attacked Pearl Harbor. He had immediately tried to enlist but had failed his medical exam because of poor eyes. Determined to play an active part in the war, he joined the American Field Service, a civilian organization that sent Americans to the British forces as ambulance drivers. His group was dispatched in the spring of 1942 by ship to Egypt, where they were assigned to the British Eighth Army fighting Rommel's forces in the Western Desert. After a year in which he saw active fighting at El Alamein and across North Africa, he tried again to enlist in the American army, this time in Algiers. Again he was turned down for eyesight.

Next Welles enlisted in the SBS (Special Boat Service), an elite special raiding force of the British Army. After training in Palestine he took part in British behind-the-lines operations against German-held Greek islands in the Aegean, as part of a raiding group under Lieutenant Colonel George Jellicoe. Welles was part of a small group put ashore on the German-held island of Rhodes on a reconnaissance mission. Separated and cut off when the British party withdrew, he spent three weeks in hiding, part of it in a farmer's manure pile, before finally stealing a boat in which he escaped to Turkey.

In early 1944 Ed Welles tried for the third time to enlist in the American army. This time he found OSS in Cairo eager to have him, and his transfer from the British forces was quickly arranged. He was put on a plane for Italy where he joined me. Welles would have been an excellent officer from the very beginning of the war had he not failed his eye exam for induction. I used him for assignments that should have had officer rank to gain the support and respect of the Partisans. But he did very well without the gold bars. We finally got him a commission, and in the final months of the war he had his own mission with a Partisan corps.

British Major Roberts, a part of Wilkinson's Austrian group, arrived with Welles. In the next weeks he kept us amused with his stories of SOE activities in Britain. In 1942 Roberts had been given the job of looking after a group of Spanish toughs who had been collected by SOE to sabotage the railroads in Spain in the event Hitler invaded the Iberian peninsula. They had completed their training and continued to get into all sorts of trouble with local authorities as month after month they were kept on standby against the possibility that Hitler would invade Spain—as he had done in Vichy France after the Allied landings in North Africa. Roberts was at his wit's end trying to keep the Spaniards out of further trouble. He took them back to Scotland for refresher courses in sabotage and night infiltration. They went through parachute school again. The final blow came when one of them slipped into the Spanish Embassy in London and spilled the beans to Franco's ambassador, telling him that they were being trained by the British to blow up neutral Spain's railroads. Roberts said all hell broke loose as the Foreign Office tried to explain away this "warlike act" to Franco, whom they were trying to keep out of Hitler's camp. Roberts was quickly transferred to Peter Wilkinson's Central European group and found his way to us.

■ The Partisans of the Fourth Zone made a major contribution to the war effort by their almost continuous attacks against the railroads during the summer months. Our attacks against the two north-south rail lines in mid-June closed the alternate western line to Vienna at least until December and probably to the end of the war. The main Vienna line was cut from June 19 until it was reopened on July 23. In addition, the large quantities of explosives and guns dropped during June and July were used to make many smaller attacks. Our attacks on the Zidani Most–Ljubljana section alone continued to restrict its use by the Germans. During one 15-day period in July the cumulative result of 6 separate attacks closed the line for a total of 11 days.

Cuts continued on the other lines as well. Our objective, of course, was to make those demolitions that would take the longest to repair while exposing the Partisans engaged to the least danger. But these two objectives were usually in conflict, and the best targets were increasingly strongly guarded.

Major bridges such as those across the Sava were ideal, but they too were becoming well guarded. Track and roadbed couldn't be protected at every point with the troops available to the Germans. They had to concentrate their manpower on the most vulnerable targets. The cut of a single rail could, of course, be made in a few minutes with a pound or two of plastic. But the Germans, in response to that kind of attack, became masters at quick repairs—usually they had the trains moving again in a few hours.

Mines containing several pounds of plastic were placed under the ties and set to detonate by the weight of a locomotive. When it worked it often derailed the train. Cuts of rails on straightaway track, unless a meter or so of rail was cut out and removed, were not effective because a moving locomotive was likely to jump across the break. But a cut in the outside rail on a curve would cause the locomotive to use its own momentum to derail and possibly to turn over.

Where the Partisans had the time and the manpower a very effective technique was to rip up the track and the ties for several hundred feet, stack the ties three or four high, balance the rails on top and set the ties afire. Because the ties were impregnated with creosote they would burn with an intense heat, sufficient to make the rails cherry red and soft enough to bend the ends down with their own weight. The twisted rails were impossible to use again and either new ties and rails had to be brought in and laid, or the bent sections cut out and the straight ends welded together. On the double-track lines the Germans were often forced to take remaining good rails from one damaged track to repair and reopen the other.

We also used our explosives to blow rocks on the sides of steep cuts down onto the tracks. Where the cuts were deep enough the line could be blocked by a jumble of blasted rock 30 to 40 feet high. To slow repairs the Partisans often were able to post snipers nearby to harass the repaircrews. As we had learned, stone viaducts required thousands of pounds of explosives. Steel truss bridges were far easier to destroy with small charges: the crucial beams to be cut were less than an inch thick, while stone columns were measured in feet. But they soon became well defended and very costly in men's lives to attack.

British PIATs and American bazookas—both antitank weapons that used the hollow-charge principle to penetrate steel armor—were dropped to us and I often tried to interest the Partisans in using them against steam locomotives. I argued that Partisans could hide in the forests along the tracks and at 100 yards hit engine boilers and explode them. But I never was able to persuade them to try.

OSS had developed an ingenious gadget for blowing up trains inside tunnels where it would be difficult and time-consuming to clear the wreckage. The devices used a photoelectric cell that reacted to the sudden change from daylight to the darkness of a tunnel. Slow changes in light, such as at sunrise or sunset, would not trigger the explosion. The detonator fired after a delay sufficient to get the train well inside the tunnel. I asked for and received some of them and explained how to use them. I don't think they were ever used successfully, possibly because of the difficulty of installing the devices and explosive charges while trains were standing in rail yards and well guarded.

Another useful device was the time pencil. We used them to delay the detonation of explosives after they had been put in place. The "pencil" was a copper wire and a glass capsule of acid inside a metal tube. When the capsule was broken by crimping the tube, the acid would eat through the wire, which when severed would initiate the explosion. Different colored capsules contained different acid strengths; by selecting the right capsule the delay could be timed. The shortest was 15 minutes, the longest 24 hours.

In messages to us, both OSS and SOE used code names for individual pieces of equipment. The British were more prosaic in their selection—using names of fruits and vegetables. The Americans were more colorful, with terms such as "Who me" and "Hedy Lamarr," the GIs' favorite pinup girl, for their array of sabotage devices. It was a little startling to receive the message "Sending you 15 Hedy Lamarrs tonite."

I now became aware that the dimensions of my world had shrunk to the mountain ridges immediately surrounding us, and to the rail lines that lay beyond them. Nothing beyond that perimeter had reality. Only the BBC, when we were able to pick it up, brought occasional fragments of news from the outside world.

Railroad demolitions became our stock-in-trade. The mission we had been sent to do in support of the Allied campaign in Italy had been successful, although not as successful as it could have been. The fall months would tell quite a different story.

8

The Partisans Organize a
Shadow Government

W hen I arrived with the Partisans in the spring of 1944, I had almost no knowledge or understanding of their organization and operations. Now, in midsummer, I had begun to put together what I had observed, and to understand that both organization and modes of operation were dictated by their particular military and political goals.

The most important activity was political—to gain and hold the loyalties of the civilians. To achieve this goal they used both the positives of propaganda and political action and the negatives of discovery and punishment of those who secretly or openly helped their enemies.

They needed an armed Partisan force to cause the occupiers to withdraw from the more remote areas and thus to prevent the liquidation of their political movement. This could only be done by repeated attacks against small and isolated German installations rather than by defending territory from attack by the better-armed German forces. For the first two years of the war the Partisans' sole source of weapons was their enemies, the Germans and the Italians. Only in the fall of 1943 did weapons from abroad begin to arrive. The Partisans would have preferred to receive weapons from the Russians, but as this was not forthcoming they welcomed British and American support.

By now we had come to know, and to a degree assess, the Partisan officers with whom we worked. The Fourth Zone headquarters consisted of the commander, his deputy, the commissar, a chief of staff and a small operations staff, a head of intelligence, a supply officer, a chief courier, and a propaganda unit. A Partisan guard company provided immediate protection for the headquarters as the brigades were dispersed and able to communicate only by courier, or later by radio.

Before February of 1944 there was no central command for Partisan units operating in Stajerska. The transfer of the Fourteenth Division from Dolenjska in March signaled a basic decision to give high priority to strengthening the Partisan presence in Stajerska. All the area odreds, the three brigades of the Fourteenth Division, and the two independent brigades were placed under the Fourth Zone command. Instructions to the new command were to expand their area of operations and to bring new recruits into the brigades. The Slovene headquarters sent in a new command team under Mile Kilibarda, a Serb, who, we had been told in Dolenjska, was experienced in leading larger Partisan operations.

The Zone political commissar (and later the commander) Joze Borstnar was an early Partisan. He was a big man with swarthy complexion and black curly hair. He was about thirty and before the war had been a railroad employee, with little formal education. He appeared to me to be anti-American and anti-British, suspicious and bureaucratic, and was far from easy to work with. Talking with him often seemed like a one-way street—he seldom was forthcoming or responsive.

The deputy commander, Alois Kolman-Marok, was a tough, experienced, and aggressive fighter. His war name, Marok, derived from the word "Morocco," where he had served before the war in the French Foreign Legion. He was a skilled horseman; I often saw him riding at a gallop among his struggling troops, urging them on with both encouraging and abusive language. He was killed in combat in the last few months of the war.

Dragomir Bencic-Brkin became Zone commissar when Borstnar

became the commander two months after our arrival. In his early thirties, he had been an engineer before the war and a Partisan since 1941. He was of slight build, handsome and blond. I found him soft-spoken and outwardly friendly. He was often visibly embarrassed when he had been ordered to be noncooperative or when I reproached him for Partisan obstructions to carrying out our jobs. When he knew I had a head of steam about some specific difficulty he would often avoid seeing me rather than face my protests.

Another of the Partisan officers with whom we dealt regularly was Franc Primozic, the operations officer during most of my months in Stajerska. I found him cooperative and helpful within the limits of his orders and I suspected that he was the ablest of the military leadership. His critical analysis of the failures of the brigades on the first round of attacks against the rail targets was perceptive and sound.

The propaganda unit, called "Agitprop" in Communist jargon (a combination of agitation and propaganda), was the largest part of the staff, and had a central role in the organization. Its missions were to build political support and to expand recruiting throughout the area in which the Partisans operated. Although we were constantly on the move, typewriters and hand mimeograph machines were carried along. Single-sheet newspapers were written, duplicated, and distributed to the armed brigades, the local odreds, and clandestinely into the German-held villages and towns.

One poor Agitprop Partisanka who weighed scarcely a hundred pounds carried her portable typewriter as well as her pack. Often toward the end of a long march she was visibly exhausted. I would take the typewriter away from her in spite of her protests and carry it myself. As soon as one of the Partisan officers spotted me with the typewriter he would rush up, grab it from me, and give it to one of the headquarters guard company. It wouldn't then be long, however, until I would see it back in the Partisanka's hand as she struggled to keep up with the column.

A Slovene priest who had joined the Partisans was an important part of the effort to win the support of the peasants. He often traveled with us and heard confessions and conducted services in the little chapels as we moved through the mountain hinterlands. He also spoke at political meetings organized by the Agitprop sections to counter the peasant fears of Communism. I had the feeling he was on a very short tether and was given detailed instructions on the party line before each meeting.

All of the Partisan units held political instruction sessions daily. Agitprop members regularly conducted political meetings in the nearby villages as a part of consolidating the support of the peasants and building a shadow political structure throughout the German-controlled area. Clandestine political cells were organized in the cities, and penetrations of German military and civil organizations provided us with early warnings of planned German attacks.

I once asked Ales Bebler, a Partisan colonel and a leading member of the Communist Party of Slovenia, under what conditions he would send an armed Partisan brigade into a new area. His answer was that he would need at least six months to "prepare the people politically" to support the Partisans before he would consider sending in an armed unit.

Bebler was a person with whom I could have relaxed and wide-ranging conversations, and I always enjoyed talking with him. He was 37, older than most Partisan leaders, having spent two years in Moscow in Comintern schools and later three years in the International Brigade in the Spanish Civil War.

"Preparing the people politically" meant sending in clandestine workers who would recruit civilians into the Liberation Front, hold small secret meetings, recruit informers in the local police and military units, and gradually build a supportive underground structure. It also meant creating a secret counterintelligence organization to uncover and eliminate enemy penetrations into the Partisans' own organization.

This intense preparation before introducing armed Partisans was carried out under the most favorable circumstances. In 1944 the war was clearly coming to an end, and by now nearly all the Slovenes believed the Germans would be defeated. The Partisans were openly supported by all three major powers fighting the Axis: Britain, the United States, and the Soviet Union. Chetnik strength in Slovenia was almost nonexistent. Almost all of the organized indigenous opposition to the Partisans in Slovenia was by now collaborating with the Germans and there was no longer any viable opposition untarnished by the stamp of collaboration. Yet in spite of these favorable circumstances, Bebler believed it would take at least six months to organize sufficient civilian support in a new area of operations. Bebler also said that one of the hardest tasks since the beginning of the struggle had been to continue to convince the Partisan troops that the war could not possibly last more than another six months.

■ Any Allied statements of admiration of the Partisans, especially those by Churchill, were eagerly and prominently quoted. But reports of Allied fighting against the Germans were given very minor coverage, if any. Partisan speeches, political-hour instruction for the battalions, and propaganda handouts reflected the conflict between their dependence on the West for arms and fear that the Allies would somehow frustrate their ultimate ambitions to rule the country alone.

The Allied planes that night after night dropped desperately needed supplies were of course evident to the Slovene population, and even more so to the Partisan battalions, but the Agitprop workers tried to minimize their dependence on us as best they could. The story was spread widely among the Partisans, for example, that these arms, medical supplies, and clothing from the West were not gifts, but would have to be paid for at full price at the end of the war. Of course it was not true. To the Western capitalist Allies the blood of the Partisans was not sufficient payment, they said.

At Slovene headquarters Lieutenant Colonel Peter Moore observed that "no single mention has ever been made of the extensive Allied help to the Slovene Partisans." Although the Partisans gave no recognition in their internal news sheets to the British and Americans for the large volume of supplies coming in by air, they were vociferous in their demands that BBC report in detail their own exploits.

They were also violent in their criticism of BBC any time the Chetniks were credited with an operation and they were not mentioned. Both the Partisans and the Chetniks regularly accused the BBC of crediting to the other the operations that they themselves had carried out.

I finally understood that the reason for the importance of BBC reports on Partisan exploits was that the BBC provided the best radio coverage to Yugoslav towns and cities held by the Germans—people whom the Partisans had great difficulty in reaching directly. BBC reporting was thus of major importance to them to validate the size and importance of their movement to the majority of Yugoslav people who were still in German-held territory. BBC was also the most credible source of information in occupied Europe.

Actually, I found that the BBC was not as evenhanded as its reputation implied. When the British supported Mihailovic, Chetnik operations were emphasized and Partisan exploits played down. When support shifted to Tito the reverse happened.

The German propagandists also realized the importance of BBC broadcasts. They transmitted fake BBC programs with subtle deceptions interspersed with authentic news reports. They even had a fake Churchill with a voice remarkably like Churchill's own.

Because of the great store the Partisans put in BBC broadcasts describing their feats, I asked Force 399 in July to arrange for BBC coverage of the rail demolitions we had been reporting since mid-June. Four days later I received a response. "Pictures and further details required before story possible." I could only guess that my signal was forwarded to BBC, where some harried staff member hadn't looked at a map to see how impossible was his request for pictures. Nevertheless, I did later get some BBC coverage of our Partisan actions, which they heard with great pride and satisfaction.

The Partisans' propaganda attacks against their internal enemies, all of whom were lumped together as collaborators with the Italians and Germans, were constant. The role of the Communist Party in propaganda was carefully managed. On the one hand the Partisan struggle was described as a broad-based coalition of freedom-loving peoples and organizations. On the other hand the Communist Party was described as the leading force in that coalition.

Mass indoctrination was carried out through the local Liberation Councils, the Partisan commissars, and Agitprop sections of the broad organizations for youth and women. Fascism being the enemy, anti-fascism needed no definition. It was the equivalent of motherhood. Nearly every political organization had "Anti-Fascist" in its title, from the highest political organs, the Anti-Fascist National Liberation Committee (the provisional parliament) and the Anti-Fascist Council of Yugoslavia (in effect Tito's Politburo), to the village Anti-Fascist Committees, the Anti-Fascist Youth, and the Anti-Fascist Women's Organization. This litany focused attention on the full range of opposition blanketed under the term "fascist," and avoided specifics of what would come after liberation.

The Communist leadership had built a national liberation movement through a combination of its own single-minded determination and the mistakes of the Germans, the Italians, and the Chetniks. Before the war a combination of purges of the Yugoslav Communist Party ordered by the Comintern in Moscow and the arrests of party members by the Yugoslav government had seriously eroded the party cadres. Party membership was no more than 10,000, of whom many were captured or killed in the early days of the war. The successes of the Partisan movement required a major expansion of party membership in order to ensure the continued preeminence of the party in control of the resistance movement, and the continuity of party control into the postwar period of political consolidation.

Indoctrination in the principles of Marxism and Leninism was carefully limited to party members, and directed especially toward the new, younger members. This involved the clandestine publication and distribution to party cells of the principal Soviet Communist tracts. Stalin's "Foundations of Leninism" was the bible. Milovan Djilas, head of the all-important Agitation and Propaganda Section of the party, reported to the Central Committee of the party at the Fifth Party Congress:

During the entire course of the war, in all Party organizations in the Army, it was compulsory to study Marxism-Leninism and the line of our Party. At the beginning of 1943, the CC [Central Committee] sent course leaders. . . to the hqs of the various divisions and corps. The Party also worked constantly on the ideal education of the non-party fighting masses.

The "education" of the nonparty masses went very light on Marx and Lenin but heavy on Yugoslav and Slovene nationalism, attacks on the prewar government, attacks on the Chetniks as collaborators, and promises of a new, democratic government when the war was over.

I had my own experience with the thoroughness of the Communist Party in identifying itself with leadership in the liberation of the country. During a quiet period in the summer the Stajerska Partisans organized a rally in the forest for which the local civil population was rounded up. I had appeared at such rallies before, and I began to be aware that as an American officer I was being used not only as a visible symbol of Allied support for the fight against the Germans, which was fair enough, but also as a symbol of support for the Communist cause, which was not. This time I made it clear that I would not participate in any meetings in which Communist Party propaganda played any part. I would only take part in rallies at which the message was united action against the Germans. I was assured by Borstnar, then still commissar, that there would be no Communist propaganda, so when my turn came I climbed up on a raised platform from the rear and said my piece. A few days later I was given a photo taken from the audience's side showing me on the platform. On the front of the platform was the sign: "Long live the Communist Party of Yugoslavia." I had no idea what words the interpreter had put in my mouth, but I suspected considerable "editing" was done.

We have become accustomed to the special meaning Communists give to ordinary terms, but then we were hearing them for the first time. Every action of the Communist leadership was done in the name of "the people." Those whom the Partisan leadership opposed were "enemies of the people" or "traitors to the people." These included as a matter of course the king and the royal government-in-exile, Draza Mihailovic and the Chetniks, the prewar politicians who did not join the Partisans, and the various militias who collaborated with the Germans and Italians. Months later during our negotiations with Tito over Trieste, he rejected an Allied proposal, saying: "The people would never permit me to agree to that." By then "the people" had been organized into slogan-chanting lockstep. Even OZNA, the Communist secret police, was named "Department for the Security of the People" (Odeljenje Zastite Naroda).

In Slovenia OZNA was preceded by VOS, the Security Intelligence Service. As a secret police organization it apparently developed such an odious reputation that it was formally disbanded and succeeded by OZNA. However, we assumed that the personnel were largely the same. Peter Moore was incensed by Boris Kidric's denials. There was no such organization, he said. Moore knew this was untrue. During early 1944 the Fourth Zone command organized three battalions of the VDV, the Army of State Security. The Partisan history describes their function: "To act against the traitors of the Slovene people and to counteract the activities of the enemy intelligence services."

The slogan that was obligatory at the end of every report, memorandum, order, directive, even a pass, was, in Slovene, "*Smrt Fasizmu—Svoboda Narodu*": death to fascism, freedom to the nation. In Serbo-Croat, however, the same phrase meant "freedom to the people." "Democracy" was often used to indicate the ultimate objective of the revolution—but it was never defined.

Our somewhat sour observations on the politics of the Partisans did not diminish our admiration for their heroism, and for the impressive courage and fortitude of the Partisan fighters and underground workers as well as the peasants who sheltered us. Peter Wilkinson had described them as "brave to a fault."

Partisan bravery was not limited to the males. Between 5 and 10 percent of the Partisans were female. Most were propaganda workers, nurses, radio operators, and cooks, but all carried weapons and ran the same risks as the men. A few were in the combat brigades. They were very tough, aggressive fighters—up to the best of the men in bravery and fearlessness. And they had no compassion for the enemy: no prisoners taken.

■ Among the Partisans there was nothing but idolatrous praise for the Soviet Union, the Red Army, and their Russian Slav brothers. But it was not until February 23, 1944, well after the arrival of the British and Americans, that the Russians sent a military mission to Tito's headquarters. They were to be taken in and landed in a British or American C-47, but repeated snowstorms made it impossible to clear a landing strip near Tito's headquarters. The British then proposed to parachute the group as the best alternative, but the Russians would have none of it. Finally they agreed to be loaded into Allied assault gliders, which were towed by aircraft and cut loose over the snowbound landing area. The Russian mission was quite large, and was headed by a lieutenant general, and included a major general and several colonels. They were strictly military, and provided no political, or party, linkage with the Partisan Politburo.

The Partisans were thrilled by the prospect of at last having their Russian brothers and fellow Communists with them. But the relations between them soon cooled, although the Yugoslavs carefully hid this from the rest of us. The Russians apparently expected to exercise strong influence over the Partisan commanders, but the Partisans were determined to run their own show. The Russians did not help matters by belittling the Partisan war effort compared to that of Russian partisans in German-occupied Russia. One of their first actions, I was told by a British officer there, was to complain that their latrine was not built according to Soviet army specifications and to ask that a new latrine be constructed.

Lieutenant Colonel Boris Bogomolov of the Soviet military mission arrived at Fourth Zone headquarters in Slovenia in July as the permanent Russian liaison officer. He was a short, thin man in his late thirties. He had been through the siege of Leningrad and recounted harrowing stories of the starvation and suffering the garrison and civil population had endured for the sixteen months before the siege was lifted by the Red Army. He seemed to have very little to do; when things were quiet he gave classes in Russian under a tree for the girls in the Agitprop section.

One night we received a bottle of Scotch in a parachute drop, the first Scotch we had seen since leaving Italy. We decided to ration ourselves to a few swallows a night to make it last as long as possible. In a burst of Allied friendship we invited Bogomolov to join us in the first night's sip. Borrowing glasses from a peasant wife, I poured out about a half-finger in each glass, the intended ration for that day. It was superbly delicious and we first smelled it, then savored it as if it were the finest brandy. But not Bogomolov. He tossed back his glass with a flick of his wrist, put it down, and reached for the bottle. We realized that if we didn't keep up with him we would have none— that night or any night. In a half hour the bottle was empty.

CHAPTER 9

Radios, Codes, and Codebreakers

W e quickly learned that without regular radio communication with Force 399 and OSS we could neither bring in supplies for the Partisans nor carry out orders to cut the German lines of communication. We also learned the terrible price that is exacted from those who fail to observe the unforgiving laws of secret radio communication. Radio provided a superb way for us to communicate quickly over long distances. But it was also an unfailing way to reveal our precise location to the enemy. And when the codes we were given were flawed, the enemy was able to discover our plans.

Our absolute dependence on radio communications made us dread equipment failure. Several officers and agents who were sent into enemy territory during the war, both in Europe and the Far East, were powerless to carry out their missions because their radios were either lost or broken. Once out of communication, there was seldom a way to get word out for replacement of the vital equipment. One of the more dramatic cases was that of a British SOE officer, Frederick Spencer Chapman. He had stayed behind in Malaya when the Japanese overran Singapore in 1942 to organize and lead a Malay and Chinese resistance against the Japanese occupiers. His radio was lost almost immediately. Alone in the jungle for two years, he survived incredible hardship and disease through sheer determination and courage. But without a radio the suffering he endured counted for nothing except his own survival. A search party, landed by submarine in 1944, miraculously found him and reestablished radio contact with SOE in Ceylon. Not until the closing days of the war was Chapman able to call in parachute drops of weapons for the Malayan resistance.

I was lucky to have Jim Fisher as a radio operator; we became fast friends. He had the build of a football player, and a warm disposition to go with it. He was completely blind in one eye and it was only an administrative mistake that caused him to be drafted when he graduated from high school in Detroit. When the army discovered he had only one eye he was designated "for continental U.S. service only," and sent to radio school to become a base station operator. OSS was looking for base operators and interviewed candidates at the Army Signal Corps school. Jim volunteered and OSS took him.

OSS was apparently less rigorous in observing the "continental U.S. service only" restriction and sent him to Cairo to be an operator in the OSS base station there. Once in Cairo Jim found that people were being sent to the British parachute school in Palestine. He volunteered and again was accepted. We met there in parachute class, and I asked him to come with me. Thus a one-eyed man, who according to regulations should never even have been in the army, ended up as one of the best behind-the-lines operators that OSS ever had. He was awarded the Silver Star for his service. I was tremendously pleased when, after the war, he named his first son John Lindsay Fisher.

■ During the war solid-state microelectronics were unknown, as the key element, the transistor, had not yet been invented. Our radios then, both receiver and transmitter, used miniature glass vacuum tubes. In spite of efforts to make them rugged, they were both fragile and bulky. Ours in Slovenia, a British set, was the size of a small suitcase and weighed about twenty pounds. Power to operate the set was always a problem. OSS and SOE had developed several different pieces of equipment to generate the electric power needed by the radio. Because none of them could provide sufficient current directly at a constant level to power the transmitters, we had first to charge heavy wet-cell batteries of the type used in automobiles. The radio transmitter and receiver were then operated on the current provided by the battery.

One type of generator was foot-powered. It looked like a bicycle without wheels and had a small generator attached to the pedal chain. It was heavy, awkward to carry, and required a man to pump it for hours to recharge a battery. We had declined to bring one with us. The second alternative was a portable generator powered by a Briggs midget gasoline engine. It required gasoline, which had to be dropped or procured locally, and it was noisy. A third alternative was a water-wheel generator, which was in theory ideal for our area because of the abundant mountain streams, and because it was silent. One had been put aboard the aircraft that developed engine trouble and was among the cargo that had been jettisoned.

At times we had to use locally procured car batteries. When we needed a replacement battery a Partisan would be sent down the mountain to "liberate" one from the nearest German car or truck he could find. After we had finally received a miniature gasoline generator, when the charge in the battery became too low it would be carried to our hidden generator for recharging, but we were always short of gasoline. After several urgent requests, and several drops to us in which no gasoline was included, we radioed that "this could be our last contact." It was not an idle threat; it almost happened. A last alternate source of power was the local electrical supply, which we used occasionally when we were near a village that had electric lights and therefore its own power.

We always asked for reliable men to carry the radio and batteries, and explained to them that the set was the only link by which we could bring in desperately needed supplies by air. Their officers told them that no matter what happened they were expected to protect the radio and battery from being captured or damaged. Yet, on two occasions when we were surprised by a German attack, the radio was forgotten as the Partisan to whom it had been entrusted panicked and ran for cover. Once I picked up the abandoned radio and carried it into the forest.

Since the German Sicherheitsdienst (the Nazi security and intelligence service) monitored all our radio traffic, encryption of both our outgoing and incoming radio messages was obligatory. There is often confusion between the terms "codes" and "ciphers." Codes are systems in which an entire word or group of commonly used words is represented by a single number, to be found in large codebooks. Ciphers are those systems in which the individual letters in a message are either mixed up or are substituted letter-for-letter by other letters, or both. Our encryption systems were technically ciphers, although the term "codes" is often used to mean both codes and ciphers.

Our ciphers were of two types. One, called double transposition, used as a key for each message a different phrase selected from a book or a poem and required a complicated process of writing the message horizontally on a grid of graph paper and reading off the letters vertically column by column in the sequence provided by the key phrase. Double transposition meant that this process was repeated a second time, thus further complicating the task of breaking or deciphering the message by the enemy. But it was far from secure against the German code-breaking experts. For us, it was so complicated it was easy to make mistakes.

The other cipher system was called a one-time pad. We brought with us thick paper tablets each of 100 or more pages. On each page were rows of random letters written in five-letter groups that filled the page, line after line. To encipher a message we first wrote our clear text message letter-by-letter above the random letters on the pad. Then using a conversion table, which we soon memorized, we converted each pair of letters into a single cipher letter which, with each succeeding letter arrived at the same way, formed the enciphered message ready for radio transmission.

For example, to encipher the word "tonite" we would first write T O N I T E above the letters on the pad, thus:

| message | T O N I T | E |
| one-time pad | K P A F C | A |

In the next step we would use the conversion or look-up table (printed on a small square of silk), as shown in the reconstructed sample table below. We would first find T along the top of the table and K down the side. By reading both down from T and across from K we would find O at the intersection and write that as the first letter of the enciphered message. The steps would be repeated for each letter following—in this case producing the enciphered "tonite" as OMIHS A. The silk conversion table never changed and was not in itself secret. If we lost it, it would be of no use to anyone else because the security was provided by the random nature of the letters on the

	A	B	C	D	E	F	G	H	I	J	K	L	M	N	O	P	Q	R	S	T	U	V	W	X	Y	Z
A	E	L	G	R	**A**	H	C	F	N	W	Q	B	P	**I**	V	M	K	D	Z	U	T	O	J	Y	X	S
B	S	K	P	O	I	M	T	Y	E	X	B	U	F	Z	D	C	V	W	A	G	L	Q	R	J	H	N
C	N	R	K	V	U	O	X	W	M	P	C	Z	I	A	F	J	Y	B	T	**S**	E	D	H	G	Q	L
D	M	V	N	J	W	L	R	O	Y	D	U	F	A	C	H	Z	T	G	X	Q	K	B	E	S	I	P
E	P	G	M	S	H	R	B	E	Z	U	W	O	C	Q	L	A	N	F	D	X	J	Y	K	T	V	I
F	J	O	T	L	S	W	V	I	**H**	A	N	D	Z	K	B	Y	X	U	E	C	R	G	F	Q	P	M
G	H	Q	I	P	X	T	S	A	C	O	Y	R	W	V	J	D	B	L	G	F	Z	N	M	E	K	U
H	K	T	F	M	Y	C	I	P	G	S	A	Q	D	W	Z	H	L	V	J	B	X	R	N	U	E	O
I	I	U	L	W	P	S	O	R	A	Y	X	C	V	T	G	E	Z	H	F	N	B	M	D	K	J	Q
J	Q	N	J	T	K	X	M	U	V	C	E	W	G	B	S	R	A	P	O	D	H	I	L	F	Z	Y
K	Z	Y	Q	K	R	I	U	N	F	V	D	X	S	H	T	W	C	E	M	**O**	G	J	P	L	B	A
L	C	S	A	X	M	N	Q	J	U	H	Z	V	E	F	W	T	G	Y	B	P	I	L	O	D	R	K
M	W	F	H	G	O	B	D	C	S	R	T	Y	Q	X	E	U	M	J	I	K	P	Z	A	N	L	V
N	X	H	O	Q	L	V	Y	B	P	T	M	E	K	S	C	I	D	Z	N	J	W	F	U	A	G	R
O	F	D	X	B	Q	A	P	L	O	Z	S	H	R	Y	I	G	E	M	K	W	V	U	T	C	N	J
P	L	I	E	N	C	Z	W	X	B	K	J	A	O	D	**M**	S	R	Q	P	Y	U	V	G	H	T	F
Q	G	Z	V	Y	T	P	A	S	L	Q	O	I	U	R	K	F	J	N	H	E	M	C	X	W	D	B
R	Y	M	S	U	J	K	L	T	Q	E	F	G	B	P	R	N	I	O	C	H	D	X	Z	V	A	W
S	D	J	R	A	Z	Q	N	V	T	B	L	K	X	G	P	O	F	C	W	I	Y	H	S	M	U	E
T	O	C	B	H	N	U	K	D	X	M	G	S	J	E	A	Q	P	T	L	R	F	W	V	I	Y	Z
U	V	E	Y	Z	B	J	G	H	R	F	P	M	L	O	N	K	S	I	Q	T	U	A	W	X	C	D
V	R	W	U	I	V	Y	Z	K	D	J	H	T	N	M	X	P	Q	A	S	L	C	E	B	O	F	G
W	U	B	D	C	G	F	E	Z	W	N	Q	X	T	J	Y	V	K	S	R	M	A	P	I	L	O	H
X	A	P	Y	D	F	E	H	G	J	I	V	N	M	L	O	B	W	X	U	Z	S	K	Q	R	C	T
Y	B	A	X	E	D	G	F	Q	N	L	K	J	Y	I	U	W	H	T	V	R	O	S	P	C	M	Z
Z	T	X	W	F	E	D	J	M	K	G	I	P	H	Z	Q	L	O	R	Y	A	U	V	C	B	S	N

one-time pad. To decipher the message the base radio station would reverse the process, using a second copy of the same page of random letters in the duplicate of our one-time pad that the base retained. Here the first letter of the enciphered message, O, would be written above K, the corresponding letter on the one-time pad. Using another copy of our look-up table, the cipher clerk would then find column O at the top of the table and line K on the left. At the intersection of column and line, the cryptographer would find T, the first letter of the original word "tonite."

No part of the pad would be used twice, thus the name "one-time pad." As each page was used it was destroyed. But if it were not, and it fell into the wrong hands, the system would still be protected; only the messages on that page would be compromised.

In the event of an emergency in which we had lost our one-time pad we were given a back-up system based on this couplet:

> A spaniel, a woman and a walnut tree.
> The more you beat them the better they be.

How times have changed since then!

The one-time pad cipher, properly used, was impossible to break without having a duplicate of the same page of the one-time pad. Unlike other cipher systems, if an enciphered message together with its clear text fell into the hands of the enemy it would be of no value in breaking other messages done on the one-time pad. It was also much easier to use than the cumbersome double transposition. Its disadvantage was that we had to carry a bulky one-time pad or tablet. There were other disadvantages for high-volume traffic because of the problem of preparing huge quantities of random-sequence letters for the pads.

The one-time system is the only type of cipher that is totally secure. That it cannot be broken can be rigorously proven. Because the sequence of letters on the one-time pad is purely random, the enciphered letter representing an actual letter in the message will always be random. There is no secret key to uncover.

I became intrigued by the history of the one-time pad system and after the war did a bit of digging. It was not a Second World War development. Its practical and theoretical origins go much further back. The one-time pad, as we had known it, was invented and openly patented at the end of the First World War by an American engineer working for AT&T. In the interwar years AT&T tried without success to get the State Department to use the system for diplomatic messages. The German Foreign Ministry, however, quickly adopted it; but it was not until the eve of the Second World War that it came into general use.

The theory of probability on which the one-time pad is based was developed in the seventeenth century by two French mathematicians, Blaise Pascal and Pierre de Fermat. Yet for the next 250 years not one of the many people engaged in inventing cipher systems made use of this powerful theory. Instead the cryptographers produced more and more complex codes and ciphers, which became harder to break but which were not invulnerable, since they all contained a secret key or pattern that ultimately could be found.

We were given the one-time pad system by SOE and a double transposition system by OSS when we went into Yugoslavia. To our relief OSS soon parachuted to us its own one-time pad. Double transposition was a headache and subject to errors that would make the entire message unreadable. Errors in a one-time pad system affected only single letters and it was usually possible to piece out and read a message containing garbles.

Our radio transmissions were not only regularly monitored by the Germans, but our position during each transmission was determined by triangulation of our signal by two or more sensitive receivers each measuring the bearing at which our signal was the strongest. German officers interrogated at the end of the war confirmed that our locations were closely plotted as we moved. Had the Germans known the content of our messages as well as the location of our transmission signal they would have been in a better position to pick us up or to protect the rail lines we planned to attack. As it was they learned more than enough from locating our positions through our radio transmissions to cause us considerable trouble. This was one more reason we changed our location nearly every day.

Another danger was, of course, that we might be captured and forced to continue our radio contacts under the control of either the Nazi Sicherheitsdienst or the Abwehr, the German army intelligence service. Alternatively, the Germans might themselves use our set and codes to feed false information to OSS and SOE. This was, of course, what did happen in the Netherlands during the war, when Major Giskes of the Abwehr for two years ran his famous "Operation North Pole," in which the Germans controlled communications of British agents with SOE in England. As a result fifty-four Dutch agents were captured as they arrived by parachute; almost all were executed. SOE London had failed to notice that the security check of the first agent captured by the Germans was absent from all messages from him— meaning that he had been captured.

We too were given a secret danger signal to use in the event we were captured to indicate that our messages were being dictated by the Germans. Danger signals were such things as regularly mis-spelling a word in every message but spelling it correctly if we were in enemy hands. Also, if the base were to suspect we might be con-trolled, an innocuous question would be asked to which the man in the field would answer one way if controlled and another way if not. Often people behind the lines were given two danger signals, one that they could reluctantly give up to their captors under interrogation, and another that could still be used to warn their own base.

When, after the war, I reviewed my own wartime messages that were received and deciphered by the British base radio station, I found on nearly all of them the handwritten notation "Security check present." Most were signed "Sheila Mills," who must have been the code room security officer. On a very few she had noted "Security check not present." Apparently we had inadvertently failed to include it. How much of a question this raised I don't know, but presumably any doubts were resolved in subsequent messages.

In retrospect nearly all of the danger signals used by SOE and OSS had the weakness of needing almost error-free radio transmission to be spotted. But in actual operations this was most unlikely because of inadequate agent training, weak radio signals, and enemy jamming. I have been surprised on seeing copies of my own messages both as they were received in cipher and then as deciphered. Some were so garbled that it took considerable imagination to correct the errors, and some parts had been erroneously reconstructed. Under these circumstances a danger signal subtle enough to escape the enemy's notice could easily have been drowned out by the garbles.

■ On one occasion we were nearly done in when we violated our own rule of moving every day in order to stay one jump ahead of German radio position locators. We had stopped for the night at a peasant farmhouse high in the mountains. The next morning was sunny and warm. It was altogether a beautiful day and there were no apparent German moves against us. Foolishly, we decided to stay a second day. That afternoon Jim had another radio contact with Italy. The next morning I was in the front of the house when I heard aircraft overhead. I looked up and saw three German Stuka dive-bombers above us at low level. Since we often saw German aircraft passing over and they usually were not interested in us, I didn't pay much attention. Then I saw them nose over into an almost vertical dive.

They hit a farmhouse and barn no more than 400 yards away with 500-pound bombs, and then strafed the house with 20-mm-cannon fire for about 20 minutes. Obviously, our radio transmission the afternoon before had been monitored and our position plotted. All eight members of the family living there were killed in the attack, and indirectly we were the cause. We ourselves were saved only by the fact that there were two houses close together instead of the more usual one standing alone. The pilots had picked the wrong one.

Signal plans provided to each behind-the-lines operator included the frequency he should use initially to make contact with base station. A small number of additional frequencies were also included so that transmissions from the base and from the field could be tried on different frequencies in order to find the ones giving the best reception in each direction. Some frequencies, called guard channels, were monitored by the base station 24 hours a day. Emergency contacts could thus be made at any time. Frequencies for transmission were controlled by crystals that could be plugged into the transmitter, and which oscillated at precise frequencies. The difficulty for us was that the transmission frequencies available to Jim Fisher were limited to the eight crystals he had been provided, and which he carried in his pack. Some of these turned out to be useless for our location. Others were good only in daylight hours and some only at night.

Communication was, of course, by Morse code rather than by voice. Each operator tapped out his messages using a brass key similar to that used by old-time railway telegraph operators. I soon learned from Jim that each operator had his own distinctive way of keying, which could be recognized by others as unique to that operator, much as a fingerprint is unique to each individual. One base station operator, clearly identified for Jim by his "fist," especially aroused his wrath. Almost invariably, in the middle of a contact, this operator would suddenly signal, "Wait five minutes." Jim was certain the man was simply taking time out for a cup of coffee. And it usually happened when our battery was low, or in a rainstorm in a forest when Jim was trying to get his radio and as much of himself as possible under an inadequate ground cloth—almost always leaving his rear end to get thoroughly soaked.

Jim's rage increased over the months he had to work with this unknown base operator, to whom he had no way to communicate his anger. While on the nightly marches Jim would be totally consumed with plotting his revenge. His final scheme was that when he at last got out to Italy he would go to the base station and stand in the doorway until he heard the familiar "fist"—since he knew neither the name of the man nor what he looked like. When he had him identified, he would, in his imagination, walk over to the man, pick him up by the back of the neck, and without saying a word knock him cold—then walk out. He must have relived this a hundred times, savoring the thought as he plodded up and down mountain trails with nothing else to do but follow the man ahead and try to shift his pack to ease his sore shoulders and back. I never knew whether he carried out his plan when he got to Italy or what he would have done if "he" turned out to be "she."

The British often assigned young women to base stations as operators. They soon came to recognize the "fists" of the men behind the lines with whom they communicated and strong emotional attachments often developed between a woman and her agent, even though they had never seen each other or even heard each other's voice. In spite of the strictest rules against any informal "conversations" for security reasons, they often could not resist asking, in the clear, about the health and safety of their men.

■ One incident that resulted in the loss of two RAF Halifax bombers and their crews directly overhead as they were dropping supplies to us drove home the possible consequences of the slightest mistake in radio communications security. Our signal plan provided that each incoming message would carry at the beginning of the message a priority indicator so that if we were on the run and not able to decode all the messages immediately we would know which we should do first. These priorities were D, DD, DDD, and DDDD (in order of increasing urgency) and XXX indicating air operations (usually meaning that the message would tell us that a parachute drop "is scheduled for tonight").

Through what must have been an oversight, the British signal procedures provided that the priority given at the beginning of each enciphered message was to be sent in the clear (not enciphered), although it would have been simple to encipher the priority along with the message itself. We would then have needed to decipher only the first five letters of each message to determine its priority. This same practice was used throughout Yugoslavia without change during the several months I was with the Partisans, although in British operations run out of England to France, the Low Countries, and Scandinavia, the message priority was always enciphered.

This may sound like a minor administrative detail but here are the consequences. On November 6, 1944, we received an XXX priority message saying that two Halifaxes would drop guns and explosives to us that night.

We were at the drop area well before the scheduled arrival time, and soon the first aircraft arrived. After we exchanged recognition signals that confirmed to the aircraft captain that he was indeed at the right spot, he circled and made his first pass to drop containers. In the middle of the run, we heard a short burst of 20-mm-cannon fire and immediately a thin spike of flame appeared from the aircraft. After a few seconds the bomber burst into flames and made a fiery arc as it rolled over and plunged to earth about a mile away. While we were trying to recover from the horror of what we had seen, the second Halifax arrived, apparently oblivious to the destruction of the first; it too was flashing its recognition signal.

We had received on a previous drop the ground unit of a ground-to-air radio known as an S-phone. We had been told that with it we could communicate by voice with aircraft flying above us that had been equipped with the other half of the system. Jim was wearing the ground unit strapped to a harness over his shoulders. I immediately told him to warn the second aircraft that a German night fighter was in the area and to take whatever evasive action was possible. Jim's translation of this was to yell repeatedly into the microphone "German night fighter! Get the hell out of here fast!" There was no answer from the plane. Within a few seconds we heard the sound of a fighter in a power dive, then there was a second burst of 20-mm fire and the second bomber burst into flames and went down.

We dispatched Partisans on the run to the first crashed aircraft. On their return they reported that no one had survived and that no one had been able to parachute from the burning plane, undoubtedly because they were too low to get out before the plane hit the ground. The second plane crashed in nearby German-held territory. We were unable to get a report on the crew who, if they survived, would have fallen into German hands.

On the radio contact the next morning I sent as detailed a message as was possible, given the limitations of our radio and ciphers, on the night's losses. From the return message it was obvious that the RAF operational command in Italy believed that the two aircraft had collided while maneuvering to drop. My second message tried to make it clear that the first aircraft had been destroyed before the second arrived and that several minutes separated the two events. When I returned to Italy some months later and visited the Mediterranean Allied Air Command, the midair collision theory was set in concrete (or in a pile of official reports) and no one was interested in reopening the case.

I was convinced at the time (and I remain so) that German intelligence, after monitoring several months of clandestine radio transmissions from the Balkans, tumbled to the significance of XXX sent in the clear at the beginning of certain messages to us—that it meant Allied aircraft were scheduled to drop that night. This they could easily establish by correlating German observations of Allied aircraft having been in our area with radio messages directed to us that they had monitored. When they saw another XXX message to us it seems certain that they concluded they would have a good chance of making a kill by sending a night fighter over us to wait for our planes to arrive.

The lack of lightweight and rugged radios and transmitters and secure cipher systems played an important role in the early days of the Yugoslav resistance. On one hand, the operations of both resistance movements were crippled by the lack of radios and secure ciphers. On the other hand, the British were able to add significantly to their knowledge of what was going on in Yugoslavia because of the insecure ciphers of the Germans, the Chetniks, and the Partisans.

The British knew in 1943 from intercepted German radio traffic that the Germans had broken both Mihailovic's and Tito's codes, and were reading their messages to subordinate commanders. British deciphered intercepts of these German radio messages in turn provided the British with strong evidence in the early days that some of Mihailovic's subordinate commanders were collaborating with the Germans and the Italians, and with their puppet governments in Yugoslavia. They also provided Churchill and the British general staff with evidence that the Partisans were effectively tying down large Axis forces. The matter of radio codes thus had a decisive influence on policy.

CHAPTER 10

Liberation of a
Mountain Valley

ntil August 1, 1944, no liberated territory existed in the Partisan Fourth Zone within the wartime German Reich, the area north of the Sava River. A few remote mountainous areas were called "liberated" simply because of the absence of German troops. Until then the Partisans had operated only in the mountains. Every village had a German garrison and Partisan movements were primarily at night. The Partisans were dispersed in small units except when brought together for an attack on a German-held target. During June and July we remained with Fourth Zone headquarters and moved with them almost every night.

Our security lay not in secrecy, which was impossible to maintain, but in constant movement. We were dependent on an invisible screen of civilians—old men, women, and children—to warn us of approaching German patrols, or of ambushes laid for us on mountain trails. Although for seven months we were never further than five miles from the nearest German post, and often much closer, we were never caught in an ambush, and were seldom surprised. In good part this was luck; many others were ambushed by SS troops or the White Guard. The plain fact was that we could not have survived for even a week if the civilian population had been hostile.

In late July the Fourth Zone headquarters launched a daring offensive of their own. The Partisans assembled their fighting brigades to attack the German garrisons in the Gornja Savinjska Dolina—the narrow valley of the upper Savinja River and its tributary, the Dreta. Descending from the upper slopes of the Karawanken Alps and curving to the east, the valley was surrounded by high mountains. The terrain spread and opened, downstream, only at its eastern junction with another valley descending from the north. There was a reasonable chance it could remain in Partisan hands, but only so long as the Germans did not move in reinforcements from outside Stajerska.

The operation was well planned. All five brigades in Stajerska were employed. The Sixth "Slander" Brigade was ordered to attack the German garrisons at the villages of Luce and Ljubno. The Eleventh "Zidansek" Brigade was to mount a diversionary attack on Gornji Grad, and to set up ambushes on the roads leading to the three villages from the German-held towns to the west, north, and east. The three brigades of the Fourteenth Division would form a second protective barrier further to the east by laying ambushes, blockading and mining roads, bridges, and railroad sections, and launching diversionary attacks on other garrisons that might come to the relief of those at Luce, Ljubno, and Gornji Grad. In addition, the Koroski Odred high in the Karawanken Alps would block any German approaches over the high passes to the north. And the odred on the Sava would launch still another diversionary attack on the Litija garrison twenty miles to the south.

The operations began on the night of July 30. Ljubno was attacked from the north by one battalion and from the south by the second battalion. The third was held in reserve. Twelve pillboxes around the perimeter were successively eliminated with grenades lobbed into them. Under covering fire explosive charges were placed against the walls of three strong points and detonated. Prisoners were taken in two while the third went up in flames, with no survivors. The remaining strong point held out through the night and into the next day.

Gordon Bush and I observed the fighting from a grassy slope on the flank of the mountain overlooking the village. It was a brilliant

Alpine summer day. The grass was emerald green, and the panorama of the valley with its fields, drying racks, and houses was breathtakingly beautiful. German soldiers were in the Ljubno church steeple, and we were in plain view a couple of hundred yards away. Suddenly, they began firing at us. Quite irrationally, I felt outraged. We were not shooting at them! But we prudently moved a few yards away where we were out of their sights.

The attack continued as Partisans moved behind walls and houses toward the center of the village where the Germans were holed up in the remaining strong point—a heavy stone building. Soon an Italian 75-mm gun appeared on the road into the village. The gun had been dismantled in Dolenjska and man-packed piece by piece across the border, the Sava, and the mountains. It had been reassembled in the woods for the attack and brought to the battle not by a truck, or even by artillery horses, but by six strong Partisans. Together they lifted the trail of the gun, crouching behind the shield as best they could and pushing it into firing position. Not more than 200 yards from the garrison wall they stopped, rammed home a round, closed the breech, laid the gun on the wall by squinting along the barrel, and fired. The wall was breached and a second round fired, which exploded inside the building. The Partisans then stormed through the breach with Sten guns and grenades. There was not much fight left in the defenders. They filed out covered with dust, hands in the air. Several of the garrison had fled to nearby houses and continued to fight. Those houses were destroyed with explosive charges, or by setting them afire, to complete the capture of the village.

At the same time another battalion of the "Slander" Brigade attacked the garrison at Luce, seven kilometers upstream. The main German force there was holed up in the church rectory. Because of heavy enemy fire the Partisans did not take the strong point, but kept it under fire into the next day. In the afternoon they demanded and got the surrender of the garrison.

While this was going on the "Zidansek" Brigade maintained its attack on Gornji Grad. This was originally planned as only a feint. However, because the attacks against Luce and Ljubno were going well the brigade was ordered to complete the attack. The principal strong point was inside a medieval castle surrounded by a heavy stone wall. Rather than attacking it the Partisans demanded surrender, threatening to bring up their artillery—the one piece that had just been used at Ljubno to reduce the strong point there. The morning of the second day the remaining garrison surrendered.

Two attempts were made by the Germans to relieve the three garrisons, one from the west over the mountains, and one from the lower valley to the east. But the forces available to them were inadequate, both in number and fighting quality. Neither was able to break through the Partisan blockades.

At the end of the day at Ljubno, as I left the center of the village I suddenly came to an open field behind a peasant house. Several men, some in bedraggled German uniforms and some in civilian clothes, were lined up facing a group of Partisans. Two Partisans had raised their submachine guns and at that instant both opened fire on the Germans, who crumpled to the ground. Afterwards I pressed Commissar Borstnar to tell me why these men had been executed. I didn't get a straightforward answer. All he said was that they had been guilty of atrocities against the Partisans. Nor could I get an answer on whether there had been any proceedings beforehand. It turned out that of the burgermeisters of the three villages, two had been shot and one spared. The two had been "bad mayors" and one had been a "good mayor," he said. I suspected that he had earned his way by secretly aiding the Partisans in the months before.

Two years after the war I was watching a movie in New York when something on the screen reminded me of those executions. I nearly blacked out. Yet at the time in Ljubno I had not been particularly troubled by what I had seen. Psychological protective defenses were obviously at work within me at the time; two years later they had disappeared.

The Italian artillery piece was the substitute for the mountain guns that I had asked be dropped. The request had been turned down because the supply of ammunition by air was considered impractical. I disagreed. Even a dozen rounds would have made a great difference in assaulting local garrisons. Only six rounds had been used in this entire operation. I doubted that the Partisans had brought from Dolenjska more than a total of twelve rounds for the Italian gun.

The first "liberated territory" in Stajerska—in truth, inside the Third Reich itself—had been created in the Gornja Savinjska Dolina. To protect this achievement, the Partisans blew several concrete bridges further downstream across both rivers, over which armored vehicles would have to pass in order to retake the valley.

To the Partisans, it was clear that the printing press was as mighty as the machine gun. After the liberation of the valley one of the first Partisan requests to me was that a printing press be dropped by parachute. The reply to my message passing on their request was that none were available in Italy but one was being requisitioned from Cairo. I have no recollection of its ever arriving, though the Partisans did not slow their propaganda output for the local population for that reason.

We and the Partisans fully expected that the capture of the valley would provoke a strong German effort to retake it within a very few days. We therefore immediately set up a new drop point in the level floor of the valley and radioed for weapons. "Priority radios, PIAT ammo, rifles, Stens, Brens, mortars. Can take as many planes as you can send. Future operations against lines of communication depend on holding this area as base. Please send planes every night til further notice." Base Operations answered: "Your sorties stand high on priority each night. Only met [meteorology, i.e., weather] preventing at moment," but added a few days later: "Commitments in France and Italy will seriously decrease August sorties. Do not expect get you more than thirty sorties unless weather improves considerably."

Five days after our capture of the valley the returns were in. More than 200 Germans were killed in the three attacks. The Partisans had been prudent in their attacks and had not made frontal assaults against heavy fire, preferring to wait out the surrender of the garrisons. Their losses were much lower.

Also captured were a large number of machine guns, rifles, and ammunition, the equivalent of several aircraft loads by parachute. Nearly three hundred Slovene Wehrmänner (a German auxiliary force in Stajerska) were captured, all of whom, I was told, had joined the Partisans. They undoubtedly had been impressed into garrison duty by the Germans and were glad to be released. They were probably almost equally reluctant to join the Partisans, but their other options were not attractive. Some of the captured ethnic Germans were stripped of clothing and shoes, and released to walk back to Celje, their headquarters. The Partisans considered this good propaganda, as it humiliated the Germans before the townspeople who saw them straggle back in their underwear.

The disposition of prisoners taken in the operation was reported to Slovene headquarters. In his report the Fourth Zone chief of staff wrote that they had shot all the Germans taken at Ljubno because they had not surrendered immediately but had continued to resist. Because the Luce garrison had quickly surrendered on the demand of the Partisans, most of them had been disarmed and set free to go back to Celje. The commander and one gendarme were shot because they had "terrorized" the villagers. The Germans who had surrendered had been taken to Gornji Grad where the garrison was still holding out to persuade it to surrender.

In Stajerska there were only three ways to deal with those who were captured: turn them loose, allow them to join the Partisans, or shoot them. Only those of Slovene blood could be trusted to join the Partisans. There was no way to hold those captured as prisoners.

On August 13 the Partisans attacked and destroyed the German garrison at Rimske Toplice on the main rail line between Celje and Zidani Most. I radioed: "Afterwards Pzns visited German military hospital there and held political hour for German patients telling them what swine they were to kill Pzn prisoners."

■ On August 19 we received a long, seven-part message from Maclean's headquarters. On decoding we found it was a translation of an order from Tito to the Zone command which we were instructed to deliver. In it Tito directed the Fourth Zone Partisans to launch a major attack against German rail and road communications in northern Slovenia during the first week of September. The attack was to be part of a coordinated plan of action throughout Yugoslavia to destroy the lines of communication over which the German armies in the Balkans were expected to withdraw northward. OSS intelligence specialists reported that eight German divisions remained in Greece, and sixteen in Albania and Yugoslavia. Anything that we could do to delay or prevent their withdrawal and redeployment to the major Anglo-American and Russian battlefronts would be important.

I later learned that Maclean and Peter Moore had conceived of the plan, codenamed "Ratweek," reasoning that a German withdrawal from the lower Balkans would become imperative as the Red Army approached Serbia from the east. If the Partisans and the Italy-based Allied air forces cut the main railroad and roads from Macedonia north through Belgrade and Zagreb to Maribor and Ljubljana, the only retreat route left to Germans would be along the narrow roads through the mountains and along the Dalmatian coast. The former were exposed to Allied air and Partisan attack and the latter to Allied attack by sea. General Wilson, Supreme Allied Commander in the Mediterranean, agreed to order increased Allied air attacks and air-drops to the Partisans in support of the plan. Maclean, promising strong Allied air and weapons support, next got Tito's approval. This message from Tito was the only time a Partisan internal communication had come through our radio links. Usually the Partisans were very secretive about their communications.

We were told to caution the Partisan command that any reference to the plan in radio messages prior to September 1, the starting date, "will prejudice surprise." It was obvious that Maclean's staff was concerned about the near-certainty that the Germans were reading the Partisan radio traffic. Their concern was well-founded. British code-breakers were in fact reading German messages that included their intercepts of Partisan radio communications. Maclean did not have access to these intercepts because he was himself exposed to the risk of capture. But he was told of the weaknesses of Partisan signal security messages, and in turn told Tito that the British had learned from a German POW that German intelligence had broken Partisan ciphers. Even then it must have required all of Maclean's persuasive talents to convince Tito and his paranoid staff to use our communications.

If the Germans were to learn through reading Partisan messages that their own ciphers had been cracked they would of course immediately change them. The Allies would thus be denied access to all future messages while our code-breakers worked frantically to break the new cipher. This could take weeks or months. To preserve the invaluable advantage their knowledge of the German ciphers gave them, the British and Americans often refrained from using the information gained from German traffic to protect their own troops, if such use was at all likely to indicate to the Germans that their ciphers had been broken.

In his order Tito spelled out the tasks assigned to the Fourth Zone. The first priority was the destruction of the Zidani Most–Ljubljana railway and the Celje-Ljubljana road. The railway north from Zidani Most to Maribor was also to be closed. The Western Allies would deliver weapons and explosives to support the attacks.

The message ordered that the Allied liaison officers be kept fully informed of the Partisan plans and operations during this period. The order concluded:

> This order is issued through the Allied Liaison Officers and you will proceed in accordance with it. SFSN.
>
> Signed Supreme Commander Marshal of JUGOSLAVIA TITO. [SFSN was the ubiquitous SMRT FASIZMU—SLOBODA NARODU]

A radio message to us the next day said that "Allied air operations your formation area will be attacking opportunity targets reported by you whose importance overrides targets prearranged in other areas." Radio communications with both the Partisan brigades attacking the roads and railroads and our Italian base of operations would be essential if these combined air and ground attacks were to be successful. We still had not received the replacement and backup radios we had been begging for since June.

The Partisan commander, Joze Borstnar, and chief of operations, Franc Primozic, set to work planning the attacks. The Fourteenth Division was ordered to move to the eastern part of Stajerska to attack the railroads there. Two brigades were to move south to cut the railroad along the Sava River. We agreed that Bush would accompany the Fourteenth Division and Welles would go with the two brigades to the Sava. Partisan intelligence officers with the shorter-range radios we planned to supply by airdrops would be at key points to report on German movements and targets of opportunity for the Allied air forces.

The targets we jointly selected were a bridge and rock cuts on the main Vienna line and five kilometers of track to be removed and destroyed along the Sava. The major bridge across the Sava at Litija would be attacked by combined units of the Seventh Corps from Dolenjska, south of the Sava, and the Fourth Zone brigades from the north side. The main Ljubljana-Celje road would be mined, but there was little that could be done on the ground that would do more than delay major troop movements along this road.

The remainder of August and the first ten days of September were filled with preparations for Ratweek, supporting operations, and reporting results.

On August 26 I radioed: "Fourteenth Division operating eastern part of Fourth Zone are without explosives. Unless they are delivered immed to Javorski [our drop point there] these troops cannot be effective against lines of comm during coming operation." Our next nearest drop point was thirty miles away, too far to man-pack four tons of explosives in time for the scheduled operations. Our frustrations continued. On August 31, the day before the coordinated attacks throughout Yugoslavia were to begin, I signaled: "Load of rifles but no explosives dropped Javorski. Unless you get explosives to Fourteenth Div their action will be minor. They plan to attack again tunnel and bridge [that first had been attacked on June 19] but cant do it with bare hands. Send final two loads of explosives to Javorski and two to Maravce [for the brigades on the Sava]. If more available send rifles and PIATs to all areas."

BELOW: The surrender of the German garrison at Ljubno during the Partisan liberation of Gornja Savinjska Dolina, August 1944; townspeople watch from the edges of the village square (*Lindsay*)

OPPOSITE: The Stampetov viaduct on the Ljubljana-Trieste rail line, blown up in 1943 by the Fourteenth Partisan division, which was transferred to Stajerska in February 1944 (*Lindsay*)

BELOW: Engine and railway cars derailed on the Ljubljana–Zidani Most line, summer 1944 (*Museum of the People's Revolution*)

ABOVE: Derailed engine and railway cars on the Ljubljana-Maribor rail line, late in 1944 (*Museum of the People's Revolution*)

OPPOSITE: A daylight parachute drop of supplies by Allied bombers near Okonina in the Gornja Savinjska Dolina, fall 1944—a rare event, since nearly all drops were made at night (*Lindsay*)

The reply September 1 was heartening. "Four sorties explosives arranged for tonite." On the afternoon contact that day: "Two Dakotas Maravce two Javorski TOT 2040 GMT onwards. Fires LOVE [the letter L] of twelve. Air letter HOW ground WILLIAM. Ensure correct fires." But on the next day, September 2, the incoming message read: "Have been trying for last four nights to get two loads mainly explosives to each Javorski and Maravce. Hope they will succeed tonite. Have two more standing by for tomorrow in case of failure to either point."

Another exasperated plea for radios went out on September 2: "We have been using MI-6 radio, Pzn generator, and German batteries since arrival. We first requested radio equipment to replace lost equipment in May. Since then eleven separate messages have been sent to you asking for radios but to date nothing has been received. [MI-6] considering move to another area. This will leave us without set." We finally received one set on September 10—and continued to argue about our need for a backup.

The reports on the results of the attacks ordered by Tito were disappointing. The brigades operating against the Vienna line did not attempt to attack again, as planned, the tunnel they had blown in June and the bridges they had failed to cut. Instead, they concentrated on ripping up sections of track. These the Germans promptly repaired, keeping at least one track open. The brigades also reported they were unable to get near the bridge at Tremerje south of Celje, another of the agreed targets. The bridges and tunnels were now well guarded, a reaction to our attacks in June.

The operations against the Sava line appeared to be more successful. The Partisans destroyed 1,500 meters of track either by blowing the roadbed and retaining walls into the river or by dropping rock from the sides of cuts onto the track to a height of more than 15 meters. Three smaller bridges were also blown.

Bush and Welles returned to Zone headquarters on September 11, and I reported their observations: "Welles reports opns on Zidani Most–Ljubljana line effective. However bridge over Sava near Litija not attacked although Hun in this area numbered between one and two hundred only. We believe they could have done this job successfully. Brigades in this area now moved back from RR to attack Mozirje garrison. Bush back from Fourteenth Division reports Pzns made no serious effort to cut Celje-Maribor line [to Vienna] except on one and two September when they removed fifteen hundred meters of track. After that no attacks were made although we had provided explosives. Traffic now believed moving uninterruptedly. Jerry making offensive in Pohorje and division has moved to area east side RR."

Life magazine war correspondent-photographer John Phillips had come from Italy into liberated territory south of the Sava, and accompanied the Partisan brigades from there for the attack on the Litija bridge. Although the attack failed, Phillips got some good pictures of Partisan activities and *Life* carried a picture article describing the action—and saying incorrectly that the bridge had been destroyed.

Jim Goodwin, Allied liaison at Slovene Partisan headquarters, had come up to join in the action, and was wounded in the leg when he took over command of one of the Partisan units when its officer was killed.

After repeated Partisan failures in the fall to do more than minor damage on the Zidani Most–Celje–Maribor line I finally recommended Allied air attacks on major targets as the only way to seriously interdict German north-south traffic. In response the Allied air forces bombed and destroyed one span of the rail bridge over the Drava at Maribor. Subsequently the key bridge at Zidani Most was also destroyed from the air.

In the midst of all this action a cipher clerk in Force 399 managed to turn at least some things upside down. He, or she, transcribed a deciphered message from us as "attacks against Zidani Most–Ljubljanal ineffective," and edited it to read "ineffective" instead of our intended "attacks against Zidani Most–Ljubljana line effective." The spacing between words should have given a clue. Force 399 replied sharply that our message directly contradicted our previous message. Baffled, we found no contradiction.

During June, July, and August the Fourth Zone Partisans had aggressively and enthusiastically responded to our proposals to cut the rail lines. In spite of some failures they had become effective once we were able to get explosives and weapons to them. These main lines had been denied to the Germans for a large part of the three-month period. But now, in September, with many more men under arms, and after a hundred or more airdrops, they were perceptibly less aggressive. We began to suspect that the Partisan brigades were under orders to attack the rail lines only if they were sure they would have few if any losses, and to avoid major targets that were defended, no matter how important.

It crossed my mind that the orders from Tito transmitted through us might have been secretly modified by Tito in a subsequent message through the Partisan radio link. In reviewing the Partisans' own history of the Fourth Zone years later, I found no mention of any special actions having been taken against the rail lines in that first week of September. Tito's message through our channels could have been meant simply to convince Maclean and the rest of us of their commitment to attacking the German routes of withdrawal. Reports from British and American officers with Partisan units further south were that several opportunities to block German withdrawal in their areas were not seized. In some cases the German withdrawal proceeded without opposition.

Equally disturbing, our relations with the Fourth Zone commissar, our principal contact with the Partisan command, had undergone a marked change. We were no longer treated as close allies and friends. Borstnar had moved from being Zone commissar to Zone commandant in August, and Dragomir Bencic-Brkin succeeded him as commissar.

■ On September 11 and 12 the Partisans launched new attacks to drive the German garrisons out of Mozirje and two other key towns at the lower end of our liberated valley—the Gornja Savinjska Dolina. By eliminating these garrisons the Partisans would make the liberated territory more secure from surprise attacks launched from only a few miles down the Savinja valley. These garrisons, like the garrisons of Ljubno, Luce, and Gornji Grad taken six weeks earlier, were manned in part by SS troops and in part by the Wehrmann- schaft. The latter, largely older Slovenes recruited to German service, did not have their hearts in the fighting. Most, rather than fight to the finish, surrendered when they found themselves surrounded by attacking Partisans.

In each of the three garrison towns the defenders were concen- trated in the strongest and most easily defended buildings, such as the churches and schools. Pillboxes had been built around the perimeters of the towns. Some were earth and logs, others were of heavy concrete. Several rings of barbed wire protected the strong points and slowed sudden charges by Partisan units.

The Partisans attacked under cover of night, first knocking out the pillboxes, then bringing the strong points under fire. Walls were breached by placing explosive charges of 10 to 25 kilos of plastic against them. The Partisans' single 75-mm artillery piece was again wheeled out to break open the walls of strong points that could not be reached by Partisans carrying explosive charges. Ambushes were set on all approaches to the towns under attack to prevent German reinforcements from relieving the besieged garrisons.

Mozirje, the nearest and strongest garrison, was attacked the night of September 11 by the "Slander" Brigade. By dawn most of the town had been taken. The enemy remained holed up in and around the church. When daylight came the Partisans withdrew out of range and prepared to resume the attack after darkness returned. The re- maining German forces, seeing no relief columns arriving, were not prepared to face a second night of attacks. They gave up at 5:30 P.M.

That same night the "Tomsic" Brigade attacked the garrisons in two villages farther down the valley where it broadened into an open plain. Both were captured. The "Zidansek" Brigade had been ordered to capture a third strong point in the lower valley. Just before the at- tack, however, the Partisans learned that the garrison had been rein- forced the day before. Rather than risk heavy losses the order was changed to limit the attack to a diversionary feint from the perimeter.

These attacks accomplished the basic objective of extending liberated territory further east, to the beginning of the lower Savinja valley. The Partisans lost only 15 killed. They reported they killed 96 enemy and took 330 Slovene prisoners. Again they demonstrated their prudence by not committing their forces in frontal assaults against entrenched enemy forces.

Again the captured Germans were shot. Most of the Slovene Wehrmänner who were taken prisoner were recruited into the Partisans. The Partisan operational report after the battles said:

> Eight Wehrmänner who had resisted to the last, who had caused suffering to our people, and who, according to the testimony of the townsfolk, had also been informers, were shot.

At the end of the fight the Partisan units withdrew to the mountains north and west of the valley. The day after their withdrawal strong German columns moved in from the east and reoccupied Mozirje and the other two villages. One reconnaissance patrol probed further into the liberated valley to within four miles of Ljubno. The Germans remained for two days, then withdrew after looting stores and homes and taking a large part of the livestock.

With the valley in our hands daily life became easier. We did not move into the villages but remained in peasant houses on the lower mountain slopes between the Savinja and the Dreta rivers. But we moved less often and the food was more plentiful. Although autumn had just begun, winter would come early in the mountains, and the prospect of not being constantly on the move through snow and ice was very attractive.

We occasionally visited Gornji Grad and were warmly welcomed by the villagers, who were mostly women and children. I remember particularly Nata, a friendly woman in her thirties at the inn. She had been in one of the German concentration camps and on her forearm was tattooed in green a five-digit number—her proof of imprisonment, of which she was very proud.

We expected a strong German reaction to liberation of the valley to come almost immediately. But it did not come until late October, nearly eleven weeks after the valley had been liberated. Instead of moving against us from Celje at the lower end of the valley, three columns of Germans attacked from the west. One column of a thousand men and two tanks came along the road across the ridge at the headwaters of the Dreta. Two smaller columns came over the mountains from the north into the upper end of the Savinja valley. All of the liberated territory was reoccupied.

The Partisans and most of the villagers and farmers withdrew to the mountains overlooking the valley. While we watched, the Germans torched the houses in each village. Clouds of smoke rose vertically above the flames, then drifted horizontally until they merged into a single dark brown cloud stretching the length of the valley. It was sickening to watch as the homes and possessions of those who had taken us in were destroyed.

Soon it became clear that this was a punitive sweep and that the Germans would withdraw quickly. Partisan units moved to positions on the steep forested slopes on either side of the road through which the Germans would withdraw westward to their base at Kamnik. As they retreated they came under heavy crossfire and suffered substantial losses fighting their way out. Most of those that were captured were held a day, interrogated, then stripped of their clothing and boots and sent barefooted in their underwear back to their barracks. The German authorities, to hide the humiliation from the townspeople, ordered the shutters drawn on all the houses they had to pass before reaching the barracks.

When we returned to the valley floor we came on the wrenching sight of villagers sifting through the still-warm ashes for metal utensils and bits of pottery that had not burned. Nails were recovered from the ashes of the wood they had held together, straightened and laid aside for rebuilding. Shards of pottery bowls were collected and later reassembled like three-dimensional jigsaw puzzles; they were held together by pieces of wire twisted tight around the outside of the bowls. I had seen destruction like this fairly often before, as the Germans burned the isolated farmhouses where we had been sheltered when we lived in the forest, but never on this scale.

Ever on the lookout for supplies for the Agitprop section, the od-red on the Sava now attacked a paper mill and "liberated" several tons of paper along with a small printing press. A print shop was immediately set up in the liberated valley to augment the German duplicators that had been used in the forest.

Although the valley had returned to Partisan control, there were increasingly ominous reports that the Germans were bringing new combat troops from the Balkans into the area, and that a drive to eliminate the Partisans in Stajerska would soon be launched. We could not understand why the Germans had allowed us to continue to use our valley as a base to receive large parachute drops, and to attack the key railroads over which they would have to withdraw their large forces still in Greece and Yugoslavia.

■ As additional aircraft were assigned to air supply operations, and as the number of airdrop points increased, the packing and dispatching of loads became a major management problem. It became increasingly clear that neither we nor base Air Operations had more than the vaguest understanding of each other's problems, capabilities, or limitations.

Each of us on the ground wanted our own loads delivered just as we had asked. But this created new and ever greater complications. The loads had to be assembled and packed before the night's schedule of drops was set at noon, then delivered to the proper aircraft before they were scheduled to take off at dusk. Weather was always fickle and loads for us might have to sit around for days waiting for weather in our area to open up. We were told by base operations that bad weather in the southern Alps continued to limit air operations to us. Meanwhile the planes had to be available for drops to other areas and loads for them had to be ready.

The Force 399 base operations tried to meet the problem by setting up standard loads that could be prepacked and delivered anywhere. One was explosives, one was weapons, and one small-arms ammunition. By the fall we were getting a lot of these standard loads, which helped us but didn't meet our urgent priorities. It seemed at times that total tonnage delivered rather than meeting priority requirements was the objective in Italy. Medical supplies also came in standard packages. But they always seemed to contain the less-needed items such as bandages, and to omit the antibiotics, anesthetics, and other supplies needed for surgery in our hidden mountain hospitals.

In view of their problems, base operations must have thought we were as unreasonable as we accused them of being. There was no sense in taking back to Brindisi a planeload of supplies if the right drop area couldn't be found. From time to time we were getting supplies requested by another Partisan group and they were getting our priority loads.

Base operations couldn't be expected to appreciate the deep frustration of a Partisan brigade that had been waiting for days for desperately needed supplies, only to receive supplies they couldn't use—as was the case with the hundred men without weapons who waited eight days for a drop of arms. When it finally came five planes dropped only the standard ammunition loads—and no guns. Our radio communications were limited to very brief messages, both for security reasons and to conserve our batteries, and even though we tried to explain our situation, our pleas were not getting through to people who assigned the aircraft and the loads.

In my communications to Italy I was also operating, as I discovered, under a misapprehension that may or may not have further confused matters. I had gone into Slovenia assuming from my briefings in Cairo and Italy, as well as from the terms of my appointment as senior Allied officer with the Fourth Zone Partisans, that Force 399 was fully an Anglo-American operation.

I also assumed that copies of my messages over the Force 399 radio link were automatically sent to OSS. I was surprised when Welles arrived carrying a letter from Lieutenant Deranian of OSS saying this was not so. "The so-called Allied mission is in reality not 'Allied' at all," he wrote, "but it is strictly British; and American officers assigned to it are on more or less 'detached duty' status with it. The Command of the Mission is strictly British. I didn't like it but

Brigadier Maclean has said that this is the way it is, and no one on an equal level or higher denies it."

■ One package air-dropped in the early autumn of that year was clearly not aimed at Partisan capabilities. Its arrival reminded us that outside our violent world peaceful procedures were still taking place. The package contained absentee ballots for a full U.S. Army battalion for the coming presidential election. There were no instructions, however, on how these ballots, after being marked and sealed, were to be delivered back to the army. I could only guess that the president, or the army general staff in Washington, had ordered that all U.S. troops, no matter where they were, must receive their absentee ballots. No exceptions and no excuses would be tolerated. The battalion-sized package was probably the smallest they had, so they sent it along. We put the ballots to good use as toilet paper, which was always in short supply.

CHAPTER 11

The Lure of Austria

During the last eighteen months of the war the penetration of Germany, including Austria, became the prime OSS and SOE target for the organization of intelligence and resistance nets. Sweden and Turkey were possible routes into Germany for legal travelers, but there were not many who would qualify. For clandestine penetration of the Reich the problem was a different and a difficult one. Bill Casey was responsible for OSS penetration efforts based in Britain. Allen Dulles, director of the CIA under presidents Eisenhower and Kennedy, ran the intelligence operations into Germany from Switzerland.

There was still another potentially important springboard for such operations: Partisan-held territory on the Austrian and Hungarian borders of Yugoslavia. Although the Partisan Fourth Zone area of operations lay largely outside the borders of prewar Austria, it was almost completely within the borders of Hitler's wartime German Reich. In Stajerska we provided the point of penetration closest to central Austria and to the interior of Germany. We had regular radio communication with Allied headquarters. We were able to receive parachute drops of men and supplies where an organized resistance provided local security. As the crow flies, we were closer to Berlin than to our air supply base at Brindisi.

The British, American, and Soviet clandestine services thus regarded our position as one of great potential as a final staging point for penetration of the Reich for both intelligence agents and the development of resistance groups. Since we were already inside the Reich, the border controls that elsewhere were barriers to the movement of agents from adjoining occupied countries could be avoided. In addition, we had regular courier lines set up from liberated Yugoslav territory south of the Sava, outside the German border.

Stajerska thus appeared to have unique capabilities to support the penetration of Germany itself. My orders from Fitzroy Maclean's headquarters, given to me before leaving Italy, included a task that had been added in ink: I was to develop the potential to penetrate both Austria and Hungary. OSS had given me similar instructions.

At first, enthusiasm ran high in both the British and American services. It would soon be replaced by frustration and tragedy. The British SOE was the first of the clandestine services to set up Austrian operations in the Fourth Zone operational area. Lieutenant Colonel Peter Wilkinson and Major Alfgar Hesketh-Prichard had gone to Tito's headquarters in central Yugoslavia in December of 1943 to obtain his approval to use the Partisan Fourth Zone as a transit point into the Reich. In 1942 when Wilkinson was head of the Central European section of SOE, he and Hesketh-Prichard had worked with the Czech intelligence service to organize the assassination by Czech agents sent from London of Obergruppenführer Reinhard Heydrich, the German "Protector" of the remnants of Bohemia and Moravia. Heydrich, known as "hangman Heydrich," was one of the most odious and hated of the Nazi SS leaders. The Czech government-in-exile in London had insisted on the assassination attempt even though they knew it would bring down on the Czechs the most frightful retribution. In retaliation for the operation, the Nazis shot all the male inhabitants of Lidice, imprisoned the women and children, and completely razed the town.

Tito approved Wilkinson's plan to use Slovenia as a base. So Wilkinson and Hesketh-Prichard set off on foot, still in winter, for Slovene Partisan headquarters in Dolenjska in southern Slovenia.

Here they reconfirmed Tito's approval with the Slovene Partisan leadership. This done, their objective became Carinthia, on the north side of the Karawanken Alps, where a small Partisan detachment, the Carinthian (Koroska) Odred, under the control of the Fourth Zone, was based high on the forested mountain slopes. Wilkinson and the Partisans agreed that the best route to the Koroska Odred was through the Partisan-held area in Primorska, prewar Italian territory inhabited by ethnic Slovenes.

After one abortive attempt to cross the Karawankens in the middle of winter Wilkinson decided to return to Italy to organize the support that would be needed to exploit the opportunity he now saw to move agents north into prewar Austria. He missed his rendezvous with a submarine pickup on the Adriatic coast and ended up retracing his march back to Tito's headquarters, where he was flown out to Italy from a clandestine landing strip. All told, he had traveled 1,500 miles in enemy-occupied Yugoslavia, mostly on foot, the rest in peasant farm wagons.

On his arrival back in Italy Wilkinson reported his optimism for penetrating Austria via the Slovene Partisans: "The Slovenians are only too willing to cooperate in this penetration, since it asks nothing of them which is in any way incompatible with their own interests, and helps widen their sphere of influence."

The Slovene Partisan leaders were also optimistic about the possibilities. In January 1944, they issued orders to the Fourth Zone to expand the operations of the Koroska Odred northward into the Drau, or Drava, River valley. This was to be the advance base for the river crossing. The odred's strength was less than 200 men, and they badly needed weapons to supplement what they had captured. The delivery of arms from the British became the quid pro quo for cooperating with Wilkinson.

On May 15 Lieutenant Colonel Charles Villiers, Wilkinson's deputy, dropped to the Slovene Partisans in Primorska. He and Hesketh-Prichard, who had wintered there, then set out across the Karawanken Alps headed for the Koroska Odred. I had been told before leaving Italy that a British officer using the name "Buxton" was being dropped to the Partisan Ninth Corps and that I should expect to see him in Stajerska. Shortly after I returned with the Fourth Zone headquarters from the Pohorje to the mountains above the Gornja Savinjska Dolina (in late June 1944, a month before the liberation of the valley) a courier arrived with a message for me from Villiers written in grubby pencil on a torn notebook page. He had arrived at the odred and proposed that we meet at a place he designated in the mountains between the villages of Solcava and Eisenkappel.

The note was signed "Buxton," but beneath the signature he had written "Grenadier Guards"—one of the elite British guards regiments. Disguise his own name he would, but "Grenadier Guards," never. Our meeting took place without incident and we worked out plans for the coordination of our individual operations as well as our joint strategy to gain Partisan support. Villiers was a graduate of Eton and Oxford in the 1930's, and had been in the evacuation of the British army from Dunkirk in 1940. He had joined SOE in London in 1943.

The Partisans were now eager to themselves develop an Austrian resistance. Slovene headquarters on May 25 instructed the Koroska Odred to move aggressively. "Your task is to assist the development of a Partisan movement in Austria under the leadership of the Austrians themselves at all costs. The aim must be to encourage the development of a Partisan movement all over Austria."

After receiving our first drops of guns and explosives and after our first attacks against the rail lines, I began to piece together what I could find out about Partisan capabilities for Austrian penetration and about the existence of an Austrian resistance. A party of fifteen men from the Koroska Odred had crossed the Drava in March and were in the Saualpe mountains just to the north of the river. Villiers and Hesketh-Prichard were now with the odred and were pushing the commander to put Hesketh-Prichard across with a second party.

They were enthusiastically optimistic about the opportunity this seemed to present, as well as about the willingness of both the Fourth Zone headquarters and the odred to work with them. It was the beginning of summer and there would be at least four months before the first snow fell during which to organize secret political groups among the rural population and to enlarge the armed Partisan group with local recruits. Direct radio communications with SOE Italy would be set up so that drops of agents, weapons, and supplies could be made to Hesketh-Prichard in the mountains north of the river. Their ultimate hope was to find or to create a separate Austrian resistance, and thereafter to cut the umbilical cord of dependence on the Slovene Partisans.

I learned from the Partisans of the existence of an Austrian Freedom Front, an underground organization in Klagenfurt, Villach, and Völkermarkt in the Drava valley. What I didn't know was that it was largely a notional organization and under the control of the Yugoslavs. Caught up in the euphoria of a potential Austrian resistance, I radioed OSS Italy saying the opportunity looked very promising and proposing that until an OSS Austrian party arrived I would develop contacts with the Austrian Freedom Front and work with the British already on the scene.

Although my message produced no response, I did stir up competitive instincts and the bureaucratic concern for turf within OSS Italy. A memorandum from Robert Joyce, OSS senior intelligence officer for the Balkans, reported my radio message, saying: "We understand that the British are at present making a maximum and urgent effort to penetrate Austria and Hungary. . . . The urgency of our getting into Yugoslavia the [Captain Charles] Fisher and [Major Gilbert] Flues teams cannot be overestimated." Captain Fisher had been waiting since May for Tito's approval to come to the Fourth Zone to organize OSS penetration into Austria; Major Flues was also waiting to go to Partisan Sixth Corps in Slavonia to set up penetrations from there into Hungary. The bureaucratic reaction also found its way into Joyce's memorandum: "Major Lindsay is a member of the SO branch and as such the penetration of Austria for intelligence purposes does not properly fall within his competence." Joyce apparently was unaware that my orders from both OSS and the British included a directive to explore this possibility.

The clandestine services of both Britain and the United States were organized into individual sections, each with its separate mission and wanting to have its own men on the ground—and, I suspected, as colored pins on their wall maps. These included the separate German and Yugoslav sections of OSS, SOE, and MI-6. The OSS sections for Special Operations and for Secret Intelligence cut across the geographical divisions. There was also a separate Allied organization called A Force, one of whose missions was to aid downed flyers to evade capture and prisoners to escape from German prison camps.

During the summer and fall I tried in several signals to convey the problems caused by overlapping jurisdictions of these several separate organizations as well as the severe limitations on what could be done from the Fourth Zone. But it had little if any effect. The pressures were heavy to penetrate Austria and Germany, and the British and American sections responsible for those operations were loath to entrust their activities to someone under the direction of the Balkan Operations sections.

The Partisan atmosphere of optimism soon changed. While maintaining an outwardly cooperative attitude, the Partisan leaders began to hedge and to raise obstacles. In early July I radioed to SOE: "Partisans promise cooperation but [I] believe they desire to be in a strong position relative Austrians at end of war so they can secure most favorable border. This may affect extent of real aid." In response to a proposal from SOE to set up a permanent base in the Pohorje from which to send agents north I replied: "Pohorje very unfavorable for permanent party. They will run most of time." We had just come from there.

There were serious limitations on the use of our area as a base that were not apparent until we bumped our heads against reality. First, the Partisans were in the forested mountains and regularly on the move in close proximity to German units. The valley that the Partisans, with our logistical support, had liberated in August was not as firmly held as the two Slovene areas south of the Sava. At any moment we might have to resume our clandestine forest existence—as events were to demonstrate to us. This severely limited the number of Allied officers and agents that could be located in Stajerska.

Another limitation was that in the summer of 1944, as the war against the Germans appeared to be drawing to a close, the objectives of the Allies and those of the Partisans increasingly diverged. The Partisans' postwar objectives included the immediate occupation and annexation of a slice of southern Austria, while Allied policy was to concentrate single-mindedly on the defeat of the German armies, postponing all consideration of possible border revisions until the postwar peace treaties were written.

In my conversations with the Partisans it became increasingly clear that they were also fearful there would be an Allied landing in Istria, at the head of the Adriatic, and a move by Allied forces across Slovenia. I sensed that they viewed any such developments as jeopardizing their final political control of Slovenia at the end of the war. When they met in Italy in August 1944 Churchill had told Tito such a landing was a strong possibility. So in the minds of the Partisan leaders it was a major threat. It also turned out that OSS General Donovan's decision to send an intelligence mission to their enemy Mihailovic deeply angered Tito. In retaliation the Partisans were ordered by Tito to cut their cooperation with us to the barest minimum.

Finally, a limitation little understood by the headquarters of the Allied clandestine services was that almost nothing could be done without the approval and support of the Partisans. We were literally never out of sight of at least our individual Partisan couriers or bodyguards. We were told they were there to provide us with constant protection. Their other purpose, however, was to see to it that we had no contacts that had not been authorized by the commissars of the units we were with. The Partisans were, in fact, in a position to block any activity they deemed not in their own interests. Our Allied intelligence organizations, in contrast, continued to believe that we ought to be able to mount operations north on our own and without the knowledge of the Partisans.

We in the British and American clandestine services wanted to use the Partisan base in Stajerska for the penetration of Austria and Germany, but to free ourselves from Partisan control as soon as possible. We were fully conscious that any appearance of Yugoslav sponsorship of our penetration agents, because of both the Communist leadership of the Partisans and the openly stated Partisan objective of annexing prewar Austrian territory, would be a distinct liability with Austrians and Germans we were trying to reach. It became demonstrably the intent of the Partisans to prevent us from developing any independent resistance in southern Austria which they did not control. They wanted a clear field to occupy and annex southern Austria as quickly as they could, relying on their physical control of the area to ensure that their long-term claims would be recognized. The existence of an independent Austrian resistance would inevitably have diluted their own claims.

Since late June the Partisans had repeatedly emphasized that the Koroska Odred was very short of weapons and that they would be better able to provide a river crossing party if we sent them more arms. The odred commander wanted the loads dropped directly to him. Although we were now delivering a substantial amount of weapons to the Fourth Zone drop points, the delivery of additional supplies to the odred became the precondition that would have to be met before the British parties would be sent north. During July and August seventeen planeloads of weapons and supplies were delivered directly to the Koroska Odred by Wilkinson. But still there was no agreement to put Hesketh-Prichard across the Drava River.

Armed with these air-dropped weapons, the Koroska group was expanded to 800 men. Slovene headquarters now changed its Austrian strategy. Suddenly in August the order came to reduce the group back to 200 men. The others were transferred to the brigades of the Fourteenth Division. The Slovene wartime records now available strongly suggest that the Partisan high command had concluded that the clandestine development of an Austrian resistance movement was not in the cards. Their available manpower should instead go to strengthen the brigades in Stajerska so that they could move in force into prewar Austria when the war ended. With the Allied advances in France in August and the recent Russian advances, the end of the war might come in a few weeks. Both the British and later the Americans had supplied several planeloads of weapons on the understanding that the Partisans would cross the Drava with the SOE and OSS parties. Now the base for that crossing was itself in jeopardy.

A second stalling tactic was also used with Villiers and Hesketh-Prichard—that it was now too dangerous for them to cross the river and that the Partisans were responsible to Tito for their safety. They would have to wait until the situation became more favorable. There was no question that it was dangerous, but it would become more dangerous as the days and weeks passed.

■ Up-to-date German documents, safe addresses, and wartime Austrian clothing were necessary for any agent moving by road or rail or staying even for a night in a town or village in Austria. In 1944 the Germans tightened their grip on Austria by periodically changing the documentation required so that anyone not having the most recent stamp on their identification documents would immediately be taken in for questioning. The only alternative was to go as part of an armed Partisan band living by their wits in the mountains and forests. This had severe limitations for obtaining intelligence on the German military and defense organizations. The rural peasant areas where Partisans could survive were so isolated from the rest of Germany that they would have little opportunity to obtain the kind of military and technical information needed by the Allied armies and air forces.

Somehow a report had gained currency in the Allied intelligence services of the existence of an armed Austrian resistance group. In July we received a signal from OSS asking for information about the Free Austrian Brigade, which was known to be operating somewhere in the mountains of southern Austria. I replied that we had no information that even suggested the existence of a Free Austrian Brigade operating independently from the Fourth Zone Partisans. This was followed by one or two other queries from OSS, to which we gave the same answer. Unable to get any confirming evidence from us, a final message directed us to report in full detail the date and the circumstances under which the Free Austrian Brigade had been destroyed. Some staff officer, having created a Free Austrian Brigade, now had to find a way to get it off his order of battle and his war room map.

In early summer a signal came in from SOE with a plan to drop to us two agents who had been recruited by ISLD (Inter-Service Liaison Department, the cover name for the Cairo-based branch of MI-6), and who were to go north into Austria. We were asked to provide German documents, clothing, and a safe address in Vienna. I answered saying that we could not provide documents or safe addresses. We were living in the forest and on the run most of the time. Agents should not be dropped to us unless they came with documents, clothes, and safe addresses and could immediately go north on their own.

I heard nothing further and assumed the operation was off because we could not provide the cover they needed. To my surprise, during the next supply drop the two men came floating down from the sky along with the parachuted containers carrying weapons and explosives for us. I had not even been told in the operational signal that morning that bodies as well as supplies were being dropped, although my original orders stated all personnel drops would be cleared with me in advance. I explained to them the limitations of our situation and then explained their objective of going north to Vienna to the commissar of the Partisan command, asking for any help he could provide, which was almost none.

Both men were Austrians recruited from a German prisoner-of-war camp and had been given the cover names of Smith and Black. We arranged for them to go to the Koroska Odred where Villiers and party were now installed. Apparently they did not conduct themselves there in a manner to give either Villiers or the Partisans any confidence in their intelligence, reliability, or sense of security. The Partisans rightly refused to work with them and they started back to Fourth Zone as the first leg of the trip back to Italy.

On the way they were surprised by a German SS police patrol while they rested outside a mountain farm. Smith escaped and made his way with a courier to us where he reported that Black had made no effort to escape when the SS patrol came in sight. Instead, he sat quietly waiting for the Germans. He was last seen being marched off, hands tied behind his back and his rucksack hung around his neck.

Within hours a strong German column of several hundred headed for the odred. Villiers, Hesketh-Prichard, and the odred officers barely escaped being surrounded and captured. Black had spilled his guts freely and quickly to the Germans on the location of the odred, and on the presence of the British party. This episode confirmed the Partisan distrust of Austrians and made it even more difficult for us to gain their support and cooperation for our Austrian efforts.

The Partisans did in fact have access to some useful German documents taken from Slovenes who deserted the German army and joined Partisan units, as well as from civilians seeking refuge. But we found out that these were being sent to Slovene headquarters. Bencic promised he would give us some from the next batch collected. But it did not happen. An order from Slovene headquarters to the Fourth Zone and the Koroska Odred had directed that the British and Americans be given only military information on the enemy. No political intelligence and no information on the Partisan forces was to be provided. And under no circumstances were we to be given any information on the Partisan intelligence organization and on the sources of the intelligence they gave us. This was interpreted by the Zone commissar to mean no German documents as well. There was little doubt that documents were available, however.

Villiers returned to Wilkinson's base in Bari, Italy, in September while Hesketh-Prichard stayed on in Carinthia, pushing to be quickly put across the Drava by the Koroska Odred. But the Partisans continued to stall, saying the crossing was still too dangerous and the German security forces too strong. The fifteen Partisans who had already crossed on March 15 had their hands full in just surviving.

■ OSS had not told me before we left Italy of the party under Captain Charles Fisher mentioned in Joyce's memorandum, and their plans for Austria, although they were then in Italy waiting for clearance from Tito's headquarters. When approval was at last given in August, we were still not told. The first we knew of Charles Fisher and his Austrians was when they appeared, twelve strong, on September 12 with their Partisan escort from Dolenjska. I was appalled by the problems of protecting such a large group. Charlie Fisher had confidently expected that the Partisans had a going operation north of the Drava that was in touch with the Free Austrian Brigade. He had intended to set up a base with us and to infiltrate nine of his men with the help of the Partisans and the Austrian Brigade.

He was quickly disabused. The group had no plan, no Austrian clothes or documents that would pass even the most cursory inspection. They had a few names and addresses, dating from prewar days, of people who might give them shelter if, after five years of war mobilization, they were still alive and at the same location. OSS had sent them in with these instructions:

> a. Obtain on the spot information concerning travel and living controls, rules and regulations, required documents, means of communication, cover and similar data necessary for a successful penetration of the respective areas, and
> b. make initial contacts through Partisan or other channels with labor and resistance groups in the respective areas and arrange for reception and protection of additional teams in those areas.

The men with Fisher had been recruited and trained by the Labor Desk of OSS, whose job was to use American trade-union people to contact and work with what remained of prewar independent labor organizations and socialist parties in occupied Europe. It was basically a sound idea, though the execution was bad.

General Donovan had appointed Arthur Goldberg, before the war a labor-union official and attorney, to head this part of OSS. He was commissioned with the rank of major. His OSS Labor Desk was a quasi-independent organization whose lines of authority ran directly to the overseas OSS bases. Even there they maintained a high degree of independence from the other branches of OSS, especially Secret Intelligence and Special Operations. Edward Mosk, the Labor Desk head in Italy, developed his own operational plans, trained his agents, and sent them off on their assignments. All of the nine men from the Labor Desk who arrived with Fisher had been born in Europe. Three had served in the Spanish Republican Army, and one in the International Brigade during the Spanish Civil War. Three had been merchant seamen.

Charles Fisher himself, Lieutenant Robert Quinn, and Bob Plan (war name "Perry"), his radio operator, were under the SI Austria section. Fisher had his own SI mission to contact the Austrian resistance and develop opportunities to support its expansion. He also had been given responsibility for the other nine, though they had their own radio communications back to the Labor Desk. It became clear to me that they did not accept Fisher's authority, which soon led to trouble. The Partisans, however, held Fisher responsible for the group, and ultimately looked to me as the senior Allied officer. Fisher soon realized that conditions were far less promising than he had expected. Within two weeks he saw for himself the obstacles—both the Partisan unwillingness to help and the severe German controls. The Koroska Odred now played the same game with Fisher they were playing with Villiers and Hesketh-Prichard: Send us weapons and supplies and we will try to put your men across the Drava.

In late September, Franc Leskosek-Luka, a senior member of the Slovene Partisans who had been given overall responsibility from Slovene headquarters for the Austrian operations, came to Stajerska. His presence gave us the opportunity to press for increased Partisan activity against the rail communications. I radioed the results of the meeting: "Our relations with Partisans, which had deteriorated considerably last few weeks, now greatly improved." We had pushed hard on Luka to increase the attacks on the railroads. In response he directed attacks on the rail line between Maribor and Klagenfurt, and increased operations against the double-track lines. Luka also directed one battalion to cross the Drava with Hesketh-Prichard.

Though somewhat encouraged by this development, Captain Fisher concluded that the outlook for sending the Labor Desk men north was remote. He radioed: "We are stalemated here. No Austrian Brigade to provide entry of men into Austria." He told OSS headquarters that he was sending back to Italy four of the nine Labor Desk men because there was no possibility of getting them further north. He held the others in the event "something opened up."

Mosk of the Labor Desk was upset that his operation was being aborted by Fisher, who was not under his control, although his own men had radioed: "It is impossible to go further north because of the absence of Austrian resistance groups. The only possible way to pass is with secure and more recent documents and by railway." Fisher was ordered not to send them out until he provided a satisfactory explanation of his decision. When at last the four did leave, it developed that one of them got drunk and attempted to rape a Partisanka in Zadar, on the coast—whence, by my orders, he was sent the rest of the way to Italy under arrest.

By mid-September Charlie Fisher thought he had secured the approval of Bencic, the Zone commissar, to send three men on a reconnaissance north as far as the south side of the Drava. However, the Partisans continued their delaying tactics and the men did not start north until late in October.

As the summer and fall progressed, the Partisans' position on Austria hardened. We were even obstructed in learning of events in Austria by the refusal of the Partisans to permit us to see and question persons escaping from that nation. This was so even in the case of downed Allied airmen and escaped Allied POWs who had come out of Austria with the aid of the Partisans. Of over 100 Allied fliers and escaped POWs brought from Fourth Zone to Slovene headquarters in November, we saw only 11.

In early October Zone Commissar Bencic came to see me alone. He told me that Art, one of the remaining five from the OSS Labor Desk, had come to him and revealed that he was a member of the American Communist Party. He then spun a tale that he knew from his time in Italy that the OSS and the American government had no intention of helping the Partisans, and that the weapons being dropped were deliberately defective. He suggested that I be removed (presumably to be shot in a fictional brush with the Germans) and that he, as a reliable member of the Communist Party, would then take over the liaison mission and the radio link with Italy. By now the commissar and I had been through some close shaves together and we had developed a mutual respect. He was so shocked by this that he immediately came to tell me.

When I confronted Art he readily admitted what he had done.

There was no alternative to sending him back to Slovenia over the courier line and reporting the episode by signal to OSS. Under similar circumstances the Partisans wouldn't have waited five minutes before shooting him. I sent as full a report as possible within the limits imposed by our communications. The next move was up to OSS. To my surprise there was no response; I was not even asked for further details about the incident.

When I was at Slovene headquarters three or four months later I asked if Art had arrived and what had been done. There was no record that he had arrived there, and no one recalled seeing him or being informed about the incident from OSS. At OSS headquarters in Italy in February of 1945 I again inquired and had the radio message files searched. I knew only his assumed name, which was almost certainly not his real one. No record of my message or of any others relating to it was found. The file apparently had been purged. The trail was cold (and still is, despite the declassification in recent years of most OSS records). A British message from Hesketh-Prichard describing the affair did, however, survive in British archives.

■ Early in the summer an Austrian turned up at the Fourth Zone headquarters saying he represented a group of Austrians in Graz who had formed a clandestine resistance cell and wished to make contact with the Americans they had heard were with the Styrian Partisans. In this case the Partisans had brought me into the discussions, in which we were told that the Graz group intended to move to the Hochschwab, a range of the Alps northwest of Graz, to form a partisan group. They wanted to have a radio and operator with them so that they could communicate directly with the Allies and, if possible, arrange supply drops. This looked like the first real opportunity to start resistance in Austria proper and I was enthusiastic about the possibility. We reported it to OSS Italy and requested a radio and German-speaking operator to be dropped to us.

The Fourth Zone commissar at first wanted to have nothing to do with the group but later agreed to allow the operator to be dropped to us. His disdain for the Austrians was apparent. The Partisans continued to have a low opinion of the Austrians and their willingness actively to resist the Germans. "No Austrian has so much as raised a pistol against the Germans," said Commissar Bencic.

This time we did receive a reply. It was favorable, but said it would take two or three weeks to prepare and drop the radio and operator. In light of this the man from the Graz group decided to return and to send another to take our radio operator to the group when he arrived. A couple of weeks later a second man arrived from Graz to pick up the radio operator, saying that the Graz group had meanwhile moved to the mountains to set up their resistance group. As the operator had not yet been dropped the second Graz courier had to wait with us.

A few days later, one of our Partisans returning from a patrol spotted the man and immediately reported that he was a Gestapo agent. They were from the same Austrian village. The Partisans, interrogating him, learned that the first man had been caught by the Gestapo on his return trip and had been broken under their interrogation. The Gestapo then substituted their own man and sent him to us posing as the second representative of the Graz group. When our radio operator arrived he would go north with the Gestapo agent.

The Gestapo's plan was to substitute their own radio operator for ours and to introduce him into the Graz group after having obtained from our operator his codes and ciphers. They would allow the group to continue and to expand, having penetrated it with their own operator, and induce OSS to send further supplies and liaison officers by parachute. Thus they would control both the group itself and the radio communications with OSS. It was to have been a classic *Funkspiel,* literally "radio game," or double-agent operation.

Yet, because of the Partisan opposition to other Allied attempts to penetrate Austria, there remained the possibility that the story had been deliberately altered, or completely fabricated, by the Partisans in order to demonstrate that they were trying to cooperate with us in spite of the enormous problems. A couple of months later Charlie Fisher reported that Bencic had told him the same story as an example of the extreme difficulties of supporting Austrian groups.

Throughout my entire time in Stajerska only one person was dropped to us who was completely prepared with documents, clothes, and safe addresses. He was a young courier being sent to Cardinal Innitzer in Vienna. He left us almost immediately to go down the mountain to a nearby railway station where, in the garb of a cleric, he boarded a train direct to Vienna.

CHAPTER 12

Failure in Austria

T he Germans took Partisan activity in Styria and Carinthia increasingly seriously. In August 1944, Heinrich Himmler, head of the Sicherheitsdienst, the Nazi secret police, declared the area a special security zone. Anti-Partisan activities were greatly increased. Lower Carinthia and Styria, he ordered, would be defended as resolutely as East Prussia. We received an increasing number of reports of heavy German patrol activity along the Drava itself.

The Partisan decision to put Hesketh-Prichard across the Drava was finally made in the fall. Roughly a hundred men in three separate groups were to cross, the second of them with Hesketh-Prichard, into the Saualpe range. I saw him just before he departed in mid-October. He had decided to go alone, and had sent his two radio operators back to Italy. Having been turned down by the army as physically unfit when the war began, he was now embarking on one of the most physically demanding missions one could imagine. He was a skilled radio operator and had been directly involved in the development of the Eureka homing beacon we used for bringing in airdrops and the S-phone by which we could communicate securely by voice with aircraft overhead. As he was leaving he told me he doubted that he would survive because snow was now on the ground at the higher levels, and tracks that could be followed would be left in the snow. But he was determined to make a try. He had spent five months waiting for the Partisans to agree.

The crossing was made. He went on with the Partisan unit into the Saualpe. Radio contact with him continued for a few weeks, then stopped and never resumed. His last message was sent on December 3. After weeks of radio silence Wilkinson's Bari base assumed that the radio might have failed or been lost and attempted to reestablish contact by dropping a replacement radio blind into the area in which he was last heard from. I was later told that two radios along with food and clothing were fitted into the external wing tanks of a long-range fighter and cushioned so they could take the shock of being jettisoned and landing in the snow without parachute. On a clear winter day the aircraft circled at low altitude over the area hoping to see some sign from the ground. None was seen. When fuel reached the point at which the pilot had to leave for home the wing tanks were dropped with the hope they would be seen and opened by Hesketh-Prichard's group. The mission failed, as no radio contact was subsequently made.

At the end of March 1945 the Fourth Zone commissar received a letter by German post from Mirko, the commander of the Partisan group with Hesketh-Prichard, saying they were living high up in the Saualpe unable to do any sabotage. "No sign of Austrian resistance but some French and Russian workers joining." The resistance group in the Hochschwab had been wiped out by the Germans, Mirko wrote. When the Partisans' own radio or courier communications were unavailable, as in this case, the Partisans occasionally sent letters through the German postal system, using innocent addresses. The Fourth Zone Partisans said there was a possibility of getting a letter back to Mirko if Colonel Peter, as Wilkinson was known to the Partisans, wanted to arrange a monthly supply sortie or send a message to Hesketh-Prichard. This indicated he was still alive. Was he? Or was this a cover-up of his earlier death?

In Maribor the following July, after the war had ended, by chance I saw and recognized Mirko on the street. In a brief conversation he told me of the death of Hesketh-Prichard in a fight with German security troops in the middle of December. Mid-December was clearly inconsistent with the letter reported to have been received the end of March implying Hesketh-Prichard was still alive. In answer to my question Mirko said yes, they had seen a fighter drop its wing tanks in December. But no, it had never occurred to them that the tanks might be meant for them and they had made no effort to recover them.

British SOE officers believed that Hesketh-Prichard was probably killed by the Partisans themselves. One hypothesis was that he was eliminated to prevent the organization of an Austrian resistance that could contest their claim to annexation of a part of southern Austria. Another was that he was determined to continue north when the Partisans decided to withdraw back across the Drava. As the chance was great that alone he would be captured and interrogated, thus jeopardizing the safety of the Partisan unit, their secret river-crossing points, and their civilian supporters, they could not risk allowing him to remain alone. The truth remains one of those tragic mysteries of war, for I have never been able to learn of any hard evidence supporting any of the hypotheses.

By late October it was clear to both the British and the Americans that the penetration of Austria from the Fourth Zone base had failed, both for intelligence and to stimulate resistance. Hesketh-Prichard and the Partisan unit with him had been unable to spark any Austrian support in the brief time they had been across the Drava. Had he been permitted to cross the Drava in the late spring, he and the group would have had the summer and fall to organize resistance before the winter snows, and the story might have been different—although that seems unlikely.

Two of the OSS Labor Desk men who had arrived with Captain Charles Fisher—Julius Rosenfeld (Rosie) and Ernst Knoth—on October 21 finally received Partisan permission to make a reconnaissance to the north. But they got only as far as the Koroska Odred. Five days later they reported that the odred commissar would provide support for them to cross the Drava "if they are supplied promptly" with additional weapons, boots, and winter clothing. But heavy German activity prevented them from going further. Again they waited. On December 18 Rosie and Ernst radioed they had been running from the Germans for ten days. "[We] are exhausted and starving. Cannot go on any more. We have to sleep in open and our equipment is all lost. This contact comes by Partisan radio and they won't promise any more contacts." And on December 21: "We are completely exhausted. Our work is failure. Germans destroyed all Partisan forces."

In January Bob Plan radioed from the Fourth Zone that he believed Ernst and Rosie were in a hidden Partisan hospital in the mountains with frozen feet. During the remainder of the winter there was no further word of them. After the end of the war in May we were unable to find any trace of them. Plan believed that they may have threatened in desperation to leave the hospital on their own, and that the Partisans shot them to protect the secret location of the hospital. Plan also reported that during the winter the hidden Partisan hospital was discovered by the Germans and set afire, burning alive all the wounded Partisans there. It is possible that Ernst and Rosie perished with them. A wounded British pilot we had tried unsuccessfully to evacuate from a makeshift airstrip at Recica may also have died there.

For the British and Americans there was now no hope of doing anything more than surviving and waiting until spring. Both SOE's Wilkinson and Howard Chapin, OSS's Austrian chief in Italy, decided to stop trying to use the Fourth Zone as a base for Austrian operations. Peter Wilkinson, commander of Special Force I of SOE (the Austrian section) in his operational report of December 1, 1944, concluded:

> No attempt can be made to form Austrian resistance groups until the end of March [when the winter snows begin to melt and air supply by parachute again becomes possible]. Assuming that the war in Germany is then drawing to a close, it seems unlikely that there will be sufficient time left to arm or organize any sufficient numbers.

OSS Major Gilbert Flues and his group of Hungarian agents, who had gone to the Partisan Sixth Corps in Slavonia in August to try to penetrate Hungary, had been blocked completely by Partisan intransigence. They too were withdrawn in December.

There was now no alternative to blind drops. All our tries in the summer and fall of 1944 to put agents across the Drava from the Fourth Zone had completely failed, primarily because of Partisan intransigence, but also because the agents were ill-prepared. As a consequence we had no groups with radios on the ground north of the Drava who could set up reception parties to whom agents could be dropped. Blind drops had the advantage of putting agents across the Drava and much closer to their destinations. But they also had the great disadvantage of having to rely on the skill of the aircraft navigator to drop his party precisely on target after flying hundreds of miles in the dead of night with nothing but celestial navigation, an inaccurate estimate of winds, and a magnetic compass to guide him.

A particularly fruitless operation began on February 7, 1945, when OSS dropped a three-man intelligence team across the Drava into southern Austria. It demonstrated again the crucial importance of managing every operational detail with the greatest care. The 25-year-old team leader, George Gerbner, was an American who spoke German, Hungarian, and French. He was also trained as a radio operator. The team radio operator, 20-year-old Alfred Rosenthal, spoke German and Italian. The third team member, Paul Krock, was an Austrian in his middle thirties who had deserted from the German army to the Italian Partisans in Italy and had fought the Germans in Florence.

The operational plan was to drop the team in the vicinity of the Austrian town of Freiland, an area Krock knew well and where he had many friends and relatives. He would lead Gerbner and Rosenthal to a remote alpine pasture area where there were several huts used to store hay that were deserted in the winter. He was then to make careful contacts with some of his friends and begin to build a local intelligence net as well as to arrange for food and additional secure hideouts for the two Americans. OSS believed that several thousand British POWs were being used as farm labor in the area to replace the able-bodied men who had all been drafted into the German army. Discreet contacts would be made with the idea that this potential for support might somehow be used.

The night of February 7 was clear and moonless. The team, together with their equipment in six padded bundles with parachutes, climbed aboard an RAF Halifax bomber at the Brindisi air base. The Halifax was over the target area at 23:50 hours. Krock sat on the side of the hole used for dropping to try to identify any ground landmarks. On the first pass scattered clouds obscured the ground. The plane circled and returned 25 minutes later. This time the ground was clear and Krock, looking down through the hole, was certain he had identified the lights of Freiland a few miles from their target. The OSS officer in the plane later reported: "He was so sure of himself he would have jumped there without waiting for the OK from the navigator."

On the third pass a white snow-covered field surrounded by dark forest was clearly visible. Krock dropped through the hole and three supply packages were then dropped. The third was so large that it had to be carried by two men to the hole and pushed through. I doubt that the men in the plane realized how far the plane had traveled (at 120 miles per hour) between the time Krock dropped and the last package was pushed out. If the interval had been only fifteen seconds, the third package would have landed a full half mile beyond Krock. In deep snow this was a long way to go to find it, to hide or carry away its contents. Tracks would have been left in the snow for a German plane to see the next morning.

The Halifax now circled for the next pass. Krock had been instructed to show a continuous beam from his flashlight if the drop point was safe and rapid on-and-off flashes if there was a problem. In that case the plane would return after 20 minutes to give him the time to find a better point for the others to drop. On its return the men in the Halifax saw a single continuous light and the two Americans dropped through the hole. Gerbner had "hesitated so we decided to come back for an additional run for the remaining packages." These were dropped on the fifth pass.

The aircrew and the two accompanying OSS men returned to Brindisi, confident they had reached the target and made a successful drop. Together they finished off the bottle of operational whiskey they had taken on the flight for the jumpers. The base radio station listened daily for the team's first transmission. Nothing was heard. Then nine days later, Captain Douglas Owen and Bob Plan at Fourth Zone reported that Gerbner and Rosenthal had been picked up by Partisans south of the Drava, and near the Zone headquarters. It remained a mystery where Krock, who was not heard from again, had been dropped.

It seemed unlikely that Krock had been able to avoid capture. Almost certainly he had not been able to find and hide all three containers that had been dropped with him. The sound of a four-engine bomber circling repeatedly at less than 1,000 feet would have alerted the German security forces, who would be out at dawn with ground parties and light aircraft. Krock's tracks in the snow and the three containers and parachutes dropped with him on the same pass very likely would have been found by the Germans.

It also seems probable that after dropping Krock the Halifax did not return to the same spot but rather to one some miles away. A steady light was seen on the ground, but was it Krock standing in the snow or some other light elsewhere? Had he been instructed to flash one Morse-code letter if the drop was safe, and another letter if it was not, the Halifax crew would have known with near certainty they were indeed at the same spot.

The only way in a blind drop at night to be certain that men and equipment were not spread over a very large ground area was to drop men and equipment all in a single pass. Or if that could not be done—and it was hard to do in a Halifax—men and equipment should have been dropped in self-contained groups. Since two of the men were operators, each should have been dropped with a radio and the minimum equipment for his survival.

In this operation the two radios and part of the equipment were dropped with Krock, the only one of the three men who was not trained as an operator, while both Gerbner and Rosenthal were dropped on the third pass without any of their equipment. They were extremely fortunate to be so far from their target as to land south of the Drava in Partisan territory.

During the winter and spring both OSS and SOE dropped intelligence teams at several points in Austria. Those that survived produced some useful intelligence, but its value to the Allied spring offensive in Italy was marginal. The operations were on the whole no more productive than our efforts to cross the Drava from Stajerska.

■ While the British and Americans were encountering reverses and, occasionally, semi-successes, the Russians, operating through the ostensibly disbanded Comintern, also had their eye on the Fourth Zone as a staging area for the penetration of Austria. All through the war in communications with the Yugoslav Communists the code word "Grandfather" had been used for the Comintern. Some of the messages were assumed to be directives to the Yugoslav Politburo from Stalin himself. Dusan Biber of Ljubljana's Institute of Current History has put together the story of the Russian activities that were carefully concealed from us in 1944.

In May of that year "Grandfather" radioed Tito's headquarters in Bosnia saying that they were much interested in establishing land contact with the Austrian Communist Party through Slovenia. In June Franz Hönner, a member of the Central Committee of the Austrian Communist Party, arrived at Tito's headquarters from the Soviet Union. From there he proceeded north to Slovene headquarters, where he remained to coordinate Yugoslav and Austrian Communist Party activities.

In June of 1944 an advance party of 27 Austrian former POWs led by Siegfried Fürnberg parachuted from Soviet planes to Slovene liberated territory in Dolenjska south of the Sava. (By 1948 Fürnberg had become general secretary of the Communist Party of Austria.) In late fall, as the "Austrian Battalion," they moved north to Stajerska, and then across the Drava at about the time Hesketh-Prichard crossed with another unit. They too found it impossible to stir up local support and, confronted with winter snows and the beginning of a German offensive against the Partisans, soon returned to Stajerska, where, until the end of the war, they fought alongside the Partisans, under Partisan control.

At the time the existence of this group was carefully withheld from us. We did learn, however, that a Partisan group had liberated about a hundred Soviet prisoners working in a mine near the Drava. Lieutenant Colonel Bogomolov, the Russian liaison officer at Fourth Zone, told me that unlike British and American escaped prisoners and airmen, whom we asked the Partisans to send south to Slovene headquarters for evacuation, Soviet escapees were ordered to resume fighting in place. "Why should I send them out?" he said to me. "The Germans are here. Why not fight them here?" It is probable that these men joined the combat group sent by Moscow. At the end of the war this "Austrian" battalion had expanded to about 500 men, but it was firmly under Slovene Partisan control.

Partisan policies in respect to Austria and a possible independent Austrian resistance appeared to vacillate. On one hand "Grandfather's" directives were to support a separate and independent Austrian resistance and to avoid inflaming the border question. This they had tried to do in the early months of 1944. But they also pursued aggressively their claims for a piece of Austrian territory.

In the end all of the Austrian thrusts, by the British, the Americans, the Partisans, and the Comintern, failed for lack of support within Austria, and because of aggressive German efforts to penetrate and eliminate the probes launched from the Fourth Zone. At that point the Partisans abandoned efforts to build an Austrian resistance and reverted to their all-out drive to occupy and annex parts of the valley of the Drava as the Germans surrendered.

■ Until the end of the war we remained puzzled that no Austrian armed resistance had developed of sufficient strength to make any appreciable contribution to the defeat of the Nazis. In most of Austria forested mountains and isolated alpine peasant farms could provide food and shelter for armed resistance. The terrain was very much like that of Stajerska. Indeed, much of Austrian terrain was even better suited for guerrillas than Stajerska, a relatively small area squeezed between two rivers and crisscrossed with roads and railroads. At their height Partisan forces there totaled nearly 6,000 men and women. Mountainous Austria could have supported a much larger resistance. If a strong Communist or non-Communist armed resistance were to have developed in Austria it would have received the political and material support of the United States, Britain, and—if it was Communist-controlled—the Soviet Union as well.

The reasons resistance had not developed were probably several. Many Austrians were ambivalent about their relation with Germany. They were not a subject people occupied by a foreign power; they had been united with Germany in 1938 with the support of a large part of the population. Most of those who were anti-Nazi had concluded that it was safer to wait for liberation by the Allies than to take up arms. They were survivors, not fighters. Most of the few who did go to the forests were evaders bent on avoiding being sent to fight on the eastern front.

Unlike most of the Slovenes, the Austrians in the Drava valley opposed active resistance because it would bring down on them the full power of the Nazi police and the terror of reprisals, including the shooting of hostages. They were thus more likely to collaborate with the police and to inform against the resisters. It is probably this factor as much as any that made it impossible in the summer and fall of 1944 for the Carinthia-based Partisans and Hesketh-Prichard to build a clandestine civilian support structure north of the Drava. Civilian support was essential if armed resistance was to survive and flourish there.

From Switzerland Allen Dulles, head of OSS operations there, reported similar frustrations in his contacts with the Austrians: "Experience has taught us that potential opposition groups are not courageous enough to risk contact with outside parties. Since they think the end is only a matter of time, they would rather bide their time and thus avoid getting into trouble."

The penetration probes launched from Stajerska by the Partisans and by the British and ourselves carried the added burden of the ethnic antagonisms between the Slovenes and the Austrians in the border areas. This was exacerbated by the open claims of the Partisans for annexation of Austrian territory. In March of 1945 I radioed from Belgrade: "During an informal discussion of Austrian occupation plans and in response to my query whether the Yugoslavs might move into Klagenfurt and Villach after the collapse, General Vladimir Velebit stated, 'Certainly we shall occupy them, they belong to us. But in addition we want to occupy a portion of enemy territory.'" The Yugoslav claims continued to be made in spite of the instructions received from Moscow to avoid the subject.

Lack of strong indigenous Austrian leadership was another factor contributing to ineffective resistance. Those few Austrians who fought the Germans in the Drava valley fought not as an independent Austrian Brigade but under the command of the Slovene Partisans. Far-left leadership was increasingly isolated because of the approaching Red Army and the fear this produced in the largely conservative Catholic population. Strong leadership from socialists and Catholics also did not develop. There was no burning national cause to enlist the commitment and, among those opposed to the Nazis, few were ready to take very real personal risks.

The Moscow Declaration of the Allied powers in 1943 had expressed support for Austrian independence and called on the Austrian people to work for their own liberation. Such resistance as did develop in Austria by 1944 was very different from the pattern of Yugoslav resistance. The few armed resistance groups were small and largely ineffective. Following the Comintern line from Moscow, the early Austrian Communist organization was based not on the peasants and rural villages but instead on clandestine cells within factories and large government bureaucracies. The non-Communist resistance followed the same strategy. They all concentrated on political work, clandestine propaganda, and some industrial sabotage. Through a combination of their poor organizational security and Gestapo efficiency nearly all of the original urban resistance organizations were thoroughly penetrated by the Germans and by 1943 virtually all were rolled up by the Germans and their members either shot or sent off to concentration camps. Until the last few months of the war none of the groups that had survived or that had subsequently come into existence took up armed resistance in the mountains. Those that finally did were for the most part simply evaders. The Austrian people suffered massive brutality and terror both from the German Nazis and from their own police. But their sacrifices did not contribute significantly to their final liberation.

By agreement of Britain, the United States, and the Soviet Union, Austria was occupied by the three powers plus France, and the country partitioned into four zones of occupation. Southern Austria was allocated to the British forces and the area claimed by the Yugoslavs was effectively occupied by British troops pending the completion of the Austrian State Treaty which, due to Soviet intransigence, was not signed until May 15, 1955. The Partisans did, as we predicted, attempt to occupy southern Austria. They were successfully opposed by British forces of occupation. The Soviets gave only perfunctory support to the Yugoslav claims.

There was talk of holding a plebiscite in the disputed areas. An earlier plebiscite at the end of the First World War had gone against the Slovenes, and the Partisans probably feared that a new plebiscite would not go their way. The Slovene Agitprop slogan thus was, "We don't want a plebiscite. The plebiscite is the blood of the fighters who fell for our liberation."

CHAPTER 13

Revolution Comes into the Open

After early September our relations with the Fourth Zone Partisans became increasingly difficult. In part this was because we now had liberated territory and were no longer living cheek by jowl with the Partisan leaders. We no longer saw Borstnar, Bencic, and the other officers several times a day, nor marched side by side on mountain trails. The houses we were assigned for sleeping were usually several hundred yards from those of the Partisan staff. The supply officer arranged that we no longer ate together. These were the surface indicators. The troubles were deeper, but for the moment they were hidden from us.

When I wanted to see Borstnar or Bencic I now had to send Vlado, our liaison interpreter, to request an interview. Increasingly often he would return with the message that "it is not possible today." Sometimes an excuse would be given, sometimes no excuse. The situation became so bad that for a period of several days the British and the Americans were for all practical purposes prisoners of the Partisans. I radioed in mid-October: "We have been virtually under house arrest for the last month."

I first realized what was happening in mid-September when one day I started to walk toward the house taken over by Bencic. The Partisan guard outside our house barred my way. Thinking he was new I said "Ameriski oficir," to which he shook his head and did not move aside. Not wishing to make a fuss (or get shot) and assuming he had misunderstood his orders, I decided to wait until Vlado showed up. But he didn't arrive that day and the guard remained adamant. Next day Vlado did show up, and by then I had a fair head of steam. Since he neither had an explanation nor would or could change the guard's orders, I demanded to see the commissar immediately. Vlado went off mumbling vaguely. A few hours later back he came to say that the commissar was busy now and would see me as soon as he could.

Vlado, I later learned, was regularly sending written reports to Slovene headquarters detailing every conversation we had and every move we made. One such report came to light when it was found by the Slovene historian Dusan Biber. Vlado had reported: "Lindsay is a pro-Austrian pacifist. He spends most of his time reading the Bible." Although I had expected he would say anything to please his Communist Party superiors, this was simply nonsense. I had no Bible or any other books in my kit, which he surely knew, as he had plenty of opportunities to inspect it. He might have thought I was pro-Austrian because I had been pushing for Austrian contacts. But pacifist? What did he think I was doing in Stajerska?

I was at a loss to understand what had happened in our relations. My first thought was that something had gone wrong locally, that we had said or done something that had been completely misunderstood and at which the Partisans had taken strong offense. But I couldn't imagine what it might be. I sent off messages both to the Maclean headquarters and to OSS describing the situation. Months later Robert Joyce, the senior OSS intelligence officer for the Balkans, told me that within a period of three days all the OSS officers with the Partisans throughout Yugoslavia had reported variants of the same treatment.

After a week had passed, during which I had often seen Bencic in front of his house doing nothing, I instructed Vlado to tell Bencic I considered this was a grave discourtesy to an Allied officer. Bencic now saw me, apologized profusely, but offered no explanation. The formal, noncommunicative facade continued.

The British had much the same experience. Peter Moore at

Slovene headquarters reported: "The JANL [Jugoslav Army of National Liberation] authorities took the most elaborate steps to ensure that no British personnel should have access to the ordinary peasant or soldier in the absence of a politically reliable Pzn observer."

The British and American officers at the Sixth Partisan Corps in Slavonia were also having problems. The liaison officers from Force 399, MI-6, and OSS finally decided to have it out with the corps commander. Together they asked him what had happened to their once cordial relations. Intelligence on German moves, which was important to the Allies, was being withheld from them.

The answers were neither reassuring nor forthright, though revealing: "The Corps Commander said he regretted he could not be quite frank and tell us all he knew, but his policy was directed from above. Among the Allied higher-ups there are people who are preventing the Yugoslav people from reaching their goal for which they have fought." They would only provide what intelligence they saw fit to give us and would withhold the rest, he said. The Allied officers then asked why they had been obstructed in their efforts to send intelligence agents across the border into Hungary. The commander replied that it was impossible unless he had written orders from his GHQ. One reason, he said, was Allied relations with Mihailovic. "Until recently the Allies had given help to Mihailovic and the BBC had put out propaganda supporting him. He and his [Communist] Party could not forget these things easily and their enemies could never forget it." Finally he said members of the mission were too friendly with the Partisan rank and file. "In the future only Captain Sutcliffe may visit the Corps staff and intelligence can be collected by only one Allied officer. There will be no other contacts with the Corps."

■ One of the most attractive features of the Stajerska location was that we believed it could provide a new source of intelligence on German military movements and on the state of their war industry and civil economy. It was of great importance to Allied commanders to know precisely where every one of the 260 German divisions were or were headed. Many of these divisions were moved across the railroads and roads of Stajerska to and from Germany, Italy, the eastern front, and the Balkans. It should have been possible to positively identify each one.

In June we had quickly found that what was important to us was often of little interest or concern to the Partisans. They were intensely interested in the smallest German patrol if it was headed their way. They seemingly couldn't care less if entire divisions were moved along the Sava or across the Südbahn as long as they didn't stop to attack. One of our first requests had been to set up train-watchers around the clock on all the main lines. In mid-July Borstnar agreed to do this and our expectation was that through local stationmasters and watchers they could give us not only the number of trains and cars that passed, but also indications of what they carried. Over the weeks we continually inquired about results. Finally, reports were given to us for a week's traffic, but they gave only the number of trains and the number of cars moving each way. There was no identification of contents, such as loads on flatcars, where that could be seen by watchers. There was no identification of German troop units on the trains. We sent on by radio that report and subsequent ones. It was probably of some use to the battle order specialists. But it was a fraction of what the Partisans could have produced.

At first we blamed our lack of success on the Partisans' different priorities and on the weakness of their intelligence staff. Later it became apparent that their lack of cooperation was intentional. Defectors from the German armies sought safety here, as did downed airmen and escaped POWs. The defectors possessed hard information of value if only we could tap it. The escaped POWs and downed airmen could tell us what they had observed as they made their way south, although the latter had seldom seen very much that was important. But in the intelligence business one never knows what bit of information may be important to complete a chain of evidence.

By September most of our own airmen and POWs picked up by the Partisan units were no longer brought to us but were sent directly to Dolenjska for evacuation. Allied officers in Dolenjska were also prevented from seeing them until they were brought to the airstrip for evacuation. Such information as they possessed was thus delayed for weeks before reaching Allied officers. Apart from the damaging effect on intelligence, Partisan obstruction in these cases was also callous. Downed airmen were always reported as missing in action as soon as their aircraft failed to return to their bases. Had we been able to see them we could have reported their survival immediately to their families and to their air units.

I finally realized that the Partisan command was deliberately keeping us from seeing our own airmen and escaped POWs in order to keep from us any knowledge of Partisan unit locations and operations that these men might have picked up after they had fallen into their hands.

Every German soldier carried his *Soldatenbuch*, which recorded his present unit and his previous assignments as well as personal data. They were important both for unit identification and to provide our intelligence documentation services with the latest stamps and endorsements our own agents would need in Germany. They were easy to collect from German prisoners and from those killed, but they were almost never forthcoming. Nor were we allowed to interrogate directly German prisoners and deserters.

In July, before the Partisans began to deny us access, we had seen the defectors. One was an Austrian second lieutenant in the German Luftwaffe who joined the Partisans in July. He told us this:

> Airfield 2000 by 1000 meters 16 kilometers from Libeck in direction Blankensee is base for bomber attacks on England. Here are Heinkel 111s Messerschmitt 110s and FW 190s. South across asphalt road is complete dummy air field with wooden planes and hangars. Dummy field is lighted and main field blacked out when raided. Dummy bombed four times without damage to main field.

It was maddening that we were prevented from interrogating the many others.

Partisan intransigence had also denied us the almost unique opportunity to contact pro-Western Austrians and to carefully recruit those who had both legitimate reason and necessary documentation to travel into other parts of Germany. They alone could have obtained through observation and discreet local contacts badly needed information, such as the effects of bombing, the location of military and industrial targets, and the location and movement of German divisions.

Tito had issued a directive in late September to all Partisan commands, in which he had ordered that the Allied liaison officers be given only military intelligence on the German forces, and that this was to be provided as a "handout" from the staff. We were to be given no political intelligence and no information on Partisan units, their strength and dispositions. Above all, we were to be given no information on the sources of Partisan intelligence or on their own intelligence organization. The handouts were a one-way street. Not knowing the sources of reports, we had no way of evaluating their authenticity, reliability, and timeliness on the German targets and order of battle. For all we knew, they might have been cooked for our consumption. In my report at the end of 1944 I estimated that we had been able to get only 10 percent of the intelligence potentially available in Stajerska.

Another restrictive step was Tito's blanket prohibition against Allied personnel with family ties in Yugoslavia. The effect of the order was to make us almost totally dependent upon the Partisan interpreters, since none of us who were not of Slovene families spoke Slovene, the tongue of perhaps only a million people. Fortunately, the ban did not apply to those of Yugoslav origin already in the country. Bob Plan, an American who had been born in Dalmatia, had arrived with OSS Captain Charles Fisher in September. He became invaluable to us both as an interpreter and to pick up the undertones in the Partisan organization.

Above all, the Partisan leadership was determined that we would have no contacts with civilians or Partisans other than our approved contacts with the Zone officers. They seemed paranoid about what we might learn, although we never tried to recruit agents in Slovenia. Many Partisans, however, volunteered information to us against their orders. In contrast, Allied officers with the Chetnik leader Mihailovic reported that no restrictions were placed on their meeting with either civilians or Chetnik troops.

Vuchko Vuchkovic, the Yugoslav Canadian, had spent the previous winter on the Pohorje waiting for a parachute drop. In the summer we had sent him to one of our drop points near our liberated valley to manage the ground reception party. Without warning he appeared at Zone headquarters one day in mid-October saying he had been ordered by the Partisans to leave his post. It seemed incredible that the Partisans could have taken a step that so directly jeopardized delivery to them of weapons, medical supplies, and winter clothing. In my radio report to Force 399 I said that Vlado, the liaison interpreter, told me this was done at Tito's orders: all British and American personnel must be concentrated at Zone headquarters and we will not be permitted to have anyone at the drop grounds. The commissar, I said, has refused to see me.

Two days later I finally saw Commissar Bencic. He expressed apologies for removing Vuchkovic without telling me but insisted he could not return to the drop area.

Slovene headquarters finally realized how self-defeating this order had been, and Vuchkovic was allowed to return to his drop area. I fully expected to be told by Force 399 that there would be no more supply drops until the Partisans became more cooperative. Allied Forces Headquarters did put a hold on drops, but it lasted only three or four days and we saw no improvement in our relations with the Fourth Zone.

■ Internal security was a major problem for the Slovene Partisans. The Germans were successful in recruiting agents and informers among them. In Primorska in 1943, for instance, the Partisans discovered that a senior commissar was a German agent.

The chief intelligence officer at Fourth Zone was Kamnikar-Bojan, a tall, attractive extrovert and our official source of Partisan intelligence. Our assessment was that he was lazy and not very good at his job. We saw him regularly, but suddenly he became "unavailable." After a week or so had passed without seeing him I pressed Bencic on when we could expect him to resume contact with us. I recall that I was shocked when Bencic, after a long pause, quietly said that he had defected to the Germans. At this late date, when the Germans were losing on all fronts, it seemed inconceivable that anyone could think of defecting to them. The only plausible explanation seemed to be that he had been a long-term German agent and had skipped out when he feared he was about to be exposed.

Long after the war, Anton Bebler, son of Partisan Colonel Ales Bebler, told me that his father's real mission into Stajerska in 1944 was to uncover a top-level German penetration into the Fourth Zone headquarters. His father, he said, was armed with full authority from the Slovene headquarters to interrogate anyone and to execute the man if he could be discovered. Ales Bebler was a seasoned Communist who had fought in Spain and had been a member of the Slovene Partisan leadership since 1941. Was he on the track of Bojan and did Bojan escape in the nick of time? Bebler is now dead, and his papers are still part of the Yugoslav secret archives. Since the war Borstnar has denied that Bojan defected, saying that he was captured by the Germans and shot in May 1945. My recollection of my conversation with Bencic is strong, yet I have since found no messages either to confirm or to refute my own memory of the event.

After the war the Yugoslavs discovered that the Germans had run a very skillful deception in Stajerska that caused the Partisans to believe that there were German agents within the Partisan command. At least one Partisan officer was shot and others were removed from their posts as a consequence of the deception.

■ Besides our frustrations with the Partisans, we continued to have problems in air supply. Radios, both for us and for the Partisans, were only one of the urgent needs unfilled by Force 399's Base Operations. The maddening part was that there was seldom any acknowledgment of our requests. It was like dropping pebbles in a well and hearing no splash. Had we been told why our priority needs were not delivered we would have been able to explain the delays to the Partisans. Undoubtedly the British supply officers in Italy were as frustrated with my increasingly intemperate signals as we were with failures of supply.

What appeared to me as lack of response to our requests came to a head over a desperate need for antibiotics in our hidden hospitals. I had first radioed a request in June. After repeated requests and more than fifty sorties to us we received a message from Base Operations that the antibiotics had not been on the immediately preceding drop because the planes had flown from Foggia. We could not understand why this prevented the delivery of antibiotics. Only later we were told that in order to increase the tonnage being delivered to Yugoslavia, northern Italy, and Greece the air groups at Foggia flew only prepacked standard loads. Special orders all were packed at the Brindisi base. If we had known that it would have mitigated the Partisans' and our frustration. In my desperation, I went around the British command channel and radioed OSS, Bari, on October 19 for help, giving them the history of the antibiotics case. One of the staff officers of Force 399 responded to my complaint in a memo to OSS:

> It is extremely difficult to explain to Lindsay by signal the difficulties experienced this end in giving him the support he deserves, both for good work he has done and the strategic importance of his mission. These difficulties will inevitably appear to be quibbles when judged from the field but they have, in fact, been very real, and have been exercising our minds for some time.
>
> The following are the principal snags which have hindered us supporting Frank:
> (a) Weather—Stajerska is a notoriously bad weather area;
> (b) Range—60 Group has been unable to reach Stajerska from Brindisi and 267 Squadron is normally committed elsewhere. The squadron has no bomb racks [to carry rifles and machine gun containers] and they cannot be fitted without withdrawing aircraft from service for 120 hours.

Brindisi was thus the only air base able to make up special loads. And only the British Halifaxes and American Liberators based there were capable of reaching us from that distance.

Because of these problems in communicating, Bush and I decided that he should go out to Italy, via the courier line, to explain to the Air Operations staff there our situation and to try to work out better procedures for airdrops. By the time he was ready to return by parachute, Tito's order restricting Allied officers to the major commands had taken effect, and I canceled his return. I would no longer be able to send him out with the brigades on operations. He did, however, succeed in getting across a better understanding of our difficulties in receiving drops. Air support thereafter improved. But there was no corresponding improvement in our relations with the Partisans.

By December 1944 we had delivered by parachute to Stajerska approximately 50 tons of explosives, as well as weapons, medical supplies, boots, and clothing for 4,000 men—not much for a modern army, but it made for a major increase in the Partisans' capabilities.

The strained relationship with the Partisans had still another facet. In early 1943 and 1944 landing strips had been laid out in several liberated areas in Yugoslavia. Using these dirt fields American C-47s flown by British and American aircrews were able to land supplies rather than use the less efficient parachute drops. The planes could also then evacuate Partisan wounded, downed Allied bomber aircrews, and escaped Allied prisoners of war to Italy. Although we were at the extreme range for such aircraft, we too sought to prepare a landing strip in our small liberated valley. The RAF, which controlled these operations, insisted that a qualified air force officer be dropped to approve the strip and to supervise the first landing.

In those days an ingenious optical device was used to guide pilots making clandestine night landings. It consisted of 3-inch glass crystals, each cut in pyramidal shape and mounted on a metal stake that could be pushed into the ground. Ten or more were used to mark a runway in a field for the pilot. The crystals were cut so that they reflected light coming from any direction directly back to the source of that light and nowhere else. The pilot of the plane coming in for a landing in the dark wore a tiny light mounted on a band around his forehead. The light from that lamp would be reflected directly back to his eyes, no matter at what angle he was in relation to the landing strip. But since the light was reflected only toward the source of the light, the crystals were invisible to any other observer.

Before coming in to Yugoslavia I had had a demonstration of the system. It was impressive. The crystals marking the runway stood out clearly as long as the light was on one's own forehead. But if the light was moved as little as a yard to the side the crystals became invisible. With this system no lights need be placed on the ground and the reflected light could be seen by no one but the pilot. We expected that the RAF officer who was scheduled to drop to us would bring a set of these crystals with him.

By September I had obtained enthusiastic Partisan agreement for such a landing strip near Recica in our liberated valley, and had found a level field of adequate length and providing sufficient clearance from the surrounding mountains. Not only would we now be able to get supplies, but we would be able to evacuate the wounded. An RAF pilot, bailing out of his damaged fighter over us, had had one leg nearly severed by the tail of his plane. A Partisan surgeon had saved the leg and put it in a cast, but there was no way he could get out except by aircraft pickup. There were also between 20 and 30 badly wounded Partisans in the vicinity of the airstrip we wanted to get to hospitals in Italy. If we could evacuate them and still hold the strip there were, I reported, about 150 more in the hidden mountain hospitals that we would bring down for an evacuation.

We now needed only the final Partisan approval for the RAF officer to come in to supervise the landing. Without explanation, the commissar suddenly reversed himself and refused permission in spite of his earlier enthusiasm. I argued with him for a month before I finally gave up. The wounded pilot had been sent back to the hidden Partisan hospital.

In mid-November I learned quite accidentally that a Partisan major had arrived from Slovene headquarters a few days earlier. Subsequently, he sought me out quietly to tell me that he had been sent to lay out a landing strip on the very same field we had selected. He had been directed by both Zone Commissar Bencic and Slovene headquarters Commissar Kidric to keep this secret from us. The strip was a thousand meters long and even had lights for night landings. The Partisans still made no mention of this, but one day the Russian liaison officer, Lieutenant Colonel Bogomolov, told me casually that he had inspected the strip and that it would be ready in a week.

Since Bogomolov had told me about the strip I could now confront Bencic without compromising my first source, the Partisan major. I tried for several days without success to see the commissar to ask for an explanation. When I finally saw him he was both embarrassed and defensive. He admitted the existence of the secret strip but said this was Yugoslav territory and the Partisans were within their rights to do as they pleased. He now agreed that the strip could be used to bring in Allied planes to evacuate the Allied and Partisan wounded.

For the next two weeks mud on the landing strip and bad flying weather conspired to prevent use of the strip for evacuation of Partisan wounded and the RAF officer. We requested C-47s with fighter escort, which would have been able to take everyone awaiting evacuation. When Force 399 advised us on November 29 that they planned to send a Beaufighter with fighter escort to pick up only the RAF officer I replied:

> If you send Beaufighter to pick up one RAF man most urgently request you send additional planes with same escort to evacuate Partisan wounded. It will jeopardize relations with Partisans if you land on field they built and take off with our man leaving more seriously wounded Partisans behind. Further this landing will blow field to Germans and will make subsequent landings more dangerous.

The flying weather continued bad although the strip had dried enough for a landing. We were told that a landing would be made on short notice. Calder, the RAF officer, was brought back to the strip. He lay in an open farm wagon filled with straw as we waited. But no aircraft arrived. The strain on Calder must have been great but he kept up a good show of spirit. The cut nerves in the wounded leg must have been giving him fits. Every few minutes he would ask Welles or me to move his leg "just a bit" to ease the pain.

On December 3 Force 399 signaled that the RAF had agreed to our request to evacuate Partisan wounded. "Hope land Dakota [C-47] when weather better." The next day we signaled: "Five hundred Hun in strong attack occupied hills commanding strip at Recica. Impossible land planes. . . . Calder has been taken back to hospital in mountains." Had the Partisans agreed to landings in mid-September we could have evacuated the RAF officer and several planeloads of wounded Partisans. As it turned out, the landing strip was never used. It was taken by the Germans a day later.

■ The question remained as to why the Partisans had at first welcomed the possibility of landings, then inexplicably refused to allow us to bring in Allied planes, and then in mid-November secretly completed the strip without telling us. Professor Tone Ferenc of Ljubljana University recently found a partial answer in secret messages exchanged between Slovene Partisan headquarters and the Fourth Zone:

October 29. Slovene headquarters to Fourth Zone: Immediately arrange airfield for heavy aircraft and report.

November 11. Fourth Zone to Slovene Headquarters: Airfield 46 19°20' north, 14°55' east near Recica. Work started. Seven days needed. Measures 1,000 meters by 110 meters.

November 12. Fourth Zone to Slovene Headquarters: For Politcommissar Kidric. Herewith landing information. Coordinates and description will be sent by Lt. Col. Bogomolov to Moscow. Landings in the evenings and darkness. Fighter escort needed. German planes sometimes patrol the sector. Signals on the ground: six fires in straight line. Plane should signal AA. Ground reply SS. For security reasons before landing bomb Celje, Sostanji, or Dravograd. All agreed with Lt. Col. Bogomolov. Report immediately if this information is to be sent to Stoner and Moscow. ["Stoner" may be a corruption of Honner, the general secretary of the Communist Party of Austria, who had been sent from Moscow to Slovene headquarters to supervise the penetration of Austria.]

November 12. Fourth Zone to Slovene Headquarters: Supply drops becoming urgent. Austrians who are already here cannot be provided with clothing or arms.

November 27. Fourth Zone to Slovene Headquarters: Airfield near Recica completed. Temporarily too wet, snow and rain. Will report when fit.

Kidric was also the secretary of the Communist Party of Slovenia and the political head of the Slovene Partisan movement. Fourth Zone would have sent a message for his personal attention only in the most unusual circumstances.

There are two possible explanations of this incident. Both may be right. One is that Moscow asked the Partisans to lay out the strip so Austrian ex-POWs in Russian hands could be airlifted by Russian aircraft to reinforce the Austrian *Kampfgruppe* (combat group). A first group of ex-POWs had already been dropped by the Russians during the summer in Dolenjska south of the Sava and had now been moved to Stajerska. At the time I was of course unaware of this Soviet-sponsored effort to penetrate Austria. However, the need for the landing strip could have easily been avoided by a parachute drop.

The other possibility was that this was part of a Russian and Partisan attempt to anticipate a possible Allied push through Slovenia. We knew that the Partisans expected such a move and feared it would upset their own political control of Slovenia and Croatia. The airstrip would make it possible to quickly call in a detachment of Soviet troops to form a "political" barrier to an Allied advance through Stajerska into Hungary after a landing in Istria. It would be very difficult for Allied troops to push past even a small detachment of Soviet troops without a serious political incident with Moscow. Either or both may have been the explanation. At the time I could not dismiss the second possibility, which caused me to send a priority message of warning to Italy.

During the course of the Second World War Churchill was often charged by both the Americans and the Russians with advocating Allied landings in the Balkans, though he has denied this in his history of the war. However, he repeatedly proposed a landing in Istria at the head of the Adriatic and a move through the Ljubljana Gap.

At the Quebec Conference in 1943 between Roosevelt and Churchill and later at the Teheran Conference of Roosevelt, Churchill, and Stalin it was decided that no Allied Balkan operations would take place except for commando raids on the Dalmatian coast, air and sea supply operations to the Partisans, and aerial bombing of strategic targets. This left open the Ljubljana Gap possibility, however.

Tito, too, opposed a Balkan strategy, although for different reasons. He remained concerned that if a landing in force was made on the Dalmatian coast, the Western Allies would be in a stronger position to influence, if not dictate, the shape of the postwar government in Yugoslavia—and possibly even to force the return of the monarchy.

On August 11 and 12 of 1944, Churchill, while visiting Allied Force Headquarters in Italy, had met with Tito, who had been brought to AFHQ for a visit. Churchill had asked Tito if the Partisans would co-operate in a possible landing in Istria to open up a port at Trieste to support the Allied forces driving toward central Europe. Tito replied he would favor such a landing if the Partisans participated. However, in September, when Tito went to Moscow to negotiate the terms under which the Red Army would operate on Yugoslav territory, he told Stalin he would resist any such Allied landing, possibly because he felt confident Washington would veto it.

But the Allied drive into northern Italy had become stalled, in part by the withdrawal of seven divisions for the landing that summer in southern France, and in part by heavy fall rains. The advance was stopped for the winter in the mountains south of the plains of the Po River. This meant there could be no Istrian landing and no push through the Ljubljana Gap in 1944.

■ On October 1, the Red Army entered Serbia from Bulgaria and Romania. The Fourth Zone Agitprop section organized a major rally and demonstration that night. Several large bonfires were built in the surrounding mountains, speeches were delivered and guns shot off.

The next day I was given a copy of the mimeographed weekly six-page journal of the Fourth Zone propaganda section. It carried this announcement:

> On September 29, Svobodna Jugoslavija (Free Yugoslavia) Radio broadcast the following message:
> "A few days ago the Supreme Command of the Red Army while carrying out its offensive operations against Hungarian and German units turned to the National Committee of the Liberation of Yugoslavia with

the request to allow the passage of the Soviet troops through Yugoslav territory in order to pursue necessary military operations. After the completion of their tasks the Red Army units will immediately vacate the Yugoslav territory.

"NKOJ has accepted the request of the Supreme Command of the Red Army, adding that during the presence of Soviet troops in our territory authority will be exercised by our National Liberation Committees. The Soviet Supreme Command has fully accepted this proviso."

This was almost certainly not the way it happened. Some months later in Belgrade, I learned from Tito's *chef de cabinet* that Partisan divisions in eastern Serbia and Slavonia had been put under Soviet Marshal Tolbukhin's command. A more likely explanation was that Tito had wanted such a paper agreement from the Russians to use as a precedent with the Western Allies should they decide to land in Istria and push through the Ljubljana Gap.

On October 29 Corporal Jim Fisher, our radio operator, picked up a BBC shortwave English-language broadcast reporting an Allied landing on the Dalmatian coast. Although the place and nature of the landing were not stated, I rushed to report this to the Partisan commander and the commissar, thinking it might be part of a grand strategy by which the Red Army and the Allied forces would link up in Slovenia and cut off the German forces in the southern Balkans. To my surprise (I should have known better) my report was met with complete silence. It was not reported to the rank and file and no celebration was organized. Since there was no further mention on the BBC I assumed it had been some sort of commando raid and had been withdrawn. It was, in fact, the landing of a small British artillery unit at Dubrovnik, which Tito had agreed to accept to help block the German retreat, and which operated under Partisan control until it was withdrawn at his request in January 1945.

A few days later I learned that two Gestapo agents had been captured near our headquarters. They had been sent with the specific purpose of finding out our plans in the event of Allied landings in Istria and parachute drops in Stajerska. In my radio message I reported: "This info not given us officially but provided by Pzn staff officer who stated info passed to us contrary to Zone orders."

■ Our highly successful attacks on the rail lines in June and July had convinced the high command in Italy that the Stajerska Partisans were well worth the commitment of additional aircraft and arms. By September the aerial supply line had been turned on full blast. But the timing was late. The Partisans were gathering up the weapons and, we became convinced, were putting their attacks on hold as they buried in mountain bunkers a large part of the drops. Our reports of this change in their strategy seemed to have no effect in slowing down the rain of arms from the sky.

Typical was the experience of OSS Lieutenant Holt Green and his radio operator who, far to the south in Montenegro, learned through a friendly Partisan that Allied arms were being hidden in a nearby barn. Investigating, they found not one but several barns piled high with weapons. Green delivered a strong protest to the Partisan command. Having been thus exposed, the arms were distributed to the brigades.

Peter Moore, at Slovene headquarters since mid-October, had expressed views similar to ours in his reports:

> After the magnificent efforts of the Slovene Partisans against the railways during the summer. . . there has been a great falling off in the Partisan attacks against railways, and many lines now run uninterrupted at night. [The reason they did not run in daylight was because Allied air attacks had become so intense.]
>
> The strongest possible representations at Hq Slovenia have produced many promises but no improvements.

Moore's recommendations to Maclean, with which I agreed wholeheartedly, were two:

> a. Allied supplies should now be limited to food, clothing, and maintenance requirements for ammunition. If the decision is to send arms they should be British or American to give us some control over ammunition supply.
> b. Allied missions, especially senior officers, should be reduced to an absolute minimum. Otherwise we risk being identified with Partisan excesses against the political opposition, over which we have no control.

We continued to puzzle for a long time over the reasons the Partisans had shifted their attitude of open cooperation to one of antagonism and opposition. Although most of the wartime Partisan archives are now open, there is still no clear explanation of the relative importance of each of the several possible reasons. My own speculation at the time was summarized in my final report on the Slovene mission:

> The incidents of non-cooperation, bad faith, and obstructionism became so numerous that it is impossible to explain them as carelessness or ignorance on the part of individual staff officers. . . . We came to the conclusion that these events could only be explained by a basic Partisan policy that had become one of all obstruction short of an open break with the West and the stoppage of air and sea supplies.

If this was their policy it appeared to be successful. In November alone 71 planeloads of arms and explosives were dropped to the Fourth Zone by Force 399; this was the last month before the German winter offensive captured all of our drop points and made it impossible to set up others.

In my report I listed what I thought might be the reasons for the anti-British and anti-American actions:

> After the failure of large numbers of the opposition—White Guard troops—to come over to the Partisans in response to an offer of amnesty in September the Partisans may have realized that their postwar position was not as secure as they had thought. They were very anxious that the extent of opposition and the anti-Partisan feeling not be known to us, hence the attempt to isolate us.
>
> The nearness of the Red Army after the fall of Belgrade may have made them feel less dependent upon the Western Allies, and more willing to throw over the marriage of convenience.
>
> There appeared to be a growing distrust of the Allied postwar intentions in the internal affairs of Yugoslavia. . . . Many Partisan leaders feared that Britain would do everything possible to put the King back on his throne.
>
> Possibly the more extreme of the Communist leaders desired to undermine British and American popularity with the rank and file, by regularly putting us in the most unfavorable light possible. This is substantiated by their removal of all Partisans in contact with us who became overfriendly and who they thought had been influenced by us.

I became increasingly troubled about the Partisans on still another score: the increasing inequality within the Partisan ranks. "There is far greater differentiation between officers and men in clothing, food, equipment, shelter, and privileges than is found in the British or American armies," I reported.

> These junior officers take advantage of their authority to get for themselves the best of the meager supplies available. Nearly all officers had "Tito" jackets tailored from British and American greatcoats supplied in our airdrops, then took second greatcoats to wear over the jackets. Meanwhile, the troops shivered in ragged remnants of civilian clothes and German uniforms. At Zone headquarters all the couriers and women propaganda workers had British battledress and at the same time I saw whole fighting brigades without a single piece of Allied clothing.

I had expressed my concerns to the Partisan leadership, but there was no response.

The same situation existed in the issuing of food. Separate messes existed for officers and men and normally there was a very great difference in both quality and quantity. Officers seldom carried their own rucksacks on the march but had them carried by their personal couriers.

In my report to Maclean I wrote:

> Apparently Partisans have a definition of responsibility quite different to our concept of military responsibility. On several occasions I made requests for certain actions to the Zone commissar and to which he agreed. Later, if the action was not carried out, the reply would be in essence, "Well, I gave the order, and if it was not carried out it is not my fault. I can't be everywhere at once." One day during a drop I asked the lieutenant in charge of the area to replace a signal canopy which had been taken away by mistake. The order was passed down through six people before a fourteen-year-old boy was sent out. Meanwhile, a Mission sergeant had done the job.

As the end of the war approached in the fall the Partisan forces expanded rapidly. Many not already in the Partisan ranks joined to be on the winning side when the war ended. The Fourth Zone Partisan leadership actively recruited about 2,000 men a month in order to bring as many men as possible under their political control. The propaganda sheet distributed to the Stajerska Partisans was becoming increasingly insistent in its demands for even greater efforts at recruiting:

> If in places our mobilization is not proceeding as well as it could, the cause lies in our political activists and military units being unable or considering it unnecessary to continue making every effort in order to ensure its complete success. The terrorist methods used by the occupying authorities against the local population are but a weak excuse for evading the mobilization. . . .
>
> These [who] by postponing their enlistment in the National Liberation Army aggravate their guilt before the Slovene people thus sinking into the morass of complete betrayal.

It became increasingly apparent to me that the objective of the Partisans' recruiting drive was not only to strengthen the brigades for occupation of southern Austria, but was also to bring every able-bodied man under Partisan discipline and control by the time the Germans were defeated. The Partisans were positioning themselves for the final showdown to control the country when the war ended.

As a consequence the Partisan forces in the Fourth Zone had become too large and cumbersome to be effective, especially against the railroads and roads over which the German forces in the Balkans were retreating. A smaller force could more easily emerge unexpectedly to destroy their objectives quickly and then be lost in the mountain forests. A smaller force would not put such heavy burdens on local food supply and airborne weapons supply. And, as would soon be demonstrated, a large, unwieldy force was highly vulnerable to a determined German attack.

Yet despite the increasing preoccupation of the Fourth Zone Partisans with winning the final phase of the civil war and with preparations for their advances into Austria and northeast Italy, they had made major contributions to the overall Allied war effort by their highly successful attacks against the key rail lines during the summer. Although many opportunities were missed in the fall months, not a single train moved across the main double-track line along the Sava

River running west to Ljubljana and northeast Italy from early September until mid-December—and it probably remained blocked for even longer. The parallel single-track line along the Drava River was cut intermittently from June to December, with delays of a few hours to a day. Occasional cuts in the single-track line east from Maribor to Hungary were also made during the fall.

■ In the relative quiet of our liberated territory in late summer and early fall, I had time to reflect on what I had learned.

First and foremost, I was struck by the very great differences between "regular" war and a guerrilla war—between the Allied-German war I had left in Italy and the Partisan war of which I was now a part. In Italy foreign armies, supplied from their home countries with everything they needed, fought each other the length of the country. The Italians, now out of the war, were in the main spectators whose role was to try to keep out of the way of the fighting. A hundred miles across the Adriatic the Partisans fought at first almost exclusively with internal supplies and captured weapons. Only after two years of fighting did supplies come from the Western Allies in significant amounts.

Here, in contrast, the civilians played a critical role. Their support was crucial to success. They provided the intelligence screens that surrounded and protected the armed Partisans, as well as the food and clothing, the shelter and the recruits, without which the Partisans could not have survived. The Partisans had no already organized government to provide them with the resources to fight the war. They had to create from scratch all the institutions needed to support their armed brigades—taxation, administration, even newspapers.

Tactics, too, were different. It would have been disastrous if the Partisans had tried to stop the Germans in direct confrontation. The better-armed Germans would have quickly finished them off in pitched battles. The tactic had to be to avoid entrapment and destruction at all costs.

This strategy was fundamentally different from that of modern highly mechanized warfare in which the objective of each side was to defeat the enemy by massive assaults. Partisan strategy was often misunderstood by the Allies. Enthusiasts, such as Churchill, claimed the Germans and Italians had been evicted by the Partisans from two-thirds of Yugoslavia. Skeptics said they had simply withdrawn and could return any time they wanted to. The skeptics were more nearly right, but they failed to recognize that it was taking larger and larger forces that the Germans could ill spare to blunt the Partisan attacks, especially against their lines of communication.

CHAPTER 14

The German Winter
Offensive Begins

Except for one punitive sweep into our liberated mountain valley, the Gornja Savinjska Dolina, the Germans had left us pretty much alone all through the fall and into the beginning of winter. I felt we must be living on borrowed time. The valley became our base for receiving a large number of airdrops and for attacking the main German rail lines and roads. These the Germans would need to control as their armies retreated into Germany from the Balkans, and as they shifted their divisions between the eastern and Italian fronts to meet Allied attacks. The nearer the front lines approached our area the more precarious our own situation would become.

Throughout the fall intelligence reports filtered in of German fortifications being constructed both along the Sava River to the south and the Drava to the north. At the end of September the Germans occupied the Pohorje, the mountainous area that had been our summer base for attacks against the north-south rail lines. We had set up our first regular drop point there to supply the arms and explosives needed to support these attacks. I reported to Maclean on October 4 that "the Germans have strong concentrations in the Pohorje and have forced the Partisans to evacuate."

On October 6 a Partisan intelligence penetration into the German headquarters in Maribor reported that six enemy divisions were being concentrated in Stajerska between the Sava and Drava rivers. Two German Croat divisions (German officers, Croat men) would be deployed along the Sava and four German divisions between the Sava and the Drava.

On October 9 I radioed Italy that Partisan intelligence reported the Third Gebirgsjäger (Mountain) Division to have moved in along the north side of the Drava. The Twenty-fifth SS Polizei Regiment was at the town of Celje immediately to the east of us. The headquarters and one regiment of the 538 Grenzwacht (border guard) Division was also at Celje. The three battalions of the regiment were located at points around our liberated valley. A battalion of the Spanish Blue Division was at a town a few miles south of Celje. Franco had sent the Blue Division of so-called volunteers to fight alongside the Germans in Russia. Why it had turned up in Stajerska was not clear.

The next day I radioed that 15,000 local civilians had been forcibly mobilized to construct a defensive line of bunkers and pill-boxes along the Sava. "All boys fourteen to sixteen and women sixteen to sixty have been mobilized for work this line." In a second message that day I radioed: "Pzns have reliable info that Huns plan heavy offensive against Fourth Zone. Most urgent you either send stores [requested in earlier messages] soonest or advise immed so Partisans will not count on them."

The expected German offensive against us still had not materialized but the tension was mounting daily. On October 16 the Fourth Zone Commander Borstnar and Commissar Bencic, the Russian Lieutenant Colonel Bogomolov, and I were up on a high ridge overlooking our mountain valley. It was a sunny fall day and the farms and villages below almost glistened. Suddenly at noon we heard aircraft below us and watched as three large planes below us circled over our main drop area on the valley floor and began discharging streams of parachutes. The others in the group were certain it was a German paratroop attack. A similar surprise attack had been launched by paratroopers against Tito's headquarters at Drvar in Bosnia only a few months before. Tito and his staff, the Anglo-American mission, including the prime minister's son Randolph, and the Russian mission had barely escaped capture.

It was with considerable difficulty that I persuaded the group that they were American Liberators responding to my urgent requests for guns, ammunition, and medical supplies. It was unusual for us to receive a drop in daytime, and when we did, only well-armed bombers were used because of the danger from German fighters. We normally would have received advance notice of the drop that day, but occasionally our drop point was given as an alternate to incoming aircraft in the event they could not find their primary drop points. On the following day several Liberators also made a daylight drop to us. This time I was in the valley floor at the drop point. One aircraft, after dropping its load, circled back and fired a red flare, meaning trouble, as it passed over us. It failed to gain altitude and appeared to crash land a mile or so away. I sent Partisans running with a few pounds of explosive to rescue the crew and destroy the electronics before the Germans reached the plane. The explosives probably weren't necessary, but I was not taking a chance should there be secret electronics relating to navigation or bomb sights aboard. All the crew were safe and uninjured. One of the four engines had failed just at the time of the drop, and the pilot had been unable to feather the propeller on the dead engine to reduce the drag and couldn't climb out of the valley on the remaining three engines. By the next day the aircrew was headed south on foot along the courier line to Slovene Partisan headquarters where they would be flown out to Italy.

Other things also contrived to frustrate the drop operations. On November 9 I signaled Base Operations: "Night fifth Pzns and Germans were having a small battle at Poezela northwest of Celje. During the excitement someone set fire to a barn and a few minutes later one of our aircraft dropped its chutes to Germans."

The German troop buildup continued into late November. By mid-November the Partisans had confirmed that approximately 9,000 additional German troops had arrived, probably from the Balkans, in the Celje area alone. Celje lay at the lower end of our valley, which was completely open to any German move toward us from that direction.

■ On October 24 we received an operational priority message over the OSS radio link from headquarters Caserta:

FOR: Lindsay

FROM: Glavin and Chapin [respectively, OSS commander, Mediterranean Theater, and head of the Austrian section]

This is an urgent request and I would like a reply immediately. I'm anxious to know if it is possible for you to move near Zagreb with W/T operator and make contact inside the city. It will be a very important and highly secret mission!!

A senior German general, Lieutenant General Edmund Glaise von Horstenau, German military plenipotentiary with the puppet Croatian government with whom OSS Switzerland had secret contact, wished to discuss surrender and had asked for a secret meeting with an American officer.

At first I was skeptical because of Glavin's condition of high secrecy. Zagreb was almost 100 miles away as the crow flies, and probably twice that distance on foot—much of it through German-held areas. I believed that this was an unrealistic idea of headquarters officers who had little understanding of the real problems we had to live with. We were completely dependent on the Partisans for guides and patrols whenever we moved. I replied that I could get to Zagreb but that it would be impossible to make contact with a German general without the knowledge of the Partisans.

Lieutenant Colonel Howard Chapin, head of the OSS Austrian section, accepted this view, saying that discussion by OSS Colonel Ellery Huntington at Partisan headquarters with Tito was approved without revealing any more information about the contact than was absolutely essential. I would be given further instructions by radio. Tito was then told of the proposed contact and gave his approval both for the contact and for my move from Fourth Zone to Zagreb.

Captain Charles Fisher would take over my responsibility for American intelligence contacts with the Fourth Zone, since his origi-

nal mission of penetrating Austria had been so completely blocked by
the Partisans. In line with a high-level decision taken earlier to withdraw the American officers from the British-controlled mission under Maclean, it had already been decided that the Anglo part of my
Anglo-American responsibilities in the Fourth Zone would be assumed by a British officer. There were already four British officers at
Zone headquarters. All were concerned primarily with Austria.
Roberts was part of Wilkinson's SOE Austrian operation; Whitfield
and Parks were MI-6; and Mathews was A Force, the prisoner escape
organization. Because of Partisan intransigence none of them had
any possibility of doing their own jobs. We all recognized that a
much smaller party could represent all the various Allied interests,
especially after the Partisans had imposed such extreme limits on our
operations. Instead of dropping yet another British officer, any one of
them could have taken my job as Maclean's representative to the
Fourth Zone. But our joint proposals that this be done met with no
favor. It would seem that the charters of each parent organization
were to be kept pure and inviolable.

I therefore pointed out to OSS that a British replacement would
have to be dropped to me before I could leave for Zagreb. Force 399
now proposed to drop a Major Saunders and Captain Owen to replace
me, and two radio operators to replace Jim Fisher. Douglas Owen and
one radio operator were scheduled to arrive November 11, but because
of weather did not get in until November 19. Saunders was never able
to get in. Because of the German offensive begun on December 4,
there were no longer any secure drop points to receive him.

With Owen on the ground I was free to leave. But we still hoped
to have a pickup aircraft land on our ill-fated strip at Recica to evacuate the wounded. If I could go out on this plane I could be briefed in
Italy on the Zagreb mission and then drop directly to the Croatian
Partisans near Zagreb. We waited day after day for the weather to
clear and the mud in the landing field to dry. Then on December 5
the Germans took the hills overlooking the Recica strip and that door
closed. The overland march to Croatia was now the only open route.

I left our British colleagues with the same respect and admiration that I had conceived for Bill Deakin when he briefed me in Cairo eight months earlier. Although there was considerable friction between the Americans and the British at our respective headquarters—primarily over differing policies regarding Tito and Mihailovic—relations among those of us in Stajerska were uniformly good. I was therefore understandably and profoundly touched when, years later, Peter Wilkinson sent me a copy of the last letter Alfgar Hesketh-Prichard wrote to him—from Stajerska—before his death: "Here we really can't keep anyone with dignity," that valiant gentleman wrote, "while Lindsay is doing the only real job and already has Squadron Leader Mervyn [Whitfield] plus radio operator plus Gatoni, Maj. Mathews of A Force and his own WTO [wireless telegraph operator] and Lieutenant Bush (coming out with this letter)." Referring to the OSS Labor Desk men, he continued: "It is a godsend to have Lindsay fix everything as it would be a disaster if they [the Labor Desk agents] came to Trigger [the planned SOE advance base across the Drava]. The more I see of Lindsay the more I like him and the more I respect his wisdom as 'coordinator' here. He is a very 'safe' man to have represent us here."

Hesketh-Prichard also paid Edward Welles a high compliment in that letter to Peter Wilkinson: "The more I see of Welles the better I like him—the Winterburn type, only better." Winterburn was the British commando sergeant who had escaped from POW camp in Breslau and made his way on prison-forged documents to us in Stajerska and had sought to stay with us.

In sending me Hesketh-Prichard's letter, Peter Wilkinson wrote:

This is such a splendid example of the mutual trust and cooperation which existed between all of us "in the field," whether OSS, SOE, Macmis [Maclean mission] and Clowder [his Austrian operation], I should so like to see it "on the record." There is abundant reference to the sickening intrigues, etc., Anglo/American, OSS/SOE rivalries and the rest of it in London and Washington and at Headquarters, that I think it is important for someone (I hope you) to say loud and clear that in the field it was completely otherwise and we were not only indifferent to who got the credit, but resolved above all never to let each other down.

I can only second what he has so eloquently written. Sir Peter Wilkinson has himself been a good friend of America over the many years he served in the British Embassy in Washington and as British ambassador in Vietnam and Vienna.

The Partisan leaders decided to throw a goodbye party the night before Ed Welles, Jim Fisher, and I were to leave, at the inn in the village of Gornji Grad. Normally we stayed out of the villages because of the danger of surprise attack. But the advancing Germans were still a few miles away and our sentries surrounded the village. In spite of the severe troubles between us over the previous months, we and the Partisan leaders had been through many rough times together and had built strong personal bonds.

The party was a final outpouring of that friendship and personal regard between us. Schnapps flowed freely and there were the inevitable long and flowery toasts followed by clinking of glasses and bottoms up. The toasts got longer and more flowery as the dinner progressed; I was later told that toward the end of the evening, after draining my schnapps glass I would toss it over my shoulder. Unknown to me the innkeeper's wife was right behind me to catch the glass before it crashed on the floor. Glasses were precious; there was no way to replace them.

The morning we left Zone headquarters Bencic, the Zone commissar, came to say goodbye. He said that he fully realized that our relations had not been completely satisfactory and implied that the blame was with the Partisans. He further said that although many Partisans were very pro-Russian, many others, including himself, were equally pro-Western.

The three of us and our liaison officer, Vlado, left with a patrol of ten men and one machine gun amid embraces and farewells. The next day a courier caught up with us to report that a few hours after we had departed, the German attack had forced the Zone headquarters and the British and American parties to abandon the valley and return to the mountains. They would have to stay there until the end of the war.

Our passage out of Stajerska, to Slovene headquarters in Dolenjska, and thence to Croatia began on December 6, 1944, in the midst of the German offensive. Two days after our departure and halfway to the Sava River, we had to cross the main Ljubljana-Maribor east-west road that followed the stream in a steep mountain canyon. We had received reports before we left of heavy German troop movements on it. A few hundred yards before reaching it that night a courier was sent ahead to scout the road. He soon returned reporting German troops on the road. Crossing that night would be impossible; we could not remain where we were, as we would be exposed in daylight. So we climbed back up the north slope to a remote farmhouse.

The next two nights the road was checked and found still occupied by German troops moving along it. Late that night, when we were crowded into the farmhouse, an alarmed shout came from outside. Instantly everyone started to grab packs and guns. Within a few seconds a second alarm was shouted. The Partisans panicked and ran into the night. Our radio and batteries were forgotten by the men in whose hands they had been put and Jim Fisher, Ed Welles, and I grabbed them as we went out. It turned out to be a false alarm—but everyone was very much on edge as the reports of fighting filtered in from the valley we had left and as our way across the road continued to be blocked.

I had already seen a few panics induced by sudden alarms. Each seemed to follow the same pattern. A first alarm was sounded unexpectedly, and a few seconds later, before the group had time to find out what danger had caused the alarm, a second cry was heard. Still not knowing what and where the danger was, the men had reacted in panic.

The next day, while we waited to cross the road, a Partisan battalion of over a hundred men joined us. They were also headed south. Two Frenchmen who had escaped from a German concentration camp were with them. They were gaunt, with deep-set eyes, and still dressed in the concentration-camp garb of flimsy, vertically striped blue and white trousers and tops. Their only other protection from the cold was blankets—from our airdrops—given them by the Partisans, which they wrapped around themselves. Whenever I felt sorry for myself I had only to think of them and what they must have endured. How they managed to keep up with our march I never understood.

The German offensive to the north was continuing and appeared to be aimed at cornering the Partisans with their backs against the Sava River. Our present position was becoming more untenable, and increasingly dangerous. The Partisan battalion commander and I decided we must get across the road that night even if it meant fighting our way across. Shortly after dark we moved down the wooded slope to the stream and road. It was snowing lightly. This time we found the road clear.

The road was on the south side of a rushing mountain stream that, fed by fall rains, was in full flood. We crossed on the trunk of a large tree that had fallen across the stream. It was wet and slippery with the snow that had begun to accumulate. Fortunately no one fell into the torrent below. The road was indeed clear. Because the road had been cut into the steep mountainside we could not climb the rock face of the cut at that point. Instead we followed the road for several hundred yards until we came to a small ravine that provided a way to climb into the forest above.

We were moving in complete silence, our footsteps muffled by the new snow. As we were halfway to the ravine, strung out ten yards apart along the road, I heard a single rifle shot from the direction of the head of the column. In the silence after the shot I could hear the soft clicks from ahead and behind me as the Partisans switched off the safety catches on their guns. There were no further shots, and when we reached the ravine the column turned off the road and began to climb the south slope.

After climbing for an hour or so I became aware of a faint warm glow ahead through the falling snow. As we came closer the outlines of a small wayside shrine began to take form. The shrine faced away from our approach and the glow I had seen was the yellow light of a tiny altar lamp reflected in the falling snowflakes. It was a beacon of safe haven.

Rural wayside shrines were common in this solidly Catholic area of Stajerska. Peasants who formed the protective screen around us had adopted the practice of lighting the little oil lamps in the shrines only when the nearby area was free of German patrols. An unlit lamp meant danger. We proceeded past the shrine to the nearby house where we rested and warmed ourselves by the big built-in ceramic tile stove that was always in the Stajerska peasant houses, to cook with and to heat the house. (In winter the babies and children were placed on top of the warm tiles for the night.)

The owner of the house told us that all that day there had been a German ambush hidden among the trees next to the ravine where we had left the road. The Germans had departed only an hour before we had come along. The Partisan at the head of the column, suspecting an ambush, had fired a single shot into the trees to provoke return fire before we were all caught, exposed on the road, in a direct line of fire from which there was no escape. There had been no answering fire. The image of the falling snow softly glowing in the light of the altar lamp seemed to me to capture the essence of the close relationship between the armed Partisans and the peasants who supported them.

The following night we reached the mountains above the north side of the Sava River, but again we were blocked. Couriers reported another German sweep was under way between the south bank and the German border a few miles beyond.

■ These enforced days of waiting gave me time to reflect on the months in Stajerska. The Partisan movement was far different than what I had thought it to be before my drop to Slovenia. At its core, it was a nationalist Communist political movement, not just a guerrilla army fighting a war against the Germans.

The liberated areas, which had been set up in all the principal nationality territories from the Reich border on the north to the Greek border on the south, provided the bases essential to the growth and final success of the Partisans. They became centers of political indoctrination and police control of the civil inhabitants. The local farms provided food and shelter for the Partisan brigades. Liberated areas were the collection points for new Partisan recruits as well as areas for their basic training and schools of guerrilla tactics for junior officers. In the more secure areas, dirt landing fields were laid out so that Allied Dakota cargo planes could land with supplies and take out wounded Partisans as well as downed Allied aircrews and escaped POWs. Liberated territories provided the bases from which armed Partisan operations could be expanded into new areas.

In creating these territories, the Partisans had carefully chosen remote areas away from cities and lines of communication, areas that were not important to the German and Italian occupying forces. To have denied these areas to the Partisans would have taken additional occupation forces at least ten times the size of the Partisan forces. The enemy would have had to be strong enough everywhere to meet surprise attacks, while the Partisans needed only to concentrate their limited strength for attacks against isolated garrisons of their choosing.

A key to the survival of the Partisan movement was that the German main forces were engaged against the Western Allied and Russian armies. They did not have manpower to spare for the complete pacification of the entire country. Only when Partisan activity threatened their important interests, such as the uninterrupted use of the roads and railroads, were the occupiers driven to retaliate.

Liberated territories were areas in which the German and local puppet forces had relinquished day-to-day control to the Partisans. The Axis occupation forces still came in, but only periodically and in large, well-armed sweeps. Their objective in these sweeps was to retaliate for Partisan attacks on German installations and lines of communication and to keep the Partisans off balance. They burned villages; deported or shot the peasants who had given aid to the Partisans; destroyed food and military supplies; and cornered and attacked Partisan units wherever they could. The Partisans, in turn, sought to make these sweeps as difficult and costly as possible by mining roads, destroying bridges, constructing tank traps, ambushing the Germans as they attacked, and harassing them as they retreated.

■ After we had waited two days near another mountain farm the couriers who crossed the Sava River at night brought back a report encouraging enough that we decided to cross that night. The boatmen were alerted and after dark fell we moved down to the road next to the river. The weather had turned to a light but cold rain. Because each boat would take only one or two passengers in addition to the boatmen, the crossing took almost three hours. This meant sitting huddled in the dark in near-freezing rain until our turns came to be taken across.

Sitting in the bushes for a couple of hours, teeth chattering, and thoroughly miserable, my imagination began to play tricks on me. I became convinced that as the guides moved us singly from one hiding spot to the next in complete silence I had somehow been passed into the hands of the Germans and that suddenly a trap would be sprung and I would be taken prisoner. While I was trying to work out whether I should bolt now or wait, there was a tap on my shoulder, and I was taken across the deserted road to a boat hidden in dense growth at the river's edge. Trying to get into the boat I lost my footing and went into the river up to my waist. I climbed into the boat thoroughly soaked.

The river was swift from the recent rains and the boat was carried downstream a quarter of a mile before the hard-paddling boatmen reached the other side. After I got myself off the bottom of the boat with my pack and gun I was taken back from the river to another hidden spot while the boatmen pulled the boat out of the water and carried it upstream before going back for the next passenger. Because of the danger of being surprised at any moment, there was no possibility of even taking off my boots to drain the sloshing water out of them. It was simply too dangerous, given the risk of being surprised and having to run.

As soon as the party was across and we were put in the hands of a new patrol and guide we headed across the railroad toward the foothills. After crossing the river we were wet, cold, and very tired. While still in the river flatland we stopped, hoping for rest, at a tiny farmhouse. It was after midnight and the house was completely dark.

Fourth Zone
Partisans on the
march in the
Karawanken Alps,
winter 1944–45
(*Lindsay*)

Carrying the wounded; this priest was one of very few Catholic clergy who joined the Partisans (*Lindsay*)

RIGHT: Exhausted Partisans resting in the high mountains, where they have been driven by the German winter offensive, 1944–45 (*Lindsay*)

BELOW: Winter camp, Stajerska (*Lindsay*)

The leader of the patrol banged on the door to rouse someone to let us in. Finally a window opened a bit and a terribly frightened woman implored us hysterically to please go away. There were Germans nearby and she would be sent to a concentration camp or shot for having sheltered us. This time we heeded the anguished plea and slogged on in the dark night.

The sloshing gradually stopped in my boots and my clothing slowly dried out from body heat. During the next day and night our march south continued without stop. There were German and White Guard patrols throughout the area and we were fortunately chased south, the direction we wanted to go. In the past it had usually turned out that when we were on the run we were forced to go in the direction opposite to our intended course. Although shots were exchanged from time to time, we were able to avoid any direct confrontation.

After moving all the next day through a mountainous and forested region, we came that night into a cultivated valley. In its center was the town of Trebnje, normally occupied by a German garrison. Since all the German troops were reported to be out conducting the offensive in the area through which we had just come, the Partisan commander decided we would go through the main street of the town rather than circling around it.

The password or recognition signal was given to each man to be used in the event we should have to fight in the black night when it was hard to tell friend from foe. The recognition signal and response, in Slovene of course, were one of the most complex we had ever used. As we moved down the center of the blacked-out main street at ten-meter intervals I kept repeating both to myself over and over, fearing I would forget them if we ran into trouble. I am sure that in my endless repetition I had gradually altered the words, just as in the game of whispering a sentence to the next person, who passes on what he thinks he has heard to the next until the sentence is altered beyond all recognition. Fortunately I didn't have to use it—I'm sure I had it all wrong. The German garrison was busily combing the area we had already passed through.

The night was again stormy. Rain replaced snow and turned the mountain tracks, worn deep by generations of farm wagons, into seas of mud on top of the frozen ground. Jim Fisher had taken out one of his last cigarettes, received from an earlier drop in Stajerska. In the black a Partisan marching alongside spotted the glow of the cigarette and tried, in his own pain and craving, to take the cigarette from Jim. Jim resisted and the two almost came to blows.

We continued on into the next day and finally arrived at the first outpost of Slovene liberated territory. It had been a continuous march of 33 hours and I was so tired I could barely walk. The muscles in my thighs were so sore that each step was a major effort. After a rest we continued to Slovene headquarters near the village of Semic. Ample food and uninterrupted sleep were now possible for the first time in days. Here we learned that a major German offensive in the Ardennes had been launched a day or two before and American and British forces were trying to stem the attack, which seemed to be aimed at reaching the English Channel. We would not have news again until we reached Croatian headquarters.

Captain Jim Goodwin was Brigadier Maclean's representative at Slovene headquarters when I passed through there in May. He had been wounded in September during an abortive attack on the Litija bridge, and Lieutenant Colonel Peter Moore was now head of Maclean's mission there. Moore said the Partisans in the Seventh Corps (Dolenjska) and Ninth Corps (Primorska) areas had abandoned offensive operations during the fall. As a result the Germans had retaken a large part of the territories previously held by the Partisans. The food supply for the winter was now precarious because much of it had come from the areas lost to the Germans. The Germans had reinforced their garrisons in Novo Mesto and Kocevje and were using them as bases for offensive forays into the remaining Partisan territory. They had reopened the railroad from Ljubljana to Kocevje and the road to Novo Mesto. One German attack had reached Semic itself before it was beaten back. The last offensive operation undertaken by the Partisans had been against Kocevje; it had failed. Since then the Germans had held the initiative.

The White Guard had become much more aggressive and under

German direction had organized highly mobile *pokretni*, or commando, battalions that had taken the offensive against the Partisans in the forests that before had been their undisputed preserve. Moore found it inexplicable that White Guard morale was now higher than that of the Partisans, even though their patrons the Germans were now certain to be defeated.

The Germans had effectively mobilized the conservative Catholics of Slovenia against the Partisans by playing on their fears of Communism, the advancing Red Army, and Soviet occupation. After Belgrade was liberated from the Germans in October the Communist direction of the Slovene Partisans was much more open and the Liberation Front had received less emphasis in propaganda.

Peter Moore was as unhappy as I with the intelligence collected by the Partisans. He too had been denied any indication of their sources. He said that the Russian colonel who headed the Soviet military mission had also been critical of Partisan intelligence, and of their reduction in operations against the railroads. Moore also had experienced a determined Partisan effort to isolate him and to keep him from any contacts with both civilians and the rank and file. The Partisan command had become very secretive about their troop dispositions and intentions, and no longer discussed them with him. Moore believed, as I did, that they were hoarding their weapons and conserving their strength to capture Trieste, and to liquidate the White Guard when the Germans were defeated on the main battlefronts in Italy and Germany. The pro-Russian propaganda continued unabated while the political attacks against the "reactionary" British and Americans increased in shrillness.

A splendid New Zealand army surgeon, Major Lindsay Rogers, had spent the last year in Dolenjska running a string of hidden hospitals for the Partisans. He daily performed operations on the many wounded Partisans to save their lives and limbs. He too had found the present hostile attitude almost intolerable. A commissar was assigned to these hospitals to ensure that Rogers did not recruit spies among his patients. Whenever the Partisan nurses and attendants he had trained became too friendly, they suddenly disappeared.

The last straw was when the Partisan supply officer took all the medical supplies Rogers had received from British stocks for his hospitals and said he would henceforth allocate them as he saw fit. Rogers sent off a radio message to Tito reminding him of his agreement that the Allied command would send medical supplies directly to Rogers for his hospitals. If this agreement was violated he would be compelled to ask for his withdrawal. While I was there he had not received a reply.

The deterioration of Partisan relations with the Allies had come at a time when the aerial supply line from Italy had been running full tilt. The Partisans in Dolenjska were now far better clothed and armed than they had been in May when we passed through the area on our way to Stajerska. Yet they had abandoned the offensive to the Germans and the White Guard.

■ The existence of liberated areas, such as the one in Dolenjska, provided the Partisans the freedom to move about openly in daylight. The danger was that it was so easy for the Partisans to adjust to living free from the constant and immediate threat of the German attack that elementary precautions tended to be quickly forgotten. It was a temptation to which they at times succumbed.

Supplies and food were often concentrated rather than dispersed and hidden. Headquarters staffs grew too large and tended to remain too long at comfortable villages. Equipment accumulated to a point where mobility was seriously hampered when the Germans suddenly launched attacks. In short, the discipline of living in small units in the forest, with nothing more than that which could be carried in backpacks or on pack animals, was quickly lost; it was hard to regain quickly in the face of determined German offensives. There were other compelling reasons to keep the Partisan units dispersed. It minimized the danger of German encirclement and destruction of a major portion of their forces. Dispersal kept them in closer touch with the villages where food and recruits could be found.

Yet Tito had often concentrated his main fighting forces in a single area for many weeks at a time, occupying the same village as offices of the high command. In 1944, for instance, he set up his head-quarters in the small town of Drvar. There was of course no hope of disguising such a large headquarters, if for no other reason than that the several radio transmitters of the Partisans, the Russians, the British, and the Americans were easily plotted, and the volume of messages transmitted was easily monitored, even if the Germans could not crack the codes. He had been there for at least five months when the German parachute and glider attack came. Tito and the others escaped with minutes to spare.

The year before Tito had concentrated his main fighting forces in a single area in the mountains of Montenegro, where they became an inviting target for the Germans. Tito and his forces were completely encircled by the Germans. They escaped only by heroic fighting over two months, breaking out through successive rings of German encirclement. His forces were severely weakened and nearly destroyed. Almost 8,000 Partisans and civilians were reported killed in the breakout. Lieutenant Colonel William Deakin had been with them then, and has vividly described the horrors of the fighting in his book *The Embattled Mountain.*

After the Drvar attack Tito dispersed more of his fighting units to the areas held by each of the nationalities. They no longer were in common danger, yet could be directed centrally by radio and by courier. Dispersal had its political advantages and effects. There already were Partisan units in each of the areas, but the addition of the elite fighting brigades strengthened Tito's military and political base in each important area. This had the further advantage to him of providing an active Partisan presence throughout Yugoslavia to support both political action and recruiting. The ground was thus laid for the complete control of Yugoslavia by the Communist leadership at the end of the war. Only in Serbia were the Partisans unable to establish a strong presence until mid-1944.

During our brief stopover at Slovene headquarters a few short radio messages came in from Stajerska. The German attacks were continuing with increasing intensity. An attempted breakout of two brigades to reach the Pohorje had been repulsed. All the Partisan units were now in the higher levels of the mountains and in deep snow.

The necessary authority for us to go on to Croatian Partisan headquarters, about 70 miles to the east, was received in Slovenia from Tito's headquarters, and we set off again on December 18 with a new patrol as escort. Our move to Croatia was more of what we had just experienced. By now winter had set in and the ground was frozen, making walking much more difficult, especially in deep snow, or when crossing fields not yet snow-covered where the plowed furrows were frozen hard.

Food was far from plentiful. I remember vividly arriving one evening at an isolated peasant house. The family—father, mother, and three children—had just sat down to an evening meal of beans and vegetables cooked in a single pot now on the table. There were no plates. They ate directly from the pot with spoons. When we came in the family immediately stood up, greeted us shyly, and motioned us to take their places. Each of us carried a spoon stuck in his boot top. It was often called the Partisan's secret weapon, and when we first arrived with the Partisans we were cautioned never to lose our spoons; if we did we would starve to death. I dipped my spoon into the stew. It tasted marvelous. I knew that this was the family's meal and if we ate it all they would go to bed hungry. I was determined to take only three or four spoonfuls but found it impossible to stop without one more and then a second. We did stop eating when there was about a third left in the pot, though the father and mother urged us to continue. It took the greatest willpower to put the spoons back in our boots.

After we crossed into Croatia we were again in liberated territory, and we shortly reached the town of Glina. The telephone line between Glina and Topusko, where Croatian headquarters was now located, was in working order. Our escort called in to report our arrival and we were told to wait in Glina. In about two hours, to our great surprise and joy, an American, a Sergeant Bradshaw, driving a jeep, arrived to pick us up. We actually rode the last 10 miles in sheer ecstasy as we watched the roadside slip past at an unbelievable rate of 20 miles an hour. We watched the trees speed past and silently counted the footsteps it would have taken had we still been on foot. It was our first ride since May.

We arrived at Croatian Partisan headquarters on Christmas Eve. Of course our first question was: How did an American jeep get here? The explanation was that OSS Lieutenant Colonel Lanning McFarland, his sergeant, and a jeep had been loaded into a C-47 cargo plane a week or so earlier, and landed in Croatian liberated territory. Welles, Fisher, and I were more than a little annoyed that they had not had to walk a single foot of the way.

CHAPTER 15

Ethnic and Ideological Wars in Croatia

Because of the crushing German offensive against the Fourth Zone Partisans, the trip to Croatian headquarters at Topusko, about 30 miles south of Zagreb, had taken 18 days. This was far longer than OSS or I had anticipated. Unlike in Stajerska, in Croatia the Partisans held very large areas of liberated territory. Here the revolutionary political organization was significantly more advanced. The forces were larger and better armed, and I now had the opportunity to see for myself the next step in the progress of Partisan political and military organization. But first I had a more immediate assignment—contacting the German General Edmund Glaise von Horstenau.

Glaise had been in Yugoslavia since 1941 as the representative of the German army general staff in its dealings with the puppet state of Croatia. After the defeat of Yugoslavia in 1941, Hitler and Mussolini agreed that an independent state of Croatia, greatly enlarged at the expense of its neighbors Bosnia and Serbia, would be created under the suzerainty of Italy.

Mussolini's designated "King of Croatia," the Duke of Spoleto, never once visited his "kingdom." Its actual administration fell to Ante Pavelic, the anti-Serb fascist. Hitler had little confidence in Mussolini and the Italians. He had personally selected Glaise von

Horstenau to see to it that neither the Italians nor Pavelic and his Ustashe interfered with the German army, or with the lines of communication through Croatia to the rest of the Balkans. Then, with the
Italian surrender, the Germans became the occupying rulers of Croatia. Glaise, an Austrian, had been a military historian and a cabinet
member of the prewar Austrian government. He had actively supported Hitler's takeover of Austria in 1938.

Allen Dulles, then wartime head of OSS operations in Switzerland, had made contact with Glaise von Horstenau in the summer of
1944 through an agent known as K-6, who was able to travel between
Zagreb and Switzerland. On September 27 a coded radio message
from Dulles in Bern to Colonel Edward J. F. Glavin in OSS Caserta,
Italy, had said in part:

> K-6 has reached Switzerland bearing a personal message from Glore
> [Glaise von Horstenau].
> Glore is going to cooperate with the Allies to free Austria.
> He was at Hitler's headquarters around September 10, to be dis-
> charged from the post he had held. . . [as German military plenipoten-
> tiary in Zagreb]. Nevertheless he expects to go back to Zagreb, as he is
> held in high esteem there by the Croats and also by Austrian officers as-
> signed there on duty with Croatian and Hun units in Croatia.
> He reports Germans have almost completely retreated from the Cro-
> atian coast, and orders have been issued to withdraw from Trieste and
> Monfalcone in the event of an Allied landing; and he suggests that the
> Allies would not have too much trouble in effecting a landing.
> Glore has a number of Austrian officer friends in high positions in
> Zagreb who are ready to cooperate with us. Among the most reliable
> are: Vendler [Major Metzger], Glore's personal aide-de-camp, an Aus-
> trian, and Muller [Freiherr von Polt], the assistant chief of Glore's staff.
> Glore went to Belgrade on leaving Hitler's HQ and saw Ringer [Field
> Marshal von Weichs] and Demarest [Generaloberst Löhr] there. Ringer
> is in command of the whole area NE of the Danube; Demarest, an Aus-
> trian who shares Glore's views, is in command of Croatia and the whole
> area between the Danube and the Adriatic.
> K-6 will receive an agent, radio-equipped, anytime after October 5 in
> Zagreb, to set up contact between the outside world and Glore's party.

This message was the basis for my briefing, which I received by
radio from OSS. If Glaise von Horstenau, von Weichs, and Löhr were

really prepared to surrender their commands, it would open up Croatia and Hungary and it would make an Allied move through the Ljubljana Gap a realistic option. If that option was not attractive to the Allied commanders it would at least collapse the German Balkan front. A subsequent coded message from Dulles to Glavin and Howard Chapin, head of the OSS Austrian section, provided the operational arrangements for the contact I was to set up:

> King Six should be met by the agent at the office of the Slavex Lumber Company, in the Wienerbank Verein Building in Zagreb. Assuming you know name ask for K-6 at any time during the day. "Regards from Uto" is the password. On October 5, K-6 will reach Zagreb. Will keep in contact with Glore in Zagreb informing him of our possible interest.
>
> According to K-6, the military strength of Glore lies in the fact that he believes that he can convince two each White Guard and Croatian German divisions to surrender to the Allies. (However not to Tito). . . . He recommends that an officer be sent to Zagreb to negotiate with Glore, after the agent contacts him. The officer should have sufficient rank for the negotiations.

I had very little to go on in this assignment. Because of the limitations on the length of messages that could be sent to me over our radio link, and because of concern for secrecy, I was told only what OSS decided I needed to know. The German offensive in Stajerska had made an aircraft pickup impossible and I had been unable to come out to Italy for briefings before going to Zagreb. Therefore, once contact with Glaise ("Glore") had been set up I expected to receive more specific instructions.

OSS Washington had approved the contact with considerable reservation:

> Extreme caution should be used in these dealings. Glore is an egotistical opportunist who favored the Anschluss for a long period of time. Almost completely without an ethical code. Give as little as you can and extract everything that you can.

There were also differences within OSS on whether Glaise should be used to provide intelligence or to instigate a coup or surrender. Everyone agreed, however, that my first job was to establish contact with K-6, and through him with Glaise. The policy of Allied Forces

Headquarters on German surrender terms had been clearly stated in messages to me. Enemy units in Yugoslavia would be required to surrender in place to the Allied force in the area. In Croatia this meant to Tito.

It appeared from Dulles's messages that Glaise von Horstenau's real objective was to induce the Allies to land in Istria, cross the Ljubljana Gap to Zagreb, and from there move on to Vienna before the Russians arrived. The inducement was the implied assurance from Glaise and the other German commanders that the German divisions would not oppose them.

I was relieved to know that OSS recognized the practical impossibility for me of contacting Glaise von Horstenau without the knowledge and concurrence of Tito and the Croatian Partisan headquarters. As soon as I arrived in Topusko I met with General Ivan Gosnjak, Croat Partisan commander, and with Vladimir Bakaric, commissar of the Croatian Partisans, and the leading member of the Croat Communist Party.

Gosnjak was a quiet, thoughtful man. Before the war he had attended a school in Moscow for Western party members and, like most senior commanders, had fought on the Loyalist side in the Spanish Civil War. I sensed he was much more confident and at ease with Americans than the Slovene Partisan leaders with whom I had been working. After the war he became defense minister in the Yugoslav government in Belgrade.

Bakaric was a small, dark-complexioned man with thinning dark hair and a rather puffy face. He was then 32. He smoked incessantly, and I had the impression that he was not well. He had joined the Communist underground at 21 and before the war was imprisoned for three years. He was one of the bright young men whom Tito had singled out for key roles in the party and the resistance. His father had been a judge in Zagreb and before the war, so the story went, at one time had acted to protect Tito. Bakaric was one of the original organizers of the Communist-led revolt in Croatia and spoke with the quiet confidence that this gave him.

Neither the Americans, including Dulles, nor the British then knew that in 1943 Glaise von Horstenau had secretly negotiated with high Partisan officers on a possible deal to stop fighting each other. During these meetings the Partisan delegation had proposed an accommodation in which the Germans would cease their attacks against the Partisans in return for a cessation of attacks against the railroads and mines on which the Germans depended. The Partisan delegation included Milovan Djilas and Vladimir Velebit, two of Tito's inner circle. According to messages found in German archives by the historian Walter Roberts after the war, the Partisan negotiators made it clear they regarded the Chetniks as their first enemy, and wanted to be free to turn their entire strength against them.

In his memoirs, Glaise wrote of his wartime assignment in Zagreb: "For some time I maintained a contact with Tito which, in the summer of 1943, through a disastrous combination of circumstances, was cut off." While Glaise's reliability can be questioned, his statement ties in with what Roberts discovered.

The Germans reported the proposed accommodation to von Ribbentrop, who flatly rejected it, almost certainly on orders from Hitler. Hitler was quoted as saying: "I don't parley with rebels—rebels must be shot."

Had the arrangement been approved by Berlin, the German commanders in Yugoslavia would have achieved what they desperately wanted—protection of their rail lines into the Balkans and the mines in Yugoslavia. The Partisans would also have what they wanted more than anything else. This was the freedom to devote all their strength to defeating the Chetniks, the only force that stood between them and complete power once the Germans were gone.

In light of the ceaseless Partisan charges of Chetnik collaboration with the Germans, including those made against Mihailovic personally, it was imperative for Tito that his own negotiations with the Germans be kept the deepest of secrets. In 1977 Milovan Djilas confirmed his own participation in these negotiations.

Bakaric and Gosnjak agreed to send an agent to Zagreb to do a preliminary reconnaissance. The agent soon returned to report that Glaise von Horstenau had been arrested by the Gestapo two weeks earlier. We had arrived too late. I was very disappointed. It would have been a fascinating negotiation no matter what the outcome.

The Partisan report that Glaise had been arrested, which promptly eliminated my projected contact with him, is open to question. At the end of the war Glaise von Horstenau turned up in Austria, where he became a prisoner of the American Seventh Army. In a report of his interrogation in August 1945, he described in detail his removal from his post in Zagreb by Hitler but made no mention of arrest. Had he been arrested by the Gestapo, it would seem almost certain he would have mentioned it in order to improve his status with the Allies. He did, however, confirm in his interrogation that he had gone to Vienna at the end of 1944. Surprisingly, in this interrogation he also made no mention of his abortive attempt through Allen Dulles to establish contact with OSS in Zagreb.

In his memoirs he says that he was recalled after being denounced by Pavelic as a defeatist. He also writes that he was in touch with Allen Dulles in Switzerland after his return to Vienna, but makes no mention of Zagreb contacts in the fall of 1944. Glaise killed himself while still a prisoner.

■ OSS Lieutenant Colonel Lanning "Packy" McFarland, whom I found at Topusko, had arrived only a week or so before, having flown in with his jeep. Shortly after my arrival he told me that he had received some important intelligence and must return to Italy with it forthwith. I was to stay in Croatia until his return in a few days. I knew nothing of McFarland, and his lurid past in Istanbul. But in 1949 Frank Wisner, who had become deputy director of CIA, told me the McFarland story. Wisner, a Navy lieutenant in the wartime OSS Cairo headquarters, was sent to Istanbul in 1943 to bring some order out of the chaos of the OSS station there. He knew all about Packy.

Wisner particularly relished the story of his own arrival and first day in Istanbul. Then one of the few remaining neutral cities in Europe, Istanbul was alive with Allied, Soviet, and Axis intelligence officers stumbling over each other as they attempted to recruit agents, arrange to examine each other's trash, infiltrate each other's organizations, and plant phony intelligence on each other. Wisner arrived on the train from Cairo at the Haydarpasha Station on the Asiatic side of the Bosporus. Posing as a new clerk for the American consulate, he was busy thinking how he should get to the offices as inconspicuously as possible when he was spotted by Packy McFarland waiting on the platform. Packy pulled Frank through the train window, gave him a great bear hug, and announced to the admiring throng of Turks that Wisner "is my boy."

Packy had a high-powered speedboat at the dock, and in it they sped across the Bosporus to a waiting limousine. Packy, explaining that he had an important meeting, dropped Frank off at a hotel after giving him the address where Frank should meet him at eleven that night. Frank was thoroughly shaken but, expecting some secret rendezvous, arrived at the address to find it a roaring nightclub. Frank slunk to the darkest corner of the bar and waited for Packy. Suddenly the band stopped and broke into a new piece, "Boop, Boop, Baby, I'm a Spy," in which the German and Turkish patrons joined in singing the chorus. The spotlights swung to the stairway leading to the dance floor and there was Packy, hands clasped above his head, bowing to the patrons. The story went on from there, ending in Frank's recommendation that Packy be relieved. How McFarland came to be reassigned to Yugoslavia I never learned. In Topusko, fresh from Stajerska, I knew nothing of this.

McFarland seemed eager to leave and we suspected he would not return. I was not surprised when after several days we were told I was to replace McFarland as the American liaison officer with the Croatian Partisan command as well as to be the senior OSS intelligence officer in Yugoslavia. We were by now in need of new shirts, trousers, and socks to replace our own badly worn uniforms. We went through his kit for clothing, razor blades, and such—anything we might use. We were a little surprised to find among Packy's things a pair of silver eagles—the insignia of a full colonel—and a packet of condoms.

■ Word came via our Caserta radio link that the German offensive in Stajerska was continuing with unabating fury. Some of the remaining American and British officers were now missing. A message to me forwarded through Caserta from Stajerska said British Captain Owen, my replacement there, his radio operator, and Bob Plan, Captain Charles Fisher's radio operator, were the only remaining Allied personnel with the Zone headquarters. They were using the Fourth Zone's transmitter, having lost their own in the fighting. In the fall I had had one spare radio buried (we had finally received a spare). Owen asked how to find it. I told them as best I could and said that Janez, the chief courier, knew its location. They found the bunker, opened it, and found that everything had been taken.

■ In Stajerska I had been almost completely cut off from the broader issues of U.S. and British policy debates about relations with Tito, Mihailovic, and the Russians. Here in Croatia both McFarland (before he departed) and Randolph Churchill, who headed the British mission in Croatia, filled me in on these issues. I now reported only to OSS. Incoming messages to me now dealt with broader issues than parachute drops and railroad sabotage. While we were inside the Third Reich the risk of our capture was high, and I was told only what I needed to know to do my specific job. Although Croatia was still enemy-occupied, it was much safer.

Also, the Allied organization had now been changed. In August of 1943 OSS and SOE had agreed that the then-British missions to both Mihailovic and Tito were to become joint Anglo-American missions. Although the intent was to have equal representation of British and American officers, and to share a base radio station in Cairo, OSS was very much the junior partner. The plan had been that half the missions with Partisan groups would be headed by a British officer and half by an American, each with a junior officer from the other service. But it didn't work out that way. This was primarily the fault of OSS in not assigning a sufficient number of officers, and of not sending as Maclean's American deputy a senior officer who had both the depth of background in irregular military operations and the understanding of Communist organization possessed by Fitzroy Maclean.

By 1944 the nature of the civil war in Yugoslavia had begun to penetrate in Washington. But there was still impatience with these internal Balkan quarrels. Washington believed everyone should be pulling together single-mindedly to defeat the Germans. The concept that the world was divided into major theaters of war, each with its Supreme Allied Commander, was accepted without question as the way the war should be run. In such a scheme, Tito and Mihailovic obviously should be placed under the Supreme Allied Commander in the Mediterranean. Roosevelt accepted the idea and proposed that a line of demarcation be drawn between the Chetniks and the Partisans, the Chetniks to operate to the east of the line (in Serbia), the Partisans in the rest of the country.

The president believed that the Yugoslavia affair called for someone with a strong personality on the ground to knock sense into the warring leaders—to order them to stop fighting each other and to fight the Germans in their separate areas. Roosevelt wrote Churchill a proposal to this effect, offering General Donovan as the man who could do the job. Churchill quickly replied that he already had very competent officers on the ground in Yugoslavia; he believed Donovan would be redundant. The exchange illustrated the inflated view in Washington and to some extent in London that the two mortal enemies could be forced to sign a truce, and to accept Allied direction and control.

By the spring of 1944, General Donovan and the State Department became increasingly uneasy about American participation in a combined mission to the Partisans. There now developed a basic divergence in the policies of the two governments. The State Department strongly believed that neither the Chetniks nor the Partisans could claim the preponderant support of the Yugoslav people, and that the United States should not take sides in the civil war. They wanted to support with arms all groups fighting the Germans but not go beyond that. It was an unrealistic view that continued to govern American policy till the end of the war. As Linn Farish had pointed out, our weapons would be used by the two factions primarily against each other.

The State Department policy was given to OSS in a memorandum from Cavendish Cannon, a senior Foreign Service officer on the staff of the American political adviser at Allied Forces Headquarters in Italy: "The United States does not intend to intercede in the political affairs of Yugoslavia. . . . Our interest is in establishment of a representative government, upon the liberation of the country, according to the freely expressed desires of the people concerned." This was pretty lofty stuff to those of us who lived with the day-to-day vilification by both sides of the other as traitors, and the increasing tempo of their civil war. We couldn't see how the people would be able to freely express their desires for a postwar government without a full-scale Allied military occupation, with freedom of the press and pluralist political organizations imposed by the Allies. That, plainly, was not in the cards.

The British, on their side, believed that Tito would win and that by giving him their sole support they might be able to retain some influence in the country. Churchill was also trying to graft the government-in-exile onto the Partisan Liberation Front. The official American view, via Cannon, rejected the British policy: "We should decline to become associated with [the British position] purporting to be on a joint basis in which the undoubted American prestige in Yugoslavia would be exploited and American responsibility engaged, unless we really know what is going on."

Donovan, with the support of the State Department and the Joint Chiefs of Staff, set up a separate American military mission to Tito and withdrew the American officers in Maclean's mission. The British mission, as executive agent of the Allied command in the Mediterranean, retained the responsibility for supplying the Partisans and for controlling all air and sea deliveries.

Donovan appointed Colonel Ellery Huntington, a lawyer and investment banker whom he had known in New York, as head of the new American mission to Tito. Huntington insisted on reporting directly to Donovan, bypassing OSS headquarters for the Mediterranean. Although the objective of the mission was to provide military and political intelligence, Huntington radioed from Tito's headquarters that he would send no intelligence reports until all the supplies he had requested had been delivered. Less than four months after arriving in Yugoslavia he wrote Donovan that the fighting was over and his assignment was completed (although the Germans still held more than half the country), and departed for Washington. Lieutenant Colonel Charles Thayer was a fortunate choice as his replacement. He was both a Foreign Service officer who had served in the Moscow embassy before the war, and a graduate of West Point. With this background he was a perceptive observer of the Communist move to power in Yugoslavia, and a qualified opposite number for Fitzroy Maclean—whom he had known in Moscow.

But it was not only of Packy McFarland's past that, arriving from Stajerska, I was ignorant. An episode more pertinent to policy had preceded my arrival by about a month. Again, I only caught up with it long after the fact. While in Yugoslavia many years after the war, with a group from the Council on Foreign Relations led by George Kennan, I spent an evening with Leo Mates, a postwar Yugoslav ambassador to the United States. In the course of our conversation, Mates recounted a secret meeting between Ellery Huntington and Ivan Gosnjak, the Croatian Partisan commander, for which Mates, a trusted Croatian Partisan leader, had been called in to interpret.

Huntington arrived at Croatian Partisan headquarters in November or early December of 1944, said Mates, stating that he had a top secret message that could only be disclosed to Gosnjak. Huntington, on being received, said that he had been directed to present a plan for an Allied landing on the Istrian peninsula and movement across Croatia to Zagreb. He was there to seek Gosnjak's approval and active support. Gosnjak consulted with Tito's Partisan headquarters by radio. He then replied to Huntington that the Partisans would agree to the plan only on condition that the infantry units all be Yugoslav and under Yugoslav control. The highly mechanized part of the force, including armored divisions, artillery, and motorized supply, could be British and American. But the Partisans would accept no Allied infantry divisions.

Mates told me that their private reasoning was that they could not accept the war ending with the northern part of the country under the control of the Allied armies. If the infantry divisions were their own forces, and if they had the agreement of the Allies that political control of the area would be theirs, they felt that this was an acceptable risk. The counterproposal was transmitted to Huntington. Subsequently he received a response, which he passed to Gosnjak, stating that no Allied commander could accept responsibility for the safety of his troops if he did not control the entire force, including the infantry divisions. That ended the matter. Huntington departed and there was no further communication.

This was a curious proposal, to say the least. If it was serious, why was it not made as an Allied proposal through Fitzroy Maclean directly to Tito? Churchill and Field Marshal Alexander had advocated such a move, while the American Joint Chiefs of Staff had fought it. Why did the head of the American military mission make such a proposal through a back channel to one of Tito's subordinate commands? The OSS archives so far declassified contain no mention of such an exchange. Mates is regarded as very straightforward and reliable; there is no plausible reason for him to invent such a story. But Fitzroy Maclean says he never heard of such a meeting.

Mates's own surmise was that Roosevelt sent Huntington to Croatian Partisan headquarters with a proposal he knew would not be acceptable. He did this in order to get a turndown from the Yugoslavs that he in turn could use as an argument with Churchill to kill Churchill's proposed Istrian landing and movement through the Ljubljana Gap.

I am inclined to disagree with Mates's conjecture because Roosevelt tended to defer to Churchill on Balkan matters, reserving only the right of veto. Further, he could not use Gosnjak's counterproposal with Churchill without revealing that an end run had been made around both Churchill and Maclean. It seems more likely to me that it was Huntington's own idea, cooked up with someone on the American side of the Mediterranean Allied Forces Headquarters. It is at least consistent with Huntington's open advocacy of a Balkan landing. Still, it remains one of the inexplicable and puzzling incidents of the war in Yugoslavia.

■ Life in Topusko was positively luxurious compared to Stajerska. The Croatian Partisan headquarters remained there for the nearly two months of my stay. Topusko had been a spa of sorts and the hot mineral baths were still working. It verged on high living to lie in a deep tiled bath soaking up the warmth of the water for as long as I liked while it snowed outside. Food was plentiful, though it was mostly bread, meat, and potatoes.

My job now was to obtain intelligence on German armed forces from the Partisans, and to report on Partisan military, political, and economic developments. Our continuing responsibility was to collect information on the German order of battle. This was the military term for the identification, location, and fighting strength of the divisions and other formations of the enemy forces. The intelligence supplied by the Croatian command was substantially more complete than in Slovenia, but in accordance with Tito's order it was limited to German order of battle. Again no sources were ever provided, so we had to be content with the daily handout. We continued to receive signals from OSS either asking follow-up questions on what had already been sent in or asking for information on entirely new subjects. After several frustrating attempts to deal directly with the senior Partisan intelligence officer I radioed OSS:

> Following is situation under which we work; am permitted to talk only to chief of staff or commissar. Have been refused permission to work directly with intelligence officer who speaks English. Consequently your questions are put thru inexperienced interpreter to chief of staff who does not know answers but makes notes to pass to intelligence officer. Most replies to specific questions are met with statement quote all our info goes into daily intelligence report which you receive. We have no further info unquote.

We found as little offensive fighting in Croatia as we had found in the last few months in Slovenia. The Germans were now making a major effort to extricate themselves from Yugoslavia. Our hope was that with the Allied weapons already provided the Partisans would be able to keep a large number of Germans from reaching Austria, Italy, or the Hungarian front. In early January about 10,000 enemy troops were caught in the Bihac pocket, which two years before had been the Partisans' provisional capital. The Partisan strength around this pocket was substantially greater than that of the Germans. I asked the chief of staff if the Partisans would be able to contain the enemy in the pocket and prevent their withdrawal north. His answer was the standard answer we had heard so often: "If we are supplied with the guns and ammunition we can do it; otherwise no." The supplies already delivered included 84 American 75-mm howitzers as well as rifles and machine guns for several thousand men. I noted in a radio report that no offensive operations had been undertaken in the preceding two weeks, although the Germans were actively trying to get out.

Exchange of prisoners between the Germans and the Partisans became an occasional alternative to shooting. The Croatian Partisans delighted in telling me about one exchange. It was agreed in advance that the exchange would take place in a deserted area on the edge of liberated territory. The Germans, in order to underline their superiority, had agreed to exchange twenty Partisans for a single German officer. As they arrived at the designated spot the Germans found the Partisan guard smartly lined up. All were women dressed in neatly pressed German officers' uniforms. The Germans swallowed hard but went through with the exchange.

■ OSS was increasingly interested in political developments in Croatia. The Partisan political organization in Croatia was by now well established. The steps by which the Partisan movement was becoming the de facto government of Croatia and of all Yugoslavia were carefully planned. A part of their strategy was to get rid of all remaining elements of prewar political parties that might contest their drive for total power.

Before the war Vladimir Macek had been the highly respected head of the Croat Peasant Party, the leading party in Croatia. At the beginning of the war he had been put under house arrest by Pavelic, and had remained stubbornly neutral in the wartime conflicts within Yugoslavia. Because he was held in such high respect among Croats, Macek was potentially a major obstacle to the consolidation of Partisan power in Croatia. The Partisan strategy to forestall such a possibility had two parts. One, a violent smear campaign against Macek and other Peasant Party leaders as German collaborators, was in full cry when I arrived in Croatia. One of the propaganda attacks against the Croat Peasants concluded, ominously: "The National Liberation Movement grinds slowly, but it grinds to dust."

The other strategy was to bring into the National Liberation Front a splinter element of the Croat Peasant Party, along with elements of other prewar political parties. This allowed the Partisans to claim that the Front represented all political groups except the collaborators. Those in the other parties who did not come into the Front were automatically branded as traitors. But, with the exception of the Communist Party, all party representatives in the Front were required to forswear independent political action. They were simply window dressing.

Bozidar Magovac, a close associate of Macek and prewar editor of the Peasant Party newspaper, had come out of Zagreb in 1943 with the intent of setting up a collaborative working arrangement with the Partisans. The Partisans quickly capitalized on his arrival by making him head of the pro-Partisan splinter of the Croat Peasants and vice president of the National Liberation Front. Later they became suspicious that he might not be fully under Partisan control, and placed him under secret house arrest on the island of Vis. I radioed in January 1945:

> In May 1944 Pzns found he [Magovac] apparently [had] given instructions to his party not to support Pzns too strongly and that Croat Peasants would return to power when Allies reach Zagreb.

My message continued, saying that a year later the Macek group, unaware that Magovac had been put under arrest, had sent the son of

Stjepan Radic, the founder of the Croat Peasant Party, to the Partisan command to strengthen the relations between the two groups. He also was put under arrest.

Allied officers on Vis (Tito's island headquarters from June until September 1944) told me that representatives of the Croat Peasants and other splinter parties were introduced to them as the leaders of these parties within the Liberation Front. After the meetings they would be returned to their Partisan guards. The fiction of the multi-party Front was thus maintained for British and American consumption. When the Western Allies found they had been duped, respect and support for the Partisans dropped another notch.

After hearing the anti-Macek propaganda for several days, I asked Vladimir Bakaric what actual evidence they had on him. His response was that the only thing they had against Macek was that he had not openly supported the Partisans. They had no evidence of collaboration with the Germans or Pavelic. I came to know and like Bakaric as one of the very few commissars with whom I could have an open and civilized conversation and not be subjected to the usual propaganda and abusive charges. After the war he became prime minister of Croatia and a close adviser to Tito.

■ The Fascist state of Croatia, created by Hitler and Mussolini, contained a mixture of Serbs, Croats, and Muslims. They formed an archipelago of separate ethnic communities. Individual villages or clusters of villages were exclusively or predominantly Serb, Croat, and Muslim. The ethnic hatreds that fueled the communal violence seemed deeply imbedded in the souls of the inhabitants.

The hatred of the Muslims by the Serbs and Croats probably had its roots in the repressions of the Ottoman empire. The Serb-Croat antagonisms seemed to have come from the thousand-year conflicts between the Eastern and Western branches of Christianity—Byzantium in the East, Rome in the West.

The German and Italian atrocities committed against both groups, and fascist sponsorship of the Ustashe government of Croatia, were major factors in triggering the ethnic terror. The Ustashe, now the rulers of Croatia, were bent on creating an enlarged, ethnically pure Croatian state. They set out to purge systematically the Serb population: deporting large numbers to Serbia, forcing others to convert to Catholicism, and slaughtering the rest.

Some of the Serb Chetnik units responded in kind with acts of terror against both the Croat and Muslim populations. Villages were burned and men, women, and children killed. The Serbs called their terror "ethnic cleansing," a term used again in 1991 and 1992.

The Croat Ustashe, with German and Italian support, had gained a greatly enlarged Croatia that included Bosnia-Herzegovina and parts of Serbia. The Chetniks envisaged an enlarged Serbia, including Bosnia-Herzegovina, Dalmatia, Yugoslav Macedonia, most of Croatia, and parts of Albania. A map circulated by the Chetniks in 1941 showed their objective for a Greater Serbia covering about three-quarters of all of Yugoslavia. Maps 2 and 3 illustrate the extreme positions of both sides.

The complex patterns dividing the Yugoslav peoples were even further exacerbated by German recruitment of large numbers of Serbs, Croats, and Muslims into openly collaborationist military units under German officers. These forces, some originally intended to be used against the U.S.S.R., were instead employed within Yugoslavia primarily against Partisans but at times against Chetniks as well.

The Partisans were not averse to the use of violence and terror, but employed these means against their ideological opponents: the occupiers and their collaborators and the Chetniks. They consistently opposed ethnic conflict. Both their propaganda and the multiethnic composition of their leadership demonstrated their commitment to a multiethnic Yugoslavia.

■ The British mission at Topusko was headed by Major Randolph Churchill. The Partisans were flattered to have the prime minister's son with them but they were put off when he told them what he thought of them, which was seldom flattering. He was one of the most aggressively rude men I ever met. He once told me that whenever anyone was rude to him he was immediately three times as rude in return. He was sure to win out. No one could possibly best him.

Evelyn Waugh had been with Randolph in Topusko until a week before I arrived. The Partisans told me that they had discovered he was acting as a courier for the Croatian Catholic hierarchy, smuggling messages to the Vatican, and that they had thrown him out. Actually he had been ordered out by Force 399. In his diaries Waugh covers his weeks with Randolph with almost daily entries: "Randolph drunk again." One entry continued: "Later he became abusive, and later comatose." In the weeks we overlapped Randolph and I often spent the evening together in the peasant house allotted to him. His radio operator and batman had been told to sleep in the corncrib although there was plenty of room in the house and it was bitterly cold. The owners of the house had been moved out and we never saw or heard of them.

In the evenings after several shots of liquor Randolph would often launch into a speech to an imaginary House of Commons (he had been elected a Conservative MP). As he paced the floor declaiming he would often refer to Henry Wallace (Roosevelt's vice president, whom he loathed), with a pointed comment about the century of the common man. (Wallace had written a book called *The Century of the Common Man.*) Then, bowing low to an imaginary Lady Astor, he would add, "and not forgetting the century of the common woman."

Randolph also filled the evenings with stories of British and American wartime politicans. They may not have been accurate but they were always colorful. His reminiscences about his father were fascinating. One was about a speaking trip in Canada that his father had made in the Thirties, when Prohibition in Canada had not yet been repealed. Randolph, who had accompanied him, had the daily assignment of buying two bottles of Canada Dry soda, half-emptying each, filling them with bootleg brandy, and placing them on the lectern. As Winston spoke, he would open a bottle and refresh himself with what the audience thought was carbonated water.

One evening Randolph recounted the origin of the Allied demand for unconditional surrender that had been announced at the

Casablanca Conference in 1943. Unconditional surrender became a controversial issue both during and after the war. Those who were critical argued that by ruling out a negotiated surrender of the Axis powers the war would be prolonged to the bitter end, since there was no incentive to those in power, or in command of troops, to negotiate an armistice to end the war earlier.

Randolph had attended the conference as an aide to his father. His story was that the entire schedule of the Casablanca Conference had been devoted to military decisions, the most important of which was the decision to invade Sicily. An hour before the meeting was scheduled to end with a press conference the press relations staffs reminded Churchill and Roosevelt that they would be expected to make some newsworthy announcement. Since they could not reveal their military decisions, Roosevelt said, "Why not call for unconditional surrender?" According to Randolph, his father felt very uneasy about it, but since he had nothing to offer in its place he reluctantly went along with Roosevelt—and later greatly regretted it.

Randolph was also concerned by the plight of the Jews in occupied Europe. While I was with him he arranged with the Partisans for the evacuation to Italy of over a hundred Jewish refugees who had collected in Croatian liberated territory.

■ The Partisans missed no opportunity to indoctrinate every group in the liberated areas, even the children. On Christmas Day the British, American, and Russian missions pooled their supplies for a party for some 150 orphans who were under the care of the Anti-Fascist Women of Croatia. The women insisted on organizing a program for the party.

One part of their program was a play in which the children were arranged in rows on four benches of increasing height to represent keys of a typewriter. Each child wore a placard with a letter representing a key. The play began with a discussion among the children about writing a letter to "Dear Marshal Tito." All agreed except little E. The other children then began to type the letter as each child stood and called out his or her letter. Little E, when E's were called for, refused to participate. When the letter was finished the head of the Anti-fascist Women held up a card showing the typed letter with all the E's missing. The kids then turned on little E and berated her for not participating. Finally she burst into tears, said she would write her own letter, and proceeded to pop up and down, shouting "E" each time. When the card was held up showing only a string of E's, the kids all shouted at her in derision for presuming that she could write a letter all by herself. Finally, little E took her assigned place and the letter was written, showing conclusively that only by being part of the system could anyone hope to accomplish anything. There was no place for individualists like little E.

The play was followed by a song to Tito, the chorus of which was:

Oh thou Tito, oh thou Tito,
Our white violet!
How we love you, how we love you,
All the youth!

The program ended with the children singing another of the oft-repeated songs: "Tito Is My Mother and My Father." A message from Randolph to Maclean concluded: "A grand time was had by all except Jesus Christ who must have thought from the songs that it was Tito's birthday that was being celebrated and that the Prince of Peace was born not in Bethlehem but in Zagreb."

Revolutionary Communist objectives were also a part of the indoctrination. This continued in spite of the directives from Moscow to emphasize a common liberation front with all parties, and to avoid emphasis on the role of the Communist Party and the objective of a postwar Communist government. Although at the national level Moscow's directives were followed to some degree, at the operational level revolutionary objectives were more out in the open.

The expansion of the Communist Party and the indoctrination of its members, especially its wartime adherents, was another matter. Before the war the Yugoslav party was a tiny group with little influence within the country. The party was rent by the Moscow purges and by resulting purges of its own leadership ordered by the Comintern.

The success of the Partisan movement required a major expansion of party membership in order to ensure continued party control of the movement into the postwar period of political consolidation. This involved the clandestine publication and distribution to party cells of the principal Soviet Communist tracts, of which Stalin's *Foundations of Leninism* was the most important. Great distinction was made between the education of party members and propagandizing the rank and file. For the latter, national liberation, not Leninism, was the diet.

Nearly every major Partisan unit had its own printing press, which it regarded as more important to protect than even the few pieces of mountain artillery captured from the enemy (as was brought home to me by the Partisan request, immediately upon our liberation of the Gornja Savinjska Dolina, for a printing press). During the early days of the war the Partisan high command moved from place to place as they were attacked by the Germans, carrying with them in a truck a large printing press and several thousand unbound copies of the *Short History of the Communist Party (Bolshevik)* they were in the process of completing. Both the press and the books soon had to be buried during a German offensive. Djilas later commented that they treated it "as if it were Holy Scripture." Tito summed up the importance of indoctrination, saying they sought to instill in their units the strictest possible discipline, not by extra drills, but by ceaseless political instruction.

■ Toward the end of January, Randolph received a radio message from Field Marshal Alexander, the Supreme Allied Commander in Italy, ordering him to come out forthwith. Randolph assumed he was to accompany his father to a meeting with Roosevelt and Stalin. It turned out to be the Yalta Conference in the Crimea. He set off in a jeep in deep snow headed across the Dinaric Alps for the Dalmatian coast, where he was to be picked up by an aircraft and flown to Italy. He soon returned. The snow on the road was too much for the jeep. Four days later he set off on horseback in a blinding snowstorm with a mounted Partisan escort.

When I came out three weeks later I stopped off at the British liaison mission with a Partisan corps in the mountains halfway to the coast. The mission was headed by an ebullient Irishman, Major Arnold Breene. Breene told me he had received a signal from Alexander saying Major Churchill was on his way to the coast and directing that he be given all possible assistance. Breene and his radio operators calculated the time when Randolph would arrive. They then subtracted a few hours and at the computed time began to consume all the liquor they had on hand, both air-dropped Scotch and local slivovitz. Their timing was perfect. They had consumed the last drop at just the moment Randolph arrived, blue with cold and dying for drink. Breene and his boys, filled with booze, thought Randolph's plight the funniest thing imaginable. Randolph, in a high rage, had to push on through the snow without so much as a swallow. It was the first time anyone had got the better of him.

■ The Russians had sent a large military mission to Croatia: six officers and a number of enlisted men under a full colonel. They were quite friendly and I met with them often. There was none of the suspicion and secretiveness we encountered with the Partisans. Conversation with the Russians was about jeeps, Detroit, American automobiles, Hollywood, Rockefeller Center, American houses, and the Moscow and New York subways. They gave me the identification and location of several German divisions in Hungary and in Yugoslavia along the Hungarian frontier, I passed to them our information on German order of battle, and we both profited. They appeared to have almost nothing to do, although they probably were much more in the confidence of the Partisans than we were.

Both then and later in Belgrade I was struck by the distance between the Russian senior and junior officers. When I saw them in their requisitioned peasant house, only the colonel and two majors were present. No matter what time of day we had to have at least one round of vodka or slivovitz. If my timing was wrong I would have to listen to a full hour of Radio Moscow reading the awards of military decorations for that day. When the time came for the broadcast the colonel would clap his hands and a captain would appear, salute, and stand stiffly at attention. The colonel would direct him to turn on the radio and the captain would then stand at attention during the entire broadcast unless released by the colonel.

One day the colonel came to see me in high excitement. In the endless list of decorations that had been announced that day from Moscow he insisted my name had been read as having been awarded the Order of Kutuzov. I insisted that it must have been a mistake. "Weren't you in Iran and the Caucasus in 1942?" "Yes." "Then that's you." We had to have a drink right away. And that was the last I heard of the matter.

■ During the winter of 1944–45 serious concerns developed in the staffs of the Allied commands that the Germans, especially the Waffen SS, planned a final stand in a mountain redoubt in the Bavarian and Austrian Alps. Here, it was rumored, they would establish secret bases and conduct guerrilla warfare against the Allied armies that had captured the plains of Germany. Because I had just left a Partisan group that had fought a guerrilla war in the Karawanken Alps I was asked to prepare what the British called an "appreciation" of the likelihood of such a development, and of the strategy to counter it. This gave me the impetus to think through what I had learned about guerrilla warfare in the last year. Having been on the side of the guerrillas, it was intriguing to put myself on the side of the occupiers.

From what I had seen of the Nazi SS troops in Stajerska their aggressive fighting spirit had not been diminished by the defeats of the main German armies by the Western Allies and the Russians. The alpine terrain, as we had found, was ideal for guerrillas.

The factors against a prolonged holdout in the mountains were that the final defeat of the German armies would release hundreds of thousands of Allied combat troops to attack and overwhelm any remaining guerrilla units, even though a large part of these forces might need to be sent to fight against Japan. In Yugoslavia we had survived only because Hitler could not spare the troops to eliminate us. But the crucial factor would be the civilians on whom the guerrillas would have to depend. I could not believe that once the main German armies had surrendered the civilians would support a fanatical SS guerrilla war. War-weariness was already so intense that they would have no stomach for enduring further conflict. The SS threats of violence against them would certainly coerce many to provide some degree of grudging support. But I doubted any wholehearted support would exist. The only caveat would be that if the Allied armies resorted to widespread violence and terror against the civilians, they could be driven in despair to support the Nazis. In short, any significant postsurrender guerrilla resistance seemed highly unlikely. Small groups of SS would certainly try to evade capture, especially by the Russians—but their motivations would be survival and escape abroad, not continued fighting.

If the rumored armed redoubt did materialize, aggressive Allied action, I wrote, would be essential. Small, highly mobile combat units of a hundred or so men should constantly be on the move through the mountains to locate and engage the guerrillas. Constant aggressiveness would deny the guerrillas any respite and would keep them on the run, forcing them to lose contact with their civilian warning network. In Stajerska we had found that when the Germans did this they nearly wiped us out. We were saved because their offensive sweeps rarely lasted more than a week or two. The German *Gebirgsjäger* (mountain troops) and the Nazi SS were the only ones who dared to leave the roads and come into the mountains after us.

Allied treatment of civilians would be the key. Any breakdown of discipline among the occupying forces toward civilians could quickly increase civilian support for the guerrillas. Civilian support of guerrillas had to be punished, but it had to be done within a framework of law in which personal guilt had been clearly established. Wholesale reprisals against civilians, such as the Germans had used in Yugoslavia, would only drive them to support the guerrillas and would cut off the intelligence that only they could provide to help isolate, track down, and eliminate armed resistance.

When the end of war came, all German resistance collapsed. The redoubt was never manned. The war-weariness was simply too great to support any further fighting.

The only use made of the German and Austrian redoubt area was as a hideout for Nazi bigwigs trying to melt into the rural landscape. In the weeks following the end of the war OSS Captain Rudolph von Ripper mounted a one-man hunt in the mountains behind Salzburg. He would leave the town in the morning clad in lederhosen, Austrian loden hat, and climbing boots, and carrying a hunting rifle. In the evenings he would return, usually with two or three Nazi prisoners who had been hiding out as woodcutters in the forest.

The only real preparations for a Nazi mountain redoubt were at Hitler's Berchtesgaden headquarters near Salzburg. A few weeks after the war ended I visited the bombed-out chalet there that was Hitler's personal living quarters and office when he was in Bavaria. Directly behind the wrecked chalet was the entrance to a tunnel deep into the mountain.

An American M.P. stood guard at the entrance to the tunnel. A small, neatly lettered sign next to him read: "Off limits to all personnel except field grade and general officers." I felt outraged that this spot, the ultimate objective that so many thousand American G.I.s had fought to reach, should be so restricted—but my curiosity overcame my outrage and I went in.

Two hundred feet in from the entrance there were two right-angle jogs in the tunnel where machine-gun ports behind thick concrete walls covered the tunnel entrance. I found it astounding that Hitler apparently was preparing to hole himself up inside a mountain, guarded by machine-gun positions, while all of Germany was being occupied by Allied armies.

Inside the mountain were many rooms and connecting tunnels in the process of being furnished. Equipment for a hospital was still crated. A reel of silent-movie film was strewn down one corridor. Curious, I picked up a torn end and looked at it against a light on the wall. The picture was of a group of German officers looking up into the sky. Another set of frames showed an approaching formation of bombers. The caption read: "Ach, das kann nur die Amerikaner sein." (Ach, it can only be the Americans.)

■ In mid-February of 1945 I received orders to leave Croatian headquarters and to go across the mountains to an airstrip near Zadar on the Dalmatian coast to be picked up by an Allied aircraft and flown to Italy. I was not told why I was to leave, nor where I was being posted. Sergeant Bradshaw drove me in our jeep across the mountain roads. Fortunately there was a gap in the German lines. Everywhere there was destruction. Nearly all the villages had been burned out. Abandoned German vehicles were overturned along the roadside. Many had burned. Bloated carcasses of horses were strewn among the vehicles. Much of the destruction had been done by Allied fighter bombers based in Italy that had strafed and bombed German convoys struggling to escape northward to Austria and Germany. It was painful to witness so much desolation dealt to such a brave people in so beautiful a land.

CHAPTER 16

Tito's Government Takes Control in Belgrade

he plane taking me from Zadar to Italy landed at Bari on February 19, 1945, in an unusual February snowstorm. Also aboard were wounded Americans and Partisans. It had been nine months since the night we had dropped to the Slovene Partisans. As the plane touched down I suddenly realized I had made it back in one piece.

After a night in Bari I flew on to Caserta near Naples, which had become the headquarters of Field Marshal Alexander, now the Supreme Allied Commander Mediterranean. OSS had taken over a nearby silk mill and convent as its own headquarters.

I was not prepared for the size of the headquarters and knew no one by sight, although a few names were familiar from radio messages. The headquarters had been set up after I had gone into Yugoslavia the year before. It was unusual for a wartime overseas headquarters in that it included many attractive and intelligent women civilians who ran the central registry and some of the staff and research activities. I felt very much like the country boy who had arrived unannounced at a sophisticated diplomatic reception in London or Washington.

The officer who took me to a large officers' mess for lunch asked as we ate how I liked the salad dressing. This seemed a rather strange question, but I mumbled vaguely "fine." He went on to say that "Colonel Obolenski mixes it himself." This seemed even stranger. Finally I learned that it was Prince Serge Obolenski who, before the war, had managed the St. Regis Hotel in New York. Obolenski was more than a hotelier. He had parachuted into Corsica as the Germans were withdrawing.

Also at lunch that first day I met Walter Carpenter, the senior OSS medical officer. Walter was a pediatrician from New York Hospital, low-key, outgoing, and slightly overweight: "See Captain So-and-so to get your blood pressure checked and see me about five." He had a bottle of operational whiskey in his desk drawer and we had a drink together while he inquired about what I had been doing in Yugoslavia. At the end of a rather rambling conversation he said, "If everyone comes back from operations in as good shape as you I will recommend it as a health cure!"

During the next few months as I came to Caserta for brief visits I saw the important job he was doing. OSS was not without its personnel difficulties, and behind-the-lines operations often produced severe emotional problems both for those on operations and for those who dispatched them and received their radio messages. Often they waited and worried over the fate of those who never came on the air after they were dropped behind the German lines or those whose radios suddenly went dead. Carpenter was uniquely positioned as a medical doctor to tap into the OSS organization at any point and to talk with anyone from corporal to colonel without violating the lines of military command. He spotted emotional problems and was able to quietly work out solutions, before they exploded in a highly charged organization.

■ The senior officers on the OSS staff concerned with the Balkans were Robert Joyce, a Foreign Service officer on detached duty with OSS; Lieutenant Colonel William Maddox, in civilian life a member of the Yale faculty; Robert Wolff and Stuart Hughes of the Harvard faculty; and a Marine, Lieutenant John Gardner, a professor of psychology.

Joyce and Maddox proposed that I return to Yugoslavia, this time to Belgrade, to replace Lieutenant Colonel Charles Thayer as head of the American military mission. Thayer was returning to the United States in preparation for going to Vienna as head of OSS there. He would also serve as interpreter to General Mark Clark, who had been designated the American member on the four-power Allied Control Commission for Austria. It was a chance to see the final stage of Tito's revolution, and I accepted.

Thayer thought the job deserved the rank of lieutenant colonel. He radioed Colonel Glavin, head of OSS in the Mediterranean theater:

> I recommend that Lindsay be promoted to lieutenant colonel when he takes over mission. His Soviet opposite will be a major general and his British opposite an air vice marshal. While the Soviet mission is probably more active due to proximity of Soviet troops, our mission has many more functions at present than the British and will probably continue to as peace approaches.
>
> While I am confident Lindsay is intelligent and able enough to establish his own position once he is known, I also feel sure that to have him start from scratch so to speak as a major is asking a good deal.

The promotion was approved a few days later.

I was only 28, but promotions in wartime were often very rapid, in part because of the explosive wartime growth of the military services and in part because of luck: being in the right place at the right time.

Before returning to Yugoslavia, I was given three days' leave in Capri in Mrs. Harrison Williams's elegant villa, which she had loaned to General Donovan for the duration. Even this was interrupted by a querulous radio message from Thayer wanting to know why Lindsay was lolling around in Capri when he was needed urgently in Belgrade.

I arrived in Belgrade in early March (although I cannot pin down the exact date). Thayer and I would overlap for several days before he departed for the United States.

■ Belgrade was a dreary city. It must have been dreary even before the war and now it carried the additional scars of German bombing in 1941, of Allied bombing in 1944, and of Russian artillery bombardment and Partisan and Russian infantry assaults in October.

ABOVE: Marshal Tito explaining Partisan military operations against the Germans to Field Marshal Sir Harold Alexander, Supreme Allied Commander Mediterranean, during a visit to Tito's headquarters, February 1945 (*Lindsay*)

OPPOSITE: American, British, Russian, and Yugoslav senior officers at Belgrade airport, waiting to greet Tito on his arrival in March 1945. Foreground, from left: U.S. Lieutenant Colonel Charles Thayer, Soviet major generals Lototski and A. F. Kiselev, U.S. Captain William Cary, U.S. Lieutenant Colonel Franklin Lindsay, British Air Vice Marshal Arthur Lee, Yugoslav Lieutenant General Arso Jovanovic (Tito's chief of staff) (*Lindsay*)

RIGHT: Partisan Lieutenant General Arso Jovanovic, Tito's chief of staff, and Franklin Lindsay at luncheon at the American Military Mission, Belgrade, spring, 1945 (*Lindsay*)

ABOVE: Brigadier Sir Fitzroy Maclean, Russian Major General A. F. Kiselev, and Marshal Tito at a luncheon at the American Military Mission, Belgrade, spring 1945 (*Lindsay*)

OPPOSITE: Tito's bodyguard waiting in a captured German "squad car" outside the American Military Mission in Belgrade while Tito lunches with Allied officers, March 1945 (*Lindsay*)

ABOVE: Yugoslav, Russian, British, and American officers at Tito's victory celebration at the palace of the former regent, Prince Paul, after the final German surrender, Belgrade, May 1945 (*Lindsay*)

OPPOSITE: Tito with his favorite stallion on the grounds of the palace of the former regent, Prince Paul, Belgrade, spring 1945 (*U.S. Army*)

After the city was liberated the German armies retreating from the Balkans held on a defensive line about fifty miles northwest of Belgrade. This front remained until the final battles of the war began in April 1945.

I now met for the first time Brigadier Fitzroy Maclean, for whom I had worked most of the previous year. He was a very tall and thin Scot. At only 34, he was already at the upper end of the age bracket into which most Partisans and Allied officers serving with them fell. Although I found him warm and friendly, many of the Yugoslavs said they found him impassive and aloof. Milovan Djilas described him as "this reserved, cold-blooded Scot."

Shortly after arriving in Belgrade I was invited to dine one evening at Maclean's mess. All his officers appeared to be old friends and several had been together in North Africa fighting against Rommel's forces. These British officers who were drawn to irregular operations seemed not only to have been together in early wartime operations but also to have had many close school and family ties. In contrast, in three years overseas I had met only one person I had known before the war. A day or two after the dinner I was told quite informally that, despite being a "colonial," I had apparently passed the test of social acceptability and that I would be invited back.

From his prewar years in the British embassy in Moscow, Fitzroy had gained an understanding of militant Communism and fluency in Russian. He was both an experienced diplomat and a veteran of behind-the-lines raids in the Western Desert. I was told that he had spent the hours of his first flight before dropping to Tito's headquarters calmly studying a Serbo-Croat grammar. When told the C-47 was over the target he had put away the book, walked to the open door and jumped into the night. On dress occasions, such as the day Tito gave him a Partisan decoration, he appeared in a kilt—to the considerable puzzlement of the Yugoslavs.

By this time U.S. and British relations with the Partisans had further deteriorated. Our interactions were best described as formal and distant. My meetings with the Yugoslavs were arranged by appointment and usually dealt with problems arising between the American and Yugoslav military. There were no longer the close and friendly relations that had existed in the early days in the forest.

Tito had moved into the beautifully appointed palace, the Beli Dvor or White Court, that formerly belonged to Prince Paul, the ruling regent after King Alexander's assassination in 1934. I marveled at how Tito, the peasant's son, Commmunist underground organizer and Partisan leader in the forest, had so quickly adapted to life as the ruler. Personal vanity was apparent in his new uniforms. They were perfectly tailored and generously adorned with gold braid and his marshal's insignia of rank. One uniform he often appeared in was a gray tunic, dark blue riding breeches with red stripes on the sides, and black riding boots. Another was all white with gold braid and gold insignia. His overcoat almost touched the ground. His visored cap carried much gold. Only the five-pointed red star was a reminder of his Communist career.

He was a gracious host who entertained well, and his buffet tables were always loaded with delicacies of every variety, including Russian vodka and Caspian caviar. He adapted so easily that it seemed he might have been born a Hapsburg prince rather than the son of Croat peasants.

Tito's commitment to the Communist Party began early. When war came in 1914 he was called up for service in the Austro-Hungarian army. He was soon sent to the eastern front where he was wounded and taken prisoner by the Tsar's army. Excited by the revolution that swept Russia in 1916, he escaped and made his way to Petrograd in time to take part in the first of the Bolshevik demonstrations that later led to the fall of the Kerensky government and the capture of the revolution by the Bolsheviks. In 1917 he joined the Soviet Red Guard and finally returned to Croatia in 1920, an enthusiastic Bolshevik.

After resuming his old trade as a mechanic he joined the Yugoslav Communist Party. But by 1921 the Belgrade government, throughly alarmed by the Bolshevik call for world revolution, outlawed the party. The tiny Communist Party then had to learn to carry on its work under the threat of arrest and imprisonment.

By 1927 he had become a full-time party worker and secretary of the party in the Zagreb area, when he was arrested and served a six-month prison term. He was again arrested for illegal party activities in 1928. This time the prison sentence was for five years. As with so many young revolutionaries, imprisonment provided Tito the opportunity to study Marx, Lenin, and Stalin. A fellow prisoner, Moshe Pijade, later a member of the Partisan leadership and the party theoretician, was his principal instructor.

On his release from prison Tito continued his advance in the Yugoslav party and in January 1935 went to Moscow as a member of the Balkan secretariat of the Comintern.

With the outbreak of the Spanish Civil War, Tito was ordered by the Comintern to provide Yugoslav recruits and to send them (illegally) across the Pyrenees to fight on the Loyalist side. Of the 1,500 or so who went to Spain, nearly half were killed; the survivors returned to fight again in their own country. These experienced fighters became the backbone of the Partisan forces, in which they were known as "the Spaniards."

As we learned more of Tito's early background, his complete loyalty before the war to Leninism, to Stalin, and to the Comintern became apparent. He had accepted and defended every shift in the party line Moscow had laid down, including the Stalin-Hitler pact.

Physically Tito was of medium height. His complexion was not swarthy; rather, he appeared to have a perpetual tan, which he had not lost in the months since he had come in from forest life. His eyes were arresting, an intense pale blue. In the mountains he had been lean and even hollow-cheeked; now he was already putting on weight. That, coupled with his new uniforms, sometimes gave him an unfortunate resemblance to Hermann Göring. During the spring the U.S. Air Corps sent in a camera team to Belgrade. After taking pictures of Tito in his office, the photographer asked him how else he would like to be photographed. He immediately asked for a picture on one of his horses. An aide had a white stallion saddled and brought to the garden where Tito was photographed, both standing with his horse and mounted.

The Yugoslavs were already hard at work building Tito into a larger-than-life world image. Honor guards, flags, uniforms, parades, speeches, books, and quotations by the great man were fulsomely deployed. One day I received a call from the general staff saying Tito would arrive back in Belgrade the next day. As head of the military mission I was told I was expected to be at the airport to greet him when he stepped off the plane. Together with the top party, government, and military leaders we all waited in line for our turn to shake his hand before he was driven off, surrounded by his bodyguards.

May Day in 1945 was the first time in history the Communists could celebrate openly. A five-hour parade, which Tito and top party leaders reviewed, featured an estimated 70,000 soldiers, workers, peasants, and children; enormous portraits of Tito and Stalin, thousands of red flags, and one lone American flag. The approved slogans for the day, shouted in unison, were "Belgrade-Moscow," "Tito-Stalin," "Long Live the Red Army," and "Long Live the Communist Party." I missed the show, having been in Rome that day. Marine Captain William Cary and Navy Lieutenant Robert Miner of our military mission were there to see it.

■ Ever since the creation of Yugoslavia, the question of the autonomy of the Serb, Croat, Slovene and Macedonian ethnic nationalities had been a burning issue within the country. It was also a key issue within the Yugoslav Communist Party. During the early revolutionary period the Comintern regarded national and ethnic antagonisms as exploitable to further the revolution. It set up as the party line support for the breakup of Yugoslavia into independent nations. During this period, in which revolution was the key objective, cooperation with any other party, especially the Social Democrats, was forbidden.

The rise of fascism in the 1930's caused the Comintern to reverse its position. World revolution had to be shelved for the time being in favor of strengthening the European democracies to resist Hitler and to protect the Soviet state as the base for future revolutionary advances. Communist parties were told to end their isolation, put off their immediate revolutionary goals and make common cause not only with Social Democrats but with all "antifascist" parties. The breakup of Yugoslavia into its component ethnic nationalities was now to be opposed rather than advocated. In short, the royal Yugoslav government was not to be "destabilized" by further support of separatism for each ethnic denomination.

Up until 1937 the Yugoslav Communist Party had been torn by dissension and was pitifully weak and largely irrelevant. For years, the leadership had been outside the country, moving from Budapest to Vienna to Paris. As a consequence they were out of touch with the internal party organization and were viewed with contempt by the Comintern and Stalin. The Comintern seriously considered dissolving the Yugoslav party at its Seventh Congress but instead decided to purge the existing Yugoslav leadership, make Tito head of the Yugoslav party and tell him to build it into an effective organization. Tito and Edvard Kardelj were the only Yugoslav party leaders to survive the Moscow purges.

Tito made clear his philosophy of revolutionary leadership:

I left for Yugoslavia to reorganize the party. This reorganization ran along the following principles:

First, the Central Committee should be located inside Yugoslavia, working among the people. It is impossible to expect a workers' democratic movement to succeed if its leadership is far from the arena of struggle. That is the elementary condition for the successful work of such a movement. To await instructions from outside, to use someone else's head instead of one's own, is deadly danger for every such movement. . . .

Political exile spells ruin for a political worker. It is better if he is in his own country, among his own people, where he can fight together with them, where he can share good and evil together with them, even if his life is in the balance, rather than to roam about, far from the movement, far from the people. Hence, upon becoming secretary-general. . . I brought the headquarters of the Central Committee back to Yugoslavia after six years of wandering from country to country.

When Tito assumed leadership of the Communist Party in 1937, the party line had become strong support for a single federal republic. During the Partisan period Tito made Yugoslav nationalism one of his central planks. The revolution he led evolved into a postwar federal government embracing all the national groups. I was surprised to learn that before the war the Communist Party was the only Yugoslav party that drew its membership from the entire country. All the traditional parties, such as the Slovene Socialists, the Croat Peasants and the Serb Peasants, were based solely in a single ethnic region.

The Moscow party line again shifted abruptly after the announcement of the Soviet-German pact. The war between the Axis and France and Britain had become a war among imperialist powers that was of no concern to the Communists. Once they destroyed each other, they would be ripe for revolution and the Communist Party was ready to pick up the pieces. In Yugoslavia Tito instructed the party to support the pact and to keep the country from becoming embroiled in the war. The subsequent German attack on the Soviet Union shattered this neutrality and Moscow urgently ordered Tito to form Partisan units and attack the Germans in Yugoslavia.

After the German retreat from Belgrade in October 1944 the consolidation of the Partisan revolution entered its final phase. It had been well planned, its groundwork skillfully laid.

During the months I was in Slovenia and Croatia I had been able to watch the step-by-step preparations. Now it was being carried to completion with thoroughness, efficiency, and ruthlessness. No element of internal society or of relations with the Allied powers was overlooked. It may have been mismanaged, but it was certainly thorough.

As the Germans withdrew northward the Partisan leadership moved quickly to eliminate all armed opposition from the Chetniks, and from the Ustashe and White Guard collaborators. While we were in Bari the year before, waiting to parachute into Yugoslavia, Linn Farish had told me that the Partisans were expanding eastward from Bosnia into Serbia, where Tito planned an intensive campaign against the Chetniks. "Tito," he said, "is sending several of his best officers into Serbia within the next few weeks." Farish planned to drop to this group and go with them into Serbia.

The Chetniks were quickly defeated by swift, aggressive attacks by Partisan brigades and by adroit political isolation of the Chetniks from Western support. Contrary to the expectations of many Westerners, almost all armed resistance to Partisan control collapsed as soon as the Germans were gone.

A major threat to Tito's postwar control was the ethnic conflicts, chiefly between the Serbs and the Croats. The strong Communist Party leadership in each of the national ethnic areas acted quickly to defuse the threat of separatism, and to preserve a united Yugoslavia under Communist control.

During the war Tito had worked to build local liberation committees in liberated areas into regional and national shadow governments. Now he simply turned the Partisan committees and councils of liberation into the formal government of the nation. He co-opted splinters of the major prewar political parties into the National Liberation Front on terms that permitted no independent political activity outside the Front. All other political activity was branded as collaborationist and ruthlessly suppressed. Thus a facade of democracy and national unity was created while all power was held by the Communist Party.

Latent internal opposition was contained by proclaiming universal military service and drafting all manpower of active military age into the armed services, where they could be both indoctrinated and controlled. This was the same technique I had seen used in Stajerska the year before. The civil population was mobilized into mass organizations where they were both politically "instructed" and carefully watched.

A monopoly of press and radio was held by the Communist Party and the captive Liberation Front, and it was used to brand all internal opposition as Axis collaborators. It was used as well to attack Britain and America and to minimize pro-Western sympathies. Military and economic support received from the Western Allies was either ignored or deprecated as niggardly. Britain and America were regularly attacked as hostile monopolist capitalist regimes run by "reactionary elements." It seemed to me that the Communists failed to see the irony of these attacks while building a hermetically sealed political and economic Communist Party monopoly.

Economic control was quickly installed by sequestration, and later by nationalization, and by branding any economic activity undertaken outside of state control as economic sabotage punished by prison and execution.

All in all it was a masterful performance: internal opposition was subdued and Allied support retained without sacrificing an ounce of national independence from the West.

■ Shortly after I arrived in Belgrade and before Thayer left, U.S. General Ira Eaker, commander of the Allied air forces in the Mediterranean, flew in for a visit to Tito. As part of the visit we arranged a luncheon at the American military mission to which Tito and his top commanders were invited. The preparations for Tito's visit were remarkable. A week before the luncheon, two protocol officers from the Foreign Office arrived at the mission to consult on the guest list and the seating. They wore the traditional diplomatic uniform: black coats, striped trousers, and silk handkerchiefs protruding from the left sleeves of their coats. We heard that they were the only two in the Foreign Office that survived the purge when the Partisans arrived in Belgrade. They were the only ones regarded as truly indispensable.

The day before the luncheon, an officer of Tito's personal security guard arrived and asked to inspect the premises for bombs and other hazards. It was a very thorough inspection. The morning of the luncheon Tito's chef arrived to supervise the food preparation and I was later told by our cook that he tasted every dish that was to be served to Tito before it left the kitchen. That morning the buildings near our mission building were evacuated and searched. A wedding in the Orthodox church across the street was postponed and a machine gun was installed in the church tower. Guards with rifles were visible on the roofs of all the other surrounding buildings.

An hour before the lunch the streets between the palace and the mission were roped off and soldiers were placed at intervals of 100 yards along the entire route of at least a mile. Tito arrived and left in a prewar Cadillac that, it was alleged, had been given to him by Stalin. More probably it had been "liberated" from a wealthy Belgrade collaborator. He was preceded and followed by open German command cars that must have had eight or ten armed men in each.

The guest list included Tito's chief of staff, Arso Jovanovic, and several top Partisan commanders and Central Committee members, Major General Kiselev, head of the Russian military mission, and Brigadier Maclean. On the American side Eaker brought his deputy and, to our surprise, Thornton Wilder, who was on the Allied forces staff as a cultural adviser. The Yugoslavs were currently producing *Our Town* for Belgrade Communist audiences. It was about the only piece of American culture allowed to compete with the full menu of heroic Soviet and Partisan plays. It seemed that the principal American influence had come from Jack London's adventure stories of the American West. On learning I was an American, both Partisans and civilians would often proudly announce they had read Jack London. At the luncheon itself there was small talk through interpreters, followed by short speeches extolling the military virtues of the Yugoslavs and the Allies.

When the time came for Tito's departure, the Cadillac was brought to our entrance, the motor running. Tito jumped in quickly, and the driver accelerated with tires screaming. The guards were caught unawares and the drivers of the two command cars started after Tito's car. The last we saw were guards running to get aboard as the two cars took off.

■ The Partisan leaders were midstream in the transition from Partisan administration of isolated liberated areas to an entirely new structure of government and society. So in addition to military liaison with Tito's staff we were increasingly concerned with political and economic affairs.

A small unit of the OSS Research and Analysis Office provided much of our political and economic reporting. It was headed by

Navy Lieutenant Robert Miner. Michael Petrovich and Alex Vucinich brought academic backgrounds as well as fluency in Serbo-Croat. Their job was to analyze the press and propaganda output and the speeches by Tito and other top leaders. They also developed informal contacts with Partisan leaders to the extent they were allowed to talk to Americans, and with others in Belgrade who could tell us what was going on. Our purpose was to gain clues to the policy directions in which the new government was moving.

Our principal source of enemy battle order intelligence in Belgrade was the Partisan intelligence service, and we attempted to use our own information on German units, sent to us from our headquarters in Italy, to exchange for Yugoslav battle order information on enemy forces still in Yugoslavia. Only by sifting and cross-checking many intelligence clues from many sources could our experts build up a reliable picture of enemy forces, or order of battle.

Our battle order expert was Sergeant Yeiser. We told the Partisans he was Captain Yeiser so that the Partisan intelligence staff would condescend to at least talk to him. Before the war he had been a music critic for the *New York Times* and was now a first-class battle order expert.

Marine Corps Captain William Cary was our executive officer. A law professor before the war, Bill had combed the Marine Corps regulations on uniforms and found that the senior Marine in a country prescribed the uniform to be worn. Since he was the only Marine in Yugoslavia he obviously qualified as the senior. Having established his authority he bought a elegant fur pelt and had it sewn onto his Marine overcoat collar. He was an impressive sight.

■ The Russian military mission in Belgrade was, I found, more rigid and wooden in its relations with the British and ourselves than the Russian missions I had known in Slovenia and Croatia. Its members were behaving more like Cold War Russians than the Russians of wartime.

We had scheduled an evening reception for the Yugoslav senior officers and the British and Russian missions. A buffet of cold meats and canned food from Italy was laid out, along with vodka, slivovitz, and any other drinks we could round up. The British and Yugoslav officers arrived singly or in groups of two or three. The Russians arrived late and in formation. Led by Major General A. F. Kiselev and his deputy, also a major general, twelve or so officers marched in the door, did a left face and saluted. Our other officers and I greeted them and everyone moved to the food and drinks. They had brought no one below the rank of major, although we had invited their junior officers as well.

After a couple of hours the party was going quite well, with lots of individual toasts and "bottoms up." I was chatting with a Russian colonel in my pidgin Russian. He had just poured another glass of vodka and was raising it to his mouth, ready to down the glass, when he stopped short and slowly put the full glass on the table. I happened to be standing where I could see, out of the corner of my eye, a Russian officer across the room. He was looking in the direction of my colonel and had been slowly shaking his head. This obviously was the political commissar being sure that drink would not loosen my colonel's tongue.

Shortly after, a signal must have been given, because the Russians lined up again, shook hands and marched out.

Our relations with the Russian military mission had now become more adversarial. As the Russian armies advanced westward during the last months of the war, British and American bombers often made emergency landings behind the Russian lines if they had been damaged and were unable to get back to their own bases. Many of these bombing missions were made at the specific request of the Russian army commanders. The Russians sent most of these downed aircrews east to Odessa for return by ship to the West, a trip that required up to three months. In Belgrade we tried to get the Russians to send these airmen out through Belgrade, a much shorter route. General Kiselev, head of the Soviet mission, told us he had worked out such an arrangement with the headquarters of Marshal Fyodor Tolbukhin, commander of the Russian armies now advancing against the German army in Hungary, but the Odessa route continued to be used.

One B-24 Liberator, however, landed in Yugoslav territory only thirty miles from Belgrade, and we were able to pick up the crew before they were sent to Odessa. As the aircraft was not seriously damaged, we arranged to bring in a repaircrew from Italy and subsequently a ferry crew to fly the plane out to Italy. The aircrew, accompanied by Captain Eugene O'Meara of our military mission, drove by jeep to the aircraft but found a Russian guard on the plane who prevented them from taking it. Although O'Meara did not speak Russian, he was able to talk the guard into letting him see the guard's orders and to copy the Cyrillic characters. When translated they said, "Re airplane 'Liberator.' Give it to 45AD18VA. The representative will be there on the first day possible. Do not surrender it to American air representatives."

With this in hand I jumped in a jeep and drove to the Russian military mission, which was housed in a large villa. I asked General Kiselev, commander of the mission, for an explanation, and asked that the guard's orders be changed immediately. He had no explanation but said he would take it up with Marshal Tolbukhin's headquarters. After failing to get any response from Kiselev in spite of several follow-ups, I saw Tito's deputy chief of staff, General Velimir Terzic. My instructions were to be tough. Was this Yugoslavia or was it now part of the Soviet Union? I asked. If it was Yugoslavia I asked for a Yugoslav escort to accompany our aircrew and to ensure we were not further obstructed by the Russians. If I was mistaken and the plane was in Soviet territory we would take the matter up in Moscow. I got no response, but obviously he was chagrined by his inability to respond.

Finally, I was told by Allied Forces Headquarters Mediterranean to send a letter of protest directly to Marshal Tito. After reciting the several attempts to get the plane released, I pointed out that the United States was still fighting a war against the Japanese and we needed to take the plane without further delay. I then said we had obtained clearance from his own general staff and had so advised the Russian military mission. I had been directed to say we intended to take the plane within 24 hours and expected that there would be no further obstacles.

Again O'Meara drove to the plane and again the Russian armed guard prevented us from taking it. It was only after two and a half months that the plane was finally released by the Russians through intervention with the Soviet high command in Moscow by General John R. Deane, the head of the American military mission there. Later I learned that more than 25 American B-17 and B-24 bombers were taken over by the Russians before we were able to learn of their whereabouts. Their crews were sent out through Odessa and reached the nearest Allied officer many weeks later. During this period they had not been permitted to communicate with us or with their own commands. This incident undoubtedly troubled the Partisan high command as one more humiliation at the hands of the Russians, but they were not yet willing to reveal that humiliation to us. I was later told by a senior Yugoslav officer that the Partisan Third Army that had participated in driving the Germans out of Belgrade had been placed under Marshal Tolbukhin's command.

After the Yugoslavs' open break with Moscow in 1948 many similar humiliations were publicly disclosed in the charges and counter-charges between the two Communist parties and governments. One was over the conduct of the Red Army troops in Yugoslavia, where shooting, wholesale looting, and rape regularly occurred. When Tito complained, through Milovan Djilas, Stalin's response in essence was: How dare you insult the Red Army!

We soon found it necessary to keep our jeeps in locked garages or under armed guard to protect them from the Russian troops. Major Toby Milbank, one of Maclean's officers, surprised three Russian soldiers using a hacksaw to cut a padlocked chain on his jeep and got a cracked skull when he tried to stop them. Captain Cary had been shot at by drunken Russian troops and a Yugoslav attendant at our garage had been killed by Russians when he tried to keep them from stealing one of our jeeps.

The thievery was not limited to the Russians. An American fighter plane had made an emergency landing in Partisan territory in Bosnia. Later it was briefly seen by one of the American mission personnel as it landed at Belgrade, where it was immediately rolled into a closed hangar; the Partisan insignia was then painted over the American identification. When I left Belgrade we were still haggling with the Yugoslav staff to get it back.

Another confrontation occurred on June 5. Colonel John Clarke, who had returned to Belgrade as the British military attaché, and I were summoned to the office of General Jovanovic's deputy. He stated that Allied aircraft were flying over Yugoslav territory and were buzzing Yugoslav troops. This, he said, "would not be tolerated." Henceforth Yugoslav territory and areas occupied by Yugoslav forces in Venezia Giulia and Austria would be prohibited areas. Any Allied aircraft violating this order would be forced to land by the Yugoslav air force. Any overflights of transport aircraft would require permits, which could be applied for three days in advance.

We told him that any attempted enforcement of this order before we had communicated it to Allied Forces Headquarters and received their reply could have unfortunate consequences. Furthermore, British and American transport aircraft were flying regularly to Belgrade and providing the only access from the West, bringing people and supplies. He agreed to withdraw the order on transport aircraft and to delay the rest until headquarters replied. I asked if the order applied equally to Russian aircraft—in answer to which there was only silence.

I could well imagine American and British fighter pilots happily buzzing the irate Yugoslavs now that the war was over. But I could also understand that men who had risked their lives and lost their comrades over Yugoslavia while on missions supporting the Partisans would feel equally irate at such an order. The issue was papered over for the time being with some limited restrictions on overflights, but it simmered under the surface with the Yugoslavs, and an unarmed American transport plane was shot down by them in 1946.

A sign of Tito's effort to maintain a degree of independence from Moscow was his insistence on approving in advance all Allied bombing targets in Yugoslavia. Marshal Tolbukhin had asked the American Fifteenth Air Force in Italy to bomb railroad bridges and yards in northeastern Yugoslavia near the Hungarian border. This was to support his drive on Budapest. In spite of the request from Tolbukhin, Tito withheld his approval because the targets were in inhabited areas. It was only after assurances from the Americans of minimal damage that he relented. This veto power given to Tito was unique. In contrast, I was told by Lieutenant Colonel John Bross, head of OSS in London, that de Gaulle was never given such veto authority in respect to bombing targets in France. This was another signal we missed that Tito's nationalism could lead to a later break with Stalin.

■ With the withdrawal of the German forces major food shortages developed in many parts of the country. UNRRA, the United Nations Relief and Rehabilitation Administration, was not yet organized to provide help. The Allied military government in Italy offered to supply food from its military stocks, provided observers would be allowed to check on the distribution within the country to be sure it was not used for political purposes. Tito flatly refused to accept observers on the grounds that it was an invasion of sovereignty. "The people would rather starve," he said, "than accept relief on such conditions." Given the weight of the food on his palace tables at receptions, there was little danger the top Partisans would starve, however.

The Allied counterargument was that a civil war had divided the country and it was reasonable to ensure that Allied food was not being used as a political weapon. Tito stonewalled and the standoff continued. The Belgrade press denounced the Allies for deliberately bringing about starvation. The Allied command in Italy was apparently more sensitive to the large-scale starvation that was threatened than was Tito. It took more than four months to resolve the impasse. Tito finally agreed to a limited number of Allied observers. Only then did Allied food begin to reach Dalmatian ports. Subsequently all UNRRA aid, without which the economy would have collapsed, was distributed through the new government. At the same time UNRRA was being denounced in political meetings as "the Trojan horse of

American capitalism." James Klugmann, a member of the British Communist Party and one of my briefers in Cairo, now arrived as a senior member of the UNRRA mission in Belgrade. The mission was headed by a Soviet colonel.

■ The problems of money and currency were still unresolved by the new government. We needed dinars to buy local provisions and to pay our local help. We had tried to exchange dollars for dinars but the Belgrade national bank told us they were unable to do so until the official exchange rate was set. After repeated calls to the bank they finally agreed to issue dinars to us, for which we would deposit dollars at a rate of exchange we pulled out of the air. When the rate was finally set we would adjust our accounts up or down accordingly. We continued to draw dinars on this arrangement because the legal rate was still not set.

Finally, the bank official with whom we were dealing confessed to one of our officers that the bank was running out of dinars. The Germans, he explained, had taken the bank's printing press and plates with them when they retreated. It would be a favor to him if we got our dinars on the black market. There was a flourishing market of people desperate to get dollars and the rate was much higher than the one we had agreed on with the bank.

I had resisted our supply officer's earlier proposal that we go to the black market. This, I thought, would be playing into the hands of the Partisan authorities, who would love to catch us at it and use it in a huge propaganda attack against the capitalist plutocrats. Now, however, with the bank's blessing, we began to get the dinars we needed illicitly.

A few days later Vladislav Ribnikar, editor of *Politika*, a strongly pro-Communist Belgrade newspaper, came to lunch with us. During the lunch he mentioned he had heard we were dealing on the black market. Fully expecting an attack, I was ready with our explanation. Instead he said he had to import his newsprint from the Romanians and they had just told him that from now on they would only sell to him if he paid in dollars. Since we were in the business it would be a favor to him if he could sell us dinars for dollars. Although his rate was slightly less favorable, it seemed prudent to deal with him.

Ribnikar had been a secret member of the Communist Party since before the German invasion. He and his wife had provided an early meeting place in their villa for Tito and his Politburo before they had gone to the mountains in 1941. He had inherited *Politika*, the largest Belgrade daily before the war, and was now publishing the paper as (formally) an independent, though it was hard to distinguish it from *Borba*, the official paper of the Communist Party.

The peasants from the nearby villages became increasingly unwilling to bring their produce to the Belgrade market because they could buy nothing they needed with the dinars they received. They were raising only enough for themselves and to barter locally. Since our only access to Allied supplies was by air across German-held territory, we had to get food supplies locally if we could. Our mess sergeant and general factotum now made foraging trips to the countryside. He either bartered the limited supplies he could get from Italy, such as salt, or paid the peasants dollars if they would not accept dinars. Many civilians in Belgrade were reduced to bartering their household possessions for food.

■ I received brief radio reports from time to time that the friends I had left in Stajerska were still under heavy attack by the German forces. Driven into the higher levels of the mountains, they had all they could do to survive and were unable to mount any operations. Had it not been for General Glaise von Horstenau's request for an American with whom he could negotiate a surrender, I would have been there with them.

CHAPTER 17

The Defeat of the Chetniks

In addition to the control of the all-encompassing National Liberation Front, Tito's strategy to gain absolute power had two other essential elements. The first was the total elimination of the Chetniks as a political and military force. The second was the isolation and then the removal of the ministers of the London government-in-exile forced on him by Churchill. First he turned his attention to the Chetniks.

Tito's determination to crush the Chetniks and OSS's determination in 1944 to have an intelligence mission with them caused a major crisis between the Partisans and us. By 1944 one of General Donovan's principal objectives in pushing for American parties in Yugoslavia was to use Chetnik-held areas in Serbia and Partisan-held areas on the Austrian and Hungarian borders as bases from which to send agents into these two countries and through them to Germany and Central Europe. My base in the Karawanken Alps was one of two places held by the Partisans from which these penetrations could be mounted. The other was a Partisan group in Slavonia on the Hungarian border.

All during the previous summer we and the British had run into a wall of obstruction and nonsupport from the Partisans. Now, in Belgrade, I learned what had happened when from Stajerska the previous fall Captain Charles Fisher and I reported to OSS and Force 399 that the Fourth Zone was completely blocking our efforts to send intelligence agents into the Austrian provinces of Germany. On September 21, 1944, Major Stafford Reid, Colonel Huntington's deputy with Tito's headquarters on the island of Vis, had taken my message to General Dusan Kveder, Tito's chief of operations, and asked that an order be issued in Tito's name to the zone commander and commissar to assist rather than block our efforts. Tito had already given oral approval to Huntington and Maclean and this was a request to confirm it in writing.

Kveder responded, "I don't know whether you or your mission fully realize it, but your whole support from the Partisans has been very considerably affected by that gesture of sending representatives to our most bitter enemy, Draza Mihailovic. Perhaps you don't realize it, but that very action on your part has traveled from one end of our large army to the other and has raised very considerable doubt in the minds of our soldiers and headquarters as to the sincerity of the American interest in our popular movement."

Reid pointed out the substantial material support being provided by the British and Americans, and reminded him that no supplies were being sent to Mihailovic. When he pressed for the written authorization, Kveder replied, "Quite frankly, we are not interested in what you are planning to do in Austria and Hungary. We are having our hands full with the enemy in our own territory and our political enemies at the same time. . . . ."

Subsequently there had been no relaxation of restrictions on us at the Fourth Zone, nor in Slavonia on the Hungarian border. On November 18 I had radioed both OSS and Force 399 from Stajerska: "Situation here hopeless due complete lack of cooperation with Pzns."

It was not until Field Marshal Alexander came to Belgrade to see Tito in February 1945 that we were able to get the authorization from him that Reid had tried to get six months before. By then it was too late. The Stajerska Partisans had been routed by the Germans and infiltration into the Reich was no longer possible.

The OSS mission to Mihailovic certainly exacerbated our difficulties with the Partisans, but the causes were deeper. I believed that the basic problem was that we were dealing with a revolutionary leadership whose antagonism toward the West had been set in concrete by years of Communist indoctrination in Leninism and Stalinism.

Many years after the war I asked Mitja Ribicic what he thought had been the root of our Austrian problems in Stajerska. Ribicic had been commissar of the Koroska Odred, with which we had tried to work on the penetration of Austria. His view of the OSS mission to Mihailovic was that it was not an important issue with the Fourth Zone Partisans. "There were no Chetniks in Stajerska and we heard little about Mihailovic," he said. "I think the reason for your problem in getting into Austria proper was that we didn't want you to find out how weak we were across the Drava."

■ The Mihailovic affair illustrated how very difficult it is for a foreign power to maintain useful relations with both sides engaged in a bitter civil war. Exclusive British support for Mihailovic in the first two years of the war made him more stubbornly resistant to British efforts to form a united resistance. In the same way British support exclusively for Tito after 1943 gave him the confidence to reject similar proposals both from the Russians and from the British.

In December 1943, the British had concluded that Mihailovic was not fighting the Germans and began to consider withdrawing their military mission and materiel support. It took until the following spring, however, to get them all out. The OSS officers attached to the British mission were, as a consequence, withdrawn as well.

The second American mission to Mihailovic was approved by Roosevelt after considerable discussion within the State Department and with OSS. Unlike the earlier joint mission with the British, this one was to be entirely American. The mission, led by Lieutenant Colonel Robert McDowell, was strictly limited to intelligence collection and to evacuation of downed Allied aircrews. Roosevelt approved the McDowell mission on March 22, 1944. Learning of this, Churchill called Roosevelt, strongly opposing the mission. Roosevelt called it off, but in July Donovan got Roosevelt to reverse his decision again. Roosevelt directed that the mission be solely for intelligence. McDowell was to make it clear to Mihailovic that no political or military support was implied.

On August 26, McDowell, two junior officers, and a radio operator landed in a C-47 on a clandestine field near Mihailovic's headquarters in Serbia. They had made six abortive attempts and had been able to land only on the seventh try. Churchill had instructed SOE, who controlled air operations to Yugoslavia, to delay McDowell's flight, "the greatest courtesy being used to our friends and Allies in every case, but no transportation."

Churchill now protested to Roosevelt again. If they each backed different sides they would lay the scene for civil war. And again Roosevelt reversed himself, ordering McDowell out. It was only six days after McDowell had landed but it took him two months to get out. Maclean thought he was deliberately delaying. He reported to the Foreign Office that he had been privately informed by an American officer that a plane had gone in to pick up McDowell but he had refused to come out. However, I have found no OSS record supporting this. Mihailovic was being hotly pursued by the Partisans and it might have been impossible to stop long enough to arrange an earlier clandestine pickup.

McDowell returned to Italy on November 1, predicting that after the Germans left there would be two years of civil war unless the Western Allies intervened to enforce peace. In the event, the Partisans very quickly finished off the civil war and dispersed the Chetniks. McDowell was also wrong in believing Britain and the United States could enforce peace between the two enemies. It took more than 50,000 British troops to expel the irresolute Communist-led Greek resistance from parts of the city of Athens after the Germans withdrew. It would have taken a much larger force to enforce a cease-fire in Yugoslavia and it would have become a one-sided protection of the weaker Chetniks from the Partisans.

■ As might be expected, Mihailovic made maximum political capital of McDowell's arrival. On September 5, only eight days after the C-47 bringing McDowell touched down near Mihailovic's headquarters, Tito formally asked the British and American military missions to transmit to their governments his charge that the Western Allies were still sending supplies to Mihailovic despite their statements to him to the contrary. In this protest he said: "Draza Mihailovic [is] in open collaboration with the German occupier. It can have an extremely unfavourable effect on the feelings of the truly patriotic forces, that is to say the majority of the people of Yugoslavia, toward the Allies." General Wilson, speaking as the Supreme Allied Commander, responded to Tito, refuting his assertions and suggesting that Tito use the weapons we had given him to get on with the job of blocking the German retreat from the Balkans. Again the conflict was between the Allied objective of destroying the German armies and Tito's objective of completing the revolution.

The pressure from the Partisans continued. On September 14, 1944, General Koca Popovic, one of Tito's top commanders, had shown Colonel Huntington a Chetnik propaganda flyer that he said had been taken from a Chetnik prisoner. The leaflet read, in part:

TO THE SERBIAN PEOPLE

The delegates of the Allied American Government and personal representatives of President Roosevelt, a proved friend of the liberty-loving small nations, have arrived. . . .

American Colonel McDowell is personal representative of President Roosevelt and will, in direct contact, interpret the wishes, intentions and sympathies of the American people and its President toward the democratic guerrilla movement of the Jugoslav Army in the Fatherland and its leader, General Mihailovic.

The leaflet asserted McDowell had brought a personal message to Mihailovic from Roosevelt.

Allied America is ready to give soon visible proofs of its sympathies for and approval of our honorable and long national struggle by offering armed help, which will enable us to crush at last, in common fight, National Socialist Germany, her satellites, and her direct and indirect helpers.

The Serbian people, the peoples of Jugoslavia, must be ready to march with new armament toward final victory!

Long live the allied American people!
Long live American President Roosevelt!
Long live our Allies!
Long live the fighting Serbian people!
Long live federal, democratic and social Jugoslavia!
Long live the Jugoslavs, American and world democracies!
Forward, into the last battle for the final victory of the
    national ideals!

In view of the short time between the arrival of McDowell and the "captured" leaflet being shown to Huntington at Tito's headquarters, some thought that it could have been written by the Partisans in order to provoke McDowell's recall.

At the same time the Partisans launched their final drive to eliminate the Chetniks and link up with the Russians for a combined attack on Belgrade. On September 13 the British liaison officer with the Partisan units attacking Mihailovic in Serbia reported, somewhat gleefully, by radio:

No. 324. Mihailovic headquarters overrun. Mihailovic escaped with protection (corrupt group) [meaning 5 letters in the message were undecipherable.] American Colonel and two officers with him. . . As we have hopes capturing Mihailovic please augment true picture.

No. 326. Have all Mihailovic's documents. These confirm American mission with him. Please clear situation with [Tito's headquarters] and have orders for their disposal on capture.

Colonel John Clarke, Maclean's base commander in Italy, replied rather sternly.

You must reassure us that Partisans are making Belgrade their military objective and not Mihailovic. We appreciate temptation of latter objective but it is your duty to discountenance it. You as British liaison officer must not embarrass us by saying "We have hopes of capturing Mihailovic."

The Partisans went for Mihailovic and drove him out of Serbia but did not capture him. They then moved their main forces to link with the Russians driving into Yugoslavia from Romania and with them took Belgrade.

■ During 1944 the Romanian oil fields and refineries at Ploesti became a prime target for the American Fifteenth Air Force based in Italy. The routes out and back crossed Partisan and Chetnik areas in Serbia and Bosnia and aircrews were told to parachute in these areas if they were unable to make it back to Italy. Since the withdrawal of the British-American mission to Mihailovic large numbers of American airmen had been picked up by Chetnik units. An OSS group was sent in with McDowell specifically to arrange clandestine airfields where C-47s could land and pick them up.

The two OSS air rescue officers on the ground were impressed with the care the Chetniks took of the downed airmen. Men without adequate weapons, clothing, food, and medical care would nevertheless fight the Germans and Partisans to rescue and protect the Americans. The OSS men became personally embittered when the evacuation planes arrived either empty or with clothing and food only for the Allied airmen awaiting evacuation. This, in their view (and in mine), was a shoddy way to treat the Chetniks for risking their necks on our behalf. The orders were to strictly observe the American commitment to the British and Tito that no support was being provided. At the same time Allied aircraft were regularly dropping weapons to the Partisan forces close by, who without a moment's consideration used them to subdue their prime enemy—the Chetniks.

In the four months the OSS team was with the Chetniks 340 American airmen and several British, Russian, French, Italian, and Polish escapees were flown out of Chetnik territory in Allied C-47s. Yet no supplies, not even food and medical supplies, were provided in return. An even larger number had been rescued by the Chetniks in 1943.

During the winter and spring of 1944–45 some small Chetnik groups were still in the hinterlands, and an active underground existed in Belgrade. Many rumors reached us that when the leaves returned to the trees an active revolt against the Communists would explode. But when the leaves returned nothing of the sort happened. We reported that large numbers of people were strongly opposed to the emerging Communist rule: some of them were disillusioned Partisans and some were former quislings and Chetniks; and many had been neutral in the civil war. But the opposition had no political program to offer except opposition to the Communists and a lingering hope that Britain and America would somehow in the end intervene.

The Western Allies had faced two issues in deciding whether or not to support Mihailovic. First, was he aggressively fighting the Germans? Second, was he actively collaborating with the Germans as Tito repeatedly charged? These were quite separate issues, yet they were often lumped together in Allied thinking.

There was near-unanimity among Allied officers that for whatever reasons Mihailovic was not actively fighting the Germans. According to OSS Lieutenant George Musulin, who was with the Chetniks in the winter and spring of 1943-44, the last Chetnik-initiated attack on the Germans was in October 1943.

Mihailovic had said almost from the beginning that the price of attacking German forces was terrible retribution against the Serb peasants—a price he was unwilling to pay. The American and British officers who had been with Mihailovic believed that this was his principal reason for limiting his attacks on the Germans. Lieutenant Musulin said Mihailovic had told him his objective was to preserve the Serb population ethnically and numerically against the Croats. British Colonel Bailey said much the same.

Mihailovic's attitude is summarized in his own message to his corps commanders in May 1944. Musulin had surreptitiously obtained the text.

> The attempt of the Communists to penetrate into Serbia has been repulsed by us and [we will continue] until their extermination. . . . German forces have not interfered with us in this last operation even though we do not have any contact or agreement with them. So that we will not [jeopardize] operations against the Communist group, it is necessary to stop all operations against the Germans. . . .
>
> Let it be known that we have large number of enemies. We cannot fight against all simultaneously. Now, the most important enemies are the Communists.

Mihailovic believed to the very end that the British and American forces would land and occupy Yugoslavia, and when that day came he would mobilize his forces to aid in expelling the Germans. As late as the spring of 1945 he still believed the Allies would land and save him.

■ The charge of Chetnik collaboration with the Germans was quite different from the charge that they were not actively fighting them. As in all civil wars, the objective of eliminating the internal enemy and gaining control of the postwar government was paramount and pursued single-mindedly by both sides. This meant using whatever support could be extracted from outside parties to gain advantage over the internal enemy. Tito used the charge of collaboration against Mihailovic as a political tool to deter the British and the Americans from providing even psychological support to Mihailovic. He could only justify to the British and the Americans his armed attacks against the Chetniks by making the charge that Mihailovic was a German collaborator. Therefore, Tito argued, his attacks against the Chetniks were the same as attacks on the Germans. Also it would be harder for the Allies to defend their support for Mihailovic if he was a collaborator than if he was simply curbing his attacks to minimize German murder of Serb peasants.

Complaining about the McDowell mission, Tito had said to Maclean, "Allied policy is all the more inexplicable since the fact of Mihailovic's collaboration with enemy was now universally accepted." There was also a bit of implied blackmail: "So long as there were American missions on [both] sides it was difficult for me to allow Colonel Huntington facilities I would otherwise like to give."

Accommodation with the enemy was quite different from collaboration. Both Tito and Mihailovic sought accommodation with the Germans. As described in a previous chapter, in 1943 Tito had secretly sent his representatives to Zagreb, where they proposed to the German high command an agreement in which they would stop attacking German lines of communication and major garrisons in return for which the Germans would stop their attacks on Partisan liberated areas.

On the Chetnik side there were undoubtedly many degrees of accommodation and collaboration. Unlike the Partisan forces who were under strict central discipline, our OSS officers reported that the individual Chetnik units exercised much greater independence and often made their own arrangements with the Serbian quislings, with the Italians, and with the Germans.

Musulin said that during his months with Mihailovic he had seen no evidence of collaboration. However, he said, "Mihailovic himself told me that he had men who were assigned to beg, borrow, buy, or steal ammunition from the German dumps. Peasants told me that truckloads of ammunition were piled along the road by Germans. The Germans would then drive away and Chetniks would appear to haul the ammunition away." It is not likely the Germans would have done this if they had thought the ammunition they left would be used against themselves.

A few weeks after the end of the war I was in Salzburg on temporary duty for a few days. Here I spent an evening with Hans Herwarth von Bittenfeld, a German wartime army officer who had been a diplomat in the German embassy in Moscow before the war. Herwarth was highly regarded by the Americans. He had secretly kept Charles Bohlen in the American embassy informed of the progress of the secret negotiations between Molotov and von Ribbentrop that culminated in the nonaggression pact that allowed Hitler to attack Poland, and thus set off the Second World War. By chance Lieutenant Colonel Charles Thayer, my predecessor in Belgrade, had spotted Herwarth, whom he knew from prewar Moscow days, in a group of surrendered German officers and had him freed.

That evening Herwarth told me that during the war he had been a staff officer at the German High Command on the Eastern Front. While on leave he had gone to Belgrade to visit his father-in-law, Field Marshal Maximilian von Weichs, commander of German Armies Southeast. Von Weichs told him that members of his staff were going to a meeting with Chetnik officers. Would he like to sit in on the meeting? He told me that the Chetnik officers said, in effect, to the Germans: "You are our enemy, you have invaded our country, we abhor having to deal with you, but we are forced to do so in order to get guns to fight our greater enemies, the Communists." Mihailovic was not present, but Herwarth said the Chetnik officers appeared to speak for Mihailovic and the German officers appeared to accept that they spoke for him.

Tito was determined to keep from us the extent to which the Partisans were fighting the Chetniks rather than the Germans as well as the extent to which they were using Allied weapons to do so. This undoubtedly was one factor behind Tito's campaign to restrict our contacts and movements with his units and to bring the maximum pressure on us to withdraw all American officers from Mihailovic's forces. In contrast, even after Allied support was stopped in 1943, Mihailovic and his commanders allowed American officers complete freedom to talk with all ranks and with civilians.

■ By spring of 1945 the Chetniks were routed as an organized fighting force. Individuals and small bands were either captured or on the run to escape capture.

Late one evening in Belgrade Robert Miner, one of our mission officers, came into my combination office-bedroom, carrying a note written in pencil on a torn piece of paper. The note read: "To any Americans: —— [A Serbian name] has risked his life to save mine. Please give him any help you can." It was signed and under the signature was "1st Lieut. U.S. Army Air Corps."

Miner said the man had somehow got into our building through a back door or window, having evaded our Partisan guards. He had presented the note to Miner and asked for asylum. He was, he said, from the remnant of the defeated Chetnik forces and he was certain he would be shot if he were captured. His only hope was to get our help and protection to get him out of the country.

The note was almost certainly authentic. But there was no certainty that the man who brought it was the same person who had rescued the American officer. The note might have been taken from a captured or killed Chetnik and was now being used by an agent of OZNA, the new Yugoslav KGB, to entrap us into trying to help the man. If we were to try to smuggle him out of the country, the secret police would move in at a criticial moment, having obtained "evidence" that the United States was still supporting the Chetnik resistance against the now legal Communist-controlled government.

We briefly considered radioing Allied Forces Headquarters in Italy for instructions, but quickly discarded that alternative. Based on instructions earlier to the OSS air rescue team with Mihailovic we would be ordered not to help the man in any way. Our first emotional reaction was to try to help and hope that the man was authentic and not an OZNA agent. But the more Miner and I tried to find a solution, the more it became evident that the odds were very much against us.

First, it seemed almost impossible that the man could have entered our building without the knowledge of the Yugoslav guards around us. That made it likely that he was a police agent posing as a Chetnik on the run. There was no way we could verify his story. We couldn't confront him with the Air Corps lieutenant, who was by now in Italy or back in the States. Since we had no independent knowledge of the circumstances under which our officer had been rescued, we had no way of testing the man's story. Either we had to believe him or reject his story.

Second, unlike an embassy, our military mission had no diplomatic immunity. The secret police could have demanded we turn over the man, and if we refused, they would have either blockaded our building, ordered the mission to leave the country, or, if we refused, forcibly entered the building.

We could try to smuggle the man out in some sort of box we would take to the Belgrade airfield when the next American C-47 flight came in. But this would have required approval of Allied Forces Headquarters in Italy and a carefully coordinated scheme to surreptitiously get him aboard a U.S. aircraft. Reluctantly, we concluded that any attempt to help him would almost certainly either fail, or worse, blow up in our faces if he turned out to be a police agent.

Miner went off to see the man, who was having a late meal in our mess room. When he learned we wouldn't help, he got up, cursed us roundly and went out into the night. A minute or so later Miner heard a shot in the dark alley. The man was either shot by the Partisan guards or had shot himself. We were unable to learn which.

I have always been very troubled by the thought that he might have been a real Chetnik, and by our own refusal to help him. Yet I was never able to see how a plan to get him out secretly could have been successful.

Mihailovic and a few loyal survivors were pursued into the Bosnian forests, where they successfully eluded Partisan forces until captured in March 1946. After a public show trial he was condemned to death and shot. American liaison officers as well as downed American airmen who had been saved by Mihailovic's forces asked to testify on his behalf, but were not permitted to do so. It was a tragic end for those who had fought a civil war and lost.

CHAPTER *18*

Communist Rule Becomes Absolute

T he third element of Tito's strategy to gain unchallenged power was to deny the representatives of the London government-in-exile who joined the Belgrade coalition government any power or influence whatsoever. Under an agreement forced on both Tito and the royal government by Churchill, with support from Stalin and Roosevelt, the king was barred from returning until a plebiscite had been held. During the interim period a regency council would hold the royal authority of the king.

Shortly after I arrived in Belgrade Thayer and I received an invitation to attend the investiture of the regents appointed to represent King Peter. The ceremony was held in the great hall of one of the old government buildings. The center of the hall was filled with high-ranking Yugoslavs, mostly Partisans and representatives of the Liberation Front. Foreign representatives were arrayed along the sides. Tito did not attend, apparently wishing to give the regents as little legitimacy as possible. The three regents, two of whom were Partisans, were appropriately dressed in formal diplomatic attire, and we in the military were in the best of our well-worn uniforms.

A large part of the ceremony was conducted by the Catholic bishop and the Orthodox metropolitan of Belgrade. It was a colorful occasion with the bishop and the metropolitan taking turns in performing their separate rituals. I had a sneaking suspicion that each was trying to outdo the other in the splendor of their embroidered robes, mitres, crowns, incense vessels, and other symbols of office and ritual. If so, the metropolitan won hands down. In comparison the poor bishop seemed like a country parish priest.

The ceremony was one more step in the validation of Tito's control of the country, which had already been decided in the forests and villages during the past four years. It was also a step in the process by which Churchill recognized and accepted the reality of Partisan power while seeming to uphold the legitimacy of the monarchy and the royal government-in-exile. Months earlier in Italy Churchill had told Tito that "chivalry demands that we should not let the King down." Yet he recognized that the reality of Partisan power could not be denied.

Under the formula worked out to paper over Tito's de facto control it was also agreed that a united government under the regency would consist of 28 cabinet ministers, of whom all but 6 would be chosen by Tito alone. The 6 were selected from among the exiled political leaders and representatives of other parties by negotiation between Tito and Ivan Subasic, the prime minister in the last royal government—but there would be no negotiation on the 20 Tito nominees. Tito was to be prime minister and defense minister. Milan Grol, head of the Serb Peasant party-in-exile, would be deputy prime minister and Subasic would be the foreign minister. Most importantly, AVNOJ, the Anti-Fascist Council of National Liberation, would itself become the legislature of the new government. Under pressure from the three Allied governments Tito had agreed to enlarge AVNOJ by adding members of the last prewar legislature who could be found and who were not tainted by collaboration with the occupiers. It proved a meaningless gesture.

The king himself, when confronted with the British-engineered agreement between his prime minister Subasic and Tito, said it seemed to be a polite way of getting rid of him. I thought this was precisely what Churchill had intended. Both Thayer and I had been instructed by OSS and the State Department not to participate in any of these negotiations, to avoid any implication that Washington approved of them.

The process by which the British government under Churchill had pressed for and brought about a united Yugoslav government seemed to me to be a curious one. The early efforts of the British, backed by the Russians, were understandably to get the Partisans and the Chetniks to stop fighting each other and combine to fight the Germans. The Soviets were also concerned that Partisan emphasis on political organization and on the civil war with the Chetniks would divert them from military action against the Germans.

But in 1943 the British had already recognized that a united resistance to the Germans was hopeless. Maclean, in his first report after arriving at Tito's mountain headquarters, had said, "There seems little doubt that nothing short of large-scale armed intervention [by British and American forces] will prevent them [the Partisans] from taking power in Yugoslavia as soon as the Germans are finally driven out." In February of 1945 he reaffirmed this position. "It has long been clear that they [the Partisans] and they alone would control the country once the Germans withdrew and that we should therefore sooner or later have to deal with them as the rulers of Yugoslavia."

Given this conclusion, which Churchill appeared to fully accept, I was puzzled as to why the British and Churchill himself had expended so much effort and political capital over so many months to bring about a paste-up job almost totally without substance. The original objective of uniting all resistance in Yugoslavia had long before been acknowledged as impossible. The charade of unity no longer seemed to serve any purpose.

Churchill himself became more and more frustrated with the impossible task of restoring monarchs to their thrones. He had been told by SOE officers with Greek partisans that the majority of the population did not want the Greek king to return from exile. In the midst of negotiations with Tito and Subasic he received another warning from SOE officers in Albania telling him that there too the people had had enough of kings. His exasperated minute to Anthony Eden, the foreign secretary, began "Another King down the drain!"

and ended: "As for 'no significant group wanting the King back,' there are very few countries in which anybody wants anyone back. Please talk to me about this."

■ Churchill had become increasingly disenchanted with Tito. The reports from British and American officers with Tito's headquarters and with Partisan commands increasingly reflected our concerns that a totalitarian Communist government would be the final outcome. But when Churchill asked him this question face-to-face, Tito reassured him, saying, "I am rather perturbed about all the questions which are constantly being asked about Communism in Yugoslavia. I have stated quite categorically that we don't intend to introduce it."

The reality was that Tito became prime minister, and of the 28 ministers all but three were Partisans or members of the Liberation Front. The key Ministry of Internal Affairs went to Aleksandar Rankovic, one of Tito's principal lieutenants. OZNA, the secret police, was under this ministry, and was responsible for rooting out all opposition to the National Liberation Front, as well as any remaining opposition to Communist control within the movement itself.

The Communist Party, operating through the National Liberation Front, controlled the entire political structure from village committees to the national parliament. The army and the secret police were an integral part of Partisan power. All the press was completely controlled by the Agitprop sections of the party. Maclean and others had reported this fully to London, as we had to Washington. Under these conditions there was little reason to think that anything would be changed by the addition to the government of a few lonely politicians returned from exile abroad. At the insistence of the British the agreement between Tito and Subasic for a combined government carried these provisions:

> The new government will publish a declaration containing basic principles of democratic liberties and the guarantees for their realization. Personal freedom, freedom from fear, freedom of religion and conscience, freedom of speech, the press, meetings and associations, will be especially emphasized and guaranteed, and in the same way the right of property and of private initiative.

No such statement was ever published.

At Yalta the United States had joined Britain and Russia in calling for the rapid implementation of the Tito-Subasic agreement for a merged government. The three powers went further by pledging to help all the occupied nations to form interim governments broadly representative of all democratic elements and to make possible free elections. By these actions the United States had endorsed the provisions of the Tito-Subasic agreement, and was in effect a co-signer on the agreement that appeared to guarantee both individual and political freedoms. It also gave the men who returned to Belgrade to join the government assurances that they could have substantive roles in the new government.

The exiled politicians who were to join the cabinet arrived in Belgrade very soon after the investiture of the regents. We reported by radio to Caserta and Washington almost daily on the reception and acceptance of the London members of the new government. Immediately they found themselves isolated and cut off from their potential supporters. The committee of AVNOJ (the Partisan assembly that was to be the new legislature) set up to nominate additional members from the prewar parties was made up entirely of Communists. They delayed acting for months; meanwhile AVNOJ proceeded to pass a series of far-reaching laws that were so general as to enable the Tito government to do essentially whatever it wanted. For example: The "Law for the Suppression of Economic Sabotage" defined sabotage as "every activity or lack of activity which aims to hinder, obstruct or endanger the correct and speedy work of economic enterprises or institutions as well as everything else which might damage the interests of the national economy or programs." This included "undertaking agricultural activities contrary to government plans" and use of "irrational methods of production or distribution." Public prosecutors were placed in all the government offices, labor unions, newspapers, and front organizations to ferret out "enemies of the people."

Milan Grol, leader of the prewar Serbian Democratic Party and now vice premier, had no party organization to provide him political support. His party had ceased to exist. The party's prewar newspaper was no longer published and Grol's efforts to restart it were blocked by the Partisans. A Partisan guard posted outside his office took the names of all visitors. Grol and those who visited him were convinced that their names were given to the secret police. He told me that he believed that his office was bugged. It probably was.

Within two months after joining the merged government Grol and Juraj Sutej, a fellow minister representing the Croat Peasant Party, both told me of their feeling of complete despair and impotence. They were even afraid to see Allied representatives openly. We now were forced to arrange clandestine meetings with them. Grol said he had discouraged his followers from taking political action for fear of personal reprisals against them.

In a subsequent meeting Grol said he had seen Tito for an hour and had protested in the strongest terms the laws against speculation and sabotage and their enforcement by the People's Courts. He told Tito the People's Courts had no standing in law. Rule of law administered by competent judges was necessary. Tito had responded by saying he would personally look into the matter, and by admitting that some injustices might be done by the People's Courts.

Grol had also urged that a general amnesty for opponents of the regime be proclaimed, saying that otherwise civil war might result. According to Grol, this was discussed at a later cabinet meeting where it was strongly opposed by Kardelj, the most influential member after Tito. Nothing came of these discussions, Grol said.

Tito usually reserved for himself the role of the statesman, leaving the hatchet work to his Politburo colleagues. In public statements he continued to promise freedom of the press, speech, religion, and assembly, and that the use of arbitrary measures would be avoided. In the talks that the other Allied representatives and I had with him he was usually reasonable, conceded mistakes by overzealous underlings, and promised to personally look into the matters we raised. Yet extreme totalitarian measures continued without abatement. We gained the strong impression that several of the other senior members of the party leadership were more zealous than he, and would often act to set limits on his more pragmatic approach to issues.

Ivan Subasic, prime minister in the London government-in-exile, had become foreign minister in the new government. He too was largely ignored by Tito and his associates. Vladimir Velebit had become the deputy foreign minister and it was with him, rather than with Subasic, that the British and the Americans dealt on political matters. Very early in the war Tito recognized that Velebit was his most effective representative to the West, and had sent him to General Wilson's headquarters in Cairo in 1943 and later to London.

Subasic, Grol, and Sutej all told us they were considering resigning to protest the failure of the government to carry out the spirit of the declaration at Yalta on the liberated European nations. In my report of these conversations to Caserta and Washington I concluded, "They want to know what if anything America is willing to do to enforce the British-American-Soviet declaration." While I could not tell them, the answer had to be "little or nothing." We had been party to a commitment that could not be enforced short of a major military operation.

Grol resigned in August. Subasic and Sutej, fellow members of the Croat Peasant Party and also ministers of the new government, resigned in October. All three were placed under house arrest the following month.

National elections for the Constituent Assembly were held on November 11, 1945. The two opposition newspapers that had managed to start that summer were banned by the government the week before the election. A single slate of candidates presented by the Liberation Front was overwhelmingly elected.

Michael Petrovich, a member of our research and analysis staff in Belgrade, later wrote:

> The highly threatening tone of many campaign speeches of the government's Popular Front, slogans such as "Ballots for Tito, Bullets for Grol" and the unmistakable impression that all who voted against the government would be considered traitors only helped to create an atmosphere of widespread fear. A hidden but very real fear of a bloody civil war of retribution, particularly between the Serbs and the Croats, inspired many to vote for the Popular Front which supported a vigorous policy of reconciliation between these two Yugoslav peoples.

Tito later openly admitted that the total exclusion of the "exile" ministers from participation in the government was deliberate:

> We could not during the period of joint government make any concessions to those elements in the government who actually represented the interests of the overthrown monarchy, the bourgeoisie and their patrons abroad, international reaction. . . . Even at this period our adversaries both in the country and abroad still cherished illusions about "who would beat whom." But we had no such illusions, we knew how this whole thing could end.

■ During the winter and spring of 1944-45 consolidation of Partisan control continued vigorously, especially in the cities and towns most recently liberated. In Belgrade we heard nightly gunfire that we presumed to be the discovery and liquidation of those identified with the Chetniks, German collaborators, or others regarded as "unreliable" and potential resisters of the Communist regime. We believed that thousands of people had been arrested by OZNA, the secret police, immediately after the departure of the Germans from Belgrade. Those that had committed atrocities or had been collaborationist leaders were quickly shot. But most were subject to long interrogations during which the names of others were extracted. Then they were released after they gave assurances of positive loyalty, and that they would not participate in any unsanctioned activities. The principal purpose of these arrests and interrogations was to impress on those even thinking about active opposition how utterly impossible it was.

The Communist Party alone kept its separate identity, and its membership was limited to those of demonstrated loyalty to the party. The Front took the place of all of the prewar parties, since it was said that members from each of these parties were in the Front. Tito explained that it was not the time "for playing politics." The Liberation Front would, he said, "manage the entire political life of the country."

After the liberation of Belgrade, the many organizations within the Front that had been started early in the war were rapidly expanded to take in every citizen not under charges of collaboration. This was a means of enlisting their positive commitment to the regime and as a control to prevent any opposition that could seriously challenge the regime. These organizations included the Anti-Fascist Women, the Anti-Fascist Youth, the labor organization, the cooperative organizations, the teachers' organization, and even the Red Cross.

We reported to Caserta how the formation of a unified labor organization had been orchestrated. It was typical of the steps to political consolidation. First an unpublicized decision was taken within the party leadership to create a comprehensive labor movement. Next popular demonstrations were organized throughout the country demanding a unified labor movement. These demands were then reported prominently in the press in Belgrade and other cities. Next Moshe Pijade, the principal party theoretician (and Tito's prewar mentor in prison), published an article in *Politika*, one of the two leading newspapers, responding favorably to these popular demands for a single organization for all workers, to include even the intellectuals and state employees. "Any separate group," he said, "would be the enemy not only of the syndicate movement but also of the National Liberation Front as well as the body politic." The next move was the convening of a national conference of labor delegates to ratify the party line laid down by Pijade and to appoint an "action committee," as the syndicate's nucleus, all by acclaim.

All persons were enrolled in one or more mass organizations under the control of the party and OZNA. In the cities cells were set up in each city block, which all inhabitants of the block were required to join, to attend regular meetings and participate in "spontaneous demonstrations" denouncing the "enemies of the people." Block meetings were held regularly for discussion and study of politically approved propaganda materials. At any time an individual block could be called out to demonstrate. Placards were provided and slogans handed out that were to be shouted in unison. Our military mission was often the focus for such demonstrators, who stood in the street and shouted slogans such as "We want Tito, down with the reactionaries."

"Spontaneous demonstrations" were a favorite device for involving the rank and file in support of the new regime. At almost any time, day or night, we would see dejected groups of 20 or 30 men and women slowly walking down nearly deserted streets carrying placards demanding or denouncing this or that and mournfully chanting their slogans. The block leader could always be spotted as the one trying to inject into the group a little enthusiasm or outrage, depending on the issue they had been given. One poor fellow privately complained that because he was the tallest he was always assigned to carry the flag. While attendance was not mandatory, the block leaders were in a position to "evaluate enthusiasm" and to control ration cards and other necessities for survival.

All men from 18 to 35 who were still around were called up for military service in order to bring them under organized control. During the spring the UNRRA (the United Nations Relief and Rehabilitation Agency) personnel for Yugoslavia had arrived in Belgrade via the American Air Transport Command's C-47s. In late April one of their senior people, an American, came in to see me and to report a disturbing incident that two of his people, both Americans, had observed. The UNRRA men had been in Montenegro and had happened to see several hundred draftees being marched north. One of the draftees, apparently hoping to escape, had thrown a grenade at the Partisan guards, killing two. In retaliation the guards opened fire on the entire column and killed most of the draftees.

■ From the earliest days of the Partisans the press had been a central part of the movement. Djilas, a member of the Politburo and Tito's propaganda chief through most of the war, described the duty of the press:

> It objectively reports what is going on in the world; at the same time it interprets and explains these events. It tells the masses what they should do with regard to these events. It shows them the path they should follow, the political stand they should adopt. It finally teaches the people and popular organizations how to approach this or that political question—and expose the enemies of the people. It admonishes you, in-

structs you—asks you each day whether you have done your job and whether you have corrected your faults.

Permission to publish was limited to the Communist Party and to organizations within the Liberation Front.

Milovan Djilas had been one of Tito's closest associates and, in 1943, the courageous commander of the column carrying the wounded when the main Partisan force broke out of the German encirclement in Bosnia. We found him to be one of the most uncompromising of the Partisan leaders in his embrace of Communism and his rejection of "bourgeois" Western society and values. In a conversation with one of the other senior Communist leaders in Belgrade I probed the basis of Djilas's anti-Western views. His explanation was prophetic. Djilas, he said, was "the purest of the pure." In a strange way I thought he probably was.

The former Royal Cavalry School was just outside Belgrade and of course had been taken over by the Partisans. It had a good stable and I was asked if I would like to ride there. I needed a pair of boots and the liaison staff arranged to have a pair made. The bootmaker, having measured my feet and selected the leather, announced proudly that he would make them "just like Comrade Djilas's boots."

■ The Communists had totally defeated the Chetniks, had isolated and then forced out the three ministers from the government-in-exile, had established control over all press and radio, and had achieved a complete and total monopoly of power within Yugoslavia.

The European war ended on May 8, 1945. The day after I was summoned by the chief of staff, General Arso Jovanovic, and told to close the military mission and leave the country without delay. I responded that it was already my intention to leave on July 4 (and I kept to that schedule). I expressed my admiration for the great contributions the Partisans had made to the victory over fascism. I then said that because he, Jovanovic, had made no mention of the value of Allied cooperation and support during the war I felt compelled to do so. I reminded him that that support included a very large volume of supplies provided the Partisans by air and by sea; the evacuation by

Allied aircraft from clandestine fields behind German lines of more than 12,000 wounded Partisans for treatment in our military hospitals in Italy; and air strikes in support of Partisan operations. His response was that it was the Partisans' right to receive this support and our duty as allies to provide it. In any case it was less than it should have been. Therefore no expression of appreciation was called for.

Jovanovic had been a captain in the Royal Yugoslav Army, serving for a time under Mihailovic. When war came he was one of the leaders in the initial Partisan-led revolt in Montenegro. Later in the war he became Tito's chief of staff. He was cold and rigid in bearing and, according to Djilas, was not liked by the field commanders. They preferred to deal directly with Tito and this Tito encouraged.

He was tall, thin, and bleak-looking. I had never seen in him an ounce of warmth, humor, or friendliness. Brusqueness and rigidity were, to me, his principal characteristics.

Jovanovic was one of the few Partisan leaders who later defected to Moscow after Tito broke with Stalin. At the time there was a brief announcement from Belgrade that the defection had occurred and that Jovanovic had been killed as he tried to escape across the Yugoslav-Romanian frontier. Several years later, during a trip to Yugoslavia, I was told about the incident by one of the senior party members. Four of the defecting party members, including Jovanovic, planned their escape using the cover story that they were going boar hunting (a popular sport in Yugoslavia) in the region near the Romanian frontier. They drove to a village near the border and left their car and driver, saying they would be back from the hunt at the end of the day. The plan was to go to the border area and slip across. When they got to the border, by sheer chance, Jovanovic's bootlace became undone and he stopped to retie it while the others went ahead. At that moment a Yugoslav border guard came into Jovanovic's view. Without hesitating, he drew his pistol, fired at the guard and missed. The guard reacted by firing at Jovanovic with his submachine gun, killing him. The irony is that had he kept his nerve and identified himself as General Jovanovic, chief of staff of the army, the guard would have fallen all over himself in saluting. He could have simply explained the cover story of boar hunting and the guard would have left in confusion to tell his comrades at the barracks that evening that he had personally met the chief of staff.

■ As our problems with the Yugoslavs grew, we began to pick up echoes of a secret order reported to have been issued to senior commanders and commissars by the Yugoslav general staff, stating that the British and the Americans were now the enemies of Yugoslavia and that the West might soon be at war with Russia. One report said that each officer shown the order was required to sign a secrecy agreement in the presence of an officer of OZNA, the security police. We were never able to track this down, but we continued to get reports that the Yugoslav officers talked of a coming war with the West. One possible explanation is that they were reflecting the often-expressed views of Germans that Germany and the West would unite against the Russians.

Tito and the Communists had completed their conquest of the country, and now controlled the entire nation without serious challenge. The next step was to expand their borders into prewar Austria and Italy.

CHAPTER 19

The Cold War
Begins in Trieste

O n May 3, 1945, only one day after the surrender of the German armies in Italy and five days before the final surrender of Germany, the first face-to-face East-West confrontation, which was to grow into the Cold War, began in Trieste. As early as the spring of 1944 the Fourth Zone Partisans had made it clear to me and to others that they intended to occupy and annex to Yugoslavia the entire prewar Italian province of Venezia Giulia, including the cities of Trieste, Gorizia, and Monfalcone. The Americans and the British also planned to occupy those cities and the surrounding territory, and to oppose any change in Italian borders until a postwar peace conference. But although we (the British and the Americans) had foreseen that Tito would make a grab for Trieste, no plan had been agreed upon to deal with it when it happened.

Venezia Giulia had been a part of the Austrian Empire since the fourteenth century. Trieste was the southern terminus of the Süd-bahn, the main railroad from Vienna—the same railroad that I had spent most of the year before trying to blow up. After the First World War and the defeat of Austria-Hungary, Trieste and the surrounding territory came under Italian rule. The border was well to the east of Trieste and deep into ethnic Slovene and Croat territory. The whole area contained a mixture of Italians, Slovenes, and Croats, but the

Map 7: Prewar and postwar (1954) boundaries between Italy and Yugoslavia.

rural northern and eastern parts were predominantly Slav while Trieste and the cities to the south and west were predominantly Italian.

The Yugoslav Partisan claims to the entire area were based in part on ethnic grounds, in part on the old Austro-Hungarian border lying to the west of Trieste and in part on raw power: to the victor belongs the spoils. To those of us in Belgrade it was certain that unless the Allies negotiated, or simply declared unequivocally, a line of demarcation between areas to be occupied by the Anglo-American forces and the Yugoslavs, we would find ourselves in a frightful mess. The dividing line between Axis areas to be occupied by the Western Allies and by the Russians had already been agreed to for both Germany and

Austria. Only the Allied-Yugoslav line of demarcation in prewar Italy had been left unsettled.

After the Italian armistice in 1943, Tito's National Liberation Council had proclaimed the annexation of the prewar province of Venezia Giulia, which included Trieste, although the Germans had quickly moved in and occupied it after the Italians surrendered. The Comintern in Moscow, however, told the Partisans that their claim was "premature." Washington and London then allowed the issue to drift until 1945.

During the year before the German surrender, Allied policy was marked by bold statements followed by indecision and vacillation. In August 1944 Churchill told Tito that the Allied military government would administer all of Venezia Giulia, although without prejudice to Tito's ultimate claim. Tito violently protested and asserted that as one of the victorious allies he had a right to share in the occupation of the region. Churchill told him that wouldn't fly with the Americans, who were determined not to prejudice the ultimate decision of a peace conference.

The matter was left hanging. The next time it was raised was at Yalta in February 1945. Foreign Secretary Anthony Eden now proposed a demarcation line by which the Yugoslavs and the Allies would share in the occupation, but this too was rejected by the State Department. Again no decision was reached.

The divergence between Allied military and political objectives was left unresolved until the crisis was in full flame and the initiative had been lost. The State Department in Washington, initially supported by the Foreign Office in London, was firmly wedded to the principle of self-determination promised in the Atlantic Charter. This was to be ensured by Allied military occupation of all defeated countries until the conflicting claims for territorial change had been carefully weighed in the presumed quiet and detached atmosphere of the peace conferences. Therefore Washington held firmly to the position that all of Venezia Giulia, up to the 1939 Italian-Yugoslav border, should be placed under Allied military government.

The Yugoslavs did not suffer from any vacillation. Their strategy to counter an expected Allied military occupation was to build secret Communist-controlled liberation committees in all the cities, towns, and villages of the area, and to organize armed Partisan groups in the rural and mountainous areas to the east, north, and south of Trieste. At the moment the Germans withdrew toward Germany, the liberation committees, aided by local Partisan units, would rise up to seize Trieste and the other cities and towns in the region. They would thus confront the Anglo-American forces with a fait accompli.

Having watched the Partisans build their liberation committees in Yugoslavia into effective instruments for the control of the civil population, I had no doubt that they could use the same iron tactics in and around Trieste. Although it would be easier if the newly formed Yugoslav army, now equipped with heavy weapons, were in military occupation, the Yugoslavs were prepared if necessary to exercise that control of the population even under the nose of an Allied military occupation force, just as they had done under German and Italian occupation. It was this possibility that we found difficult to get Allied diplomatic and military policy makers to focus on before it happened.

Field Marshal Harold Alexander, having received no political instructions from the Anglo-American Combined Chiefs of Staff, developed his own purely military requirements. He also proposed a line of demarcation between the areas to be occupied by the two armies. The political objective of holding the entire province in trust for a peace settlement was not relevant to his own military needs for a supply line to Austria.

In late February of 1945, Alexander came to Belgrade to see Tito. Probably the most important subject discussed was Tito's request for Allied arms and supplies for 30,000 men to support an immediate attack on the northern Adriatic islands and the part of the Dalmatian coast still held by German forces. This was in addition to the existing British commitment to equip and maintain 300,000 Yugoslav Partisans with infantry weapons, medical supplies, radios, clothing, and boots.

At the meeting Tito also asked for arms and equipment for an additional force of 100,000 men to be used, he said, to pursue the German armies into the Reich. The Yugoslavs also presented this latter requirement to the Lend-Lease Administration in Washington. The list was pages long and included more than a kilometer and a half of gold braid in addition to artillery, tanks, gasoline, food, and 10,000 trucks. No action had been taken on this list by either government by the time the war ended.

Alexander said he would do what he could to meet Tito's immediate requirements. Within days after the Belgrade meeting, a large volume of supplies was delivered to those ports on the Dalmatian coast already held by Tito's forces. This was done, I was told, contrary to Churchill's instructions. When informed of Tito's requests he had sent a minute to Eden, saying: "Surely no more."

OSS Captain Rex Deane, at the Partisan-held port of Zadar, reported to us in Belgrade in early April: "LCT [Landing Craft, Tank] boats are pouring in vehicles, tanks and weapons for the Fourth Partisan Army." An American tanker was anchored in the harbor to provide gasoline and oil for the Partisan trucks and tanks. The tanker also fueled an RAF fighter-bomber squadron that was supporting the Yugoslav advance.

After Alexander left Belgrade he reported to London: "I have today returned from a most successful visit to Belgrade. I found Marshal Tito very friendly, sensible and cooperative. He has agreed to all the proposals I made to him. . . . From a purely military point of view I can get all I require." Tito had not even hinted that he intended to use Alexander's arms and supplies to get to Trieste ahead of the British Eighth Army.

■ In April of 1945 the final climactic battles of the war in Europe began. On April 14 Alexander launched a massive spring attack to destroy the German and Fascist Italian divisions defending a line in the hills and mountains south of the Po valley.

The race to gain control of Trieste and the Italian province of Venezia Giulia was now on. The New Zealand Second Division had crossed the Po river on April 28 after breaking through a series of strong, well-dug-in German defense lines. Having broken into the clear, the New Zealanders were ordered to head for Trieste without stopping to mop up pockets of German resistance on the way. They covered the distance of about 150 miles from the Po River to Monfalcone on the western edge of Venezia Giulia in less than 5 days.

Tito launched his own offensive when the Allied offensive began. Soon he was back to Alexander, asking for more supplies for his Fourth Army, now attacking northward in Dalmatia. Without this help Tito said his offensive would have to be halted. Alexander sought guidance from the Combined Chiefs of Staff. He favored giving Tito what he wanted, telling London: "If I have to negotiate an agreement with Tito over Venezia Giulia it will be easier for me to get what I want from a grateful Tito who will be under some obligation to me for the help I have given him." Alexander also told Churchill that with additional Allied support Tito would draw off into Yugoslavia German forces opposing his own advance. The Allied supplies continued to flow.

But instead of concentrating on the German forces within Yugoslavia, the Yugoslav army, largely equipped by Alexander, bypassed the Germans wherever possible. The cities of Zagreb and Ljubljana, and major German forces still in Croatia and Slovenia, were left on the vine. The German Ninety-Seventh Army Corps north of Rijeka was also bypassed. Yugoslav columns crossed over the Adriatic islands to Istria while others outflanked the German corps by heading north, then turning westward to Trieste.

In the last weeks of the war I had become increasingly involved in trying to get high-level attention on the row that was certain to erupt over the control of Trieste and Venezia Giulia. Frustrated by the lack of a firm Allied decision, on April 27 I wrote to Richard Patterson, the newly arrived American ambassador in Belgrade:

> It is of the utmost importance immediately to establish a line of demarcation between the Allies and the Yugoslav troops. With both sides now racing to occupy as much as possible before the other side arrives, it is quite possible that an extremely difficult situation will arise. The possibility of local armed conflict between the two is not to be overlooked.

In the areas occupied by the Allied forces the Allies can either recognize the incumbent Italian civil administration and work through them—leaving themselves open to the charge of dealing with Fascists and collaborators, or they can recognize the local Partisan committees—thereby acknowledging, to a degree, the claim of the Yugoslavs to this area. If the Partisans are selected as the local administrative agents under the authority of the Allied Commander, trouble is almost sure to arise. It seems probable that these Committees would continue to take their orders through secret Yugoslav channels, while officially recognizing the Allied authority. They would use this interim period to establish and consolidate their hold on the area in order to influence and control the final decision on their claims at the peace conference. In so doing they will do everything they can to discredit the Allied occupation in the eyes of the local inhabitants and the world in general.

The time had passed, I argued, when it would have been possible to get Tito's agreement to Allied control of all of Venezia Giulia and to withdraw from territories already taken by his forces. Their population was predominantly Slovene and Croat, and he had already claimed them by annexation. It would be better to settle for a line of demarcation east of Trieste that roughly followed the ethnic boundary between the Italians and the Slavs. We should insist on complete Allied military and civil control west of this line while allowing the Yugoslavs to occupy and administer the much larger and predominantly Slovene and Croat territory east of the line.

Ambassador Patterson asked me to go to Caserta and Rome to see if a decision could be reached with Alexander's Allied Forces Headquarters and with Ambassador Kirk, Alexander's American political advisor. He wired Kirk his concurrence with my recommendations, but by the time I reached Italy the two forces were already approaching Trieste.

In Rome on May 1 I was caught in the midst of a huge May Day Communist demonstration, the first since Mussolini had come to power. As the crowd surged through the streets, my American army car was surrounded and stopped by a sea of shouting demonstrators. I was astonished by their gay, light-hearted holiday mood. I rolled down the windows and clasped the outstretched hands of those pushing against the car. I was even bussed by two or three pretty Italian girls. This was not the sort of demonstration I was used to. In Belgrade the mood of the crowd, egged on by the leaders, would have been grim and anti-West, and the car might even have been overturned.

■ Meanwhile, within the Venezia Giulian cities of Trieste, Monfalcone and Gorizia, Italian and Slovene undergrounds were rising against the Germans and against each other. On April 29 the Yugoslav Liberation Committee proposed to the Trieste Committee for National Liberation (CLN) that the two together assume control of the administration of the entire province of Venezia Giulia. The CLN, whose members included the major Italian parties less the Communists and Fascists, set as a condition that the flags of both Yugoslavia and Italy fly over all public buildings. The Yugoslavs demanded that only their flag with its red star be flown. The CLN wouldn't agree, and with a force of 2,000 to 3,000 men, they set out to take Trieste and hold it until the Allies arrived. But German units holed up in some of the docks and public buildings and refused to surrender.

The Central Committee of the Slovene Communist Party now radioed instructions to Trieste: "Only two days left for the occupation of Trieste. If not, others will get it. Begin with the rising. . . . Make sure you stay in command in the course of the rising."

By April 30 the Yugoslav Fourth Army was approaching the outskirts of Trieste and by the next day their leading elements linked up with the Slovene Partisans within the city. We British and American officers in Yugoslavia had been reporting since September of the previous year that the Partisans in Slovenia and Croatia had largely quit fighting the Germans. We had concluded they were conserving their forces, and our supplies, for a final move into prewar Austria and Italy. Now the evidence was clear.

The leadership of the CLN in Trieste tried desperately but unsuccessfully to contact the New Zealand division, which at that moment had arrived in the Venezia Giulian city of Monfalcone 20 miles to the west. According to the account of Colonel Geoffrey Cox, the division intelligence officer, General Bernard Freyberg, the commander of the

New Zealand division, was persuaded by the local Partisan commander in Monfalcone to halt the division and remain there that night. The commander of the Yugoslav Fourth Army, he reported, would meet Freyberg there at 8:30 the next morning. "Better to spend the night here," he said. Freyberg waited until midafternoon the next day, but Yugoslav General Petar Drapsin failed to show up.

Tired of waiting, Freyberg ordered his division to move on to Trieste; the lead tanks arrived in time to attack the last two German pockets in the city. The division could have entered Trieste 24 hours sooner but General Freyberg was understandably eager to avoid a confrontation that could easily have resulted in nasty incidents.

We debated afterward whether Freyberg had been deliberately stalled so that the Yugoslavs could have an extra day to nail down their control of the city. Or was it simply inefficiency and confusion on the part of the Yugoslavs? I suspected it was the former. From the time the Yugoslavs had entered the city on May 1, the day before Freyberg's arrival, they were busy stacking the deck by arresting the pro-Italian CLN resistance leaders who had first taken over the city government. They then installed their own Communist-controlled Liberation Committees as the provisional government.

By May 3 both armies were in Trieste and the Yugoslavs had their Liberation Committees in place in the Piazza dell' Unita and were running the city. Armed Partisans patrolled the streets and the Yugoslav flag with its Communist red star had been raised over every school and public building in the city and surrounding countryside.

Freyberg was now confronted by an immediate problem. Did he accept the Yugoslav civil government until he received instructions from Alexander or did he install an Allied military government? He had no instructions and decided to accept the Yugoslav administration pro tem rather than to try to force his own military government on the Yugoslavs.

It still was impossible to get an agreed decision out of Washington or London on what to do. The Yugoslav Liberation Committees were left in place as the civil administration while negotiations on Yugoslav military presence continued. They made the most of it by taking over control of all press and radio, and by organizing a labor syndicate to which everyone from intellectuals to laborers had to belong. Local block committees and committees to purge the fascists—meaning all those opposed to their annexation of Trieste—were quickly set up. The CLN leaders they could find were arrested; the others went into hiding.

The issue that had proved to be so intractable was whether Allied military policy should be based only on military requirements, as Alexander wanted, or on broader political objectives. The State Department continued to oppose sharing the occupation of the province with the Yugoslavs, still arguing that all prewar Italian territory should be occupied by the Allied forces. Eden and the Foreign Office had now shifted their position to favor Yugoslav occupation of the larger Slav part of the province. Still no instructions were forthcoming.

■ With the arrival of the New Zealand division in Trieste, the reality of the Yugoslav determination to use every strategy in the book to secure control of the area and of its population became clear. Colonel John Clarke, fully expecting trouble, had headed for the Yugoslav Fourth Army headquarters as it approached Trieste. At the Yugoslav command post he found General Jovanovic, Tito's chief of staff, as well as General Drapsin, the army commander. Barely acknowledging his arrival, Jovanovic attacked: "In the name of Marshal Tito I wish to make the following energetic protest: That the Allied troops withdraw immediately to the line previously agreed upon, namely the Isonzo River." He went on, "You are getting in the way of operations we are undertaking to the north. . . . You are interfering, too, with our civilian administration." There had been no agreement on the Isonzo as the limit of the Allied advance. It was simply a bluff.

Clarke said he would pass the message. "I replied [to Jovanovic] that as there were no Germans left between Trieste and the Isonzo I could not think what these operations could be. He looked embarrassed and said he had evidence that we used Italian fascists in preventing an anti-fascist demonstration in Gorizia."

Later in the day a similar protest from Tito arrived at General Freyberg's headquarters with a covering note from the chief of staff of the Fourth Army saying that the Yugoslav army "would not be responsible for anything that might happen" if Freyberg did not withdraw. Freyberg immediately sent John Clarke back to Drapsin with the message that he would ensure that no trouble was started by his forces, "but we should certainly defend ourselves with great effect should the forces [under Drapsin's command] dare to dispute our presence by force."

The following day Drapsin met with General John Harding at Thirteen Corps headquarters, where Harding agreed that until the issue was settled at a higher level, the Yugoslavs would administer the entire province of Venezia Giulia including areas in which Allied troops were located. Harding made it clear Allied troops would remain, but made no mention of the Allied interest in occupying the area until the final disposition would be made at a future peace conference. He said to Drapsin, "I and my officers and troops are soldiers, and are not interested in the political future of this country. . . . My orders to my troops are that they are not to intervene in any local matters."

After the meeting John Clarke said, "The only decision reached was on the football match between British and Yugoslav armies."

Again, the British commander was on his own and without instructions. But the effect was to guarantee the Yugoslavs permanent control of the area east of Trieste and to give them more time in which to nail down their political control in Trieste itself.

Clarke radioed an urgent request to me to come to Trieste. General Kveder, whom I had known in Slovenia the year before, was now the Partisan commander in that city. Clarke thought I might have some influence with him based on our earlier time together. I had doubts that any British or American officer could have any influence in that quarter.

But before I could get to Trieste the center of action shifted to Belgrade and Caserta. There began a series of exchanges of messages between Tito and Alexander aimed at resolving the border issue. Our military mission in Belgrade became one of the main channels for communications between Tito and Alexander. Each message seemed to be dispatched or received in the middle of the night. After one of Alexander's messages was deciphered I would drive in a jeep to Tito's residence, the prewar palace of the Regent Prince Paul, to deliver the message to Tito's personal staff. The messages each way became stronger and stronger and each started with variants of "I am surprised and shocked by your last message."

Tito's first message was short and sharp:

> This moment I have received a signal from my Fourth Army saying tanks and infantry units of the Allied Forces which are under your command, without any previous notice have entered Trieste, Gorizia and Monfalcone, the cities which have been liberated by the Yugoslav Army.
>
> Since I do not know what was meant by this I wish you would give me your immediate explanation of the matter with expedience.

Alexander replied on May 4:

> 1. I have received your message of 3rd May. I am astonished at your apparent failure to honor the agreement we made at Belgrade.
> 2. The agreement was that as the Port of Trieste and the rail and road communications from Trieste to Austria via Gorizia and Tarvisio are essential to maintain my advance into Austria, I should have full control in these areas. You further offered, and I accepted, that any of your forces in these areas would be put under my command.

Alexander pointed out he had provided Tito with large quantities of munitions, medical supplies, and food as well as the support of strong air and naval forces.

> 4. So far, however, you have taken unilateral action by ordering your troops to occupy territory as far west as the Isonzo River.
>
> . . .
>
> 6. I have ordered my troops to maintain their present positions in the Trieste, Monfalcone, and Gorizia Areas.

Alexander still believed he could negotiate his demands with Tito, but it was a price neither Britain nor the United States would be willing to pay. On May 5 he cabled the prime minister: "I believe that he will hold to our original agreement if he can be assured that when I no longer require Trieste as a base for my forces in Austria he will be allowed to incorporate it into his new Yugoslavia."

I in turn was surprised that Alexander had gotten so far out of step with the Allied governments, who were by now firmly committed to preventing Tito's de facto takeover. Given the seniority and outspokenness of his two senior political advisers, Harold Macmillan (himself later British prime minister) and Alexander Kirk, a hardnosed senior American diplomat, it was doubly surprising. Churchill quickly responded by telling Alexander to make no such proposal.

I continued to be the one to deliver Alexander's messages to Tito and to receive his responses. On May 5 Tito continued the exchange:

To Field Marshal Alexander:
I was surprised at your readiness to express your doubts as to the respect on my part of the agreement we made in Belgrade. I am even more surprised owing to the fact that I am not bound solely by the military responsibility as Commander in Chief but also by the responsibility as Prime Minister who must first of all take care of the interests of his country. I am even more surprised because in my signal of May 2nd I underlined that I am keeping my word given in Belgrade, namely that you may use the ports of Trieste and Pola as well as the line of communication leading toward Austria for supplying your troops.

. . .

The occupation of the territories in question by our troops has not as you know purely a military character but also a political one. Yugoslavia is very much interested in this territory not only as a victor on the side of the Allies in the war against Italy but also because these territories were unjustly annexed by Italy as a result of a former peace treaty. I consider that a great injustice is done to our martyred country when one recognizes only her duties and not her rights of an allied nation at war.

Tito acknowledged the military supplies and equipment provided by Alexander that made it possible for the Yugoslavs to reach Trieste before the Eighth Army.

I am once more expressing to you my thanks for having fulfilled your promise and given the necessary war material to our Army so that it might carry out its tasks which are mutually profitable to us and to our allies.

But the grateful Tito that Alexander was counting on to ease negotiations was not visible.

> My troops have been ordered to hold the whole of the occupied territory and not to impede in any way your troops on their way towards Austria along the line of communication foreseen by the agreement. The port of Trieste is also at your disposal.
> With respects, signed J. B. Tito, Marshal of Yugoslavia.

After these exchanges Alexander decided to send his chief of staff, Lieutenant General William Morgan, to Belgrade to try to resolve the impasse directly with Tito. His instructions to General Morgan were to negotiate a purely military agreement for the control of the port of Trieste and the lines of communication to Austria.

■ Air Vice Marshal A. S. G. Lee and I met General Morgan and Brigadier General A. L. Hamblen, an American on the Allied Forces Headquarters staff, at the Belgrade airport. Lee had replaced Fitzroy Maclean as head of the British military mission. Morgan was a small man with full white hair, pink cheeks, and a trim military moustache. Most arresting were his blue eyes. He was every inch a British general yet I immediately found him easy to talk with despite the wide differences in age and rank. After a preliminary talk Lee and I accompanied them to meet with Tito. Morgan's aide, who stayed outside the meeting room of the White Palace, struck up a conversation in French with the commander of Tito's personal security guard. Morgan's aide later told us the guard commander had said to him: "Are the Western Allies so weak and exhausted they must come to Belgrade to negotiate with us?"

Tito sat in the center of a long table. Four senior Partisan generals, now in smartly tailored grey uniforms with the insignia of general on their collars and sleeves, were arrayed along Tito's side of the table. These new Yugoslav uniforms, rumored to have been tailored in Moscow to Tito's specifications, bordered on the gaudy, with their generous use of gold braid. They were not what one would have expected from the leaders of a people's revolution, fresh from fighting in the forest. General Morgan sat opposite Tito with Hamblen, Lee, and me alongside.

Morgan presented the proposals Alexander had sent him to negotiate. The first was a line of demarcation which would divide Venezia Giulia into two zones of occupation. It became known as the Morgan Line, and paralleled the rail line and road from Trieste to Austria, varying between two and ten miles to the east. This was also a rough approximation of the Slovene-Italian ethnic boundary. Nearly all of the region except the cities of Trieste, Pula, Monfalcone, and Gorizia was in effect being given over to exclusive Yugoslav control even though the disclaimer was often repeated that the line would in no way prejudice the final peace treaty. In the areas east of the line, the Yugoslavs were the only occupying force. They were quickly installing their Communist government and internal security police.

The other elements of the draft agreement were by now quite familiar. The area west of the demarcation line would be under Alexander's command; Tito would withdraw his forces east of the line; and Alexander would govern the area using an Allied military government. He would use any Yugoslav civil administration already set up and "working satisfactorily."

The Tito I knew was a man of great composure and presence. This day he fidgeted throughout Morgan's explanation of the proposed agreement, lighting one cigarette after another, sticking them in the miniature pipe he used as a cigarette holder, then snuffing them out after a few puffs. He repeatedly shifted his position in his chair and appeared to be very ill at ease. My feeling at the time was that he expected an ultimatum from Morgan that he knew he would have to accept.

When Morgan finished without an ultimatum, Tito immediately counterattacked, rejecting Morgan's proposal. The problem was now a political and not a military one, he said. Venezia Giulia and Trieste were Yugoslav territory. They had been liberated by his army. He pointed out that Alexander's March statement to him was based on the Allied military requirement for the Trieste port and rail facilities to support a continuing military thrust northward into Austria and Germany. The war, however, was over, and that rationale no longer existed. He also spoke emotionally of the tremendous losses the Partisans had suffered at the hands of the Italian and German occupation forces in Yugoslavia. The Partisans had won the war in their own country and had every right as victors to occupy and annex Trieste, Venezia Giulia, and Istria.

He repeated his earlier proposal to assume full political and military control in Venezia Giulia, including Trieste. He would gladly make available such road and rail facilities as the Allies might need to supply their forces of occupation in Austria and Germany.

When he finished, had Morgan said that he was sorry, but that Tito would have to accept Alexander's proposal, I felt sure Tito would have done so. Instead, Morgan replied that he had no authority to modify Alexander's proposals, but he would be glad to carry the Marshal's proposal back to Alexander. Tito now quickly became his usual confident and gracious self: his immediate crisis was over. He spent the rest of the meeting and a subsequent one expanding his proposals and answering Morgan's questions.

At the end of the meeting, General Morgan said that in order to be sure he correctly conveyed these proposals he would write them up as he understood them and submit them to Tito for his approval before his departure. This task of drafting fell to me. Much as I disagreed with the turn the negotiations had taken, it was too late to retrieve Morgan's offer. We should not have been put in the position of drafting Tito's proposals and then asking him to approve our draft.

I have a vivid memory of Tito and Morgan sitting side by side in the back of an open German staff car as they departed for a tour of the sights around Belgrade while I set to work to draft the memorandum. The next day my draft was reviewed and approved by Tito with changes to underscore that the territory was Slovene, and that because of their sacrifices in the Allied cause the Partisans had the right of occupation. Morgan returned to Italy with Tito's proposal to report to Alexander and to the Allied governments.

■ The Yugoslavs had convinced themselves that they had become the co-equal of the United States, Britain, and the Soviet Union. At the height of the crisis a lead editorial in *Borba*, Belgrade's Communist newspaper, said that the great contribution of the Yugoslav Partisans to the war effort in Istria and the Slovene littoral was "the best guarantee that no power on earth will be able to stop these regions from joining Yugoslavia." The editorial asserted that their army had become the fourth largest United Nations army in the world—presumably after those of Britain, the Soviet Union, and the United States, but omitting both Chiang Kai Shek's and Mao Tse Tung's armies in China.

In my subsequent talks with the Partisans they asserted they had earned the right to sit at the same table as the Big Three and to participate fully in postwar territorial arrangements. They saw no difference between their right to occupy territory their troops had taken and the right of the British, Americans, French, and Russians to occupy Germany. While they conceded that a plebiscite in Trieste would favor Italy, they held that Trieste, southern Austria, and bits of other bordering states were theirs by right of conquest. Italy, on the winning side in the First World War, had successfully asserted the same argument to gain a large piece of Venezia Giulia inhabited by Slovenes and Croats.

The Allies still regarded the Partisans as a band of irregulars who had made a useful but peripheral contribution in a backwater theater of the war. The Big Three simply assumed they would settle the postwar map among themselves, just as they had directed the war against the Axis. It was a shock to each side to find how different were the other's perceptions.

For the next month the Trieste issue remained unresolved. It was pushed back to the State Department and the Foreign Office. Meanwhile the confrontation in Trieste became more acute. The Yugoslav Communists exploited to the utmost their civil government structure that General Freyberg, and then his superior General Harding, had agreed would temporarily remain in place.

The Yugoslav objective was to eliminate any potential leadership that might challenge their continuing control in the areas into which the Allied troops had moved. Edvard Kardelj, Tito's alter ego in the Politburo, had instructed the Yugoslavs in Trieste that as soon as the city was occupied, all the Italians who had settled there should be "driven out without any discussion."

Those of us who had seen the effectiveness with which the Partisans had set up their political controls under the noses of the German occupiers saw clearly what they were up to. National liberation committees composed of Communists and those who accepted Communist orders were set up in every community. Peoples' courts and epuration (purging) commissions handed out sentences to those who were considered potential threats to their control. We received reports from our OSS officers in the area that several thousand people had disappeared, presumably to prisons in the areas beyond the control of Allied forces, although many of them were later released. Participation in regularly scheduled anti-Allied demonstrations was required. Food ration cards were used to enforce the rule of the liberation committees.

The Yugoslavs clearly understood the nature of the contest. Their Liberation Council of Trieste called a snap election, which they fully controlled, for a constituent assembly. The assembly in turn elected by acclaim a permanent body called the Consulta. The Liberation Council was then confirmed by the Consulta as the governing body of the city. Kardelj sent urgent instructions to Trieste. "The main thing is democracy and authority in the hands of the Consulta. If the English succeed in organizing these [Italian] democrats formally against the Consulta, then they will take the authority from the Consulta and we will lose the fight in Trieste. . . . We have a few days time. . . . Get them [the Italian Communists] to defend the Consulta against the English. Do not irritate the Italians by constantly stressing the *Slovenian* littoral." The technique was the same as I had seen in Slovenia, in Croatia, and in Belgrade. Power would be in the hands of the Communists. Fellow-travelers or dupes would be used for window dressing.

While General Morgan was in Belgrade, Edvard Kardelj radioed

Tito from Trieste complaining about the Yugoslav army's lack of aggressiveness in Trieste:

> English throwing troops against Trieste and making demands which mean the liquidation of our control of Trieste. Up to the present Arso [Yugoslav Chief of Staff Jovanovic] and the others have done nothing at all to carry out your order that they close the crossing over the Isonzo. There are none of our soldiers there at all.

The British and American governments now finally began to understand what they were up against. The Yugoslav military forces would not be moved out of the western area of Venezia Giulia except by superior force. Truman, reversing his earlier position of avoiding involvement in Balkan politics, now told Grew to "throw them out." In late May Truman agreed with Churchill on a show of force and additional British and American divisions were moved up to the Isonzo River. The two governments now saw the issue in the much larger context of not setting a precedent by giving in to unilateral force.

The policy of postwar containment of Communist expansion was now taking form. Churchill cabled Truman on June 2:

> If it is once thought there is no point beyond which we cannot be pushed about, there will be no future for Europe except another war more terrible than anything the world has yet seen. But by showing a firm front in circumstances and locality which are favorable to us, we may reach a satisfactory and solid foundation for peace and justice.

The show of military force finally induced Tito to accept the Morgan Line and jurisdiction of Allied forces west of the line on condition, he said, "that representatives of the Yugoslav army be allowed to take part in Allied Military Government, that Yugoslav units be permitted to remain in the territory under Allied control and that the Allied command act through civilian authorities already established."

Kardelj sent a message to Boris Kidric, the leader of the Slovene Communist Party who was directing political operations in Slovenia: "We will try to secure as much responsibility as possible for our army within the framework of the joint military administration and as great independence as possible for [our] civil authority."

Tito's conditions were unacceptable to Washington and London and on June 2 the final Allied demands were given to Tito in Belgrade. They were accepted by Tito one week later, presumably after he had found that the Russians would not back him to the point of risking military conflict with Britain and America.

London and Washington had still not fully appreciated the danger of Yugoslav subversion of Allied control if they allowed the Yugoslav civil government to remain in place. Article 3 of the Belgrade agreement would cause continuing trouble:

> 3. Using an Allied Military Government, the Supreme Allied Commander will govern the areas west of the [Morgan] line. . . . Use will be made of any Yugoslav civil administration which is already set up and which in the view of the Supreme Allied Commander is working satisfactorily. The Allied Military Government will, however, be empowered to use whatever civil authorities they deem best in any particular place and to change administrative personnel at their discretion.

The agreement also provided that General Morgan and General Jovanovic, the respective chiefs of staff, would meet to work out supplemental accords to implement the agreement. The meeting was set up near Udine. John Clarke and I were ordered there from Belgrade to take part in the negotiations. Field Marshal Alexander sent his mobile headquarters for the use of the Allied negotiating team. The mobile headquarters consisted of several army trucks on which had been set camouflaged boxlike offices and sleeping quarters with built-in bunks. They were elegant by my standards and very comfortable. The negotiations themselves were conducted at a long table under a tent in a field.

Jovanovic had been a regular officer with the prewar Royal Yugoslav Army and had joined the Partisans very early in the war. Perhaps because he felt that he more than the others had to demonstrate his loyalty to Tito and Communism he was one of the more difficult Partisan leaders to deal with. He was always grim-faced and I had never seen him unbend or even smile. His speech was direct, aggressive and often abrasive. Unlike Tito and some of the more secure Communist leaders with whom one could, at times, have friendly give-and-take, he would never unbend; it seemed impossible to break through his hard shell.

The Yugoslavs, having been forced to give up military control of the western sector, now concentrated on preserving their Liberation Committees, police force, and people's courts as the civil governing authority, with the intention of winning Trieste at the peace conference. The crucial Article 3 of the Belgrade agreement, Jovanovic argued, provided that the Yugoslav civil government must remain in place as the sole civil government of the region. He refused to accept that the last sentence gave Allied military government the final authority on both the form of civil government and the personnel used. The rest of the implementing agreement was accepted by both sides after tedious negotiations.

The next day Belgrade issued a public blast. "The Allied military delegation has not accepted the proposition of the Yugoslav delegation in connection with the recognition of the existing civil authorities that had been guaranteed by paragraph 3 of the Belgrade agreement." Tito formally protested to Truman and Churchill.

The Yugoslavs had told me at the beginning of the crisis that they expected support from Stalin. In fact, he sent a relatively mild note to the president and prime minister but made no further effort on behalf of the Yugoslavs. And he had waited until after Tito had been forced to withdraw from the disputed area to dispatch this note. The lack of strong Soviet support for Tito could have been because Stalin had bigger fish to fry in Germany. As the war ended the American forces had advanced deep into the agreed Soviet zone of occupation and had not yet pulled back behind the line of demarcation. Stalin may have reasoned that if he backed Tito to the hilt over Trieste the Americans could become very sticky about withdrawing from the area in Germany allocated to Russian occupation.

■ When I returned to Belgrade after the implementing agreement had been signed, I found great bitterness and hostility among the Yugoslav leadership. They referred to the basic June 9 agreement as the "Belgrade diktat." They told me "the Allies treated us as if we were impotent Italians or beaten fascists."

Tito told me that he had made an agreement with the Allies over

Venezia Giulia and he intended to keep the agreement. This, he said, included all provisions except recognition of their civil administration, about which no agreement had been reached. He implied that Article 3 of the Belgrade agreement he had signed was not in effect, nor would be without a further agreement.

The Yugoslav leaders with whom I talked when I returned to Belgrade said they believed that the real reason the Allies would not agree to Yugoslav annexation of Trieste was that they wanted to deny Yugoslavia and Russia a major port on the Mediterranean. In the internal American and British cables and in the exchanges between them that I saw at the time, as well as in our meetings, this was a consideration. However, there was never any proposal to deny them the prewar Italian port of Fiume (Rijeka) to the east of Trieste. The reasons advanced at the time in the cable exchanges were that there should be no change in borders prior to the postwar peace conferences; that the Trieste population was Italian; that in light of Italy's early surrender and subsequent support of the Allied war effort, the city should not be taken from Italy.

The Soviet Union was faced with a dilemma over Trieste. If Moscow backed Tito it was sure to antagonize the Italians—and this could have weakened the Italian Communist Party, which then had a large popular support and a chance to come to power in the forthcoming elections. So when the chips were down Moscow tilted toward the Italians rather than the Yugoslavs. Tito was furious and publicly stated: "Never again will we be dependent on anyone to support our national rights." Stalin in turn was outraged at Tito's statement, which he assumed was directed at Moscow. His ambassador in Belgrade conveyed this privately in unvarnished words. Again we had missed a clue that nationalism was stronger than international communism.

The same strength of leadership that was a necessary element of Tito's internal victory was also at work in his relations with the superpowers in both the East and the West. He had become his own man.

CHAPTER 20

In the Wake of the Hot War

he conflict over control of Trieste was still far from settled. The Yugoslavs had now turned to vitriolic propaganda, strikes, and clandestine threats against the populace to subvert the functioning of Allied occupation.
The British ambassador, Ralph Stevenson, recommended to Harold
Macmillan, British political adviser to Alexander, that I be appointed
political adviser to General John Harding, the military governor of
the Trieste territory and commander of British Thirteen Corps, when
our military mission in Belgrade was closed the end of June. General
Lyman Lemnitzer, the American deputy chief of staff at Allied Forces
Headquarters, had made the same proposal to OSS. I agreed to go
back to Trieste, but only until a Foreign Service officer arrived, arguing that it was no post for an amateur. I wondered if the reason the
British advocated the assignment of an American to the otherwise
British command was to share the troubles of the Trieste occupation.

Jim Fisher and I got permission from the Yugoslav general staff
to drive from Belgrade to Trieste. The ever-present Yugoslav liaison
officer came with us to ensure we had no unauthorized conversations
along the way. When we reached Slovenia Jim and I wanted to take
the road that led through the Stajerska mountains where we had
spent so much time with the Slovene Partisans. We had both hoped

to see again the mountains we had climbed over, the forests in which we had hidden, and the villages over which we had fought. More important, we hoped to learn the fate of our friends, the officers and men who, we had learned from radio messages, had disappeared in the December German offensive. But the Yugoslav authorities were adamant that our pass from Belgrade did not authorize us to take that route. I pointed out the order did not specify any precise route. But it was no use. We were sent by a roundabout way. We thought it was to avoid any contact with people we had known.

After I arrived at General Harding's headquarters it became clear why we were not allowed to go through the Stajerska area. In accordance with the Yalta Agreement that nationals of each country would be returned to that country, the British forces in Austria were turning back the thousands of Yugoslavs trying to escape the Partisans. Their principal escape route had been through Stajerska, and the Partisans undoubtedly did not want us to see the brutal treatment that was being handed out to them after they were forced back into that region.

One mixed group of 30,000 Serbs, Chetniks, Croat Ustashe, Slovene White Guards, Germans, and Yugoslav civilians fleeing the Partisans crossed the Karawanken Alps into Austria on May 7. Other groups of Cossacks, Ukrainians, and White Russians, in total about 70,000, crossed from Stajerska into Austria at several points. These men had been recruited by the Germans to fight against the Red Army. They knew what was in store for them if they were caught by either the Partisans or the Red Army. At least 200,000 more were captured before they reached the Austrian border.

Simultaneously the Partisan Fourteenth Division that had been in Stajerska with us the year before moved into Klagenfurt (as we had predicted) and had begun to take over public buildings and establish their political control preparatory to annexation of the Drava valley. Units of the British Five Corps had arrived there simultaneously and, as in Venezia Giulia, the two forces became intertwined in Klagenfurt and along the Drava valley.

In accordance with Yalta, the British now began to return the Cossacks to Marshal Tolbukhin's Third Ukrainian Front (army group) and the Yugoslavs to the Partisans. Most were either imprisoned or shot in mass executions. But after it became apparent to the British what was happening, the British authorities canceled further repatriation. Altogether some 70,000 Cossacks, Ukrainians, and Yugoslavs were forcibly repatriated. At the same time the British and Americans pressed Tito to withdraw behind the prewar Yugoslav border. When Stalin did not back them, the Yugoslavs complied and withdrew.

■ As we entered the area occupied by the Yugoslav Fourth Army in Venezia Giulia we were stopped by guards at a roadblock who asked our Yugoslav liaison officer for our passes. An officer took them into a nearby house while we were left with the guards. After an hour or so during which our liaison officer tried to find out what was wrong we were told that the passes issued by Belgrade were not valid for the Fourth Army military zone. We were under arrest until our status could be determined by further orders from Belgrade. We were then escorted to a large chalet on the shore of Lake Bled, a beautiful lake in the mountains northeast of Trieste.

If we were to be under arrest it couldn't have been at a more comfortable and pleasant place. It had belonged to the governor of Slovenia before the war. We were the sole occupants. A cook was produced for us and we ate well. We were allowed to row out to a small island on which there was a tiny baroque chapel and from which there was a beautiful view of the lake, the forested shores, and the mountains beyond. Several times I demanded to see General Drapsin, the Fourth Army commander, always without success. We remained under the surveillance of our Partisan guards armed with guns we had undoubtedly delivered to them by parachute. We later discovered that two of our junior American officers had not fared as well. They had spent five days in a Ljubljana jail because their passes were asserted to be not in order. Finally, after two days, we were told we could proceed and we left under armed escort for Trieste.

General Harding and the corps headquarters had taken over the castle of Duino about ten miles west of Trieste. It was on a rocky promontory jutting out into the Adriatic, with an almost vertical drop to the sea 300 feet below. It had been the inspiration for Rainer Maria Rilke's *Duino Elegies*. We were told that before the war the castle had been completely modernized by the American wife of the count whose family owned it. She was, I believe, the heiress to the Crane plumbing fortune. The bathrooms could have competed with the best on Park Avenue! The castle was built of oyster-white stone and was perfectly restored without visible change to the exterior. A large open terrace projected to the edge of the cliff. The senior officers of the staff gathered there for drinks before and after evening mess.

During the war the castle had been the regional headquarters of the Gestapo. Next to the main door a set of instructions to the Gestapo officers was neatly typed and set in a glass frame attached to the wall. It read like instructions in a boarding school: "Keep feet off the furniture, don't track in mud, don't leave cigarette butts around," and so on.

After dark the sea was lit by a hundred or more bobbing lights on the small fishing boats off shore. The lights, which were hung from the rigging, were there to attract fish to the waiting nets. I had a beautiful large room with windows onto the sea and was assigned a British soldier who not only brought tea at 5:30 A.M. but also shined my shoes and saw to it my uniforms were well pressed. It made me uncomfortable that a soldier who had fought at El Alamein and Tobruk in the African desert and up the length of Italy should be doing these sorts of services, but there was no sign he thought it demeaning.

General Harding's daily morning staff conferences were usually held in the garden. The business at hand was the day-to-day administration of the corps as an occupation force, and the continuing battles with the Yugoslavs. They were past masters at agitation and propaganda and the Allied command was completely unprepared for the political warfare unleashed against them.

The British and American commanders were used to imposing their military government on the defeated Italians as their armies advanced northward. There was no question who was boss and nearly all the Italians were eager to cooperate with the Allied forces. Italian civil governments accepted Allied authority. If any tried any funny business they were out. The Allied commanders assumed the Yugoslav civil government would respond to their directives in the same way. They were totally unprepared for the massive propaganda machine, and for the subversive operations launched against them. General Harding's morning staff meetings were always filled with the latest propaganda attacks against us, reports of abductions and beatings, and Communist obstructions.

Having been forced to withdraw their military forces, the Yugoslavs now concentrated on influencing and controlling as large a part of the civil population as possible. Their propaganda organs declared confidently that Allied military control was only temporary and that Yugoslavia would regain control at the peace table. The Communist press was turned loose to denounce the Allied command for failing to arrest fascists, causing unemployment, and failing to provide adequate food. The threats of eventual Communist control were exploited to coerce Italian citizens into signing anti-West petitions and into participating in mass demonstrations against Allied military control.

■ The grueling war had ended for General Harding and the soldiers of Thirteen Corps, who had fought all the way from El Alamein in North Africa to Trieste. Between the continuing problems in Trieste there was time to enjoy life. A race day was organized and we all attended. Horses had been found and amateur jockeys recruited. A racing card had been printed listing horses, riders, and their regiments and divisions. Some soldiers had, for a day, become bookies and set up shop near the track that had been laid out in a level grassy field. The Tenth Indian Division officers put on a colossal curry banquet under a large tent. It was a great day.

General Harding loved to ride and he often invited me to join him. It was usually cross-country at full speed. He had acquired (the Partisans would have said "liberated") an Alfa Romeo sports car, and the drive to the stable was along a narrow winding road cut into the cliffs above the sea. He drove at top speed around blind turns, weaving in and out of lines of horse-drawn farm wagons filled with hay, livestock, and produce. I often feared I had survived Stajerska only to die when the general careened the car over the cliff and into the sea.

■ After the British Labor Party victory in the general elections the Yugoslav-controlled press confidently predicted that the new Labor government would reverse Churchill's policy and restore "democratic institutions established by the people." However, they received a dousing of cold water when Ernest Bevin, the new British foreign secretary, gave a strong speech opposing Soviet expansion into Eastern Europe. Bevin also took the lead in ending the forced repatriation of prisoners and displaced persons to Russia and Yugoslavia.

On June 15 the Yugoslav-sponsored Trieste Communist party staged a demonstration march of several thousand people through the city. A set of demands were presented to General Harding for the continuation of the 3,000-man People's Militia as the civil police force and the retention of the Communist-controlled Liberation Council of Trieste and the Anti-Fascist Executive Committee. Together they gave the Communists complete control of the civic administration and police force.

Our intelligence reported that "approximately 6,000 civilians have been left behind" to sabotage the functioning of military government. "A fair proportion of OZNA [Yugoslav secret political police] and ex-members of the political branch of the Yugoslav army are concealed among the civil administration personnel."

Immediately after the Yugoslavs moved into the Trieste area they had arrested several thousand Italians as well as some Slovenes. There were continuing reports that many of those deported to Yugoslav-controlled territory had been shot and their bodies dumped into the Basovizza pits, natural pits in the limestone karst near the suburbs of Trieste.

In one of my reports I summarized the Yugoslav strategy to subvert the Allied occupation: "They are attempting through their underground organizations to stir up sufficient local dissatisfaction that a general strike culminating in violence can be staged successfully. So far this has not been possible because of the refusal of Italian Communists to support strike."

General Harding finally came to grips with the impossibility of working through the Yugoslav civil government and people's courts and replaced them with appointed officials. The Yugoslavs then set up secret shadow governments that effectively continued to control parts of the city and environs in spite of the Allied military government's civil administration.

After the Communist-controlled liberation committees had been replaced, Thirteen Corps military police from time to time arrested some of the more violent Communist agitators. This was grist for the Communist press, which charged that freedom-loving patriots were being held in prison by the fascist tools of the Americans and the British. I pushed General Harding to order prompt trials, or at least publish documented statements of the laws they had violated, in order to defuse the Yugoslav propaganda. General Harding, used to dealing with troublemaking Italians during the period of active fighting, could not understand why I was concerned. They had broken the rules and had been locked up—period.

■ Having been thwarted in my effort to return to Stajerska on our way to Trieste, I was still determined to know what had happened there after I had departed, and especially to learn the fate of those who had disappeared.

Edward Welles, James Fisher, and I had left our isolated mountain valley in Stajerska on December 6, 1944, to recross the Reich frontier in the midst of a determined German offensive. The story of death and disaster after our departure has been told to me by Robert Plan, one of the survivors. It is supplemented by the few terse radio messages from Captain Owen describing their struggle to survive by hiding out in deep snows in the high mountains for the remainder of the winter.

The long-expected attack in Stajerska had begun on December 4 across the entire front of the valley mouth. The immediate German objective was to reoccupy completely the liberated territory the Partisans had held, except for the one brief German incursion, since the beginning of August. The German objective was to eliminate the Partisan units as an effective force, and to remove the threat to their rail and road lines of communication leading from the Balkans to Austria and Germany.

On December 7, the day after we left, the large village of Mozirje was taken. The next day the Germans also took the landing strip at Recica where we had for so long tried to arrange landings for Allied aircraft to evacuate the wounded. Tanks, armored cars, and artillery were used to support the infantry of the Thirteenth SS Mountain Division, and the German Croatian regiments. The division had as bad a reputation for terrorism and atrocities against both civilians and Partisans as any German unit. To counter the attack the Partisan command attempted to send two brigades east to the Pohorje mountains to create diversions there. Neither brigade was able to break through the German lines and both were forced to return.

In the face of imminent attack, on December 7 the Fourth Zone headquarters and the brigades in the area broke up into small bands and dispersed into the higher levels of the mountains. By December 11 the only drop area still under Partisan control was Mala, in a remote mountain location. On December 15 Captain Owen signaled: "On run, all [radio] contacts on emergency [schedule]. Brigades departed. We at present in Menina mountains."

By this time the Germans had recaptured the entire Savinja valley and forced the Partisans to retreat in bitter weather to the higher levels of the mountains where there was little or no food. The Germans stationed troops in all the villages. Farms were either garrisoned, regularly patrolled, or burned. All food stocks were confiscated or destroyed. Captured Partisans and all civilians suspected of being pro-Partisan were shot. Plan said that just before Christmas the Germans offered an amnesty to those who would surrender. Over a hundred who did were locked up in the village of Luce. In early January all were taken out and shot.

From December 7 on the Zone headquarters moved constantly, most often in deep snow. Everyone was cold, hungry, and exhausted.

Major Mathews, a well-built man in his late twenties, collapsed in the snow, saying he did not have the strength to continue and had decided to surrender himself. A strong Partisanka pulled him to his feet and started to take his pack in addition to her own and her gun. Seeing a woman intending to carry his pack was enough to prod him into struggling on.

Captain Charles Fisher, with the Partisan headquarters on the run, could barely walk because of feet blistered raw. Before I left the Zone headquarters he had decided to exchange his OSS blucher boots for a pair of locally made Partisan officer boots, which turned out to be too small and on the forced marches hurt him terribly. Bob Plan, his radio operator, had bought a horse and saddle for him from a peasant for $100. A second horse carried their radio and batteries.

On December 24 German units launched a surprise attack on the Zone headquarters, cornered in a mountain hut, and on the Partisan battalion nearby. As the firing came close, Plan told Charlie Fisher that they should leave immediately. But just as the group started to move out the peasant wife brought steaming cups of hot soup. Packs were put down and fifteen minutes were lost. The Germans by then were in sight of the house. Seeing two saddled horses outside they began firing on the house. Owen, Campbell, and Plan escaped by crawling behind the hay-drying racks to the cover of the forest.

Charlie Fisher dropped the radio he was loading on the pack horse and fled in another direction. He also lost his cipher pad and a complete set of the clear-text messages he had exchanged with the OSS base station during the previous several weeks. After gaining the cover of the forest, he apparently fell in with a group of about fifteen Partisans trying to make their way to shelter and safety. Several days later Plan learned that the group had been captured three days later by a German patrol while trying to cross a road. All were shot two hours later. Major Mathews and Lieutenant Edward Parks disappeared during the attack.

Because of the intensity of the German attack and the large number of troops employed, the Partisans had lost contact with their civilian underground organizations. They had lost the eyes and ears of the civilian warning screen that had protected us so well in the months before. For lack of that protection they blindly fell into one ambush after another.

The only radio saved was that of the Partisans. Fortunately its transmitter signal was strong enough to be heard in Italy and it was shared by Plan, the only remaining American, and by Owen and his operator, Campbell. It was not until five days later they could stop long enough to get off a short message reporting the attack. Plan, who had a separate signal plan and emergency ciphers, had saved his crystals, codes, and emergency transmission schedule. But they all had lost everything else except the clothes on their backs.

The situation was now desperate. The Germans, employing about 15,000 troops in clearing the roads and valleys, had driven the Partisans into the higher mountains where there was little possibility of doing more than surviving. Even that was chancy. These Germans were tough, aggressive fighters, not the troops from whom we had captured the valley in August. Without supply drops of food, weapons, explosives, ammunition, and replacement radios there was little that could be done to harass the Germans. Through deaths, capture, and desertions the strength of the Partisan brigades was reduced to less than a quarter of what they had been in November. They now numbered less than 2,000 men. Some of the desertions, however, were more in the nature of temporary demobilization, as many men returned to their own mountain farms to hide out until the snows melted.

The most urgent task of Force 399 was to get emergency supplies to Owen, Campbell, and Plan, including radios, food, and clothing. Next in importance were medical supplies and weapons for the Partisans, who had lost many of their weapons during the German attack. Radio contacts remained uncertain because of constant movement. Those contacts that were made had to be held to the absolute minimum number of brief messages in order to conserve batteries and to try to avoid disclosing Partisan positions to German monitoring stations. The record of the desperate efforts to get in at least one planeload of supplies is revealed in the few stark messages that were exchanged between Owen and Force 399 during the month of January.

January 3. Owen to 399: Pls lay on emergency drop of one plane only at DZ [Drop Zone] and time to be set by us for immed use or emergency one B2 [radio] and two A3 [radios] and winter clothing.

January 5. Owen to 399: Local situation very difficult and although afraid drop will betray [our] position to Huns Zone HQ will risk two aircraft only by night with essential supplies [food, clothing, radios]. Standing by night five/six onwards at map REF [the map number and coordinates on it]. Best approach two six zero degrees. Try drop all in one run. Tell pilot not to hang around. Fires ITEM [letter I] Ground flash OBOE [O] Air KING [K]. Make every effort. Counting on these stores. Further drops unlikely for some time.

January 7. Owen to 399: Food situation getting desperate. Weather clearing. Has stopped snowing.

January 9. 399 to Owen: Weather frightful. RAF aware yr desperate plight. Doing all possible assist.

*January 12.*Owen to 399: Cloud nil. Wind nil. Cleared up over nite. Situation now so desperate will you fly this afternoon in daylight. I dare not stay here longer. If cannot fly today or early evening must cancel sorties.

January 12. 399 to Owen: Deeply regret unable to fly to you today or tonight 12th. RAF held special conference but found met [meteorological] conditions absolutely forbid operations.

January 12. 399 to Owen: [late afternoon transmission] 1100 GMT [Greenwich mean time on 13th] onwards 2 Halifaxes dropping Solcava. Confirm immediately on emergency link whether possible to receive. Impossible to send by night.

January 12. Owen to 399: [later message] Mathews and Parks wounded and taken prisoner by Hun. No news Fisher. Thanks for trying. Cancel DZ. Hold sortie until new DZ can be found. Think we are going east this time. Five feet of snow makes movement difficult and easily followed. Future contacts probably irregular.

January 12. Owen to 399: [later message] Not able to receive planes. Are moving east. Will give new DZ when poss.

Several days later the Partisans heard through the underground that Mathews and Parks had been taken to a Ljubljana hospital.

January 15. Owen to 399: All DZs at present closed. Will advise when open. Hope to open new DZ in area north Sostanji in few days where we are now.

January 19. Owen personal from Clarke [Force 399]: Much regret cancellation yr sorties for tonite. Am satisfied RAF doing all possible to assist and sorties would have flwn had failure not been certain and loss of aircraft likely. Keeping you top priority for 20 in hope you can hold drop point. Reply next sked whether possible. Try hold on until they succeed as weather seldom allows choice of specific date for sorties.

January 20. 399 to Owen: Not possible again owing met. Keeping you top priority. State daily on first morning [radio] sked whether able receive that night. Presume daylight drops still off.

January 20. 399 to Owen: [later message] Have 2 Halifaxes standing by for night 21st weather permitting. Confirm on QRX 0800 GMT 21st you can receive.

January 21. 399 to Owen: Regret met still against you. Have cancelled your two sorties until you advise us again.

January 25. Owen to 399: After much unpleasantness from Huns Zone HQ crossed into Pohorje at night. Hope to open new DZ in two days for daylight attempt to receive sorties as planned.

January 30. Owen to 399: Will be off air for several days as Pzns require full use their radio which we share. Further strong Hun action cut all internal routes and contacts. Local situation bad. DZ here unlikely for at least three days.

January 30. Owen to 399: Have now arranged 1500 sked working. Zone HQ making all out effort to open DZ soonest as they have just received rocket from Slovene HQ for not having done so before.

It was not until February 20 that the first sortie bringing radios, batteries, clothing, and food finally was received successfully. It had been more than two months since the German attack had forced the Partisan headquarters and the Anglo-American liaison parties to disperse to the snow-laden mountaintops without radios, food, or adequate clothing.

At the end of February the three brigades of the Fourteenth Partisan Division were ordered to retreat south across the Sava. During the winter offensive the Germans had combed the hiding places along the river banks and destroyed all the hidden Partisan boats. The brigades concentrated around the proposed crossing point. Owen radioed for an emergency drop of infantry assault bridging to span 65 yards. "Local commander states this is a matter of life and death for his troops as Hun now has them pinned against the river."

The rubber boats and ropes were dropped the following day. Neither Owen nor Plan nor anyone among the Partisan officers had ever constructed such a bridge. After several failed attempts to pull a rope across the swift-flowing river with one of the boats, a Partisan suggested coiling the rope in the boat and letting it pull out as the boat was paddled across. This worked and the rope was secured at both ends. Plan asked him how he knew what to do. The Partisan replied he was a deserter from the German army and that's how they did it in Russia.

Next they tried to move the rubber boats out along the rope, where together they would act as floats to support a plank bridge. The man in the first boat lost his balance in midstream, the boat was swept away, and he was left in the middle of the river holding on to the rope. To save him the rope was cut on the far bank and the man was pulled ashore. Now they were back where they started. It was growing dark, the Germans were pressing, and the commander decided not to make another try. The Partisans fought their way back to the high mountains where they remained until the end of the war.

By March the German offensive was largely spent. From that time on to the end of the war in May, neither side undertook any major actions. Although the Partisans did launch limited attacks and ambushes, their main effort was to survive in the snow-covered forests with little or no shelter. Dispersal into small units was necessary both to avoid encirclement and to find local sources of food, mostly from the mountain peasants remaining in the area who still had animals and grain.

The Partisans did fight on, as best they could. In early spring one

325

ambush they set on the road north from Celje to Austria resulted in the capture of General Konrad Heidenreich as he was driven north in his staff car. The general was brought to the nearby Zone headquarters. Bob Plan was there and wanted to interrogate him about the documents in his dispatch case. The Partisans refused Plan's request and then shot the general. Dusan Kveder, at that time commander of the Slovene Partisans, was irate because he had wanted to use the general to exchange for Partisan prisoners, including his cousin.

In retribution the Germans seized 99 civilian hostages and hanged them from telephone poles along the road. The effect on the population was not antagonism against the Partisans for having provoked the atrocity, but rage against the Germans. Nearly everyone in the area had a relative or friend who was hanged; the result of their anger was to join the Partisans to fight the Huns and avenge the deaths. The shooting of civilian hostages by the German occupiers in Serbia, Montenegro, Bosnia, and Croatia since 1941 had provoked the same reaction.

In the days and weeks following the end of the war in Europe, Allied officers made determined efforts to locate the British and Americans who were missing during the German offensive north of the Sava. No traces were ever found of those who had vanished.

Hesketh-Prichard had disappeared in the mountains north of the Drava. We believed Rosenfeld and Knoth to be in a Partisan hospital in the mountains. They too were not found. Plan said that about 20 American and British airmen were in a hidden Partisan hospital on Mozirske Planina, where one of our drop points had been during the summer months. A unit of the Fourteenth SS Division discovered the hospital in March of 1945 and set fire to it with all inside. Plan was on a mountainside nearby and watched smoke rising above the hospital. He surmised that Rosenfeld and Knoth were among those killed.

Mathews and Parks were reported to have been captured and held in a Ljubljana hospital, but as they were not found there, they were presumed to have been shot after capture. Charles Fisher had been shot after capture in December.

The tragedy was that by the time the offensive began none of them had seen any hope of accomplishing their missions and had so reported to their base organizations. At least some of them might have been withdrawn before the German attack, or better still, never sent in. I had reported several times the impossibility of accomplishing their missions because of Partisan intransigence.

■ In London in the fall of 1945 to attend the meeting of the Council of Foreign Ministers of the five major victors, I was asked by Cavendish Cannon, a member of the American delegation, for my views on future U.S.-Yugoslav relations. It was a time of frustration over the coming to power of anti-Western Communists. Some thought there was still a chance that the Yugoslav government could somehow be changed by supporting rebellion if that was what it would take. My own view was different:

> The present regime is firmly entrenched. Because of its complete political, economic and propaganda control backed up by a strong secret police, and because of the complete disorganization of the center and right parties there is no present possibility of the establishment of a liberal government supported freely by the majority of the people.
>
> Consequently, a long-term policy should be developed aiming at the ultimate establishment of a liberal government which is friendly to the United States. This can be attempted through the encouragement of legal opposition or through the support of an illegal opposition which would employ force.
>
> The [route of] illegal opposition. . . has many dangers: (a) the opposition would be forced to assume totalitarian methods and if successful would probably end in a dictatorship of the right, (b) Russia would probably intervene if the situation became serious, (c) the government would be forced to be increasingly oppressive in order to combat the danger of revolt, (d) if the revolt failed United States prestige would suffer immeasurably.
>
> It appears that the only course open is the slow and largely ineffective policy of support of a legal opposition and the support of liberal institutions. Possibly a public statement should be made aimed at discouraging illegal opposition and removing any hope of United States support to such opposition. At the same time such support as is possible should be given to the establishment of democratic institutions and the reorganization of legal opposition parties.

In this memorandum I had overlooked the potential of internal ethnic conflict as a major force in the long-term evolution of Yugoslavia. But I believe I was right in opposing the support of illegal opposition. In examining the course of other internal wars and revolutions I have come to believe strongly that no civil population that has endured the frightfulness of civil war will, in less than two generations, support a new round of armed conflict. Only after four decades passed did the first signs of new internal strife begin to appear in 1985.

■ For a time I commuted between Trieste and Belgrade. Shortly before leaving Belgrade for the last time, I paid a farewell call on Tito. During our conversation, which was much more civilized than the earlier one with Jovanovic when he ordered us to leave, I expressed a personal hope for the future of Yugoslavia. I understood the wartime need for a single National Liberation Front to bring all groups together to support the war effort. Now that the war was over, I hoped that in addition to the Communist Party other political parties would be allowed to exist independently. His reply, a combination of wry humor and seriousness, was, "Yes, that is a possibility. But the prewar parties represented the collaborators and were enemies of the people. Surely you don't propose that they be allowed to be revived? Other new parties could of course exist, but who would they represent? And what would they do? The Communist Party represents the people."

CHAPTER 21

How It All Turned Out

Not surprisingly, Trieste continued to be a thorn, and I continued to be involved from time to time.

In 1946 the United States proposed that Trieste be created as a free territory under the U.N. as a compromise on the border issue between the Yugoslavs and the Italians. The Russians had accepted the concept of a neutral territory but were trying to subvert its neutrality by insisting that the Yugoslavs be given control over the civil administration. Senator Tom Connally, the chairman of the Senate Foreign Affairs Committee, represented the United States on a U.N. committee debating the issue. At the time I was a member of the U.S. delegation concerned with the international control of atomic energy, and by chance I attended the meeting.

In response to the Russians, Connally launched into a senatorial speech extolling the virtues of a Free Territory of Trieste that would be truly neutral and independent of both superpowers, as well as of Italy and Yugoslavia. His long white curls bobbed as he became more and more eloquent. Forgetting that he was not on the Senate floor, he came to his peroration in which he described his vision: "Trieste, that jewel at the head of the Adriatic, would be free at last, with Old Glory waving proudly overhead." It didn't kill the deal but it must have confirmed to the Russians their worst suspicions of American intention to continue to control Trieste.

■ In mid-September of 1947 I was briefly back in Trieste accompanying a group of congressmen (one was Richard Nixon) from the House Select (Herter) Committee on Foreign Aid. The committee had come to Europe in response to General Marshall's proposal for a massive economic aid program for Europe. Their arrival coincided with the birth of the new territory.

As a part of the Italian Peace Treaty, the Free Territory was to come into existence at midnight, September 15, but the Russians had continued to oppose a neutral civilian governor. With the approval of Washington and London, the Allied commander in Trieste, General Terence Airey, announced that British and American troops would continue their occupation until a governor was agreed upon. The Yugoslavs held that the agreement provided for the joint occupation by both the Yugoslavs and the British-American forces. They sent a message to the Allied commander that at midnight their forces would move into Trieste. Since the agreement we had reached in Belgrade in 1945, the city had been occupied by British and American forces.

Robert Joyce, the wartime OSS intelligence chief for the Balkans, was now in Trieste as consul general. He and I thought we might well have an armed confrontation. So did General Airey, who had succeeded Field Marshal Alexander. He concluded his message to the British and American governments reporting on the crisis: "If this matter is not handled very carefully a third World War might start here."

Knowing well the capacity of the Yugoslavs to stage a violent uprising, I was concerned for the safety of the congressmen. An American destroyer was in the harbor and that evening Colonel Richard Stilwell, an American officer in the Allied command, and I went aboard to see the captain. He agreed that if violence erupted he would take the congressmen aboard.

Shortly after midnight a Yugoslav tank column rumbled up to an isolated checkpoint in the hills behind Trieste that marked the boundary of the Allied Zone. The checkpoint was manned by an American sergeant and four or five soldiers. The Yugoslav officer in the lead tank ordered the sergeant to stand aside to let the column enter the Zone. The sergeant refused and calmly set up his machine gun on its tripod in the center of the road, pointing at the tank. He then sat down behind it, telling the Yugoslav officer his orders were to let no one pass and he intended to do just that. Meanwhile he radioed for support. The Yugoslavs, who had hoped to make an unopposed sneak entry and establish themselves in the new Free Territory, backed down. Had the sergeant given in we would have been confronted by the far harder task of getting the Yugoslavs out, since they now had the preponderance of force in the Trieste area.

The congressmen, having had by sheer chance a ringside view of a Cold War confrontation, left Trieste reinforced in their view that the Marshall Plan was essential to strengthening western Europe against Communist expansion.

In 1954, after years of trying to get Soviet agreement on a neutral administrator for the territory, the United States and Britain gave up and returned Trieste to Italian jurisdiction. The far larger eastern part of Venezia Giulia, with its preponderantly Slav population, had long since been absorbed into Slovenia and Croatia without opposition from the West.

■ If the Yugoslavs proved themselves difficult toward the Western powers in Trieste in 1947, they showed the next year that they could be ruggedly independent vis-à-vis the Soviet Union as well. In June of 1948 Tito refused to subordinate the Yugoslav Communist Party to Stalin's orders. As a consequence the party was expelled from the Cominform, the organization through which Stalin controlled the foreign Communist parties.

At the time I was in Paris, working for Averell Harriman, then the European head of the Marshall Plan. We were taken by surprise by Tito's defiance. During the war there was almost complete unanimity within the British and American governments that Tito would remain completely loyal to Moscow. Many of us who had been with the Partisans had contributed to this view. We believed the Yugoslav Communists were slavishly eager to follow even the slightest whim of the Soviet dictator.

Yet even as early as November 1943, after his first few weeks at Tito's headquarters, Fitzroy Maclean had foreseen the possibility that Tito might pursue a nationalist policy independent of Moscow. In a dispatch to London he wrote: "Events will show the nature of Soviet intentions towards Yugoslavia; much will also depend on Tito and whether he sees himself still in his former role of Comintern agent or as the potential ruler of an independent Yugoslav State."

Still, by the time he came to write his final report in February 1945, Maclean had concluded like most of us that there was almost no possibility that Tito's Yugoslavia would be anything but a Moscow satellite:

> Both [Tito's] personal background and the present trend of events in Europe have undoubtedly convinced him that in all major questions of policy Yugoslavia must henceforward take her line from the Soviet Union.
>
> Its internal institutions will bear an ever increasing resemblance to those of the Soviet Union, and its foreign policy will be dictated from Moscow.

I also underestimated the latent strength of Tito's nationalism. In my own final report in 1945 I concluded:

> The basic policy of the present Government is the complete integration of Yugoslavia into the Russian sphere. This policy is being implemented primarily by the Yugoslav Communists and is not being directed locally by Russian representatives. The top Yugoslav leaders are so thoroughly indoctrinated with Soviet policies and methods that there is little or no need for day-to-day directives from Moscow.

Misreading the slavish pro-Russian propaganda of the Partisans, I believed international Communist ideology was a stronger political force than any latent nationalism within the Yugoslav Communist Party.

Stalin, we learned after the break, had been increasingly concerned over Tito's seeming independence and apparently had concluded that Tito and those loyal to him had to be replaced with men who would be unquestionably subservient to Moscow. Tito, aware of Soviet efforts to penetrate and suborn his own party and army, concluded he could only survive by refusing to accede to Stalin's demands.

The trouble between Stalin and the Cominform on the one side, and Tito and the Yugoslav Communist Party leadership on the other, had begun almost immediately after the German invasion of Yugoslavia, but it had been carefully hidden from those of us with the Partisans during the war, as well as from all but the top Yugoslav party leadership. It was only after the break that each side published parts of the hitherto secret record of communications between them. Now for the first time we could see what had actually occurred.

Immediately after the German attack against Russia began in 1941, the Comintern directed the Yugoslav Communist Party to begin operations against the Germans in support of Russia: "Organize partisan detachments without a moment's delay. Start a partisan war in the enemy's rear." To this the Yugoslav party responded wholeheartedly. The Comintern instructions, significantly, also directed the Yugoslav party to "take into consideration that at this stage your task is the liberation from Fascist oppression and not Socialist revolution." In March 1942 the Comintern repeated their guidance in a further message to Tito:

> Study of all information you send gives the impression that the adherents of Great Britain and the Yugoslav Government have some [justification] in suspecting the Partisan movement of acquiring a Communist character, and aiming at the Sovietization of Yugoslavia. Why, for example, did you need to form a special Proletarian Brigade? We earnestly request you to give serious thought to your tactics in general and to your actions, and to make sure that you on your side have really done all you can to achieve a united national front.

The Comintern also advised Tito to play down the conflict with the Chetniks: "It is not opportune to emphasize that the struggle is mainly against the Chetniks. World opinion must first and foremost be mobilized against the invaders; mentioning or unmasking the Chetniks is secondary." In spite of Moscow's directives, Tito continued to concentrate on the defeat of the Chetniks and to prepare the ground, step by step, for the creation of a postwar Communist government.

Throughout the war Moscow continued to advise Tito to avoid anything that smacked of a provisional government, to play down the role of the party, to emphasize the role of the National Liberation Front, and to emphasize that the Front had representatives of all parties and groups resisting the German occupation. Yet Tito ignored Stalin's advice. Instead he created a provisional government in liberated territory in 1943, and he made a secret proposal to the Germans the same year for an accommodation that, if it had not been turned down by Hitler, would have freed him to concentrate on defeating Mihailovic. Stalin was furious when he learned of the former; had he known of the latter he would have considered it high treason.

Another source of friction was the fact that the Russians continually put down the Partisans as uneducated and uncivilized. Molotov told Anthony Eden that he and the prime minister must make allowance for Tito's "lack of manners, which must be expected from Yugoslav peasants"—a statement echoing not only Great Russian condescension toward "lesser breeds," but possibly Molotov's own origins in the hereditary Russian nobility (he was born Scriabin, a second cousin of the composer). Russian officers with Tito often belittled Partisan fighting compared to that of the Russian partisans.

But as the war progressed Tito and his commanders had gained confidence in their own abilities. In the last two years of the war they were increasingly lionized throughout the world as leaders of the largest liberation movement in Europe. Tito, who was not without ego, had met with Churchill in Italy, and with the most senior Allied officers in Italy and Belgrade—all without the intercession or sponsorship of Stalin. Churchill said of him in a toast at an official dinner in Naples in August 1944, "Marshal Tito has shown himself to be not only a great military leader but also a statesman of outstanding character who has made a tremendous contribution toward the unification of the Yugoslav people." This accolade was given wide publicity within Yugoslavia and over the BBC. The Partisans had received no help from the Russians until late 1944, and they stood on their own feet. The situation had changed completely from 1937 when the Comintern imposed Tito, the Comintern agent, on the politically bankrupt Yugoslav Communist Party as its head.

By the time the war ended, national Communism had gradually overtaken world revolution as Tito's first objective. Although still loyal to Stalin, Tito was acutely sensitive to any act or statement, either from Moscow or from the West, that he interpreted as an improper intrusion on Yugoslav national sovereignty. By the time the Red Army reached the Yugoslav border in the fall of 1944, Tito had become enough of a nationalist to ask for a commitment from the Russians that they would not remain in occupation and that all of Yugoslav territory would remain under his political control, though his immediate purpose was to create a precedent to use with the Allies should they decide to send Allied divisions to pursue the Germans in Yugoslavia. He expressed the sense of the Partisan leadership when he said, "We have won the right to full independence and the right to take part on equal terms with our great Allies in building a new and happier Europe."

Most students of Communism agree that Tito and his close associates were genuinely shocked when the break came. They believed that they had earned the right to Stalin's trust and to a high degree of independence in managing their internal affairs, and this in no way conflicted with their loyalty to Stalin and to the Cominform.

Immediately after the expulsion of Yugoslavia from the Cominform, Eastern bloc trade with Yugoslavia was cut off. Anti-Tito propaganda blasts were launched from Moscow and the Eastern European capitals. Stalin must have expected that his denunciation of Tito would so split the Yugoslav party that he could designate a successor to Tito who would be a loyal agent in bringing the party and the government back into the fold of submission to Moscow. Instead nearly all of the leadership remained loyal to Tito, who moved quickly to round up those who might support Moscow in the struggle.

The Warsaw Pact military forces were expanded, equipped, and trained for an invasion of Yugoslavia. Troops were concentrated on the Yugoslav borders. Tito, cut off economically from Eastern Europe, was in an extremely vulnerable position.

The implications of Tito's defiance, if it were to be successful, went far beyond the borders of Yugoslavia. It was the first break in the hitherto monolithic world Communist movement. If it were allowed to stand, it would open the door for dissent among Communists everywhere, particularly in the rest of Eastern Europe.

The break was totally unexpected by most in Washington. At first the government was divided on whether the break was real or was simply a temporary quarrel. Even those of us closer to the scene—as I was, in Paris—debated the significance of it endlessly. A few even believed it was a fake to mislead and trap the West. But after a few months the view prevailed that the break was real and that it was in our interest to quietly provide support to Belgrade.

■ As the tempo of the Cold War increased in 1948, driven by the ruthless installation of full Communist governments in Eastern Europe, I was asked to join in the creation of a new postwar secret operations organization. Known first as OPC (Office of Policy Coordination—a deliberately bland name), it later became a part of CIA. Almost immediately we were directed to find ways to strengthen Yugoslav capabilities to remain independent of Moscow.

Our primary contacts were with Ales Bebler and Vladimir Velebit, both of whom I had known during the war. Bebler and Velebit had been early Partisan leaders, and they were well-educated and widely traveled. Bebler had fought in Spain, and both were long-time members of the Yugoslav Communist Party and trusted by Tito. By 1948 Bebler had left his post on the Slovene Communist Party's Central Committee to serve in New York as the Yugoslav permanent representative to the United Nations. He and I had become friends in Stajerska in 1944, and in spite of the intervening conflict over Trieste in which we had been on opposite sides, I was able to reestablish a good personal relationship with him as we explored ways in which the United States might strengthen Tito's government to withstand an attack.

Vladimir Velebit, the deputy foreign minister whom I had known in Belgrade, arrived in Washington in 1949. Velebit, now 41, had been one of the most effective men in the Partisan leadership in their relations with the West. Because Tito recognized Velebit's special skills, he had used him in negotiations with the British and Americans. For this reason Velebit had now been branded by Stalin as a British spy. Velebit, Robert Joyce (now back in the State Department), and I developed steps we might take during informal meetings in our tiny eighteenth-century Georgetown home.

Velebit told us that they desperately needed arms to strengthen their defense against the possibility of an attack by Hungarian, Romanian, and Soviet forces. Yet Tito believed that the open acceptance of arms from the United States could provide just the pretext Stalin needed for actual invasion. We agreed upon an initial secret shipment of arms. Any additional military and economic aid, we said, would have to be provided openly through the existing economic and military assistance legislation. The proposal we developed for an initial covert shipment of arms was approved by the National Security Council and the president, and five shiploads of arms in innocently marked boxes were loaded out of Philadelphia aboard ships bound for Yugoslav Adriatic ports. With this in hand Tito felt sufficiently secure to receive openly additional support from the West. Over the next ten years the United States openly provided more than one billion dollars of military and economic aid to Yugoslavia. Britain provided similar support.

Our initial arms shipments to Yugoslavia were an example of the constructive use of our covert capability. OPC had provided quick stopgap support at a critical time when Tito believed secrecy was essential. Although the program was secret, it was consistent with stated national policy as publicly enunciated by the president. For example, at his press conference on December 24, 1949, Truman had stated: "As regards Yugoslavia, we are just as opposed to aggression against that country as any other, and just as favorable to the retention of Yugoslavia's sovereignty."

In the early postwar years the White House often turned to CIA to accomplish its objectives while avoiding public and Congressional scrutiny. In recent years, as the term "covert" has come to imply something deeply improper, we have lost sight of the fact that there are important things to be done in the world that can only be done privately. It is only when covert activities are inconsistent with openly stated national policy that they do great damage when they ultimately become known either through leaks or when secrecy is no longer warranted. For example, the Reagan administration secretly supplied arms to the Iranians with the expectation of securing the release of American hostages held in Lebanon, contrary to stated policy that the United States would never make such deals. When this later became known, it turned into a national scandal that provoked Congressional hearings, the appointment of a special prosecutor, and even the indictment of a former Secretary of Defense.

General Bela Kiraly, who in 1949 was commander of infantry in the Hungarian army, later described the expansion and equipping of that army in preparation for the planned attack on Yugoslavia. He believes that the attack was finally called off by Stalin for two reasons. First, a massive purge of the Hungarian army leadership took place about the time the attack was ready to be launched. Second, the North Korean attack on South Korea began on June 25, 1950. In Kiraly's view, the American response to the invasion of South Korea signaled to Stalin that the United States would respond similarly to the planned attack on Yugoslavia, and this Stalin was not prepared to risk. Kiraly has stated that without that response "the war against Yugoslavia would surely have taken place."

One conversation shortly after the end of the war cast a new and unexpected light on Tito's decision to stand up to Stalin. During those long months in Yugoslavia, when talking with the Partisan commissars and officers, I had often felt that I was up against a stone wall, completely unable to make a dent in their unrelenting antagonism to the West. Five years later, in 1949, I was told the following story. A group of State Department officers had just met informally with Franc Primozic, then the Yugoslav minister in their Washington embassy. The Americans were eager to learn the inside story of the events leading to Tito's decision only a few months before to break with Stalin rather than accept Stalin's terms.

After describing the history of the conflict with Moscow, Primozic recounted what he said was a second factor in that decision. During the war the Partisan leaders had come to know the British and Americans who had parachuted to them and who had shared in their fighting against the Axis. As Communists they had had no previous contact with the West; they had all been underground Communist leaders, political prisoners, or in Spain, fighting against Franco. They had learned from these Allied officers for the first time about the West, its people, and its institutions.

Primozic had been operations officer of the Fourth Zone Partisans with whom I had spent seven months in 1944. We had gone through some difficult times together and had come to respect each other. I was surprised and pleased when I was told that at the meeting with the State Department officers he said that conversations such as those he had with me during the Partisan days had helped the Yugoslavs understand America and Britain and had done much to counter the Communist stereotype of the West. These wartime discussions with British and American officers, he said, had also been a factor in their decision to resist Moscow.

■ I have mentioned that Stalin had called Vladimir Velebit a British spy. In fact, I have no reason to believe he was anything but a loyal Yugoslav patriot. The charge, however, brings up another important issue from those years: the influence of Communist sympathizers in Western governments.

More than four decades after the end of the Second World War, the wartime decision by the British to drop Mihailovic and to support Tito and his Partisans still remains controversial. Those who criticize the decision often argue that the key people who recommended supporting Tito were either Communist agents or, at the least, dupes. One person who has come under attack is Major James Klugmann, who was an officer in the Yugoslav section of SOE in Cairo, and before the war a member of the Communist Party at Cambridge University. In recent years he has been accused of altering or suppressing intelligence reports from inside Yugoslavia in 1942 and 1943. His objective, so the argument goes, was to influence the recommendations of Maclean and Deakin to the British Foreign Office and Churchill to drop Mihailovic and to support the Partisans instead.

In the most famous spy case in Britain after the war, five Soviet moles were uncovered one by one over a period of several years. Their names are now well known: Kim Philby, Guy Burgess, Donald Maclean, Anthony Blunt, and John Cairncross. All were or had been in sensitive intelligence and foreign policy positions in the British government. All had been recruited at Cambridge University in the late 1930's by the Soviet intelligence service. James Klugmann was a key member of this Cambridge group and was an acknowledged Communist, so it is reasonable to assume that in the Yugoslav section in Cairo he would have done everything he could to influence British policy in favor of the Communist-led Partisans. (In the early 1950's, during Philby's two-year tour as the MI-6 representative in the British Embassy in Washington, I had often worked with him on joint intelligence matters. I was as shaken as anyone by the revelation that he had been for years a Soviet mole.)

In Cairo Klugmann had been one of my SOE briefers. I had found him a modest, kindly, even gentle man. He seemed the antithesis of most of the British officers in SOE who had eagerly sought dangerous assignments behind enemy lines. He spoke very well of the Partisans, but he made so little impression on me that I had almost forgotten him until I was told by a British officer in Belgrade in 1945 that he was under investigation as a possible Soviet agent.

During my briefings, Klugmann was strongly pro-Partisan, and I believe he did whatever he could to cause the British to shift their support to Tito. But how much influence he actually had is another question. After reviewing American and British wartime records on

Yugoslavia, I think it unlikely that Klugmann by himself was able to tip the balance to Tito and against Mihailovic. The reports and recommendations of British officers who were on the ground in Yugoslavia with Tito, especially from William Deakin and Fitzroy Maclean, carried far more weight with the Allied High Command and with Churchill than reports edited by Klugmann could ever have carried. And it is hard to see how Klugmann, sitting in Cairo while Deakin and Maclean were inside Yugoslavia, could have influenced their interpretation of events to which they were much closer than was Klugmann. The conclusion of those officers was that Tito's forces were more effective against the Germans and Italians than those of Mihailovic. British Colonel S. W. Bailey and OSS Captain Walter Mansfield, who had been with Mihailovic, both reported that Mihailovic was ineffective against the Germans. Most important, these judgments were supported by the British intercepts of German radio communications. It is now well documented that the Germans launched seven major offensives against the Partisans, each employing several divisions, which showed that significant German forces were being committed to fight them.

Whether or not Klugmann was an active Soviet agent during this period is still an unresolved question. According to a retired MI-6 officer, in private conversation, two security investigations, one in 1943 and one in 1945, concluded that he had not been an active Soviet agent. This was of course before the defection of Burgess and Maclean, the later confession of Philby, and the still later exposure of Blunt and Cairncross as Soviet agents. All were members of the Communist movement at Cambridge in which Klugmann was a leading light. Had this been known during the war, Klugmann's open membership in the Communist Party and his close association with all five would have been regarded as more serious than just a radical phase through which many university students passed in the Depression years of the 1930's. The circumstance of Klugmann's entry into wartime SOE is an example of the British "old boy" network of school and university friendships that was the source of many recruits for the intelligence and special operations organizations. Klugmann, having enlisted in the army, was in Cairo in 1942 as a corporal in the Pioneer Corps, a special unit to which those with questionable security credentials were assigned by cautious authorities. By chance Terence Airey, a senior British intelligence officer, passed him on a Cairo street and recognized him as having been at Gresham's, an English public school, in the class ahead of Airey. Klugmann had been at the top of his class and Airey thought that Klugmann's mind should be put to better use. He arranged for him to be transferred to SOE Cairo, which was then beginning to plan for the support of resistance in the Balkans. Airey went on to become a lieutenant general and the head of intelligence for Field Marshal Alexander, the Supreme Allied Commander in the the Mediterranean.

Klugmann did such a good job at SOE that he was given a field commission and had been promoted to major by the time I first met him. One explanation for the security lapse in transferring him to SOE is that British security records on Klugmann were destroyed by a German bombing attack early in the war.

■ In 1958 my wife and I were invited to attend the fifteenth anniversary of the fifth German offensive against Tito's main forces. Foreign representatives were limited to two Americans, two British, and two Russians who had been with the Partisans during the war. William Deakin and John Henniker-Major were the Brits; Ellery Huntington, my predecessor as head of the American mission, was the other American. The Russians were not expected to accept the invitation but two turned up. They were almost completely ignored.

The celebration was held at Sutjeska in Bosnia, the site of the battle into the midst of which Bill Deakin had first parachuted in 1943. The encampment was in a narrow river valley surrounded by steep mountains. It was on the face of the mountain to the west that the Partisan command had been pinned down by bombing as they tried to escape the German encirclement. Tito and Deakin had been wounded that day by the explosion of a bomb in their midst. Bill and I asked for horses and rode up to the point where they had been hit.

Bill described looking up at the cliff above them. German mountain troops were coming down the face of the cliff on ropes. The Partisan leaders and Deakin had extricated themselves only when darkness came.

The survivors of the Partisan brigades were brought back to the battle site. On the early morning of the big day we heard the wonderful Slavic marching songs growing louder in the dawn as each of the brigades, with their wartime battle flags, marched up from their encampment along the river to the field where Tito's review was to take place. They formed in long ranks across the grassy field in the bright sunlight. Tito, accompanied by Koca Popovic, one of the top Partisan commanders, walked along the long lines of former Partisans. He seemed overdressed in the heavy gray uniform that he had adopted in the closing months of the war. And he had put on more weight. Popovic, as lithe and trim as he had been in wartime, instead wore his simple Partisan uniform. I thought it too bad that Tito had not done the same—though it was highly unlikely he could have fit into it now.

To me the most touching part was that the Partisan troops had been told they might bring their children to Sutjeska. And when the brigades formed up for the review the children stood with their fathers in the ranks as Tito walked past taking their salute. It was a touch of simple human gentleness that one so seldom saw in Communist life. Yet I did not see Tito stop to recognize and greet a single man, though he must have personally known many of them from wartime days.

In the afternoon the four British and Americans and Margot, my wife, were invited to Tito's simple but very comfortable cabin at the upper edge of the encampment. He was again the gracious, friendly host we had known in Belgrade in the closing months of the war. The conversation was mostly reminiscences, although we expressed our pleasure that Yugoslavia had been successful in staying out of Stalin's clutches. In looking around the room I noticed three very good Impressionist paintings, which I was told were by Yugoslav artists. It was another indicator of the difference between Yugolavia's communism and that of the Soviet Union—where there would have been the poster pictures of heroic workers and soldiers.

I saw many friends from Stajerska, Croatia, and Belgrade, and in the evening around the campfire there was much talk of the war and of the subsequent trauma of the break with Stalin.

One high party member told me he had recently returned from Beijing where he was a member of a delegation of the Yugoslav Central Committee that met with members of the Chinese Central Committee. The break between Moscow and Beijing had not yet occurred, and the Yugoslavs were put under very heavy pressure by the Chinese to rejoin Moscow and the united Communist bloc. The Yugoslavs had resisted, and the Chinese had finally told them: "The day will come when you will come crawling back on your hands and knees begging to be taken in." My friend said by now they were used to the Russians and understood how to deal with them, but that "these Chinese are really tough." He said that at one point in their meetings one of the Yugoslavs had spoken apprehensively of the dangers of nuclear war, to which Mao had replied that they were not afraid of nuclear war. "We can take 300 million casualties and still fight and win. What other nation can do that?"

Ales Bebler, who was also at Sutjeska, recalled our clandestine shipments of arms to Yugoslavia eight years earlier. He now told me he believed that if American military power had not been in the background, the Russians would have certainly attacked.

■ After the break in 1948 between Moscow and Belgrade, it should have become clear that a monolithic Communist world empire was not inevitable. The forces of nationalism, religion, and ethnic diversity were potentially stronger and more enduring than the force of Communism. If further evidence was needed, it was provided by the rupture between Mao's China and the Kremlin that came a decade later.

Yet the myth of the monolithic Communist empire continued to dominate the thinking of many American policymakers for another two decades after the Tito-Stalin break. Nowhere did this have more devastating consequences than in our policy toward Indochina, where Ho Chi Minh and the Vietnamese Communists were regarded by American presidents and policymakers as an integral part of a united Communist drive for world domination.

The tragic failure of many in our national leadership to recognize that the myth of monolithic world Communism had been exposed and destroyed is revealed in a January 1962 letter from the Joint Chiefs of Staff to the secretary of defense and to the president. Written 14 years after Tito's break with Moscow, their assessment was of the chain reaction that could follow a loss of Vietnam:

> Of equal importance to the immediate loss [of Vietnam] are the eventualities which could follow the loss of the Southeast Asian mainland. All of the Indonesian archipelago could come under the domination and control of the U.S.S.R. and would become a Communist base posing a threat against Australia and New Zealand. The Sino-Soviet Bloc would have control of the eastern access to the Indian Ocean. The Philippines and Japan could be pressured to assume at best a neutralist role, thus eliminating two of our major bases in the Western Pacific. India's ability to remain neutral would be jeopardized and, as the Bloc meets success, its concurrent stepped-up activities to move into and control Africa can be expected.

The tragedy of this lack of understanding of communist evolution was visited, not on my generation, but on the generation coming of age in the 1960's, who were asked to fight a war in defense of a concept many believed disastrously wrong, and who were torn apart by conflicts over duty and loyalty as a result.

■ The excommunication of the Yugoslav Communist Party by Stalin caused the separate nationalities of Yugoslavia to close ranks for the common defense against the feared Soviet-led attack. Differences among the Slovenes, Serbs, Croats, Macedonians, Bosnian Muslims, and Montenegrins were submerged by their common peril. Even after the direct danger of invasion from the East had passed, there remained the Cold War conflict between East and West. This, coupled with the strong commitment to Yugoslav nationalism expressed through the Communist Party's monopoly of political organization, the press, radio, and television, continued to obscure the deep ethnic conflicts.

During the war I was well aware of these conflicts and of the violence and massacres they had let loose. But I tended to believe they were the work of extremist minorities, incited by atrocities of the German and Italian occupiers. Within the Partisan leadership I could detect only minor ethnic antagonisms. Tito's own top leadership was made up of Croats, Slovenes, Serbs, Macedonians, Montenegrins, and Bosnian Muslims. They continued to make a determined effort toward reconciliation among the ethnic groups. Yet when the external pressures were removed as the Cold War wound down, the centuries-old ethnic conflicts surfaced again. With the collapse of the Yugoslav Communist Party, the principal force supporting Yugoslav unity disappeared. The army, officered largely by Serbs and the only remaining Yugoslav-wide force, gradually shifted to supporting Serbian interests.

In the spring of 1989 I returned to Stajerska for the first time since that wintry day in 1944 when I had departed on foot to recross the German frontier. My wife and I, together with Bob Plan, my old colleague from the forest whom we had picked up in Trieste, drove to Ljubljana and then into our wartime mountain valley. I remembered the mountain slopes over which we had climbed to evade the German patrols as being high and rugged, and I was a little apprehensive that from a car they would look lower and less precipitous than I had remembered them—perhaps in the intervening years I had romanticized their grandeur. Instead they looked higher and even more beautiful.

The houses and barns that had been burned by the Germans had long ago been rebuilt. The villages were a little larger but had kept their earlier alpine character and architecture. The fields and pastures were the same emerald green and the higher mountains were coated with the remnants of the winter's snows.

Dr. Dusan Biber of the Slovene Institute of Modern History and Professor Tone Ferenc of Ljubljana University had planned our every move. I tried to remember our routes of march in and around the valley. To my astonishment, Tone Ferenc had worked it out in detail from his analysis of the Partisan operational reports now in the Slovene archives. He was able to tell us precisely where we had been as we had moved each day. I was deeply moved: there were the memories of those eventful and dangerous days, now rendered more vivid on the spot; and there was the enveloping welcome and singular thoughtfulness of our hosts who had gone to so much trouble to enliven those memories with accurate detail.

In the capital, Ljubljana, we were warmly entertained one evening by the president of Slovenia, Janez Stanovnik, at the Slovene government's guest house. At the end of the war Stanovnik had been secretary to Edvard Kardelj, Tito's closest associate. Now his bushy hair was gray and he sported huge handlebar moustaches.

Like the host, all the guests were old Partisans. Some I immediately recognized. Rudi—Viktor Avbelj—was there, looking much the same as he had when we blew up our first bridge together. In the intervening years he had served as president of Slovenia. Mitja Ribicic was there. He had been the commissar of the Koroska Odred that had responsibility for the secret crossings of the Drava River. After the war he had become prime minister of Yugoslavia under the rotating presidency in Tito's time, and was now an elder statesman. Others I had only known by reputation. Ivan Dolnicar had been with the Fourteenth Partisan division and in the years after the war had risen to the rank of colonel general in the Yugoslav Air Force. Lado Pohar had been a news reporter with the Partisans and later became director of Slovenian television programming. My Fourth Zone Partisans had become distinguished leaders of Slovenia and of Yugoslavia!

The conversation that evening was almost exclusively about the current conflicts within Yugoslavia. The rigid grip of the Slovene Communist Party and of the secret police clearly had eroded to the point of insignificance. The wartime antagonisms toward the West seemed obsolete. Even Tito could be spoken of with more candor than had once seemed possible. The qualities that had enabled him to rally the Partisans throughout the war and stand up to Stalin, it appeared, did not carry over to leadership of a postwar government. He succumbed to the sybaritic life of a secure and unchallenged potentate. Several luxurious villas and hunting lodges throughout the country were his. His huge yacht would have been the envy of the most self-indulgent capitalist multimillionaires. Meanwhile the country and the economy drifted. Many publicly owned enterprises failed to be productive. Inflation set in and unemployment increased. Tito revised the constitution to give greater autonomy to the individual republics. But the result was that no strong leadership could emerge after his death. While he was still living, his wartime reputation, together with the impossibility of any legal opposition, ensured that there would be no challenge to his authority, that no other leadership could emerge to revive the deteriorating economy. His legacy, after his death in 1980, was a weak central government and a collective presidency with a rotating chairman.

The dinner group was deeply concerned about the coming crisis in the relation of the individual republics to the federal government in Belgrade. The old ethnic conflicts, suppressed but not extinguished under Tito's long rule, were now surfacing as the most serious political problem facing the nation. Some of the guests feared a breakup of Yugoslavia itself, while others viewed a breakup as preferable to the current state of affairs. Slovenia, the richest and most productive of the six republics, was tired of subsidizing the rest of the country.

Economic decentralization was also an important issue to the Slovenes that evening. Inflation was rampant and little was then being done by the federal government to bring it under control. Unemployment was up to 14 percent and the standard of living was declining. Communism as a political and economic philosophy of centralization and monopoly power had been discredited, and was rejected by the Slovenes as a failure. It appeared from that evening's conversation that either Slovenia would get a new deal allowing it to have a multiparty government (as it did the next year), run its own economy, and keep its army draftees within Slovenia, or it would pull out of Yugoslavia.

■ With their historical roots in Central Europe, the Slovenes and Croats were moving in 1989 toward an open, multiparty political system and rejection of Communist Party rule. The Serbs, in contrast, were still under Communist control, and supported the continuation of a centralized Yugoslav nation. I hoped that the separation of the republics might be accomplished peacefully, if it came, but my memories filled me with foreboding. Soon after my 1989 trip the inherent difficulties of separation were brought sharply to mind, when the little Croatian town of Glina figured in the news.

On Christmas Eve, 1944, after an eighteen-day trip through German-occupied territory, I had arrived with my escort in Glina. Here we were given a ride for the first time in seven months (in a jeep), and found Croatian Partisan Headquarters.

Despite its location, Glina was a predominantly Serb town in the military frontier region of Croatia that had marked the divide between the Austro-Hungarian and the Ottoman empires. In 1941 it had been the scene of massacres of the Serb population by the Croat Ustashe collaborators of Hitler and Mussolini. Fifty years later, Glina was again the scene of Serb-Croat conflict. Franjo Tudjman, president of Croatia, had said publicly in 1990 that there were too many Serbs in the Croat government and had set about to replace them with Croats. In Glina Croat policemen replaced local Serbs and locked up their weapons. In 1991, after Croatia declared its independence, armed Serb irregulars moved in to control the town. The Serb inhabitants, whose memories of the 1941 Ustashe atrocities were still strong, sided with the Serb irregulars, who captured the Croat-manned police station and seized more than 200 rifles. The pro-Serb Yugoslav army then moved in to restore order, leaving the Serb irregulars in control.

Soon the fighting spread to the surrounding area, and then to other Croatian areas of mixed Serb and Croat populations. Irregular reinforcements, calling themselves Chetniks, arrived from Serbia and with the support of artillery of the Yugoslav national army took large areas of Croatia. Croat fighters responded, and the fratricidal war was on. Entire towns and villages were destroyed. Civilian prisoners were taken by each side and many were reported to have been shot; hostages were sent to concentration camps. Large numbers were forced to flee as refugees.

■ My old colleague and friend, Vladimir Velebit, wrote to me in 1991 of his anguish over the disintegration of his country:

> I thought that forty years of preaching brotherhood would shape the younger generations and would make them forget the crimes committed during the war. But a group of so-called intellectuals, whom I consider criminals, have spread hatred in such a degree that Yugoslavia can't survive as a civilized nation. I do not see a single person in Yugoslavia who has the wisdom and the authority to stop the present chaos. Yugoslavia cannot continue to exist as an entity but on the other hand it can't fall apart because the nationalities are inextricably mixed. Foreign intervention is not possible because no nation is ready to risk the lives of their soldiers to pacify the madmen in the Balkans.

His comment that "Yugoslavia. . . can't fall apart" seems to me the most painful of facts. For centuries the frontier between the Austro-Hungarian and Ottoman empires ran through the Krajina, one of the centers of the most intense violence in 1991 and 1992 between the Serbs and the Croats. Generations ago Serb men were encouraged to move with their families to this area, known then as the Frontier Region, by Vienna in order to create a strong defense line against the Turks. The result was islands of Serb population deep within Croatian and Bosnian populations.

Map 4, showing ethnic distribution, graphically demonstrates the extent to which the ethnic and religious groups have been intermixed. Yet the actual situation is even more complex. Within each of the areas of the map indicating settlement by one or another group, peoples of other ethnic and religious groups also have resided as local minorities (see table in Appendix). Short of massive population transfer, there is no possible way of redrawing boundaries that will not include large minorities disconnected from their kinsmen across these boundaries. Only Slovenia, with its homogeneous Slovene-Catholic population, has reasonably clear ethnic boundaries.

The boundary issues are further complicated by history. Over the last few centuries the individual states have alternately expanded and contracted like an accordion. At times Serbia has extended far into the present territories of its neighbors; at other times it has been shrunk to a small central core.

Religious differences have also intensified the ethnic conflicts. The Serbs and Montenegrins are Eastern Orthodox, the Slovenes and Croats are Roman Catholic, and there are large minorities in Serbia, Macedonia, and Bosnia-Hercegovina who were converted to Islam during the Ottoman rule. In each case religion served to reinforce the antagonisms among the Yugoslav nations. And with it all, tales of violence and hatred are passed from generation to generation. The terrible violence of Serbs and Croats against each other that we witnessed in the 1941–45 war became the fuel for the violence unleashed in 1991 and 1992.

General Adzic, the Serb commander of the Yugoslav army during the 1991–92 fighting, is a Serb from Croatia whose entire family was murdered by the Croat Ustashe during the 1941–45 war. Now he is converting the Yugoslav army to an army of Serbia. What seems clear is that this new violence will live to fuel still other cycles unless the chain can somehow be broken. Celestine Bohlen has put it succinctly: "One group's revenge becomes the other group's atrocity."

■ Those of us who fought the war with the Partisans had a unique opportunity to observe the Communist movement at first hand, as it grew from Partisan brigades living in the forest to the government of the nation. Those of us with the Chetniks saw them fail to win Allied support for many reasons, the most agonizing of which being that Mihailovic was unwilling to bring down on the Serb people the terrible retributions from the Nazis for all-out attacks on the German soldiers.

We had soon learned that outsiders had very limited influence on the leadership or course of events within Yugoslavia. Churchill, Roosevelt, and Stalin had all attempted to impose their own priorities and interests on the warring parties. They failed for the simple reason that men and women risking their own and their families' lives and future do so only for deeply felt commitments of their own: bringing into being a new government, removing a foreign invader, and destroying an internal enemy.

Both the Partisans and the Chetniks, locked in an internal struggle for political control of their nation, competed to get support from the Allies solely for themselves, and when that was not forthcoming, sought accommodations with the Germans and Italians that would allow them to concentrate on destroying each other.

■ In a short span of 70 years from its creation as a nation, Yugoslavia has passed through a hapless monarchy, a terrible foreign occupation and civil war, and a Communist dictatorship, to emerge into a period of economic misfortune and further ethnic strife. Yet my memories are of people who were brave, intelligent, compassionate and industrious. After the terrible succession of tragedies they have endured—some of which I have shared—I can only hope they find a way to achieve the peace and tranquility they deserve to rebuild their lives.

REFERENCE MATTER

Map 8: Political divisions within Yugoslavia, 1945–1991.

APPENDIX

Political Boundaries and Ethnic Distribution
in Postwar Yugoslavia

Distribution of Ethnic Groups in the Republics and
Autonomous Areas of Yugoslavia

Ethnic group	Percent of population	Ethnic group	Percent of population
Bosnia-Herzegovina *(18.6% of total Yugoslavian population)*		Serbia *(41.6% of total Yugoslavian population)*	
Muslims	44	*Serbia Proper (24.6% of total)*	
Serbs	33	Serbs	96
Croats	17	Muslims	2
Yugoslavs	6	Gypsies	1
Croatia *(20.0% of total)*		Croats	1
Croats	75	*Kosovo (8.4% of total)*	
Serbs	15	Albanians	83
Yugoslavs	9	Serbs	13
Macedonia *(8.7% of total)*		Muslims	2
Macedonians	64	Gypsies	2
Albanians	21	*Vojvodina (8.6% of total)*	
Serbs	5	Serbs	70
Turks	5	Hungarians	22
Bulgars	3	Croats	5
Gypsies	2	Romanians	3
Montenegro *(2.6% of total)*		Slovenia *(8.5% of total)*	
Serbs	90	Slovenes	91
Yugoslavs	6	Croats	3
Albanians	4	Serbs	3
		Yugoslavs	3

SOURCE: *Yugoslav Survey* 32 (March 1990–91), as presented in Alex N. Dragnich, *Serbs and Croats: The Struggle in Yugoslavia* (Harcourt Brace Jovanovich, 1992), pp. 194–95.

NOTES

Primary Sources

The Public Record Office (PRO—the official archives of the British government), Kew, London, holds most of the radio messages I exchanged with the British base station in Italy between May and December 1944. The PRO archives also hold the messages and report files of the British mission to Tito and those of the Supreme Allied Commander, Mediterranean, Foreign Office, and Prime Minister's Office. I have reviewed those files that pertain to Yugoslavia and have in my files copies of those messages relevant to the subjects covered in this book.

The National Archives in Washington hold messages I exchanged with OSS Italy between May 1944 and August 1945, as well as message files for other OSS officers in Yugoslavia. With the exception of approximately 20 documents still classified and unavailable, I have in my files copies of these messages and reports relevant here.

The Slovene Partisan archives in Ljubljana hold the messages exchanged between the Partisan Fourth Operational Zone and the Slovene headquarters. My own files contain copies of several of these messages and English translations as well as translations of the relevant parts of the official history of the Partisan movement.

In addition, I have in my own files many original documents.

Some of these records have been transferred to the Hoover Library at Stanford University and the balance will be transferred to that library in the near future. Unless other sources are specifically identified in the following notes, it should be assumed that these primary collections are the sources used throughout.

Chapter 2

Page 19: "set Europe ablaze": See Walter R. Roberts, *Tito, Mihailovic and the Allies 1941–1945*, Durham: Duke University Press, 1987, p.13.

Page 19: "the young man who has used the Mother of Parliaments": See Fitzroy Maclean, *Eastern Approaches*, London: Jonathan Cape, 1949, p. 227.

Page 20: "unmerciful harshness." In Directive 25 Hitler ordered the attack on Yugoslavia, saying in it "Yugoslavia. . . must be destroyed as quickly as possible."

Page 21: It is impossible to make an accurate estimate of the civilians murdered by the Ustashe. Jozo Tomasevich writes: "Yugoslav Communist and Chetnik sources usually give figures between 500,000 and 700,000 as the number of Serbs killed by the Ustashe during their rule. This figure seems to us too high. . . . The figure of 350,000. . . is a tentative minimum." (Wayne Vucinich, ed., *Contemporary Yugoslavia*, Berkeley and Los Angeles: University of California Press, 1969, p. 367.)

Page 22: On orders from Hitler, Field Marshal Keitel issued a directive that September declaring that 100 hostages would be executed for every German killed. In October the German General Franz Böhme ordered that this directive be carried out "in the most draconian manner"—that without exception 100 hostages be executed for every German killed—and they were. In Kragujevac, for example, at least 2,300 men and boys were rounded up and shot. Wartime German documents published after the war include a telegram to Berlin from the plenipotentiary of the German Foreign Ministry in Serbia: "The executions in Kragujevac occurred, although there had been no attacks on members of the Wehrmacht in this city, for the reason that not enough hostages could be found elsewhere" (Vucinich, *Contemporary Yugoslavia*, n. 74, p. 370).

Pages 23–24: The early British efforts to establish contact with Yugoslav resistance groups are described in detail in *Embattled Mountain*, by F. W. D. Deakin, London: Oxford University Press, 1971; in *Tito, Mihailovic and the Allies 1941–45*, by Walter R. Roberts; and in *Britain and the War for Yugoslavia, 1941–43*, by Mark Wheeler, New York: Columbia University Press, 1980.

Page 24: Mihailovic's relations with Hudson deteriorated quickly, possibly because he had been told by the two Royalist officers of Hudson's favorable reports on the Partisans. Hudson was soon cut off from Mihailovic and survived the winter alone in the forest. Because he now had no radio of his own the British heard nothing from him throughout the winter of 1941–42. Radio contact was also lost with Mihailovic himself during that winter and the following spring.

In February 1942 two separate British parties were sent in to find Hudson and to reestablish contact with Mihailovic. Both disappeared without a trace. Finally, in July of 1942 SOE successfully dropped a radio and operator to Mihailovic and communication both with him and with Hudson was reestablished. But no further effort to establish communications with Tito's headquarters was made until Deakin's drop the following year.

After talking with Bill Deakin I was puzzled as to why, having received Hudson's early radio messages of his favorable impressions of the first Partisan detachment he met, the British made no further effort during 1942 and the early months of 1943 to send a separate party to establish a continuing contact specifically with the Partisans. During this period further confirmation of Partisan fighting had come from radio intercepts of reports from the German army and the Sicherheitsdienst (the Nazi Party security service of which the Gestapo was a part) on their operations against the Partisans. More important, the intercepts revealed that a large number of German divisions were engaged in these operations. Under these circumstances it remains a puzzle as to why almost two years were allowed to pass before Deakin's arrival.

Churchill's very personal interest and continuing direct interventions were an important element in the evolution of British policy toward the civil war in Yugoslavia. Deakin has described to me how it came about. "Churchill's decision to propose military support for Tito was based on solid evidence from German sources, in particular 'Ultra,' MI-3 summaries [MI-3 was the organization responsible for controlling the dissemination of the information gleaned from these decoded intercepts], and memoranda of the Chiefs of Staff—first assembled at the time of operation 'Weiss' against Tito's forces [January 1943].

"Most significant was Churchill's quick appreciation of memoranda from the Chiefs of Staff on the risks of 'Overlord' [the planned invasion of Normandy]. If twelve divisions—in reserve—could be assembled in Normandy, the Allied invasion would collapse. Twelve divisions from where? Only the Balkans—in effect from Yugoslavia. Hence the role of Tito to hold them. On the basis of this accumulated evidence Churchill made a proposal, at the Teheran Conference in November 1943, that British military aid should be given to Tito, which was agreed by Roosevelt and Stalin."

On leaving Teheran Churchill stopped in Cairo where he consulted with the British military and political authorities on the implementation of the decision to support Tito. By chance Deakin had just arrived in

Cairo from Tito's headquarters in Bosnia, together with Brigadier Fitzroy Maclean. The latter had parachuted in September 1943 as head of a permanent military mission to Tito and the prime minister's personal representative. Maclean and Deakin were summoned to report directly to Churchill on the situation in Yugoslavia as they saw it.

Deakin had been Churchill's literary secretary before the war, and had worked with him on his biography of Marlborough. He has described the meeting in Cairo to me in this way: "It was characteristic of Churchill both to keep informed of the fate of his personal friends and, on occasion, to demand directly an informal opinion. This merely meant that he would then be prompted to confirm, or otherwise, from top level evidence."

Churchill now decided to send Fitzroy Maclean back to Yugoslavia as head of a permanent mission to Tito's Partisans. Maclean was both an experienced officer in the diplomatic corps and an experienced desert fighter.

Pages 25–27: Linn Farish's reports are in my personal files and in the OSS document collection, Record Group 226, in the National Archives, Washington, D.C.

Chapter 3

Pages 37–38: These and other Italian proclamations are in the Hoover Library of War, Revolution, and Peace, Wayne Vucinich Collection.

Page 39: "In the words of Milovan Djilas." Milovan Djilas, *Wartime*, San Diego: Harcourt Brace Jovanovich, 1977, p. 335.

Page 39: According to the Slovene historian Dusan Biber, Rozman was then also working for Soviet intelligence. He was killed accidentally in November 1944 by the premature explosion of a British mortar shell he was trying out. Kveder became commander on Rozman's death, and at the end of the war was the Partisan commander in Trieste before the Yugoslavs were forced by Britain and the United States to withdraw.

Page 44: The 1942 order defining the role of political commissars is quoted in Tito's Political Report of the Central Committee, Fifth Congress of the Communist Party of Yugoslavia (1948); found in Fitzroy Maclean, *The Heretic: The Life and Time of Josip Broz-Tito*, New York: Harper, 1957, p. 160.

Page 46: Tito, the Partisan staff, and the foreign missions were chased for several days. Finally they found a possible landing strip and radioed for a pickup by Allied aircraft from Italy. C-47s flew in with fighter escort, landed and carried the party to Italy. Unaccountably, a Soviet pilot stole the show by flying the American C-47 that picked up Tito himself. Tito was anxious to return to Yugoslav territory, and after four days in Italy he recrossed the Adriatic on a British destroyer to the Yugoslav island of Vis off the Dalmatian coast, garrisoned jointly by Partisans and British. This was his headquarters until the final drive on Belgrade by Partisan and Russian forces in October.

Chapter 4

Page 49: Tad Szulc in *The Secret Alliance*, New York: Farrar, Straus & Giroux, 1991, suggests that the actual organization may have been Mossad, which was then the organization responsible for rescuing Jews from occupied Europe.

Page 49: Many years later General Shlomo Gazit, former head of Israeli Intelligence, told me that the Jewish Agency had, in 1942, worked out an arrangement with MI-6 Cairo for joint operations in occupied Europe. Under this arrangement about 25 Palestinian Jews with European languages joined MI-6, with the agreement that intelligence gained from operations in which these men participated would be shared. Dan Gatoni was one of six who parachuted into Yugoslavia.

Gazit told me his true name was Dan Linar. Born in Vienna, he had escaped to Palestine in 1939, and settled at a kibbutz in the northeastern corner of Palestine called Ga'aton—from which he had taken the war name Gatoni, the name by which we knew him. Late in 1944, while in the mountains of Stajerska, he and a group of Partisans had been surrounded and captured by the Germans. The Partisans were shot, but when the Germans learned he was a Jew he was separated, apparently for intensive interrogation. He managed to escape and to survive the war. In the years that followed he rose to the rank of major general in the Israeli Army, and commanded a tank division. He died in 1987.

Chapter 6

Page 71: "Approximately 50 percent of Germany's oil, all of its chrome, 60 percent of its bauxite, 24 percent of its antimony and 21 percent of its copper were procured from Balkan sources" (Paul N. Hehn, *The German Struggle Against Yugoslav Guerrillas in World War II, East European Quarterly*, New York: Columbia University Press, 1979). A large part of these strategic materials moved across our railroads.

Page 72: At the time the Fourteenth Division arrived in Stajerska it had only 365 rifles, 34 machine guns, 3 antitank guns, and 6 light mortars. From *Narodnoosvobodilna Vojna Na Slovenskem 1941–1945* (National Liberation

War in Slovenia), ed. Zdravko Klanjscek, Ljubljana: Partisanska Kniga, 1976, pp. 713–14.

Pages 83–86: Copies of these reports from the Fourth Zone to Slovene Partisan headquarters from Slovene archives were given me by Professor Tone Ferenc of Ljubljana University and are in my files.

Page 87: A British Army officer with the Greek guerrillas, Captain D. A. L. Warren, was executed in Greece on May 14 or 15, 1944, in compliance with this order. Colonel Christopher Montague Woodhouse, wartime head of the British military mission to the Greek ELAS Partisans and later professor of Greek history at London University, discovered in 1988 that Kurt Waldheim had signed the interrogation report on Warren and concluded Waldheim must have known what would happen to Warren as a result of this report. See Woodhouse's article in *Encounter*, September 1988. See also "Waldheim Linked to Briton's Death," *New York Times*, August 11, 1988. After the war the consensus seemed to be that whether or not Hitler's order was carried out depended on the individual German officer responsible for the prisoner.

The Yugoslavs had accumulated a major file on Waldheim's activities as a German intelligence officer in Yugoslavia during the war. In 1947 they asked for his extradition as a war criminal. But before it was acted upon the request was dropped. This puzzled people familiar with the Waldheim case. Gerhard Waldheim, his son, suggested in an op-ed piece in the *New York Times* (June 6, 1986) that the reason the charge was dropped was that it was "an explosive subject inside Yugoslavia" and that "the Yugoslavs are unlikely to publish the files on my father to explain why they never pursued the allegation."

One possible explanation is that the Yugoslavs were afraid that the record would reveal the details of their own negotiations with the Germans in 1943.

Chapter 7

Page 93: Fitzroy Maclean describes this and similar atrocities committed by the Germans in *The Heretic: The Life and Times of Josip Broz-Tito*, p. 158.

Chapter 8

Page 112: The wartime guidance to BBC from the Foreign Office in respect to Yugoslavia is described in Mark C. Wheeler, *Britain and the War for Yugoslavia, 1941–1943*, New York: Columbia University Press, 1983, pp. 184–187, 192, 195, 214, 225–26.

Pages 113–14: For a description of the activities of the Communist Party during the war years, see Walter R. Roberts, *Tito, Mihailovic and the Allies*

1941–1945; Milovan Djilas, *Wartime*; and Fitzroy Maclean, *Disputed Barricade: The Life and Times of Josip Broz Tito*, London: Jonathan Cape, 1957.

Page 115: "Peter Moore was incensed by Kidric's denials." Milovan Djilas wrote after the war: "The nerve center of the entire movement was the Security Intelligence Service, or VOS. . . which was managed by Kidric's wife Zelenka, who seemed reserved and conceited, but was in fact just right for such a job, unerring and enterprising. VOS not only carried out a series of 'justifications' or executions. . . but also made arrests and conducted interrogations" (Djilas, *Wartime*, p. 339).

Chapter 9

Page 130: Such mistakes were not limited to the British. In early 1945 OSS dropped an agent with radio into Austria with the mission of contacting an Austrian underground resistance group. He was captured and surrendered his codes and the Germans continued to operate the circuit. The absence of his security check was not noticed and the Germans continued to con OSS into thinking that they were still communicating with their own agent.

The payoff for this deception (the Germans called this type of operation a *Funkspiel*, or "radio game") came when a German undercover agent posing as an OSS agent approached a member of the budding Austrian underground. The Austrian, in order to protect the group from the possibility of a German provocation, gave the German a phrase—something on the order of "The bells are ringing"—and asked that it be included in the BBC's nightly broadcast of coded messages to the undergrounds in occupied Europe. BBC broadcast the message at OSS request because OSS believed they were still talking to their own agent. The bona fides of the German agent were established when the Austrian heard his own phrase on a BBC broadcast. The Austrians thus assumed with good reason that they were dealing with a genuine OSS agent. The result was that the resistance group was penetrated and rolled up by the Gestapo, its captured members shot.

Page 130: See F. H. Hinsley, *British Intelligence in the Second World War*, vol. 3, Part I, New York: Cambridge University Press, 1984, for a full explanation of the part played by signals intelligence in Yugoslavia.

Chapter 10

Pages 132–36: Copies of the Partisan reports of these attacks are in my files. Originals are in the Slovene archives in Ljubljana.

Page 141: "Baffled, we saw no contradiction." This episode underlined the dangers in sloppy deciphering—but the revelation did not come during the war; only many years later, coming across the original message as it was decoded, did I understand how the mistake had been made.

Chapter 11

Page 149: William Casey became the Director of the Central Intelligence Agency (CIA) in the Reagan administration.

Page 154: A Force's primary function was to mount strategic deception operations in the Allied Mediterranean theater. One such operation was to convince Hitler and the German general staff that the Allied forces would land in the Balkans, thus causing the Germans to hold several divisions in Yugoslavia and Greece that might otherwise have been sent to France.

Page 159: Tito had sent this message to the Comintern in Moscow in 1942: "If the Austrian comrades so desire we are able to infiltrate them into Austria. It is possible either through the Partisan odreds, or by train. We can provide all the necessary forged documents. [signed] Valter. [the pseudonym used by Tito in communicating to Stalin and the Comintern]" (Josip Broz Tito, *Sabrana Djela*, vol. 10, p. 87, Belgrade, 1982).

Page 160: Arthur Goldberg later became a justice of the Supreme Court and U.S. ambassador to the United Nations.

Chapter 12

Page 175: Allan Dulles's comment on the willingness of Austrians to actively oppose Hitler was contained in a message from his base in Bern, Switzerland. Original in the OSS collection, Record Group 226, the National Archives, Washington. A copy is in my files.

Chapter 13

Page 183: Dusan Biber, the Slovene historian of the Partisan war, has told me Slovene archival records confirm that no OSS spies were recruited within the Partisans.

Pages 189–90: We often used the term "Hun" for the Germans. The origin is interesting. In 1900 Emperor Wilhelm II addressed German troops about to embark for China at the time of the Boxer Rebellion. He instructed them to take no prisoners so that the Chinese would remember it "for a thousand years." Concluding, he said: "You should conduct yourselves like Attila's Huns." This was told to me by John Charles Ruhl, biographer of Kaiser Wilhelm II of Germany.

Page 198: "The Italians, now out of the war. . . " As "co-belligerents" Italian units supported the Allied armies and Mussolini's blackshirts fought with the Germans. But their roles were minor.

Chapter 14

Page 216: Tito and his staff had been critical of the Slovene Partisans for raising too few brigades. After the war the Slovene leadership had asserted that the Slovenes "had created their state through their own efforts." Tito commented when he heard this: "Like hell they could have liberated themselves, if the Serbs and the Croats hadn't come to help" (Djilas, *Wartime*, pp. 339–40).

Chapter 15

Pages 223–24: Lt. General Glaise von Horstenau's memoir was published after his death: *Ein General im Zwielicht: Die Erinnerungen Edmund Glaise von Horstenau*, Vienna, Cologne, Graz: Böhlau Verlag, 1988. The interrogation report of Glaise von Horstenau, Seventh [U.S.] Army Interrogation Center, is dated August 9, 1945. It also makes no mention of the abortive attempt to arrange a contact in Zagreb in the fall of 1945.

Page 223: Wilhelm Hoettl, a senior officer in the German Sicherheitsdienst, with whom Glaise von Horstenau conferred seeking approval of the Partisan proposal, says that Glaise decided to approach Hitler through Ribbentrop. See Wilhelm Hoettl, *The Secret Front: The Story of Nazi Political Espionage*, New York: Praeger, 1954, p. 167.

Page 230: After returning from Yugoslavia I wrote Huntington telling him of the conversation with Mates and asking if he had kept a record of the meeting or could give me any background on it. I received no reply.

Page 232: ". . . although the Germans were actively trying to get out." After I had left, Croatian headquarters reported that the Bihac pocket had been taken on March 20, 1945.

Page 235: "The Partisans were not averse to the use of violence. . . " The Partisans did not hold back from provoking German and Italian retribution. During the war Kardelj, Tito's alter ego, said: "We must at all costs push the Croatian as well as the Serb villages into the struggle. Some comrades are afraid of reprisals, and that fear prevents the mobilization of Croat villages. I consider the reprisals will have the useful result of throwing Croatian villages on the side of Serb villages. In war, we must not be frightened of the destruction of whole villages. Terror will bring about armed action" (Nora Beloff, *Tito's Flawed Legacy*, London: Victor Gollancz, 1985, pp. 75–76).

Page 236: Harold Macmillan, British resident minister at AFHQ and later prime minister, wrote in his diary on June 16, 1944: "I had to put up with an hour of Randolph. . . . He has a certain charm, but his manners are dreadful, and his flow of talk insufferable. He always manages to have a row or make a scene wherever he goes" (*War Diaries: The Mediterranean 1943–45*, London: Macmillan, 1984).

Page 236: See *The Diaries of Evelyn Waugh*, edited by Michael Davie, London: Weidenfeld and Nicolson, 1976.

Page 238: "Oh thou Tito. . . " Stalin was also eulogized in song by the Partisans: "Oh Stalin, thou people's god, / Without thee we cannot live. / Let's go, brothers, let's measure the Drina, / Let us build a bridge for Stalin" (Ivo Banac, *With Stalin Against Tito*, New York: Cornell University Press, p. 7).

Page 239: The printing press story is in Milovan Djilas's *Wartime*, p. 109.

Chapter 16

Page 248: "This reserved, cold-blooded. . . " Milovan Djilas described Maclean in this way in *Wartime*, p. 403.

Page 252: "I left for Yugoslavia. . . " Maclean, *Disputed Barricade*, p. 100.

Page 253: "Farish planned to drop. . . " Linn Farish, who had spoken so movingly of the Yugoslav wartime situation when we had talked in Bari, returned again (May 1944) to Yugoslavia by parachute, this time to Serbia. When he came out to Italy two months later his depression was even greater. OSS Bari reported to OSS Algiers: "Farish and Popovich were evacuated from Jugland yesterday morning. . . he is close to nervous and physical exhaustion." Farish now wrote: "I personally do not feel I can go on with the work in Yugoslavia unless I can sincerely feel that every possible honest effort is being made to put an end to the civil strife."

On August 9 I received a radio message in Stajerska from him: "Am working with newly formed unit concerned solely with rescue evacuation of Allied airforce personnel. We plan place small parties along Austrian, Hungarian, Yugoslav borders. Could you receive my party within ten days?" He must have seen this assignment as a way of concentrating on a task that removed him from the terrible ambiguities and conflicts of the civil war. I had to reply explaining the limitations of operating in our area and discouraging his drop. He was killed on September 9 in the crash of an aircraft attempting a clandestine night landing in Greece to evacuate downed American airmen.

Chapter 17

Page 268: See Churchill's instructions to delay McDowell's flight in to Mihailovic in Martin Gilbert, *Winston Churchill: Road to Victory 1941–1945*, Boston: Houghton Mifflin, 1986, p. 729.

Page 268: Robert McDowell had been a professor of history at the University of Michigan before the war, where he had specialized in the Balkans.

When he returned to Italy after being with Mihailovic, he saw Harold Macmillan, the British resident minister at AFHQ, who afterward wrote in his diary for Monday, November 6, 1944: "Col. McDowell—a charming American professor dressed in uniform. Round the innocent head of this sweet old man has raged a tremendous storm. He has been the OSS mission to Mihailovic. The President agreed in August (with Winston) to withdraw him. But for various reasons. . . he has just come out. . . . All the real Tito fans (urged on by Brigadier Maclean) have ascribed the most sinister causes to this episode. But I feel sure that the dear Colonel was not a very mysterious or dangerous force" (Harold Macmillan, *War Diaries: The Mediterranean 1943–45*, p. 576).

Page 273: "Complaining about the McDowell mission. . . " Tito's complaint to Maclean transmitted in a message from Maclean to London is in the Public Record Office, London. A copy is in my files.

Page 274: Bohlen has described how in Moscow in 1939 Herwarth had kept him informed of the progress of the negotiations between the Russians and the Germans. Charles E. Bohlen, *Witness to History 1929–1969*, New York: W. W. Norton, 1977, chapter 5, pp. 67–87.

Chapter 18

Page 280: "Maclean, in his first report. . . " Fitzroy Maclean's reports and those of the prime minister and the Foreign Office relating to Yugoslavia are in the Public Record Office, London. Copies of the relevant documents are in my files.

Page 281: "The new government will publish. . . " See National Archives, Washington, RG226, Shepard cable series #2, Nov. 6, 1944.

Page 284: "Michael Petrovich, a member of. . . " See Michael Petrovich, *Political Science Quarterly*, vol. 62, no. 4.

Page 285: Tito's statement was made in his speech to the Fifth Party Congress, YPC, July 21, 1948. See Maclean, *Disputed Barricade*, pp. 310–11.

Page 287: Djilas's statement on the role of the press appeared in *Borba*, Feb. 12, 1945, Belgrade. A copy is in my files.

Page 288: Nine years later, Djilas broke with Tito and the party leadership for having forsaken their revolutionary ideals. In his widely read *The New Class* (New York: Frederick A. Praeger, 1957), he denounced his former comrades for having adopted a lifestyle of extravagance and high living. For the unforgivable attack he was read out of the party, and for continued attacks on the party's total monopoly of power he was imprisoned. He had retained his "purity" even in his lonely attacks on his closest wartime comrades. Of all the charges he later made against the Communist regime, the one that appeared to be the most serious challenge to the party leadership was his opposition to the single-party system and his advocacy of a second party modeled on the Social Democratic parties of Western Europe.

Chapter 19

Page 291: Internal communications among the Yugoslavs quoted in this chapter have been provided by Dr. Dusan Biber from Yugoslav archives. British and American communications are from National Archives, Washington, and Public Record Office, London. Copies are in my files.

Page 298: For Colonel Cox's account of the arrival of the New Zealand division in Trieste see Geoffrey Cox, *The Race for Trieste*, London: William Kimber, 1977, chapters 11-19.

Page 300: "You are getting in the way of operations. . . " Some 20,000 Chetniks and their families had managed to move north from central Yugoslavia to the Isonzo River to escape the Partisans. They were trying to evade the Partisans and this was another unstated reason for Partisan operations there. The Chetnik group was able to get across the river into areas controlled by the Allied army where they were interned.

Page 303: Churchill responded to Alexander's message saying: "There is no question of your making any agreement with him [Tito] about incorporating Istria or any part of pre-war Italy in his 'new Yugoslavia.' The destiny of this part of the world is reserved for the peace table, and you should certainly make him aware of this" (Winston S. Churchill, *The Second World War: Triumph and Tragedy*, Boston: Houghton Mifflin, 1953, p. 1334).

Page 307: The negotiations in Washington between the State Department, the Foreign Office, and President Truman are described in *Diplomatic History*, vol. 10, 1986, pp. 141–60.

Page 309: Churchill cable to Truman, June 2, 1945. Public Record Office, London, PRIM 3/473.

Page 312: Tito's statement and the Soviet reaction are covered in *Maclean's Disputed Barricade*, pp. 305–6.

Chapter 20

Page 315: This sorry episode is scrupulously researched in Brigadier Anthony Cowgill, Lord Brimelow, and Christopher Brooker, Esq., *The Repatriations from Austria: The Report of an Inquiry*, London: Sinclair Stevenson, 1990.

Page 315: I have since been told the castle of Duino was owned by the Hohenlohe family.

Page 328: Milovan Djilas has confirmed our own assessment of Tito's opposition to other political parties: "The formation, or rather the restoration, of the dissolved parties was not even considered; this would have disrupted the unity of the uprising, and might even have presented a lever to its enemies. The participation of individuals or groups of these parties was for show and symbolic; it broadened the base of the uprising and facilitated transitions" (Djilas, *Wartime*, p. 335).

Chapter 21

Page 330: Richard Stilwell, later a four-star general, was the commander-in-chief of U.N. forces in Korea 1973–1976.

Page 331: "Many of us who had been with the Partisans. . . " OSS Major Richard Weil, Jr., was for three weeks in March 1944 at Tito's headquarters. Weil reported on returning to Italy: "For whatever it may be worth, my own guess is that if he is convinced that there is a clear-cut choice between [nationalism and international Communism], on any issue, his country will come first." Roberts, *Tito, Mihailovic and the Allies, 1941–1945*, Durham: Duke University Press, 1987, p. 213. In August 1944 Robert Murphy visited Tito briefly on the island of Vis. After this meeting he also ventured an opinion that Tito was more of a nationalist than an international Communist (Robert Murphy, *Diplomat Among Warriors*, New York: Doubleday, 1964, p. 224). Both opinions were formed after very little contact with Tito and the Partisans. Yet they turned out to be more accurate than the conclusions of those of us who spent a much longer time with them.

Page 333: "It was only after the break that each side published parts. . . " The Yugoslav published record of the statements and messages exchanged with Stalin, the Comintern, and the Eastern Bloc countries is in *White Book on the Aggressive Activities by the Governments of the U.S.S.R., Poland, Czechoslovakia, Hungary, Rumania, Bulgaria and Albania Towards Yugoslavia*, Ministry of Foreign Affairs, the Federal People's Republic of Yugoslavia, Belgrade, 1951.

Page 334: "Churchill said of him. . . " Churchill's toast is recorded in a press release in my files. Tito's statement is also in my files.

Page 335: "We have won the right to full independence. . . " Tito's statement is in Vladimir Dedijer, *Tito Speaks*, London: Weidenfeld and Nicolson, 1953.

Page 336: "I was asked to join. . . " I served in CIA from 1949 to 1953. I resigned to join the Ford Foundation.

Page 338: For Bela Kiraly's article see "The Aborted Soviet Military Plans

Against Tito's Yugoslavia," Wayne S. Vucinich, ed., in *War and Society in East Central Europe*, Vol. 10, East European Monographs No. 74, Brooklyn College Studies on Society in Change, 1982.

Page 345: The statement of the Joint Chiefs of Staff is document 31 in *The Pentagon Papers*, New York: New York Times, 1971, p. 154.

Page 347: Not only had the Stajerska Partisan leaders gone on to higher jobs in the years after the war, several of my OSS associates had done so as well. John Blatnik, who had been in Slovenia, became a congressman from Minnesota and served many years in the House of Representatives. Allen Dulles, OSS chief in Bern during the war, had resumed his legal career and subsequently was director of the Central Intelligence Agency in the Eisenhower and Kennedy administrations. John Gardner, a Marine lieutenant at OSS headquarters in Caserta, became head of a major foundation, secretary of the Department of Health, Education and Welfare and founder of Common Cause. Charles Thayer, my predecessor as head of the military mission to Tito's forces, returned to the Foreign Service. Marine Corps Captain William Cary, executive officer of our military mission, was for years a law professor at Columbia and, for a time, head of the Securities and Exchange Commission. Robert Wolff and Stuart Hughes became distinguished professors at Harvard. Edward Welles and James Fisher stayed in government.

Among the British officers, Fitzroy Maclean returned to his seat in Parliament for some thirty years, and for a time was Parliamentary Undersecretary of State for War. Charles Villiers became a banker and later chairman of British Steel. Peter Wilkinson became a diplomat and served in Washington and as ambassador to Vietnam and later Austria. William Deakin became the first warden (head) of St. Antony's College at Oxford and worked again with Churchill on his six-volume history of the Second World War. All four were knighted. Lieutenant Gatoni—Dan Linar—became a major general in the Israeli army.

Page 349: "Fifty years later Glina was again the scene. . . " For an eyewitness account of the fighting within Yugoslavia in 1990 and 1991, see Misha Glenny, *The Massacre of Yugoslavia, New York Review of Books*, January 30, 1992.

Page 351: "Now he is converting the Yugoslav Army. . . " Misha Glenny, *New York Review of Books*, January 30, 1992.

Page 351: "One group's revenge. . . " *New York Times*, August 4, 1991.

SUGGESTIONS FOR
FURTHER READING

Among the personal memoirs of participants in the wartime conflicts in Yugoslavia are those of Sir F. W. D. Deakin (*The Embattled Mountain*, Oxford University Press, 1971), Milovan Djilas (*Wartime*, Harcourt Brace Jovanovich, 1977), and Sir Fitzroy Maclean (*Eastern Approaches*, Jonathan Cape, 1949).

Deakin, the first British liaison officer with Tito's Partisan command, arrived by parachute on May 28, 1943, in the midst of a battle for survival against surrounding German, Italian, and collaborationist forces. Maclean arrived a few months later as head of the British (later Allied) military mission to the Partisan forces. Both books vividly describe the raw political and military conflicts as seen primarily from Partisan headquarters.

Milovan Djilas was a member of Tito's top wartime command and after the war was jailed by Tito as a dissident. His detailed memoirs cover the entire period of the Partisan war. Among his other books, some written in prison or under house arrest, the most widely read in the West are *Conversations with Stalin*, Harcourt Brace & World, 1962; and *The New Class* (Frederick A. Praeger, 1957).

Fitzroy Maclean has published a biography of Tito that is also a history of the Partisan war (*Disputed Barricade: The Life and Times of*

Josip Broz-Tito, Jonathan Cape, London, 1957; also published in America under the title *The Heretic*, New York: Harper, 1957).

Tito, Mihailovic and the Allies, by Walter R. Roberts (Duke University Press, 1987, reissued) is an excellent history of the 1941–45 wars in Yugoslavia with emphasis on the relations of both the Partisans and Chetniks with the British and the Americans, as well as with the Germans and the Russians. Mark C. Wheeler, who has had access to British archives, has written a well-documented and thorough history of Britain's relations with the Partisan and Chetnik movements in the early period of the war (*Britain and the War for Yugoslavia 1941–43*, Columbia University Press, 1980). *Fires in the Night* by Fritz Molden (Westview Press: Boulder, San Francisco, and London, 1989) is a record of the Austrian resistance during the Second World War.

For those interested in the conflict for control of Trieste between the Western Allies and the Tito forces, Geoffrey Cox, the chief intelligence officer of the New Zealand Division, tells a fascinating story of the arrival of his division in Trieste to find the Yugoslav Partisans already in the city and working at full speed to control all the organs of local government (*The Road to Trieste*, William Heineman, first published in 1947). Bogdan Novak, a historian, describes in detail the prewar origins of the conflict, the uprising as the Germans withdrew in 1945, and the protracted negotiations that ended with the return of Trieste to Italy by Britain and the United States in 1954 (*Trieste— 1941–1954: The Ethnic, Political and Ideological Struggle*, University of Chicago Press, 1970). Roberto G. Rabel covers the same period (*Between East and West: Trieste, the United States and the Cold War 1941–1954*, Duke University Press, 1988). Rabel has the advantage of having written after the declassification of British and American official documents and therefore has been able to give greater insights into the decision-making process in Washington and London.

Resistance in the border area between Austria and Slovenia is described in detail by Thomas M. Barker (*Social Revolutionaries and Secret Agents: The Carinthian Slovene Partisans and Britain's Special Operations Executive*, East European Monographs, Boulder, 1990, distributed by Columbia University Press). Brigadier Anthony Cowgill, in *Repatriations from Austria in 1945* (London, 1991), describes that chapter of the end of the Second World War.

For those interested in the role of intelligence and code-breaking in the Second World War, F. H. Hinsley's five-volume *British Intelligence on the Second World War* (Her Majesty's Stationery Office) provides the most comprehensive coverage of the subject, including what was learned of events in Yugoslavia through Allied wartime successes in reading German radio messages. A very readable book for signals intelligence buffs is *Ultra and Mediterranean Strategy* by Ralph Bennett, a member of the group responsible for disseminating Ultra intercepts during the war (William Morrow, 1989). The most comprehensive is by David Kahn, *The Codebreakers*, New York: Macmillan, 1967.

Jozo Tomasevich provides a well-researched story of the Chetniks from 1941 to 1945 in *The Chetniks* (Stanford University Press, 1975). He tends to support the 1943 British decision to drop Mihailovic and support Tito's Partisans. Two recent books on the Chetnik-Partisan conflict argue the thesis that the Chetniks were done in primarily by the British decision to switch their support from Mihailovic to Tito: David Martin's *Web of Disinformation: Churchill's Yugoslavia Blunder* (Harcourt Brace Jovanovich, 1990), and Michael Lees's *The Rape of Serbia: The British Role in Tito's Grab for Power, 1943–44* (Harcourt Brace Jovanovich, 1990). Both present the case for the Chetnik cause and overlook the considerable documentation conflicting with that view. David Martin has presented an excellent lawyer's brief for his "client," Mihailovic, but it is not dispassionate history, tragic though Mihailovic's death by Tito's firing squad was.

The early postwar period in Yugoslavia is well described in *The Yugoslav Experiment 1948–1975* by Dennison Rusinow (University of California Press, 1977). "At the Brink of War and Peace: The Tito-Stalin Split in a Historic Perspective," edited by Wayne S. Vucinich (*War and Society in Eastern Europe*, vol. 10, *At the Brink of War and Peace: The Tito-Stalin Split*, Columbia University Press, 1982) provides an analysis of the political, military, and economic effects of the Tito-Stalin split. A later volume edited by Rusinow, *Yugoslavia: A*

Fractured Federalism (The Woodrow Wilson Press, 1988) provides the ethnic, political, and economic background of the subsequent breakup of the Yugoslav Federal Republic in 1990 and 1991.

The complex issues of nationalism now tearing the Yugoslav nation apart are laid out in the monograph *The National Question in Yugoslavia: Origins, History, Politics* by Ivo Banac (Cornell University Press, 1984). A more recent book, *Remaking the Balkans* by Christopher Cviic (Royal Institute of International Affairs and the Council on Foreign Relations, 1991), sets out in highly readable form the origins of the conflict up to the dissolution of Yugoslavia in 1991.

A late addition to this list—*Serbs and Croats* by Alex N. Dragnich (Harcourt Brace Jovanovich, 1992)—also provides a useful historical background to today's conflicts in the former Yugoslavia.

ACKNOWLEDGMENTS

I would like to thank the many people who helped in so many different ways to bring this book to its final form.

John A. Bross, Robert Bowie, Doris Kearns Goodwin, James Chace, Frances and Burke Wilkinson, and Walter R. Roberts read early drafts and helped shape the direction of the final product.

Sir William (F. W. D.) Deakin, Dusan Biber, Christopher Andrew, and Wayne Vucinich reviewed the entire manuscript, provided many original documents from their own collections and gave me their special insights on Partisan and Allied policies.

Tone Ferenc gave me copies of many wartime Partisan messages from Slovene archives. Stane Mervic, of the Museum of the People's Revolution in Ljubljana, has given me a collection of photographs to supplement my own. Colonel J. R. S. Clarke, Sir Peter Wilkinson, Mitja Ribicic, Robert Plan, and Edward Welles added their recollections of the wartime events we shared. Michael Straight gave me insights on James Klugmann and his role in a prewar Cambridge University group, at least five of whom became Soviet agents.

Siegfried Beer, Gunter Bischof, Kirk Ford, and Thomas Barker shared with me documents uncovered in their own research. Thomas Winship, Thomas Wallace, John Kenneth Galbraith, Adam Ulam, Harriet Relman, Ellen Hume, and Grant Barnes also read the manuscript and suggested changes of substance as well as changes that put it into much more readable form. Felicia Kaplan and Peggy Lamson read sections of the manuscript and made helpful suggestions. James McCargar and Peter Kahn made important contributions in editing the manuscript, removing redundancies, improving the organization and the flow of the text.

John Taylor, archivist at the National Archives in Washington, and G. L. Beach, head of Search Department, and Mary Z. Pain, researcher at the Public Record Office in London, steered me through the maze of historical documentary collections to find my own and related files of declassified messages and reports. Tula Connell, Carina Campobasso, and Mark Mahoney read through reams of documents at the National Archives, helping to find those relevant to the story. Dennis Skiotis searched out important materials in the vast Harvard libraries. Bozidar Pahor translated operations reports of those Slovene Partisan units with whom I had lived and fought. Olivia Radford also helped with the translation of some of the Slovene historical records.

Much of the work on the manuscript was done while I was a visiting scholar at the Woodrow Wilson Center in Washington, and later an Associate at the Center for International Affairs at Harvard. I thank both organizations for a friendly and stimulating environment in which to work.

Robert Moulton and Sanford Dornbusch guided me to the Stanford University Press. There, Ellen F. Smith has been most helpful in editing and in guiding the manuscript to its final book form, and Ann Klefstad did the copyediting in an easy and professional manner. Richard Zeeb put the several maps into finished form. Dorothy Burnett helped me proofread the typeset pages.

My wife Margot provided invaluable help in the organization and editing of the manuscript and unfailing support during the naively unanticipated length of time it has taken to research, write, and edit this book.

And of course, I assume full responsibility for all mistakes and oversights.

F. L.

INDEX

In this index "f" after a number indicates a separate reference on the next page, and "ff" indicates separate references on the next two pages. A continous discussion over two or more pages is indicated by a span of numbers. *Passim* is used for a cluster of references in close but not consecutive sequence.

Fisher, Captain Charles, 153, 159–62, 164, 203–4, 321, 323, 326
Fisher, Corporal James, 1, 3, 9, 30, 46, 50, 119, 126f, 129, 206, 313, 319, 370
Fisher, John L., 119
Flues, Major Gilbert, 153, 169–70
Force 399, 5, 29, 73, 118, 147, 186, 204, 322. *See also* Special Operations Executive
Fourth Zone, *see* Partisans: Fourth Zone
Free Austrian Brigade, 157, 160f
Freiland, 170–71
Freyberg, General Bernard, 298–301, 307
Fürnberg, Siegfried, 173

Gardner, Lieutenant John, 246, 370
Gatoni, Lieutenant Dan (Dan Linar) 49, 55, 63, 361, 370
Gazit, General Shlomo, 361
Gerbner, George, 170–72
Germany (Third Reich), 4, 21, 58; operations against Partisans, 20–23 *passim*, 33, 46f, 50, 54–57, 64, 69, 75, 102, 126, 144f, 158–59, 213–14; Partisans crossing into, 52–53; air operations, 75, 100, 126, 128–30; winter offensive, 200–203 *passim*, 209, 264, 319–25 *passim*; surrender talks, 203, 219–24; alpine redoubt, 241–43
Gestapo, 164, 176, 193, 363
Glaise von Horstenau, Lieutenant General Edmund, 203, 219–24, 365
Glavin, Colonel Edward, 203
Glina, 217, 349
Goldberg, Arthur, 160, 364
Goodwin, Captain James, 31, 39, 43, 141, 213
Gorizia, 298, 302
Gornja Savinjska Dolina, 91, 131–36 *passim*, 200
Gornji Grad (Oberburg), 60f, 132ff, 144
Gosnjak, General Ivan, 222f, 229f

Graz, 163–64
Green, Lieutenant Holt, 194
Grol, Milan, 279, 282–84

Hamblen, Brigadier General A. L., 304
Harding, Major General John, 301, 307, 313f, 315–19
Harriman, Averell, 331
Heidenreich, General Konrad, 325
Henniker-Major, Major John, 342
Herwarth von Bittenfeld, Hans, 274–75
Hesketh-Prichard, Major Alfgar (Cahusac), 150–63 *passim*, 166–68, 175, 326
Heydrich, Reinhard, 150
Himmler, Heinrich, 166
Hitler, Adolph, 20–21, 87
Hochschwab, 167
Hoettl, Wilhelm, 365
Hönner, Franz, 173
Hudson, Captain D. T., 24, 358–59
Hughes, Stuart, 246, 370
Hun: origin of term, 364
Huntington, Colonel Ellery, 203, 228–31, 269, 342

Innitzer, Theodor Cardinal, 165
Interservice Liaison Department (ISLD), 158. *See also* MI–6
Iran, 14
Isonzo River, 300, 309
Italian occupation of Slovenia, 30, 36–38, 43

Jewish refugees, 237
Jones, Major William, 27, 32
Jovanovic, Lieutenant General Arso, 256, 288–90, 300, 309ff
Joyce, Robert, 153, 179, 246, 330, 337

Kamnikar-Bojan, 184–85
Karawanken Alps, 59, 90
Kardelj, Edvard, 35–36, 252, 283, 308–9, 370
Keitel, Field Marshal Wilhelm, 358

162, 186, 203, 205, 226, 364; Labor
Desk, 160–62
O'Meara, Captain Eugene, 259–60
Owen, Captain (later Major) Douglas,
172, 204, 319–25

Parachute drops, 1–7, 25, 27, 56–57, 61,
64, 76–77, 88–89, 153, 156, 170–73,
185, 187, 194–95, 200, 201–2
Parks, Lieutenant Edward, 204, 321,
324, 326
Partisans, 5, 9–13 *passim*, 22–29 *passim*,
34–46 *passim*, 213–16; antagonism
toward Western Allies, 3, 111, 142,
155–56, 159–64, 178–79, 181–84,
188–89, 194–95, 214–15, 248–49; Allied support for, 11–12, 20, 111; relations with Russians, 12f, 107, 116,
190–91; weapons, 41–42, 73–75,
133–36; organization, 72f, 107, 197;
hidden hospitals, 93–94, 214–15, 326;
and civil population, 95, 131, 198–99,
208–9; strategy and tactics, 107, 110f,
209–10, 215–16, 232–34; and prisoners, 133, 136, 138, 144f, 232; intelligence collection, 181–83, 214, 231;
proposals to Germans, 222–23
—units: Seventh Corps, 43, 50, 213;
Ninth Corps, 43, 213; Fourteenth
Division, 72, 108, 132, 139, 141, 314,
325, 361; Sixth "Slander" Brigade,
72–73, 132ff, 143; Eleventh "Zidansek" Brigade, 72–73, 79–80,
132ff, 143; Sixth Corps, 153, 170, 180
—Fourth Zone, 40–41, 59, 61, 63, 70,
72ff, 83–86 *passim*, 104, 131f, 136–40
passim, 170, 197–98, 320–26 *passim*;
Austrian operations, 149–56 *passim*,
162–63, 166–68
Patterson, Ambassador Richard, 296f
Pavelic, Ante, 21, 219
Peter II, King of Yugoslavia, 20–21; regents for, 278–79
Petrovic, Michael, 257, 284

Philby, Kim, 340–41
Phillips, John, 141
Pijade, Moshe, 250, 286
Plan, Robert, 161, 169, 172, 183, 319–22,
326
Ploesti oil fields, 271
Pohar, Lado, 347
Pohorje mountains, 63, 72, 75, 88, 90,
200, 320
Popovic, General Koca, 269, 343
Popovich, Lieutenant Eli, 32
Primorska, 39
Primozic, Franc, 109, 139, 339
Prisoner exchanges, 232

Quebec Conference, 191–92
Quinn, Lieutenant Robert, 161

Radio codes and cyphers, 24, 118,
121–26, 128–30, 137–38, 141, 322, 363;
intercepts and code breaking, 124,
126, 130
Radio communications, 24–25, 46f, 49,
118–30, 167, 172; equipment, 5–9, 64,
102, 119–20, 129, 138, 140, 226
Raduha mountain, 90
Railroads: operations against, 10–11,
18, 34, 46, 56–57, 61, 64, 73–87 *pas-
sim*, 104–6, 136–42, 197–98
Ramat David parachute school, 15–16
Rankovic, Aleksandar, 281
Ratweek, 137–42
Recica, 188–90, 320
Reid, Major Stafford, 266
Rescue of Allied airmen, 56, 65–66,
181–82, 186–90, 210, 258–59
Ribicic, Mitja, 267, 347
Ribnikar, Vladislav, 263–64
Rijeka, 312
Rimske Toplice, 136
Roberts, Major G., 103–4, 204
Roberts, Walter, 223
Rogers, Major Lindsay, 214
Rome, 297–98

Library of Congress Cataloging-in-Publication Data

Lindsay, Franklin, 1916–
  Beacons in the night: with the OSS and Tito's partisans in
wartime Yugoslavia / Franklin Lindsay
      p.   cm.
  Includes bibliographical references.
  ISBN 0-8047-2123-8 (alk. paper)
  1. Lindsay, Franklin, 1916–   2. World War, 1939–1945—
Underground movements—Yugoslavia.   3. World War, 1939–1945—Secret
service—United States.   4. United States. Office of Strategic
Services—History.   5. Yugoslavia—History—Axis occupation,
1941–1945.   6. World War, 1939–1945—Personal narratives, American.
7. Guerrillas—United States—Biography.   8. Guerrillas—Yugoslavia—
Biography.   I. Title.
D802.Y8L56   1993
940.54´8673´092—dc20
[B]
92-36774
CIP

♾ This book is printed on acid-free paper.
It was designed by Copenhaver Cumpston and typeset
by Anne Cheilek in 11/14 Adobe Minion and Stone Sans
on a Macintosh IIci at Stanford University Press.